Guide to International Financial Management

Guide to International Financial Management

J. Fred Weston
Professor of Management
Graduate School of Management
University of California
 at Los Angeles

Bart W. Sorge
Professor Emeritus of Finance
Graduate School of Business
 Administration
University of Southern California

McGRAW-HILL BOOK COMPANY

New York • St. Louis • San Francisco • Auckland • Bogotá
Düsseldorf • Johannesburg • London • Madrid • Mexico
Montreal • New Delhi • Panama • Paris • São Paulo
Singapore • Sydney • Tokyo • Toronto

Guide to International Financial Management

Copyright © 1977 by McGraw-Hill, Inc. All rights reserved. Printed in the United States of America. No part of this publication may be reproduced, stored in a retrieval system, or transmitted, in any form or by any means, electronic, mechanical, photocopying, recording, or otherwise, without the prior written permission of the publisher.

1234567890   KPKP   783210987

This book was set in Press Roman by Allen Wayne Technical Corp.
The editor was J. S. Dietrich;
the designer was Allen Wayne Technical Corp.;
the production supervisor was Milton J. Heiberg.

Library of Congress Cataloging in Publication Data

Weston, John Frederick.
    Guide to international financial management.

    Includes bibliographical references and index.
    1. International business enterprises—Finance.
2. International Finance. I. Sorge, Bart W., joint author. II. Title.
HG4028.I53W47   658.1'5   76-46648
ISBN 0-07-069488-5
ISBN 0-07-069487-7 (text ed.)

Contents

	Preface	xi
Chapter 1	International Business Finance and Its Environment	1

International financial developments have significant impacts on the U.S. business firm. The growing dimensions of international trade and finance require American businessmen to consider international financial factors more and more. What is the international financial management function? International financial management is influenced by the environmental factors prevailing in the country of operation. U.S. government policies toward international business affect the U.S. business firm.

Chapter 2	The Development of an International Firm	13

The general steps in the progression from a domestic to a multinational firm. The scope of a firm's overall foreign operations will not develop in exact conformance with the sequence of events discussed above. The degree of development of company activities in a particular country will reflect a combination of influences. Multinational firms do affect the U.S. economy. The importance of the stage of economic development of a country.

Chapter 3	Organization and Control for International Financial Management	31

The organization of a multinational corporation. The development of a financial system by a multinational corporation. The subsidiary of a multinational corporation. The regional center as an important form of geographical organization. Planning and control systems in a multinational corporation. Measurement of performance. Evaluation of performance. Responsibility for foreign exchange losses. Transfer pricing.

Chapter 4	The International Financial System	53

The adjustment process in the balance of payments between nations. Foreign exchange systems. Factors leading to the international monetary crisis of August 1971. Efforts to formulate a viable international financial system. Proposals for reform of the international financial system.

Appendixes to Chapter 4   75

Interactions of national income, the money supply, and the balance of payments. A formal analysis of the effects of devaluation.

Chapter 5 The Balance of Payments and Forecasting Foreign Exchange Rates   81

International transactions, financial flows, and the balance of payments. Balance-of-payments statements. Construction of the balance-of-payments accounts. Balance-of-payments summary measures. Significance of a balance-of-payments summary measure. Exchange Rates. Exchange-rate adjustment processes. Illustration of arbitrage outflow—situation A. Illustration of arbitrage outflow—situation B. Historical examples of covered interest arbitrage opportunities. Equilibrium market relationships. Checklist of factors for forecasting foreign exchange rates.

Chapter 6 The Accounting Treatment of Foreign Operations and Transactions   115

Accounting systems are based on four alternative points of view. There are two basic problems in accounting for international operations: differences in accounting principles and practices between countries and the requirement to translate financial statements from one currency into another. The financial translation of accounting statements—historical background. FASB Statement No. 8 is now the governing guideline for U.S. based multinational firms as they translate the financial statements of foreign subsidiaries denominated in foreign currencies into U.S. dollars. Illustrative translation example.

Chapter 7 Government Rules and Policies Affecting International Business   145

The preservation of foreign exchange reserves. Alternative taxes and tax theories. United States taxation of international operations. Tax aspects of the selection of the operating form of foreign organizations. Items that influence the before-tax earnings of a

CONTENTS vii

foreign subsidiary. Taxation of international business by major trading nations. Information from a report to the Committee on Finance of the United States Senate. Value added tax.

Chapter 8   The Risks of International Financial Management   175

The risks of foreign operations differ in degree and kind from domestic operation risks. Discussion of risks associated with foreign activity. Environmental factors, political, social, and economic in nature, directly influence the risk exposure of a firm doing business in a foreign country. The risks affecting the returns from a foreign subsidiary are more complex than changes in foreign exchange rates. Anticipated versus uncertain inflation and exchange risk. Risk analysis concerns probabilities of unfavorable developments in relation to the position of the firm or investor.

Chapter 9   Insurance and Guarantee Programs for Foreign Operations   191

Insurance and guarantee programs involving foreign operations. Foreign Credit Insurance Association. The Export-Import Bank of the United States. OPIC offers three programs: an investment insurance program, an investment guarantee program, and a financing program using its own funds. Investment guarantees offered by the Agency for International Development.

Chapter 10   Exchange-Rate Risk Protection in Foreign Operations   211

The equilibrium relationships in the foreign exchange markets provide the framework for decision making to minimize the costs of exchange-rate fluctuations. The use of the forward exchange market to protect future commitments or receipts. The currency swap. The concept of monetary balance. Centralization and an overview of the firm's position and its alternatives.

Chapter 11   International Working Capital Management   243

Working capital management. The problem of foreign-exchange-rate risk. The international flow of funds. The management of the flow of funds. The international movement of funds — implementation of policies.

Chapter 12 Financing Worldwide Commercial Sales — 261

A proper volume of world trade is important to the U.S. and world economies. Factors affecting the volume of U.S. exports. The basic documents in normal export-import transactions are the bill of exchange, the bill of lading, and the letter of credit. Methods of financing export-import sales. Foreign trade with countries suffering severe shortage of foreign exchange. Variables in the sales transaction.

Chapter 13 Financing International Operations — 281

Summary framework of alternative financing forms and sources. Financing in an international setting. Financing subsidiaries are established to serve as a conduit in international financing. Expanding role of U.S. commercial banks and investment bankers in international financing. The Eurodollar system. The Eurobond market. International financing agencies. National development banks conduct activities to support economic growth of their nation as well as to support international business operations.

Chapter 14 The Cost of Capital and Financial Structure of the International Firm — 321

Cost of different forms of capital. The cost of equity capital. Applications of capital market theory. Leverage and the cost of capital. Illustrative calculations of the cost of capital. International financial markets and the use of debt. The sale of equity issues in foreign countries. The influence of international operations on the selection of a firm's capital structure. The determination of an international firm's cost of capital.

Appendix to Chapter 14 — 347

Illustration of the benefits of foreign investment with the market model.

Chapter 15 The Foreign Investment Decision — 353

The general principles of international investments concern comparative advantages in the supply of capital, labor, raw materials, and technology among trading nations. The U.S. position in foreign investment. The stimuli to direct foreign investment are so numerous and diverse that a single theory does not provide a complete explanation. Project evaluation in foreign investment decisions. Risk considerations are especially important in foreign investment decisions.

Chapter 16 The Finance Function in International Operations — 381

The scope of the international financial functions. The general patterns of organizational relationships in the international company. Financial policies and practices must be carried out consistently on a worldwide basis. International tax planning. Management of international cash flows and temporary investments. Financing international sales. Financing foreign operations. Planning and evaluation of foreign ventures. Central themes of this book.

Appendix   Compound Interest Tables — 395

Glossary of Symbols Used — 399

Index — 405

Preface

New developments in the field of international financial management have been accelerating. The problems of international finance have become increasingly complex and no easy solutions to international economic issues are available. The turbulence of the international economic and financial environments has had an increasing impact on all business firms, whether large or small. We have learned in recent years that no person or business firm is unaffected by the substantial changes taking place in the international financial environment.

The world has become smaller and more interdependent because of developments in transportation and communication. International commerce has increased. Most firms are now affected by international developments either directly or indirectly whether or not they are aware of it.

The central theme of this book is that the international financial markets are efficient because of informed participants. Information is rapidly reflected in these markets because of the high level of knowledge and experience of the many participants and agents. A wide range of technical and institutional factors interact in the international financial markets. The decisions of highly knowledgeable and informed participants produce systemic relationships in these markets. To earn average returns in the international financial markets, or to avoid losses, requires that a participant be informed and rational, know what data is relevant and how the data should be interpreted. Managers of firms must increasingly prepare themselves to become aware of international factors and to react to them on an informed basis.

This *Guide to International Financial Management* is designed primarily to assist nonspecialists to understand the important events occurring in the international financial environment. Our intent is to cover key concepts and decision areas. Since our treatment is brief, it is also at times simplistic. We have not attempted to give full treatment to all topics, but rather to supply a map of the very complex terrain of international finance. We traverse only the main roads to provide a first survey of the entire territory. Our objective is to open the way to more intensive exploration by further reading and analysis. For an executive or scholar with experience and knowledge of international finance, our treatment provides a review of the fundamentals. He or she will recognize that we do not attempt to be exhaustive.

The materials for each of the 16 chapters covered are composed of two parts. One part is a set of outlines of the subject matter of international financial management. These outlines are used to present the materials in compact, understandable form and to provide the necessary background for understanding and assessing international and economic financial developments. We offer a reference guide for managers who themselves are not specialists in international finance, to help them to better understand the international aspects of the operations of their business firms. The outlines seek to provide a bridge between international financial developments and the decisions required of business managers.

The second part of the materials is a set of questions and answers or problems and solutions. Much of the subject matter of international finance and economics is either relatively abstract or highly technical. By presenting problems that deal with concrete matters, we seek to provide a focus for the abstract ideas and technical materials. We have tried to make the applications relevant to decision making by managers of individual business firms, and to demonstrate how the materials and concepts of international financial management can be used.

The format of this book is designed to make it a relatively self-contained manual. The outlines and study of the applications provide the basic subject matter, while the problems and solutions suggest practical applications. Individuals may therefore use the *Guide* both as a reference manual and as an instrument for self-study.

These materials will also provide a useful supplement to existing literature in the area of international economics, international business, and international financial management. For the reader who is stimulated to pursue any of the individual topics in greater depth, we have provided end-of-chapter references in the above areas. Materials from other sources are also presented in brief compass for perspective. Our general treatment of these materials makes the book particularly useful as a supplement to other texts on international financial management. Used in conjunction with these other materials this *Guide* illustrates managerial application of materials covered on a more general basis.

To make sound decisions in response to the international economic developments of recent years requires an understanding of basic concepts and new developments. International financial events continue to be subject to rapid and continued changes. The aim of this *Guide* is to provide the key materials for understanding the events taking place and to serve as a foundation for continued study.

We wish to express our thanks to the numerous officials in government agencies and insurance organizations who have provided up-to-date information. We are particularly grateful to Professor Ian Giddy, Columbia University, and Alan Shapiro, University of Pennsylvania, whose suggestions and criticisms resulted in substantive improvements. Steven Fellows contributed so much that he deserves to be listed as a coauthor. Dorothea Sorge, Susie Chen and John Sell ably assisted in all phases of the project. Lynn Hickman and Marilyn McElroy also helped creatively. We alone are responsible for materials presented. Students and business associates stimulated us to clarify a number of areas and provided ideas on subjects they felt it was useful to cover.

J. Fred Weston
Bart W. Sorge

Guide to International Financial Management

Chapter 1

International Business Finance and Its Environment

Theme: The world is becoming one interacting and interdependent market place as a result of rapid developments in communication and transportation. Most firms are now directly or indirectly affected by international financial developments whether or not they are aware of these new influences. The international financial markets operate efficiently with information rapidly transmitted through highly knowledgeable participants. This requires that managers of firms prepare themselves to recognize the influence of international factors, to benefit from the new opportunities, and to avoid pitfalls. The finance function in its international dimensions must encompass new decision areas of increased complexity. In addition, the cultural, social, political, and economic environmental variables to be considered in international business decisions are substantially broader in range.

  I. International financial developments have significant impacts on the U.S. business firm.
    A. The noninternational firm.
      1. A customer may be affected by changes in price and availability of foreign raw materials or parts.

2. A firm may be a supplier to a manufacturer of export goods. Its volume of business is influenced by the economic environment in the countries of the manufacturer's foreign customers.
B. The international firm.
1. The purchases of a foreign customer are influenced by the economic environment in his own country.
2. The firm that imports some of its raw materials and parts is influenced by a change in price levels in the supplying country.
3. Action on the part of foreign governments may strongly affect the demand for the firm's goods or the foreign availability of its supplies.
4. Currency devaluations and revaluations materially affect profit margins and competitive ability.
C. The U.S. economy.
1. Changes in price levels in foreign countries and changes in the availability of raw materials affect economic conditions and business opportunities of U.S. firms.
   a. The increase in the price of oil caused price levels in the U.S. to rise and caused shifts in the use patterns of petroleum products.
   b. The world demand for food has placed upward pressure on grain and livestock prices.
   c. The high rate of growth in the demand for raw materials in relation to their relative inelasticity of supply has caused their prices to trend upward.
2. When foreign prices rise relative to U.S. prices, opportunities for selling abroad are improved. When U.S. prices rise relative to foreign prices, U.S. firms may find it more difficult to sell abroad and may face increased foreign competition in the U.S. market.
3. U.S. direct investment abroad and investment by foreigners in the U.S. increases competition in both foreign and U.S. markets.

II. The growing dimensions of international trade and finance require American businessmen to consider international financial factors more and more.
A. Reasons.
1. Some industries derive over 50% of their sales from exports.
2. Net profits from foreign operations for many U.S. firms exceed 50% of their total profits.
3. Private investment abroad has increased.
4. To achieve economies of mass production operations and other economies of scale to compete with foreign firms achieving economies of large size necessitates international sales.
5. Foreign funds and international capital markets are used to finance foreign and domestic operations.

THE INTERNATIONAL BUSINESS FINANCE FUNCTION AND ITS ENVIRONMENT

    6. Possibilities of higher profit margins exist in foreign countries.
    7. There is the necessity for U.S. exports to offset foreign raw material purchases and other persistent outflows such as remittances and government grants.

  B. New variables in international business operations.
    1. New cultural-institutional factors.
    2. Different legal-political constraints.
    3. Diverse labor laws and requirements.
    4. Proliferation of regulations and requirements.
    5. Differential rates of inflation in selling prices and costs.
    6. New and increased risks from:
      a. Changes in exchange rates and devaluation.
      b. Exchange controls.
      c. Restrictions on flow of funds.
      d. Expropriation.

III. What is the international financial management function?
  A. Why is it different from the domestic financial management function?
    1. The worldwide scale of operations makes the information requirements greater.
    2. The communications, planning, control, and coordination needs are also greater.
    3. Different currencies are involved and their relationships change with changing economic, financial, and political developments.
    4. The cultural, social, and political factors are different in various countries of the world; adaptation to their different environments requires that firms have different rules for different parts of their operations.
    5. The problems of measurement of performance are complicated by the different circumstances of individual foreign subsidiaries.
    6. The terms and conditions of financing and its availability are subject to continuous change, presenting new opportunities and risks.
    7. The proper balance between centralization and decentralization of strategies, policies, and operations is more difficult to achieve in international operations.

  B. What are the central external information flows that must be followed by the international financial manager?
    1. Monitoring and relating international economic and political trends.
    2. Watching trends in prices, costs, interest rate levels, and foreign exchange rates throughout the world.
    3. Noting different tax laws and procedures throughout the world.
    4. Observing competitive developments throughout the world.

C. What are the central areas of decision making that the international financial manager must coordinate with other management decision areas in the firm?
 1. In which currencies will the firm have inflows and outflows over various time periods and how will the values of these flows be affected by prospective changes in the foreign exchange values of the currencies involved?
 2. To what extent will sales of the firm involve credit extension, commercial and political risks, and foreign exchange risks? How should the nature of these risks and the alternative methods of dealing with them affect the pricing policies of the firm?
 3. Will future operations result in positive or negative balances in various countries throughout the world? Can the firm take protective actions? If so, what are the trade-offs between the use of forward markets, borrowing or lending at home or abroad, and the use of a monetary versus nonmonetary balance sheet position?
 4. What are the relations in different countries between relative price-level changes, interest rate levels, foreign exchange rates, and rates of economic activity?
    a. Implications for sales opportunities, domestic and foreign.
    b. Implications for labor costs and the supply of managers.
    c. Implications for sourcing materials and parts.
    d. Implications for costs of operations and profit potentials.
    e. Investment decisions and choice of operations in U.S. versus abroad.
    f. Forms of operations abroad.
D. Domestic economic developments that impact the financial decisions of firms cannot be understood without consideration of the international influences as well. The remainder of this chapter will deal with social and cultural factors in the environment. The following chapter will outline some important international financial mechanisms and their implications for business firms.

IV. International financial management is influenced by the environmental factors prevailing in the country of operation.
 A. Demographic, social, and legal factors.
  1. The demand in some countries that nationals be employed in the foreign-owned enterprises requires that the skills, education, and capabilities of the local population groups be evaluated.
  2. The social stratification and the social structure influence the mobility, education, and advancement potential of local employees.
   a. The degree of education and training of a local population influences its capabilities as employees and its possibilities as potential buyers of products.
   b. The degree of horizontal geographical mobility affects the freedom of an employee to move from one place to another.

       c. Vertical mobility (possibilities for moving upward in economic or social position) has a strong influence on the ability of an individual to advance in rank and responsibility. This affects the incentives for education and achievement and hence the motivation and efficiency of both workers and executives.
       d. Education in most foreign countries follows the European two-track system—one track for the elite who will be leaders of industry and government, another track of vocational-type education for future technicians. Employees who do not have the proper educational prerequisites have difficulty holding responsible managerial positions. This affects the future supply of potential managerial talent.
  3. Customs and attitudes of the people toward the particular business activity and its function or service are influencing factors.
       a. The degree and nature of government regulation.
       b. The demand for its products.
  4. Social responsibilities are required of a business within a foreign country.
       a. Cooperation in government, economic, and social programs.
       b. Fringe benefit costs of employers.
       c. Costs of pollution controls, etc.
  5. Exposure to different foreign influences during a country's formative years as well as local religious codes and attitudes cause variations in legal systems.

B. Governmental factors.
  1. Attitudes of the host government toward foreign-owned domestic businesses influence management.
  2. The political stability of the host government is important.
       a. Impact on treatment of foreign firms.
       b. Impact on economic policies.
  3. Laws and regulations affect businesses owned by foreign investors, especially concerning investment and repatriation of funds.
       a. Payment of interest to foreign lenders.
       b. Payment of dividends to foreign owners or investors.
       c. Repatriation of funds to foreign lenders.
  4. Costs of social legislation, i.e., social security taxes, vacation pay, severance pay, etc., can be higher abroad than in the U.S.
  5. Tax laws, tax structures, and local administration of tax laws may be used to discriminate against U.S. firms or U.S. owned firms.
       a. Tax officials may threaten unusually high tax levies unless side payments (bribes to the officials) are made.
       b. It is better to challenge these forms of arbitrary behavior than to compromise ethical standards of business conduct.

C. Local business customs.
1. Daily business hours and social routines vary.
2. Aggressiveness and competitive spirit fostered in the U.S. may be unacceptable in many countries.
   a. Some governments take active roles in determining a business's share of the market.
   b. Business conducted on a cooperative gentleman's agreement basis may run counter to U.S. antitrust laws.
3. Sales commissions versus bribes.
   a. Payment for the services of sales agents may be as justifiable as in domestic sales.
   b. Payments to agents for influence may become a form of blackmail that grows progressively more oppressive.
   c. Difficult judgments must be made by U.S. executives on these issues which have become highly publicized in recent years.
D. Economic and financial conditions.
1. Growth rate and stability of the local economy.
2. Soundness of fiscal and monetary policies.
3. Equity and soundness of the taxation system.
4. Tax shelters and other incentives for local investment.
E. Governmental economic and financial policies.
1. Equity in obtaining licenses to conduct business.
2. The availability and cost of local funds.
3. Stability of the local currency.
4. Convertibility of local currency into other currencies.

V. U.S. government policies toward international business affect the U.S. business firm.
A. Monetary and fiscal policies to influence the exchange value of the dollar.
B. Tariff policy and customs administration to promote equal treatment for U.S. exporters and importers.
C. Development of appropriate policies to offset foreign government subsidies to foreign producers and restrictions on U.S. imports into foreign countries (cf. policies of the Japanese government).
D. Export financing to place American exporters on an equal basis to that provided foreign firms by their governments.
E. Commercial and political risk insurance for exports to place U.S. firms on an equal basis to that provided foreign firms by their governments.
F. Tax policies to harmonize with tax policies toward foreign firms by their governments.

PROBLEM 1-1

A knowledge of demographic, institutional, legal, and government factors will significantly enhance the probability of a multinational company's success in foreign operations. Describe these factors.

SOLUTION:

1. The world can be divided into three major politico-economic ideologies: communism, socialism, and capitalism. The nature of the economic system greatly influences how business is conducted.
2. The wide variations in educational systems strongly influence the make-up of the local work force. If managers must work with more educationally privileged persons, it is extremely difficult to take persons educated in the lower echelons of the educational system, train them to greater competence, and have them become effective managers.
3. Institutional arrangements for the care of the aged, the sick, or the unemployed are developing in most countries, representing an additional cost of doing business.
4. Citizens of any country typically have a strong sense of national identity or pride.
5. Although most developed countries follow general legal systems based on English common law or on the civil law system of Latin origin, widely diverse systems have evolved in some less developed countries, strongly influenced by religion, myths, and other cultural factors.
6. The governments of some developing countries have at times adopted policies of taking over foreign industries. Sizable investments in these countries could be disastrous should nationalization take place. The possibility of unexpected changes increases the risk exposure for an investment or a firm.
7. Familiarization with established laws, regulations, and procedures are absolutely necessary before the firm reaches a decision on foreign operations.
8. The knowledge of the details of taxation, when operating in a foreign country, is crucial to the financial well-being of the company.
9. Dividend rules and regulations must be known, as well as rules affecting the movement of funds, exports, imports, competition, etc.
10. In general, the undertaking of operations in the international sphere requires a broad knowledge of factors which are not common to domestic finance. As such, a firm's international success is not dependent solely on methodologies developed domestically.

PROBLEM 1-2

Your firm is considering an investment in Peru. You have been asked to evaluate the strengths and weaknesses of the country's environmental factors as they may affect the new business venture.

1. The population is about 14 million in an area of some 500,000 square miles (about twice the size of the state of Texas). About 52% of the population is urban. Half of the total population is Indian. Peru is the

center of the old Inca Empire. The literacy rate is 61%. The rate of population growth has been over 3% per annum.
2. Half of the work force is engaged in agriculture, fishing, and forestry. Only 13% is in manufacturing.
3. Between 1970 and 1974, consumer prices rose 54%.
4. Laws were enacted in 1970 and 1971 which severely restricted foreign investment. Almost all U.S. investors will have to accept an eventual minority position on any investments in Peru. This is especially emphasized by the Andean Foreign Investment Code, effective July 1, 1971.
5. The 1970 Industrial Community Law calls for worker participation in profits, ownership, and management; compulsory contributions from the industry involved; and an ultimate goal of 50% labor ownership in the enterprise.
6. In spite of steps taken by Peru requiring liquidation of foreign currency accounts and foreign assets, and rigid foreign exchange controls, Peru's financial problems have continued to increase.
7. In early September 1975, Peruvian President Juan Velasco Alvarado was overthrown in a coup. Former Prime Minister General Francisco Morales Bermudez became the nation's new leader. Velasco had seized power himself as the result of a military coup in 1968. He had launched a far-reaching social and economic revolution in Peru, breaking the power of the landed aristocracy, nationalizing banks, mines, factories, and newspapers, and seizing the assets of Gulf Oil and other U.S. companies.

SOLUTION:

1. The high illiteracy rate and the large population growth create substantial problems for increasing per capita income. Also, the predominant Indian cultural influence may not be conducive to profit-oriented Western business operations.
2. The industrial base is not broad enough to provide the complementary manufacturing industries necessary for many production activities.
3. Peru has had a high rate of inflation, but relatively moderate by the standards of a number of other Latin American countries.
4. Enactment of investment codes clearly makes foreign investment in Peru very risky.
5. The 1970 Industrial Community Law makes ownership, management, and control of foreign investments highly uncertain and precarious.
6. Controls make repatriation of any profits highly uncertain.
7. The coup indicates political instability and lack of democratic processes for changing governments. Velasco's reforms earned him considerable popularity, at first, particularly among the impoverished Indians who make up half the country's population.

THE INTERNATIONAL BUSINESS FINANCE FUNCTION AND ITS ENVIRONMENT

As the middle class grew increasingly concerned about the social revolution Velasco's fellow military men urged him to take a more moderate course. Thus, the change in leadership indicates that a more favorable climate may develop. However, in view of the difficult underlying economic problems of the country, there remains basic doubt as to whether any government in Peru would be stable. Clearly, investment in Peru would represent a high-risk category.

PROBLEM 1-3

Your firm is considering an investment in Argentina. You have been asked to evaluate the strengths and weaknesses of the country's environmental factors as they may affect the new business venture.

1. The population is about 27 million, growing at an average rate of 1.6% per annum during the last decade. The population, mostly of European origin, is made up of a mixture of Spanish, Italian, and German.
2. Almost 80% of the population is urban. The labor distribution is as follows: 16% in agriculture, 27% in manufacturing, 6% in construction, 11% in commerce, 19% in services, and 21% in other sectors.
3. The gross national product (GNP) in 1970 was over $21 billion and had been growing at over 2% per annum in per capita terms.
4. Since 1970 the price level has been rising at a rate of 40% to 60% per annum.
5. The exchange rate has risen from 3.5 pesos per dollar in 1968 to 26 pesos per dollar during the second quarter of 1975.
6. The government has been somewhat unstable with power shifting from one group to another. The position of the present government is somewhat uncertain and both the military as well as strong labor unions are exerting pressures on government policies.

A. Indicate whether the influence of each factor is favorable or unfavorable and provide a brief explanation.

B. Present an overall appraisal of the environment in Argentina for making a long-term investment.

SOLUTION:

A. 1. The predominant European traditions inherent in the population makeup is a favorable factor. It suggests cultural attitudes that are probably consistent with profit-oriented conduct of modern business operations. Also, the relatively low population growth reduces the problem of maintaining per capita income, reducing the strain on the economy.

2. Population is a plus factor as it shows a good balance in labor distribution consisting of a relatively developed manufacturing sector and no undue dependence on agriculture.
3. GNP is favorable since real income is growing moderately.
4. The high rate of inflation is a negative factor. Misallocations, dislocations, and economic unrest result because inflation hits different groups unequally.
5. The exchange rate indicates weakness in the country's international reserve position reflecting a relatively high rate of domestic inflation. Foreign investment would again have to seek to protect itself from the high rate of domestic inflation, particularly since resulting domestic economic problems will likely result in government restrictions on repatriation of earnings.
6. Government instability makes foreign investment in such a country very risky. If accommodation is worked out with one existing government, it can be swept away when a new government comes into power. Extreme political instability of the kind experienced by Argentina is a very strong negative factor against making foreign investments.

B. The general political and economic instability in the country represents a highly unfavorable environment for long-term investments. A firm that chooses to make such an investment, however, may reduce its risk exposure somewhat by choosing to get into the kind of business operation that is consistent with the economic welfare of the country. Also, the firm should make use of the appropriate forms of insurance and guarantees discussed in Chapter 10.

PROBLEM 1-4

A number of factors influencing operations in a foreign country are listed below. Mark each with an F for favorable or a U for unfavorable. Then match each factor with a rationale given below.

1. A large Indian population continues on a subsistance agriculture basis.
2. A strong social caste system which limits mobility into the elite educational, business, and government opportunities.
3. Two distinct religious groups vying for political and economic dominance.
4. Good balance in the distribution of the work force and manufacturing activities.
5. Possesses several basic commodities and raw materials whose prices are increasing faster than the average for all commodities.

6. Population growth rate has been over 3% per annum and no strong efforts to reduce the growth rate.
7. The money supply has been growing 25% per annum and drains on its foreign exchange reserves will exhaust them in 1½ years.
8. A broad educational system and opportunity for attendance at the nation's universities is open to all who are intellectually qualified.

A. Indications of inflationary conditions and pressures for exchange controls and devaluation of the currency.
B. Indicates strong demand growth for its products which may provide foreign exchange for broader development of the economy.
C. Limits growth of managerial talent and is a potential source of unrest.
D. Provides upward social and economic mobility and increases the potential supply of managerial abilities.
E. May create strong pressures for economic growth and make it difficult to increase real national product per capita without inflationary strains.
F. Could provide local sources of required raw materials, parts, and workers with experience and skills.
G. Can lead to conflict and political instability.
H. A drag on growth in national product and a potential source of social unrest.

SOLUTION:

	F or U	Reason
1.	U	H
2.	U	C
3.	U	G
4.	F	F
5.	F	B
6.	U	E
7.	U	A
8.	F	D

REFERENCES

Several recent textbooks on international financial management providing additional materials on this and other chapters are:

Eiteman, David K., and Arthur I. Stonehill: *Multinational Business Finance,* Addison-Wesley, Menlo Park, Calif., 1973.

Rodriguez, Rita M., and El Eugene Carter: *International Financial Management,* Prentice-Hall, Englewood Cliffs, N.J., 1976.

Weston, Fred J., and Bart W. Sorge: *International Managerial Finance,* Richard D. Irwin, Homewood, Ill., 1972.

An especially good treatment of the environmental factors affecting managerial decision making in the area of international business is:

Farmer, Richard N., and Barry M. Richman: *International Business: An Operational Theory,* Richard D. Irwin, Homewood, Ill., 1966.

Chapter 2

The Development of an International Firm

Theme: A firm develops its international activities through an evolutionary process. A progression of events usually follows its initial involvement in international business. Different areas of the firm will be engaged in international activities in unequal degrees. The form of participation involves an assessment of the trade-offs of alternative approaches. The opportunities in individual countries are often strongly influenced by the stage of development of the country.

  I. The general steps in the progression from a domestic to a multinational firm.
    A. The existence or development of a strong competitive product for domestic sales is a prerequisite for international involvement.
      1. A management team capable of developing and producing a competitive product of quality is also able to cope with the many new environmental factors and uncertainties that will be encountered in international operations.
      2. A firm successful on a domestic basis is also more likely to be able to obtain the required financing to make involvement in international operations possible.

B. Importing raw materials or parts may bring international exposure to the firm. This contact creates interest in potential sources for foreign sales.
C. Exporting through brokers may be a first step in understanding the requirements of international business. It is favored under these conditions:
   1. The sales personnel of the firm have little experience in export sales.
   2. The goods sold require a knowledge of foreign markets.
D. Use of the sales personnel of the company usually follows. It is warranted under these conditions:
   1. The price of company products is lower and its quality higher than products of foreign competitors.
   2. The products are industrial goods with few customers, thus requiring a small marketing organization.
E. The appointment of a distributor or distributors in the foreign country usually follows. This broadens the marketing effort and permits cooperation between the personnel of the distributors and the sales and service personnel of the firm.
F. A foreign branch sales office may be established when a satisfactory sales volume has been achieved and the market outlook appears favorable.
   1. The foreign office enables the firm to establish more direct contacts overseas and to keep closer tabs on foreign market developments.
   2. It also allows technical service personnel to be located closer to the customers of the firm.
G. Licensing a foreign firm to produce the product abroad may be an intermediate step before actually setting up a foreign manufacturing operation. In some instances, licensing is the only method permitted by a local government that has established strong controls over imports.
   1. Licensing has advantages.
      a. It shifts concern with foreign problems from the firm to the licensee.
      b. It contributes a high return on investment to the firm.
   2. Licensing has long-run disadvantages.
      a. The foreign company becomes a potential source of competition when the license expires.
      b. Confidential information once imparted to the licensee cannot readily be recaptured.
   3. Licensing with partial ownership allows the firm to participate in long-term profits from the operation.
H. Joint ventures provide some degree of local foreign ownership.
   1. Government regulations and restrictions may require that this form of organization be used. The trend toward greater local participation is increasing. For example, Japan and Mexico permit only joint ventures in manufacturing operations, with foreigners as minority investors.
   2. Joint ventures may obtain the local goodwill and support necessary for the success of the operation.

3. This form allows smaller firms to expand abroad with minimum investment, and enables them to share the risks with foreign investors.
4. Joint ventures can produce conflicts of interest and possible loss of control for the U.S. firm. However, usually patent agreements, technical licensing arrangements, and control over the flow of information from the firm to the joint venture assures a strong voice in management.

I. Wholly owned manufacturing branch plants or subsidiaries are favored for several reasons.
   1. Administration and quality control is made easier without local partners.
   2. Maximum security of business methods and know-how prevails.
   3. Maximum flexibility on financial policy decisions is present.
   4. Potential tax advantages exist.
   5. The wholly owned approach is most suitable
      a. For relatively small scale operations of specialized production and services.
      b. In countries where local capital and managerial know-how are not developed.
   6. Majority ownership on the part of foreigners is not permitted in a steadily growing number of countries.
   7. Wholly owned manufacturing facilities are possible in most developed countries and in those developing countries whose policies are not dominated by strong nationalistic feelings.

J. Multinational management organizations fall into two basic categories.
   1. The world corporation format merges all the supporting functions for both domestic and foreign operations.
   2. The international division format separates foreign operations from domestic activities.

K. Multinational ownership of equity securities of multinational firms is an important trend in the development of international capital markets.
   1. It improves the acceptance of foreign multinational firms in those countries where their equity shares can be purchased.
   2. Worldwide share ownership is encouraged in several ways.
      a. Printing annual reports in foreign languages.
      b. Disseminating company information through foreign news media.
      c. Listing corporate securities on major overseas stock exchanges.

II. The scope of a firm's overall foreign operations will not develop in exact conformance with the sequence of events discussed above. It will be the sum total of all the activities of the firm with or in the foreign countries that are involved. Conformity is not possible due to these factors.
   A. The firm may sell to one country by means of brokers while at the same time it may sell to other countries via distributors and/or its own sales organization.
   B. It may operate wholly owned manufacturing facilities in some developed countries while manufacturing on a minority-owned joint venture basis in

other countries. At the same time, in still other countries, the firm may have goods manufactured according to its own specifications by a licensee.

III. The degree of development of company activities in a particular country will reflect a combination of these influences:
   A. An historical accident that occurred.
   B. The degree of competition which exists in a particular country.
   C. The performance of domestic firms to meet the needs and demands of customers in their country may create opportunities.
   D. The particular characteristics of the company's product may make it very acceptable in one country and not in another.
   E. The need to have a product adapted specifically to the needs of a country and the requirements for continuous service often lead to the establishment of additional manufacturing operations.

IV. Multinational firms do affect the U.S. economy.
   A. Do foreign investments jeopardize American jobs?
      1. Many foreign countries require that manufacturing be done in their country.
         a. Import restrictions prevent the importation of goods for sale.
         b. Without foreign manufacturing facilities, many overseas sales would be impossible for U.S. firms.
      2. Surveys have shown that a large percentage of U.S. exports represent sales to foreign subsidiaries of U.S. firms.
      3. Some studies have shown that foreign operations of U.S. firms create rather than diminish domestic employment.
   B. Do direct investments abroad create adverse balance-of-payments effects?
      1. Though foreign investments represent an outflow of capital at the time of investment, they also generate income during the economic life of the investment which is an annual net positive contribution to the balance of payments.
      2. Placing artificial restrictions on U.S. foreign direct investment ignores the mobility of capital towards investments of higher rate of return.
      3. If U.S. firms are prevented from entering foreign markets, the firms of other nations will take these investment opportunities. The potential income from these investments will be lost to the U.S.

V. The importance of the stage of economic development of a country.
   A. Five broad stages of development.
      1. Traditional.
         a. Low per capita income.
         b. Stagnant or declining per capita income.
         c. Population mainly in agriculture.
         d. Little international trade except agricultural and mineral products.
         e. Special social customs and political factors.

2. Transitional.
    a. Increased contact with outside world.
    b. Need to solve periodic social and economic breakdowns.
    c. Simple equipment and strategic fertilizers for productivity of agriculture.
    d. Some agricultural surplus for foreign exchange.
    e. Outside grants and some loans for roads, schools, power, and transport.
    f. Periodic political and social upheavals.
3. Take-off.
    a. Emergence of strong individual growth sectors in some parts of manufacturing.
    b. Production more diversified.
    c. More rapid rise of per capita income.
    d. Self-sustaining growth for profitable employment of foreign loans.
4. Technologically Mature.
    a. Ability to engage in all forms of economic activity.
    b. New leading sectors determined by comparative resource advantages.
    c. Emergence of national surplus over basic needs.
5. Developed.
    a. Surplus national income for consumer affluence, welfare state, etc.
    b. Must depend on emergence of new industries to sustain growth thrusts.
    c. Sound national economic policies necessary for full employment growth.
    d. Favorable foreign trade balance depends on strong research by advanced industries.

B. Implications of stage of development for planning international operations.
  1. It provides the key to identifying opportunities favorable to the business under consideration.
      a. Businesses dealing with mineral extraction and sources of raw materials would look to the nations in the traditional stage.
      b. Manufacturers of consumer durables and transportation equipment would be interested in selling to countries in the transitional stage.
      c. Take-off nations provide fine investment opportunities for firms manufacturing goods needed by these nations.
      d. Financiers seeking good foreign investments should look to take-off and maturing countries.
  2. The stage of development also indicates possibilities for growth.
      a. There are few industrial sectors with strong growth opportunities at the traditional stage. The variety of available business opportunities increases as a country moves through the transitional and take-off stages to reach technological maturity. At this point overall growth slows down.

b. The risks of investment at the traditional and transitional stages are often great. Instability and turmoil may be underlying causes of slow economic progress.
c. The key factor in the growth of a country from transitional to technological maturity is the development of domestic production facilities to substitute for imports.
d. As the country begins to restrict imports of certain goods, the multinational firm will need to rely more on joint ventures to manufacture and sell its products.

C. Technique of entry into a foreign market and the stage of development of a country.
1. Determine the proper technique of entry into traditional and transitional economies.
    a. The U.S. firm should keep its fixed capital investment low.
    b. The firm should seek agents for importing and exporting.
    c. Investment to produce exports is favorable, especially of agricultural and mineral resources, as this produces the foreign exchange necessary for further trade.
    d. Investment in production facilities to replace imports is not feasible at this stage because domestic markets are not large enough.
    e. Licensing agreements are generally not good alternatives in these early stages. They may hinder efforts to invest directly in joint ventures when the markets grow larger.
    f. The transitional stage is a good time to learn about local markets and local government regulations. Such knowledge is important for transportation, utilities, and durable goods industries which begin to grow rapidly at this stage.
2. Take-off countries offer more opportunities for investment.
    a. Long-term growth and success require an association with nationals committed to economic development.
    b. Production of goods to substitute for imports is an increasing necessity as import restrictions develop.
    c. Production of exports receives encouragement for their contribution to the foreign exchange position of the country.
3. As countries move into the technologically mature and developed stages, their dependence upon international trade decreases.
    a. Since most markets become large enough to support domestic producers, foreign exporters retain a smaller proportion of the market.
    b. Direct investment by joint venture or wholly owned subsidiary is the appropriate technique.
    c. Licensing may be the quickest way to enter foreign markets, but it also creates the greatest potential for later competition.
4. Countries in the first three or four stages are likely to favor the importation of producer durables necessary for economic growth. They may restrict the importation of consumer durables.

PROBLEM 2-1

The Agro-Industrial Machinery Company manufactures a complete line of agricultural equipments and machineries. It is currently a thriving business worth $30 million. The company has an extensive marketing/service operation in the country. It ships manufactured parts to its various sales locations to be assembled at the local plant. At one of its annual business planning sessions, it has been suggested that the company look into the possibility of expanding its sales by entering appropriate markets abroad. Areas that seem to generate much interest are the relatively underdeveloped Latin American economies which are still largely land-based. Develop an appropriate plan to enter and expand the market.

SOLUTION:

Since the company is not familiar with the local market conditions, not to mention the social and cultural influences which weigh heavily in these traditional economies, it would be wise for the company initially to locate a local dealer with strong marketing skills to penetrate each market. This should be done on a contract basis. As the company gains in sales and experience with each local market, it can at some point integrate all these individual markets and set up its own sales branch to service the entire region.

As the product is rather technical in nature and the level of technical skills is low in these countries, the company should arrange for servicing of the parts, at least in the initial stages, to assist the local dealers in their marketing efforts. This would, of course, be absorbed into the sales organization of the company when it is set up later.

The advantage of the plan above is that it affords the company time to get acquainted with the market without the risk of prematurely tying up investment funds and personnel. Of course, the main disadvantage is that the success of the plan depends entirely on the choice of dealers and their working relationship with the company.

Since the machineries and equipments can be conveniently shipped in knocked-down parts and assembled by the local dealer, operation and shipping costs are not prohibitive. There is no reason to contemplate the manufacture of these machineries locally, or to offer a license to a local manufacturer.

PROBLEM 2-2

The Clinton Business Machines Company is a very successful manufacturer of business machines and related equipment. It has recently pioneered a line of sophisticated business machines that would simplify office work tremendously. Clinton is also expanding into the more sophisticated area of small scale computerized equipment for business use. Because of its pioneering efforts in developing new and superior products, the company has been able to increase its market penetration to half of the total market for business machines in the U.S. at the present time.

The company is presented with a good opportunity to enter into the German market. A relatively successful German manufacturer of business machines has approached the company with a proposal to merge operations there. The German company would provide the people and the marketing resources while Clinton would provide the technology and the know-how. The company is contemplating the best way to join in this venture: to grant a patent license at an agreed price for royalty, or to invest as a majority interest in a joint venture. Evaluate each alternative, and then present your recommendation.

SOLUTION:

The main argument in favor of the licensing arrangement is that it represents a very high rate of return to the Clinton Company. The big disadvantage of the licensing arrangement is that it is a short-range approach, because after a period of years the licensee learns enough to become relatively independent and a formidable competitor to the company that sold the patent license. This is true whether the company selling the patent license under a royalty is an American company or a foreign company. There are other arguments discussed in the text, but these are the critical considerations.

The advantage of the joint venture arrangement to Clinton is that any knowledge gained by the German company would have to be shared with Clinton on an agreed-upon basis, with the majority interest going to Clinton. Of course, Clinton gets the greater share of the profits, too. Although the German company may not be willing to give Clinton the majority-control position, it really does not have a strong bargaining position. Clinton does have a superior product that has great potential for penetrating and capturing a big share of the European market. If the German company is wise, it will move fast and use its relationship with Clinton to expand and enter the French, Italian, and English markets.

The advantage to the Clinton Company of entering into the joint venture with the German company and giving up a small percentage of the profits is that the German company does have a marketing organization and good marketing acceptance. The German company can provide personnel in conjunction with the Clinton Company to maintain the product once it is in operation. This would enable the Clinton Company, in a relatively short period of time, to have a very substantial portion of the total European market for its product.

It is thus strongly recommended that Clinton enter into a joint venture with the German company.

THE DEVELOPMENT OF AN INTERNATIONAL FIRM

PROBLEM 2-3

The Rostow theory of stages presents a framework for grouping countries according to their level of economic development. What are these stages and what significance do they have for multinational companies planning their international investment strategies?

SOLUTION:

Rostow theory of stages and appropriate multinational company strategies:

Strategy	A Traditional	B Transitional	C Take-off	D Technologically Mature	E Developed
1.	Import raw materials.	Sell consumer durables.	Produce consumer durables.	Direct investments.	Specialty goods, such as chemicals, paints, and photographic equipment.
2.	Sell extractive machinery.	Sell transportation equipment.	Direct investments.	Joint ventures with local companies.	Licensing only when better alternatives not available.
3.	Keep fixed inventories at low level.	Sell civil works, goods, and services.	Work with nationals committed to growth in the local economy.	Capital goods investments.	Make acquisitions or purchase minority interests.
4.	Sell agricultural equipment.	Keep fixed inventory at low level.	Produce substitutes for imports.	Obtain licenses from these countries.	Sell needed commodities.
5.	Do not offer licenses.	Learn marketing problems.	Produce to expand exports.	Sell consumer durables and nondurables.	Sell high technology products, such as aircraft.
6.	Wherever possible work with the local government.	Learn mechanics of working with local government.	Joint ventures with local firms.	Sell needed commodities.	

PROBLEM 2-4

To what strategic areas should financial managers of multinational companies pay particular attention with respect to operations of subsidiaries in underdeveloped countries? What are your proposed policies to guide the planning of your corporate financial staff and management of subsidiaries in order to deal with these problem areas effectively?

SOLUTION:

A. Cultural factors.
  1. Focus on preeducational and training programs.
  2. Develop executive exchange between countries.
  3. Learn language and customer peculiarities.
  4. Participate in local cultural events.
B. Government policies.
  1. Restrictions and/or incentives provided to local industry.
  2. Effects on changing attitudes of local management.
  3. Local ownership.
     a. Enter into joint venture.
     b. Avoid political activity.
     c. Have close ties to strong political groups.
C. Inflation and devaluation.
  1. Maintain monetary balance.
  2. Obtain local borrowing.
  3. Extend credit on short-term basis only.
  4. Own real assets.
D. Revaluation. Be a net monetary creditor.
E. In short, seek to contribute to the economic well-being of the underdeveloped country. Identify with their social and political attitudes. Anticipate executive changes to benefit from them.

PROBLEM 2-5

What are some of the leading theories of foreign direct investment?

SOLUTION:

Professor Caves has set forth a theory of foreign direct investment which represents an extension of the structuralist theory for domestic markets. He summarizes his central themes as follows:

> Briefly, the argument of this paper is that foreign direct investment occurs mainly in industries characterized by certain market structures in both the "lending" (or home) and "borrowing" (or host) countries.

> In the parlance of industrial organization, oligopoly with product differentiation normally prevails where corporations make "horizontal" investments to produce abroad the same lines of goods as they produce in the home market. Oligopoly, not necessarily differentiated, in the home market is typical in industries which undertake "vertical" direct investments to produce abroad a raw material or other input to their production process at home. Direct investment tends to involve market conduct that extends the recognition of mutual market dependence—the essence of oligopoly—beyond national boundaries, (1971, p. 1).

But a number of rival theories of direct investment may also be found. Aliber presented a theory of direct investment based on exchange risks.

> The central hypothesis is that the key factor in the explanation of the pattern of direct foreign investment is that the world is divided into different currency areas and that there is a bias in the market's estimate of exchange risk. The bias in the evaluation of exchange risk determines whether a country is likely to be a source country or a host country for foreign investment.
>
> National differences in capitalization rates are the major factors that explain the country pattern of direct foreign investment; otherwise the pattern would tend to be random. The difference in pattern by industry reflects differences in the size of the host-country market and the cost of doing business abroad. Similarly takeovers can be explained by these differences in capitalization rates (1970, p. 34).

Still another view was presented by Hymer and Rowthorn in emphasizing increased competitive consequences of both the European merger movement and internationalization of business.

> Mergers and rationalizations will lead to corporate reorganization and the creation of new administrative structures more akin to those of the American corporation and better suited to multinational expansion. Or, to put the matter differently, as European firms increase in size and complexity their administrative "brain" will increase more than proportionately and their attention will focus not so much on national or European markets but on the world as a whole, including the U.S. market itself. In a sense, the vision of a firm depends on the height of its head office building.
>
> By consolidating the overseas sales of European firms, mergers will make them better able to establish subsidiaries of an efficient size. In any particular market a big firm is likely to have actual or potential sales larger than those of a small firm, either because it is already selling more in the form of exports or because it can afford to finance a costly promotion and distribution program for its products. Equally it can afford to establish a large and efficient subsidiary which can produce the output necessary to satisfy this larger market. From the point of view of both supply and demand the big firm is therefore better able to produce on an efficient scale, 1970, pp. 74-75).

Hymer and Rowthorn emphasize the rivalrous nature of foreign investments.

> Cross investment is a long-standing feature of direct foreign investment. In many industries where U.S. corporations have substantial direct investment in foreign countries, one of the leading firms in the United States is a foreign firm, e.g., oil, soft drinks, paper, soaps and detergents, farm machinery, business machinery, tires and tubes, sewing machines, concentrated milk, biscuits, chemicals, (1970, p. 81).

Further counter evidence to a simple theory of direct investment is presented by Professor Lowinger. He runs a regression to explain U.S. industries' export shares of world trade from 1968 to 1970 and changes in the relative export shares of U.S. industries between the years 1960 and 1962 to 1968 and 1970. He generally obtains high R^2 values. Generally the most powerful explanatory variable, mostly at the 1% level, is scientists and engineers engaged in research and development (R&D) as a percentage of total employment, 1967-1969. The industries with the best export performance record (and investment possibilities) are aircraft, electrical equipment, drugs, scientific instruments, industrial chemical, and machinery. Lowinger concludes:

> U.S. competitive performance in international trade is largely determined by the country's ability to invest a comparatively high proportion of its resources in the development of new products and improved processes. A high rate of generation of new knowledge whether embodied (in capital) or disembodied is typical of a high income country such as the U.S. and may be thought to be the mainstay of its comparative advantage in international trade, (1975, p. 234).

Another theory of foreign investment is the product-cycle thesis of Vernon (1966). The product-cycle thesis emphasizes that a large and rapidly growing market is a stimulus to investment. As product markets reach a maturity stage in the U.S. in which the overall growth rate slows and rivalry makes it increasingly difficult to hold market share and increasingly expensive to increase market share, foreign markets become relatively attractive. Tests of this thesis have been performed by Wilkinson (1968), Wells (1968, 1969), and Prachowny and Richardson (1975). It has been observed that this theory suggests that certain types of international investment are inherently growth-oriented. The implications of the product-cycle thesis have been noted by Dunning:

> This suggests very strongly that certain types of international investment are inherently growth oriented, not only because they are directed to industries supplying products, the demand for which increases proportionately to the growth in GNP per head (Wells 1968), but because of the various advantages, e.g., access to knowledge and markets, size,

integration, and finance, possessed by the investing companies over their host competitors. Even the most cursory glance at the structure of U.S. firms in Europe reveals that their activities are heavily concentrated in two sectors, first the science-based, or research-intensive, industries supplying both producer and consumer goods, and second, industries subject to economies of scale and producing products with a high income elasticity of demand. Between 1958 and 1964, for example, the four most research-intensive industries in the United States spent 2½ times the amount on new plant and equipment in Europe than 14 other industries (Gruber, Mehta, and Vernon, 1967). Moreover, these same "knowledge" industries (e.g., computer, instruments, electronics, chemicals, etc.), by providing a kind of infrastructure of knowledge, create substantial spillover effects, and act as a catalyst for growth which may far outweigh the initial demand-stimulating effects (1970, pp. 149-150).

Caves presents some very important insights which provide ingredients for a theory much more rich and robust than the structural theory. In observing that capital flows are not induced by availability of equity capital, he writes:

Its investments transmit equity capital, entrepreneurship, and technological or other productive knowledge in an industry-specific package: The influence of national endowments of equity capital need not dominate or even significantly influence its actions (1971, p. 3).

Professor Caves also formulates the conditions for foreign investments:

For the possession of some special asset to lead the firm to invest abroad, two conditions must be satisfied. First, the asset must partake of the character of a public good within the firm, such as knowledge fundamental to the production of a profitably saleable commodity. Any advantage embodied in knowledge, information or technique that yields a positive return over direct costs in the market where it is first proven can potentially do the same in other markets without need to incur again the sunk costs associated with its initial discovery. Knowledge would seem to be the prototypical asset displaying the character of a public good proprietary to the firm, but it is not the only one. The essential feature of an asset conducive to foreign investment is not that its opportunity cost should be zero, but that it should be low relative to the return attainable via foreign investment. . . . Second, the return attainable on a firm's special asset in foreign market must depend at least somewhat on local production (1971, pp. 4-5).

A general framework for analyzing the impact of foreign direct investment has been presented by Harry G. Johnson (1970, pp. 45-47). He suggests that if foreign investments flow into the more capital intensive sectors of the economy (including nonmaterial), the effect of the inflow of foreign capital may be to raise the return on capital and reduce the wages of labor. Within this framework his observations on arguments for restrictions of foreign direct investment because of the possibility of increased monopoly are also worth noting:

> This is a second-best argument, because the intrusion of foreign enterprises may either increase or decrease competition in the domestic economy, and if more competition is desired it can be achieved more reliably by domestic antitrust policy, or still more reliably, by reducing the tariff protection enjoyed by industries where the presence of monopoly can be verified. Moreover, the question of whether foreign ownership of part of industry leads to social loss through increased monopoly requires more careful analysis than it has usually received. Social loss would seem to require either an increase in prices to consumers above what they would otherwise be, or additional wastes of resources on the nonprice aspects of monopolistic competition. Higher profits derived from the superior efficiency of foreign firms are not evidence of such loss, but rather the contrary from a cosmopolitan point of view, reflecting the saving of resource costs through greater efficiency; and from the national point of view, there is a gain to the extent that prices to consumers are lowered, prices of domestic factors of production are raised, or the nation shares in the increased profits of the foreign firms through taxation (1970, p. 55).

The same logic is extended to the issue of the takeovers of the existing domestic firms. If the foreign firm possesses organizational capabilities and knowledge that will enable them to produce the products at a lower price, this increased competition will result in capital losses for domestic firms. They will receive a higher value for their firms if they are able to sell to a buyer who can use these resources effectively rather than duplicating them.

Other studies have emphasized managerial aspects in the expansion of multinational corporations (MNCs). For example, Mason, Miller, and Weigel write:

> Although many United States firms may not have a technological advantage over local firms, some have advantages stemming from superior management. It is widely recognized, for example, that Proctor and Gamble has a competitive advantage over other firms in the consumer products industries because of its superior marketing skills. These skills may be exploited, to some extent, by exporting. However, Proctor and Gamble may have to produce in foreign markets to exploit fully its marketing advantage. Superior marketing skill includes the ability both to identify the characteristics of market demand, and to supply the desired products either in fact, or in the mind of the consumer through advertising. Local production is an invaluable marketing aid because it facilitates adaptation of the product and marketing strategies to

changes in local market conditions. Moreover, the local plant improves the reliability of supply—a factor that is of particular importance when the product has no special technological advantage.

Other management skills also may have to be exploited by direct investment. For example, the advantage possessed by United States food processing firms such as Heinz and Del Monte is a unique capacity to organize farmers to produce high-quality products on a large scale. These skills cannot be adequately exploited in foreign countries by exporting to them because canned foods are bulky and heavy and, thus, are costly to ship. Consequently, foreign investment is necessary to exploit the organizational skills possessed by these firms (1975, p. 245).

Aharoni (1966) found that foreign investment decisions were often stimulated as a response to meeting emerging domestic problems of firms. Others have found that the growth of foreign direct investments have been in response to sales growth and cash flows in foreign subsidiaries (Stevens, 1969). The size and prospective growth of foreign markets have also influenced foreign direct investments (Gordon and Gommers, 1962). Differential tariffs may cause a shift from export to direct investment (Horst, 1972).

Thus, there are many theories of the MNCs. Each of the theories can be supported by some appropriate assumptions and some evidence can be found both to support and to contradict any individual theory. Unfortunately, the plethora of theories makes it difficult to develop a general theory. What we have is a large number of causal variables operating with widely differing strengths in greatly different combinations of circumstances. Different statistical studies, even when done carefully, will therefore yield greatly different results and a variety of possible interpretations.

REFERENCES

Excellent general treatments of the subjects of this chapter are found in:

Behrman, Jack N.: *National Interests and the Multinational Enterprise: Tensions among the North Atlantic Countries*, Prentice-Hall, Englewood Cliffs, N.J., 1970.

Bergsten, C. Fred, Robert O. Keohane, and Joseph S. Nye, Jr.: "International Economics and International Politics: A Framework for Analysis," *World Politics and International Economics*, The Brookings Institution, Washington, D.C., 1975, pp. 3-36.

Servan-Schreiber, J. J.: *The American Challenge*, Atheneum, New York, 1968.

Vaupel, J. W., and J. P. Curhan: *The Making of Multinational Enterprise*, Division of Research, Graduate School of Business Administration, Harvard University, Boston, Mass., 1969.

Vernon, R.: *Sovereignty at Bay: The Multinational Spread of U.S. Enterprise*, Basic Books, New York, 1971.

Other more specific studies, including those referred to in this chapter, are listed below:

Aharoni, Yair: *The Foreign Investment Decision Process,* Harvard Graduate School of Business Administration, Harvard University, Boston, 1966.

Aliber, Robert Z.: "A Theory of Direct Foreign Investment," in Charles P. Kindleberger, (ed.), *The International Corporation: A Symposium,* M.I.T., Cambridge, Mass., 1970, pp. 17-33.

Barnet, Richard J., and Ronald E. Muller: *Global Reach: The Power of the Multinational Corporations,* Simon and Schuster, New York, 1974.

Boarman, Patrick M., and Hans Schollhammer, eds.: *Multinational Corporations and Governments: Business-Government Relations in an International Context,* Praeger, New York, 1975.

Business International Corporation: *Organizing the Worldwide Corporation,* Business International Corporation, New York, 1970.

Caves, Richard E.: "International Corporations: The Industrial Economics of Foreign Investment," *Economica,* pp. 1-27, February 1971.

Dunning, John H.: *American Investment in British Manufacturing Industry,* George Allen and Unwin, London, 1958.

———: "Technology, United States Investment, and European Economic Growth," in Charles P. Kindleberger (ed.), *The International Corporation: A Symposium,* M.I.T., Cambridge, Mass., 1970, pp. 141-176.

Gabriel, Peter: *The International Transfer of Corporate Skills,* Harvard Graduate School of Business Administration, Harvard University, Boston, 1967.

Gordon, L., and E. L. Gommers: *U.S. Manufacturing Investment in Brazil,* Division of Research, Graduate School of Business Administration, Harvard University, Boston, Mass., 1962.

Gruber, W., D. Mehta, and R. Vernon: The R and D Factor in International Trade and International Investment of United States Industries," *Journal of Political Economy,* 75:20-37, February 1967.

Hasson, Nathan, "Concentration and Performance: A Protection Criterion," unpublished Ph.D. dissertation, Graduate School of Management, University of California, Los Angeles, Spring 1975.

Horst, Thomas, *At Home Abroad: A Study of the Domestic and Foreign Operations of the American Food-Processing Industry,* Ballinger Publishing, Cambridge, Mass., 1974.

———— : "Firm and Industry Determinants of the Decision to Invest Abroad: An Empirical Study," *The Review of Economics and Statistics,* **54**:258-266, August 1972.

Hymer, Stephen: "The Internationalization of Capital," *Journal of Economic Issues,* **06**:91-111, March 1972.

———— and Robert Rowthorn: "Multinational Corporations and International Oligopoly: The Non-American Challenge," in Charles P. Kindleberger, (ed.), *The International Corporation: A Symposium,* M.I.T., Cambridge, Mass., 1970, pp. 57-91.

Johnson, Harry G.: "The Efficiency and Welfare Implications of the International Corporation," in Charles P. Kindleberger, (ed.), *The International Corporation: A Symposium,* M.I.T., Cambridge, Mass., 1970, pp. 35-56.

Kahn, Alfred E.: "The Chemical Industry," in Walter Adams, (ed.), *The Structure of American Industry,* Macmillan, New York, 1961, pp. 233-276.

Krause, Lawrence B., and Joseph S. Nye, "Reflections on the Economics and Politics of International Economic Organizations," *World Politics and International Economics,* The Brookings Institution, Washington, D.C., 1975, pp. 323-342.

Lowinger, Thomas C.: "The Technology Factor and the Export Performance of U.S. Manufacturing Industries," *Economic Inquiry,* **13**:221-236, June 1975.

Mason, R. Hal, Robert R. Miller, and Dale R. Weigel: *The Economics of International Business,* John Wiley & Sons, New York, 1975.

Miller, Robert R., and Dale R. Weigel: "The Motivation of Foreign Direct Investment," *Journal of International Business Studies,* **3**:67-79, Fall 1972.

Prachowny, Martin F. J., and J. David Richardson: "Testing a Life-Cycle Hypothesis of the Balance-of-Payments Effects of Multinational Corporations," *Economic Inquiry,* **13**:81-98, March 1975.

Richardson, J. D.: "Theoretical Considerations in the Analysis of Foreign Direct Investment," *Western Economic Journal,* **9**:87-98, March 1971.

Rostow, W. W.: *The Stages of Economic Growth: A Non-Communist Manifesto,* Cambridge University Press, New York, 1961.

Scaperlanda, A. E., and L. J. Mauer: "The Determinants of U.S. Direct Investment in the EEC," *American Economic Review,* **59**:558-568, September 1969.

Severn, Alan K.: "Investment and Financial Behavior of American Direct Investors in Manufacturing," in Fritz Machlup, Walter S. Salant, and Lorie Tarshis, (eds.), *International Mobility and Movement of Capital,* National Bureau of Economic Research, New York, 1972, pp. 367-396.

Stevens, Guy V. G.: "Capital Mobility and the International Firm," in Fritz Machlup, Walter S. Salant, and Lorie Tarshis, (eds.), *International Mobility and Movement of Capital,* National Bureau of Economic Research, New York, 1972, pp. 323-353.

_____: 'Fixed Investment Expenditures of Foreign Manufacturing Affiliates of U.S. Firms: Theoretical Models and Empirical Evidence," *Yale Economic Essays,* **9**:137-198, Spring 1969.

Stieglitz, Harold: *Organizational Structures of Multinational Companies,* National Industrial Conference Board, New York, 1967.

Vernon, R.: "International Investment and International Trade in the Product Cycle," *Quarterly Journal of Economics,* **80**:190-207, May 1966.

Wells, L. T., Jr.: "A Product Life Cycle for International Trade," *Journal of Marketing,* **32**(3):1-6, July 1968.

_____: "Test of a Product-Cycle Model of International Trade: U.S. Exports of Consumer Durables," *Quarterly Journal of Economics,* **83**:152-162, February 1969.

_____ ed.: *The Product Life Cycle and International Trade,* Harvard Business School, Boston, 1972.

Weston, J. Fred: "A Framework for Product-Market Planning," in N. N. Barish and M. Verhulst, (eds.), *Management Sciences in the Emerging Countries,* Pergamon Press, London, 1965, pp. 1-33.

_____: "Determining the Export Potential," *California Management Review,* **8**:89-92, Winter 1965.

_____: "Do MNC's Have Market Power to Overprice?" presentation to National Chamber Foundation, "Conference on Multinational Corporations," Washington, D.C., November 25, 1975.

Wilkinson, B.: *Canada's International Trade: An Analysis of Recent Trends and Patterns,* The Private Planning Association of Canada, Montreal, 1968.

Chapter 3

Organization and Control for International Financial Management

Theme: The organization of an international firm moves from a functional basis to product and geographic grouping, and ultimately to combinations of these as the firm grows. Financial planning and control use goals and objectives, but must also emphasize the development of an effective information flow process. The evaluation of the performance of subsidiaries is complicated by the need to account for different tariffs, taxes, exchange-rate fluctuations and restrictions on the repartriation of funds.

I. The organization of a multinational corporation.
  A. One major pressure for change in the multinational firm is the conflict between the three principal projections of the firm: *central services*, *product group*, and *geographic organizations*.
    1. Central services refer to research and legal services, but may also include functional activities such as finance and personnel.
    2. Product-group organization would be in charge of a range of products no matter where the product group is produced or sold throughout the enterprise.
    3. Geographical organization would separate control over product lines and services according to geographical location.

4. Firms have been classified into four types: A, B, C, D, as categories of organization types for international operations.
B. Type-A firms are primarily single-product firms with no separate geographical or product-group organization. They are organized into functional departments.

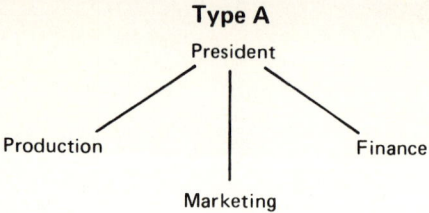

1. This would be a relatively small firm.
2. One production department would handle both domestic and foreign sales as well as foreign manufacturing activities, if any are involved.
3. The products must be relatively simple and it must be feasible to readily communicate production decisions, for example, all over the U.S. and the world.
4. The central-services organization is at the head office.
5. Links of communication in Type A are the most simple and straightforward.
6. Type A is the least stable; a merger or reorganization will quickly change it to Type B, discussed next.

C. Type-B firms comprise companies in which the geographical organization is the main link with foreign operations.

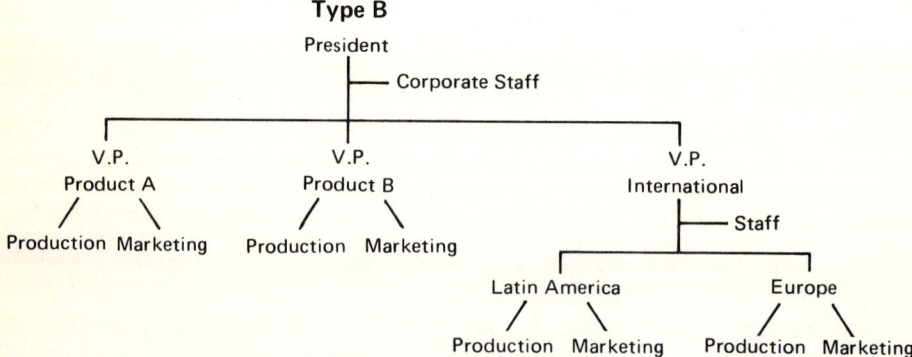

1. As overseas operations expand, they outgrow the resources of the domestic-product-group organization and an *international division* is formed.
   a. A common pattern is a product-group organization at home and a geographical organization overseas.

        b. The problem that arises from this type of structure is a block in communications with headquarters.
        c. The international division may come to be at odds with the product group, which seeks to retain control over product lines.
    2. The international operations have become sufficiently important and the problems of international operations are sufficiently distinct that they are guided by a vice-president or general manager who has an international orientation.
        a. The international division includes a staff which parallels and duplicates most of the functions of the corporate staff group.
        b. As a company develops experience in international operations, the staff functions become administered centrally at the corporate level. At this stage, the divisional staff of the international division is used by the corporate staff and corporate line officers to communicate with and control the operations that take place in the individual countries.
    3. The company will generally follow the policy of rotating its domestic management personnel.
        a. First, giving them experience in individual countries in their specific management function activities, such as production or marketing.
        b. Then later, after a manager has had some experience in general management activities domestically, he may be given responsibilities as a part of the divisional staff or general management responsibilities in an individual country.
        c. The business firm develops a group of managers who have both domestic experience and experience in adjusting to international conditions.
        d. This is an effective way to achieve coordination between domestic and international operation.
            (1) The domestic managers have had international experience and know the problems and can speak the language of the international managers.
            (2) The international managers receive their initial experience in domestic operations, so they recognize the problem of domestic operations and can think about how to relate the international activities to contribute to the effectiveness of the domestic operations as well.
D. Type-C firms have product groups organized worldwide.
    1. The senior vice-president in charge of individual products has a functional organization, such as production, marketing, etc., under him. In addition, the international activities covering different geographic areas also report to him.
        a. As products go overseas they remain the responsibility of the product group.

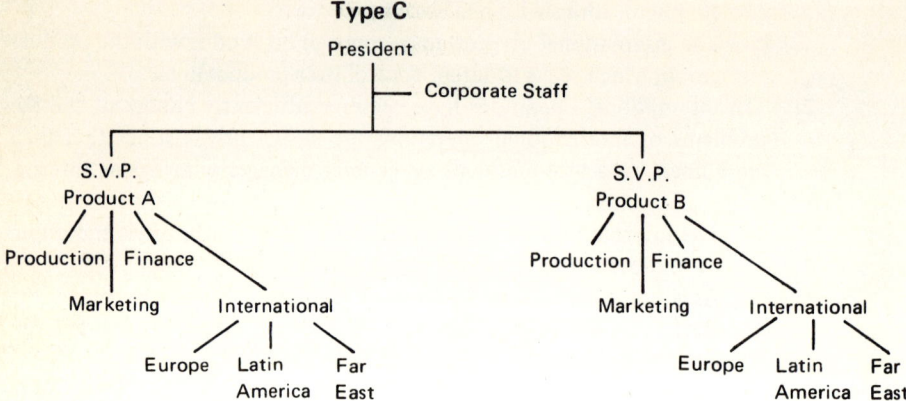

      b. Type C often has a more complex organization than Type B. There may be subproduct divisions which have foreign operations under their control.

  2. This kind of organization is likely to be found when the production methods and characteristics that appeal to consumers are essentially uniform throughout the world. A basic staple, such as cornstarch, would illustrate this kind of product.

      a. This form of organization insures that all international activities are made consistent with domestic operations.

      b. Another advantage is that sourcing for production, whether domestically or internationally, can take place wherever factors of production can be achieved most cheaply. Furthermore, production will take place where it can be accomplished most efficiently and at the lowest cost.

      c. This type of organization lends itself to standardizing production, marketing, operations, and policies throughout the world.

  3. Possible disadvantages that may evolve.

      a. Blocks in communications between the product division at the head office and its foreign operations may develop.

      b. Another concern is the waste of resources involved in setting up more than one organization in any particular foreign country.

E. Type-D firms are a mixture of the different organizations.

  1. They represent a combination of product-group and geographical departmentation.

      a. Product management will run the foreign organization and receive most services from the international division.

      b. The geographical division must promote and service new activities abroad.

          (1) It confers with the product group for recommendations.

          (2) Or the process could work in reverse.

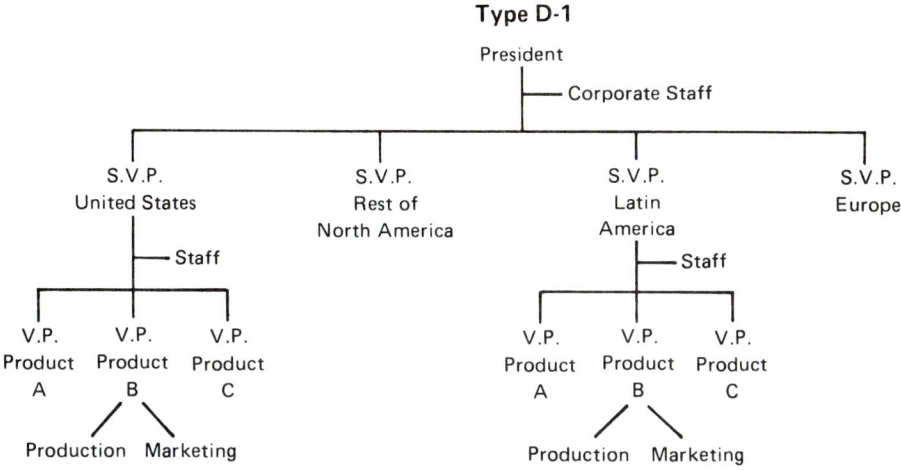

2. Type D-1 takes the Type C organization and moves the international up to the first level of grouping below the president.
   a. As shown in the diagram, there would be a number of broad divisions organized geographically. For each geographic group there is a suborganization based on product grouping. Then below each product there is likely to be functional departmentation, such as production, marketing.
   b. This kind of organization is likely to prevail in an industry, such as pharmaceuticals, where operations from beginning to end can be quite different depending upon the geographic area. For example, the processes of obtaining governmental approval for introducing and testing a new drug may differ from country to country. The size, strength, taste, and packaging of the drug might be different depending upon different countries.

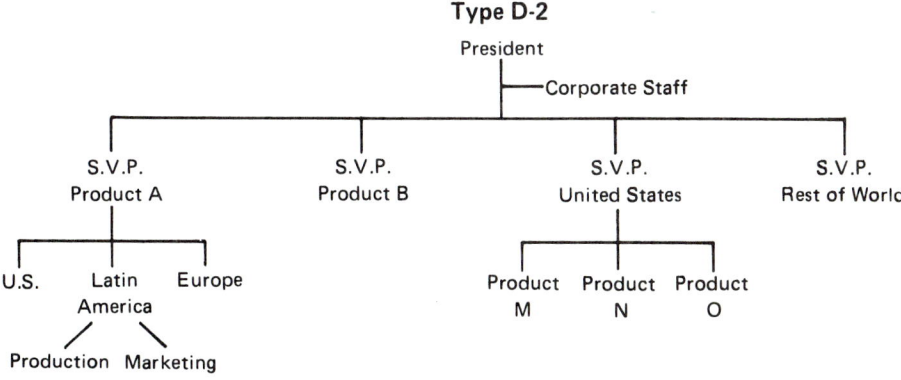

3. Type D-2 is a combination of Type C and Type D-1. Like Type C, there is product grouping for some products. For other products, there is geographic grouping as shown in Type D-1.
   a. This kind of organization is likely to occur if some products of the firm are basic staples produced and sold all over the world in the same way. That would involve the product grouping part.
   b. On the other hand, some products, such as pharmaceuticals or automobiles, may be produced differently and produced for different consumer tastes in different parts of the world, and for those products the grouping may be on a geographic basis.

II. The development of a financial system by a multinational corporation.
   A. Phase 1 is ignoring the potential of the system.
      1. During the early periods of foreign expansion:
         a. Firms do not believe that the function of international financial management requires specialized attention.
         b. There is usually just a small staff at headquarters dealing with international problems.
      2. Coordination of financial links is hindered by:
         a. Lack of foreign experience.
         b. The small scale of foreign operations.
      3. During this phase, financial managers of the foreign subsidiaries operate without close direction from the parent.
         a. Each subsidiary tends to operate independently.
         b. Subsidiaries operate to improve their individual performance, but this may be at the expense of the total profits of the system.
      4. The multinational enterprises in Phase 1 are relatively small in comparison with other multinational firms. Their foreign operations typically range from $20 million to $100 million in sales.
   B. Phase 2 is exploiting the potential of the system.
      1. As the foreign business of the firm grows, the managers in the parent organization learn the distinctions between the domestic and international sectors, and realize the increasing importance of closer control from headquarters.
         a. Multinational enterprises in Phase 2 generally range from $100 million to $500 million in sales from foreign operations.
         b. These foreign sales usually represent from 15 to 30 percent of the total world sales of the enterprise.
      2. Intercompany financial connections expand as more foreign subsidiaries are established and begin dealing with each other.
         a. At this point, the firm will generally decide to set up a strong central staff to direct the financial aspects of foreign operations.
         b. This brings the firm into Phase 2 of financial evolution.

3. In Phase 2, the central staff makes most financial decisions of importance and issues frequent orders to subsidiaries.
   a. The staff employs a "system optimization" viewpoint in making decisions for the entire enterprise.
   b. They set up policies and procedures and work with local management on the implementation.
   c. Central office retains final authority on decisions.
C. Phase 3 is compromising with complexity.
   1. Eventually, the management group at headquarters is faced with a dilemma.
      a. The scale and importance of foreign operations encourage them to keep tight control over foreign financial decisions.
      b. However, the increased number of financial options resulting from the growth in subsidiaries makes it impossible for the central staff to make a separate decision on each financial transaction.
   2. The enterprise resolves this issue by delegating more authority to the subsidiaries, and enters Phase 3.
      a. This delegated authority is accompanied by a "rule book" of standard procedures issued by headquarters. The rule book may specify items such as the limits of local borrowing, standard terms of payment on intercompany accounts, and standard rates for management fees.
      b. Central staff then reviews only major financial decisions and the results of subsidiary operations.
      c. Local management, with a larger financial staff than under Phase 2, is left with decisions on implementation within the guidelines of the rule book.
   3. Another development, generated by the increased complexity of a Phase 3 enterprise, is the creation of a regional financial headquarters.
      a. The regional financial group allows for more optimization and less reliance on decision rules for transactions between subsidiaries within a given region.
      b. However, transactions between subsidiaries located in different regions tend to be controlled by the rule book.
   4. Throughout this evolutionary process, the major factors affecting financial strategy are foreign experience and size of foreign operations.
      a. However, neither these nor any other measure fully determine the financial behavior of any given multinational enterprise.
      b. Firms of identical size and experience often behave differently.
III. The subsidiary of a multinational corporation.
   A. The subsidiary is held to have a number of advantages over local competing companies.
      1. Multinationals are generally large and possess many technological, managerial, and financial resources. These are available to the subsidiary at nominal cost.

2. Subsidiaries receive strength from the mutual support of other members of the group.
3. Economies of scale may be achieved through the group.
4. Financing by the group can provide needed funds at cheapest cost.
5. However, these advantages can be offset by the greater degree of risk and complexity in a geographically dispersed organization.

B. The foreign subsidiary will have a much simpler organization but will mirror the head office to some extent.
   1. This may not be the result of direct instructions from the head office, but by a development along similar lines of activities to facilitate communication.
   2. The foreign operations are bound to have some legal framework to comply with the fiscal laws of the home country.
   3. Though foreign branches do exist, the complications of different national taxation systems usually lead to the setting up of a subsidiary company.

C. The financial management of a foreign subsidiary is similar to that of a private company, as opposed to a publicly held firm.
   1. Most are wholly owned, or jointly owned, with a small number of companies as the shareholders.
   2. They rarely publish their financial accounts, avoid close scrutiny by the financial press, and are not concerned with large numbers of local shareholders.
   3. They can conduct their affairs with somewhat more flexibility than a public company.

D. Many of the usual measures of financial management appropriate to publicly owned domestic companies are not valid in the case of the foreign subsidiary.
   1. Many are part of an integrated system organized around broad geographical regions.
      a. Some may specialize in supplying products to other subsidiaries.
      b. Intracompany transfer pricing policies may distort the profit picture of many subsidiaries.
      c. Thus, a meaningful measure of performance will be quite difficult to achieve.
   2. Such intercompany policies can lead to conflicts of interest between the subsidiary and the host country as well as between head office and subsidiary management groups.
      a. Transfers of funds during a foreign exchange crisis is in opposition to the short-term advantage of the host country.
      b. These types of conflicts are inherent in international operations, though they need not inevitably damage either the subsidiary or the host country.

E. Management responds to these complex variables through risk-minimizing policies.
   1. They are financed with local debt, earnings, and intracompany loans.
   2. These are more easily repatriated than equity funds.

ORGANIZATION AND CONTROL FOR INTERNATIONAL FINANCIAL MANAGEMENT

IV. The regional center as an important form of geographical organization.
   A. It is designed to coordinate the activities of local companies in a group of countries.
      1. It is regarded as a unit of the head office that is nearer to the operations under its control.
      2. It bridges the gap in the line of communication between subsidiary and head office.
   B. The regional center provides a strong and experienced team for development in the area.
      1. It has expertise for setting up new national organizations.
      2. It can underpin a subsidiary where there are problems. This allows greater risks to be taken by the subsidiary companies.
      3. It meets the lack of local knowledge at headquarters and the lack of expertise in the subsidiary.
V. Planning and control systems in a multinational corporation.
   A. Policies for communication between the head office and the subsidiaries are set up.
      1. The system by which the head office collects reports from its subsidiaries constitutes a major formal channel of communication.
         a. The main problem is to make the reports meaningful and avoid disrupting the activities of the local company.
         b. A reporting system that is significant in a large headquarters can be irrelevant and burdensome in the subsidiary.
      2. Another aspect of the communications system is to ensure that the subsidiary is familiar with the policies and rules of the company.
         a. Companies with unwritten rules may actually be more rigid than those with written rules and organization charts.
         b. If a company has elaborate written manuals, it may have local management in its foreign operations.
         c. Multinational companies are likely to have a mixture of written and unwritten regulations.
   B. Tactical planning is done at the level of the subsidiary.
      1. The parent company sets guidelines, objectives, and policies.
      2. These are detailed, routine, and generally short-term.
      3. The subsidiary makes initial choices among alternative courses of action.
   C. The core of planning and control is the annual budget.
      1. Operating budget covers sales, expenses, and cash flow.
      2. Capital budget covers major investments.
   D. Parent company participation in planning subsidiary operating budgets depends on the division of authority.
      1. In industries of slow change, there is less participation.
      2. In industries of rapid change, such as electronics, operations are coordinated at higher levels.
      3. Plans with multiple objectives and multiple criteria, extending over several years, help avoid budget manipulation.

4. The budget provides the yardstick for evaluating the performance of the subsidiary.
5. Flexible budgets allow management to correct unfavorable situations.
   a. They are a means of adjusting activities of the firm to new operating conditions.
   b. They provide the head office with the subsidiary's latest view of operations and cash flow conditions.
6. Frequency of budget revisions depends on the nature of the industry.
7. Cash forecasts are revised more frequently than other plans.
   a. They are necessary to keep on top of fund transfer policies.
   b. They make most efficient use of corporate funds.

E. Capital budgeting difficulties are compounded in foreign investment decisions, arising from:
   1. Poor quality of information.
   2. Added risks.
   3. Different costs of capital in multiple environments.

F. One major issue in capital budgeting is division of authority between the head office and the subsidiary.
   1. Control over investment represents ultimate control over operations.
      a. This control is almost always held by the head office.
      b. Primary control is exerted by limiting the amount of autonomous expenditures.
   2. The annual capital budget is as much a control device as a planning device.
      a. Preparation of this budget is a continuous process.
      b. It includes a list of projects likely to begin, and amounts to be spent on unfinished projects.

G. Special problems arise in the use of financial criteria for the multinational firm.
   1. Criteria may differ at the head office and the subsidiary levels due to:
      a. Effects of taxation.
      b. Methods of financing the investment.
      c. Elements of risk.
   2. Tax differentials between foreign and home countries can cause a rate of return that is acceptable to the subsidiary to be unacceptable to the parent.
   3. Investment risk is seen differently by the subsidiary than by the head office.
      a. A high return may make an investment desirable to the subsidiary.
      b. Currency depreciation and exchange controls may make the investment unacceptable to the parent.
      c. These differences may cause the parent to vary its usual required rate of return on foreign investments.

ORGANIZATION AND CONTROL FOR INTERNATIONAL FINANCIAL MANAGEMENT 41

    4. Many companies try to avoid these risks by limiting the commitment of their own funds.
       a. They rely more on subjective criteria and field recommendations than on figures and percentages.
       b. More weight is often given to strategic, technical, or subjective considerations than to financial data.
VI. Measurement of performance.
   A. Performance measurement is the final element in a planning and control system.
      1. It helps guide future allocation of resources to the subsidiary.
      2. It helps to coordinate a group of interdependent activities.
   B. If the objective of the company is long-term profits and maximization of net present worth, performance must be judged by this measure. The difficulty is that measurement of current profits can be misleading if many current activities begin to pay off in the future.
   C. The basic measures of performance most often used are the rate of return and the performance of the subsidiary relative to a budget.
      1. The rate of return usually relates net income before taxes to either equity or total assets after depreciation as the investment base.
      2. Due to the problem of specifying the appropriate investment base, most enterprises use some supplementary device to gauge the performance of the subsidiary.
      3. The most important measure is budget versus performance, and this analysis often replaces the rate of return as the primary tool.
      4. This analysis seeks to develop a good information system and fast reaction to change.
   D. Adjustments in the financial statements of foreign subsidiaries are necessary to give headquarters a clearer picture of the performance of the subsidiaries.
      1. Profits earned by the enterprise as a whole are not easily attributable to one subsidiary or another.
      2. The performance of each subsidiary varies with the degree of other subsidiaries' integration into the system.
      3. The parent may require certain subsidiaries to engage in a series of financial relations that benefit the entire system rather than any one subsidiary.
      4. It is difficult to determine the effects on the firm as a whole if any one subsidiary were not present.
       a. Transfer of goods through the system is influenced by tax considerations and other international business factors.
       b. An affiliate in an area with low interest rates may be instructed to finance an affiliate in an area with high interest rates.
       c. Loans may be taken out in low-interest areas and sent back to the home office or to other areas.

        d. The costs and benefits of the above transactions must be assigned in order to evaluate performance.
    5. Judging each subsidiary as a profit center, without properly assigning costs and benefits, can create conflicts of interest between the subsidiary and the system as a whole.
 E. The performance of each subsidiary is also affected by the national conditions under which it operates.
    1. Barriers against transferring funds to the parent may hold down the rate of return of one subsidiary.
    2. Variations in interest rates from country to country result in unequal opportunities for various subsidiaries.
    3. Under the accounting principles of one country, a subsidiary may show a profit that could be substantially changed if expressed according to the requirements of another country. An example is the timing of the recognition of revenues, using the installment method or the accrual method.
    4. Performance must also be evaluated in light of cultural patterns and established social or business habits.
        a. Consider the productivity of the labor force.
        b. Consider the length of established credit terms.

VII. Evaluation of performance.
 A. The small multinational firm uses evaluation measures on an informal basis.
    1. Rate-of-return calculations are made on the basis of local operations alone, without reference to costs or benefits of the whole system.
    2. Headquarters generally allows the management of the subsidiaries to use their own judgment and make decisions.
    3. The informal nature is attributed to lack of foreign experience and lack of adequate staff to perform detailed reviews of the budgets of the subsidiaries.
 B. The firms of medium size use rate of return as an indicator of performance and a formal budget as a supporting measure.
    1. The close control of management over subsidiary activities reduces the importance of budgetary policies for firms of medium size. Lack of experience with a tightly controlled budget and the necessary foreign adjustments also contribute to the reduced emphasis placed on this tool.
    2. Firms of medium size generally consider the income and assets of the entire integrated system when using rate of return to evaluate the performance of a particular subsidiary.
 C. The large enterprise uses a more formal scheme of reviews and procedures to control and evaluate its scattered and diverse foreign subsidiaries.
    1. The budgetary procedure becomes the structure that guides the financial activities of the subsidiaries without the necessity of constant overview by headquarters.
    2. The large firm is likely to calculate and compare rates of return of individual foreign subsidiaries.

3. The budget is a major yardstick against which the operations of the subsidiary may be measured.
   a. Headquarters can develop supporting guidelines so that deviations from the budget can be checked.
   b. The desire to judge the relative performance of units within the network leads to the use of worldwide and regional comparisons.
   c. Management, as previously discussed, makes adjustments to operating results in light of the circumstances of particular subsidiaries.

VIII. Responsibility for foreign exchange losses.
   A. Management reaches different conclusions when evaluating a currency change depending on whether the outcome is expressed in local currency or in dollars. In practice, about half the firms judge the subsidiary in terms of local currency and about half use dollars.
   B. Enterprises that judge in terms of local currency do not believe the subsidiary has the burden for protecting against devaluation.
      1. Local management makes recommendations, but headquarters is responsible for the full range of currency problems.
      2. These enterprises use a performance review to gauge the operating efficiency of local management rather than its financial acumen in avoiding exchange losses.
      3. However, this ignores the effect of devaluation and revaluation factors upon the operating results of the subsidiary. (For example, the evaluation of a Brazilian subsidiary's profits in terms of cruzeiros not adjusted for purchasing power would overstate the true picture.)
   C. Enterprises that judge performance in terms of dollars maintain that a U.S. multinational must express the outcome of its operations in dollars.
      1. Since the entire system is judged in dollars, these firms feel that each element must be so judged.
      2. Difficulties still arise because of the 1-year period often used to measure performance.
         a. In a given year, rapid inflation can substantially increase the dollar value of local earnings.
         b. But a devaluation in the following year, brought on by the previous inflation, can substantially reduce the dollar value of local earnings.
         c. Hence, the oscillating dollar value of subsidiary profits could be stabilized if longer time periods are used as performance intervals.
   D. It is not realistic to consider a subsidiary as an independent operation when it is really an organic part of the worldwide corporate network.
      1. Use of a standard return-on-investment performance measure, even with adjustments, is a "bent measuring stick," since its use neglects the reasons for which the subsidiary was originally founded.
      2. Foreign investments by U.S. multinationals are typically defensive in nature.
         a. They are part of a long-run strategy to preserve the position of the enterprise in a world economy.

b. A foreign investment in a manufacturing subsidiary may take place when the company's foreign market postion is in danger due to the effects of tariffs, freight, and other factor costs.
c. Also, by manufacturing in a country, the firm obtains more information about local market conditions.
d. This reduces the danger of another firm moving in and capturing the market.
3. Natural resource enterprises undertake foreign investments to acquire new reserves and develop more diverse sources to match those of competitors.
E. Since the investment decision is of a long-run strategic nature, annual return-on-investment calculations are often subject to wide margins of error and ignore the intangible considerations.
1. When the foreign investment finally commences operations, those evaluating its performance tend to forget the purpose of the original investment and the melange of numbers that went into the profitability calculations.
2. The true economic benefits should be ascertained by comparing the total enterprise with and without the subsidiary.
3. In the long run, the typical formula for evaluation of performance is either some version of rate of return on investment, or a comparison of budgeted profit and realized profit.
4. There are wide differences in the form of rate of return on investment (and sales) used among MNCs. A multinational corporation can only compare its foreign subsidiary with another firm's foreign subsidiary in the same country if the definition of rate of return on investment is adjusted. Also, MNCs can only make comparisons between their own foreign subsidiaries in different countries if a consistent definition is used internally.
5. Measure of investment includes one of the following: gross assets, net assets, or equity investment.
6. Measure of return constitutes different combinations of foreign earnings, royalties, fees, dividends, rentals, interest, commission, and export profits. Some companies use measurement before taxes, some after taxes.
7. Even if measurement of performance could be standardized, acceptable levels of performance cannot.
8. The realized rate of return on investment depends on the maturity of foreign investment, the economic stage of development of host country, risks, type of operation, and other objectives including strategic objectives.
IX. Transfer pricing.
A. Unless market prices for similar products are available, some arbitrary elements will be involved in pricing the transfer of goods, services, and

technology between divisions of the same corporation (intracorporate transfer pricing) in the domestic case, and between corporate subsidiaries in different countries (intercorporate transfer pricing) in the multinational case.
- **B.** In the intercorporate case, taxes, tariffs, managerial incentives and evaluation, antitrust, risk, bargaining power, and joint-venture partners must be considered.
  1. Taxation.
     a. Tax-haven subsidiaries act as trade intermediaries to drain off income from transfer transactions between related corporations in third countries.
     b. Governmental restrictions prohibit manipulation of transfer prices.
     c. There is danger of double taxation on the same income under two or more governments.
     d. U.S. Internal Revenue Code, Section 482, provides that the IRS reallocate gross income, deductions, credits or allowances to prevent tax evasion or to reflect more clearly the proper allocation of income.
     e. Treasury guidelines state "correct price" as one which reflects an "arm's length" transaction.
  2. Tariff.
     a. An *ad valorem* tariff is based on the value of the product. It must be balanced against higher income taxes under lower transfer prices of goods.
     b. Most countries are aware of the effect of transfer pricing on tariff revenue. Importing countries can also consider revenue generation from income taxes versus tariff.
  3. Managerial incentives and evaluation.
     a. Under decentralized profit centers, transfer pricing between centers could be a major determinant of managerial performance.
     b. Domestic intracorporate transfer pricing by coordination at the corporate level alleviates some of the distortions, since each profit center is suboptimizing profit from the corporate point of view.
     c. Fixing transfer prices and sourcing alternatives (countries or locations where raw materials are purchased) can be a managerial disincentive if prices seem arbitrary or unreasonable; also, rigid control of prices loses one of the main advantages of the decentralized profit-center system.
- **C.** Transfer-pricing policies of multinational corporations must satisfy the arms-length test by reasonable and commercially defensible pricing formulae. A "reasonable" transfer price must be demonstrated for royalties, fees, management assistance, and other services without outside equivalent.

PROBLEM 3-1

Explain why the development of a financial organization by a multinational operation goes through three phases.

SOLUTION:

1. In Phase 1, the firm is new to international operations. It does not understand the situation in foreign countries. It has an exaggerated view of the risks of foreign operations. Frequently the firm takes a wait-and-see attitude: "Let's see what they can do on their own, and if they succeed, fine; however, if they do not, let them just use money that they borrowed from abroad. We won't take any responsibility."
2. In Phase 2, the foreign operations grow, and begin to contribute significantly to the profitability of the total enterprise. More and more officers at the corporate level begin to understand better the foreign operations; then there is an effort to optimize from the standpoint of the firm as a whole. A central staff including a strong financial group will begin to interact continuously with the foreign operation.
3. In Phase 3, the foreign operations now become so important that if they are not handled well, mistakes could result in substantial losses to the firm as a whole. Therefore, an effort is made to achieve tight control over foreign financial decisions. But with the growth and complexity of the foreign subsidiaries, the central staff simply has neither sufficient time nor knowledge of local conditions to make decisions on individual financial transactions. Hence, an intermediary group, such as an international division group or a regional financial headquarters group, will function as a communication link between corporate headquarters and the operations of the individual foreign subsidiaries.

PROBLEM 3-2

Describe some of the characteristics of a foreign subsidiary as compared with the department or subsidiary of a domestic operation.

SOLUTION:

1. The foreign subsidiary has access to the greater technological, managerial, and financial resources possessed by its multinational parent. The domestic operation alone does not have the equivalent strength or amount of resources that the MNC as a whole has to support a local subsidiary.
2. The foreign subsidiary is subject to a greater degree of risk and complexity arising from a geographically dispersed organization. Obviously, this is not as much a problem for the subsidiary of a domestic operation.

ORGANIZATION AND CONTROL FOR INTERNATIONAL FINANCIAL MANAGEMENT

3. The foreign subsidiary affords the multinational parent the opportunity to make use of its locational advantage to minimize total corporate costs or to maximize corporate profits, i.e., where it provides a cheaper source of material, labor, etc. The subsidiary of a domestic operation does not offer this kind of advantage.
4. Intercompany policies that seek to optimize corporate interests may lead to conflicts of interest between the foreign subsidiary and the host country as well as between the head office and the subsidiary management groups. For the foreign subsidiary, such conflicts usually center on the effects of such policies on the countries involved. For the subsidiary or department of a domestic operation, the focus of attention is on the conflict among divisions and the effect on divisional performance.
5. Policies that seek to govern the operations of the foreign subsidiary differ in focus from those of domestic subsidiaries. The former seek mainly to minimize the risk of the complex environmental factors for the foreign subsidiary.

PROBLEM 3-3

Describe the development of the regional center as an important element in the evolving organizational structure of a multinational corporation.

SOLUTION:

As the international operations of the corporation grow in scope, the need to coordinate the activities of various geographically dispersed subsidiaries also grows. The regional center is developed to meet this need on a regional basis. Regarded as a unit of the head office that is situated nearer to the operating subsidiaries, it serves as a crucial communication link between the various subsidiaries in the region and the head office. In addition, the regional center provides a team of managers that develops expertise in the area under its control. Thus, the regional center gradually evolves as an important geographical link between the head office and the subsidiaries in the region under its control.

PROBLEM 3-4

Discuss the nature of the planning and control system in a multinational firm.

SOLUTION:

A. An extensive reporting system is required by the multinational parent for control purposes. This may prove burdensome to the subsidiary.
B. Tactical planning is done at the level of the subsidiary within the guidelines and goals of the parent company.

C. The annual budget is the core of the planning and control system.
   1. Parent company participation in planning subsidiary operating budgets depends on the nature of the industry.
   2. Control over subsidiary capital budgets is almost always held at the head office.
   3. The budget serves as the basis for measuring the performance of the subsidiary.

PROBLEM 3-5

How do capital budgeting decisions become more complicated in making foreign investment decisions?

SOLUTION:

Complications arise from:
A. Added dimensions of risks.
B. Difficulty in gathering information.
C. Different criteria needed to evaluate multiple environments. This is due to:
   1. Effect of taxation.
   2. Method of financing.
   3. Risk differentials.
D. Use of appropriate cost of capital in multiple environments.

PROBLEM 3-6

Discuss the problems and adjustments required in order to evaluate the performance of foreign operations in total and in individual foreign subsidiaries.

SOLUTION:

A. There are alternative measures of performance.
   1. The use of current profits in judging performance, as consistent with the corporate goal of profit maximization, may be misleading where investments made have long pay-offs.
   2. The use of rate of return runs into the problem of the use of the appropriate investment base, i.e., equity or total assets, gross versus net.
   3. The budget has come to be the most commonly used alternative for measuring performance.
   4. There is no substitute for an effective information flow system, with informed reviews of the foreign operations.

B. Financial policies and decisions made in the interest of the whole corporation may be at the expense of some operating subsidiaries.
   1. The minimization of the total corporate tax liability through transfer pricing and other means is an important consideration.
   2. Advantages of interest differentials among countries where subsidiaries are located affect financing methods among subsidiaries.
   3. Costs and benefits of such transactions must be made to adjust for distortions in arriving at a proper evaluation of the subsidiary.
C. The performance of each subsidiary is also affected by the prevailing environmental factors of its host country.
   1. Interest-rate differentials provide unequal opportunities.
   2. Differences in accounting rules and requirements among different countries means that the profit picture has to be adjusted to make the performances of various subsidiaries comparable.
   3. Legal barriers to transfer of funds may adversely affect the operations of the subsidiary.
   4. Differences in cultural patterns and social or business habits must be considered. These affect:
      a. Productivity of labor.
      b. Ease in meeting financing requirements.
      c. Cost of doing business.

PROBLEM 3-7

Discuss the nature of transfer pricing. How must transfer-pricing policies take into consideration variables such as taxation, tariff, a sound basis for maintaining managerial incentives, and a sound basis for managerial evaluation?

SOLUTION:

In general, transfer pricing in international transactions performs functions similar to transfer pricing for domestic operations. The basic function performed is to price out the sale or transfer of goods, components, or services from one corporate division to another corporate division. In general, the correct principle for transfer pricing, either domestically or internationally, is to price transfers at the market prices of those same goods when sold by independent nonaffiliated producers. However, when similar goods are not produced by independent producers, the market price guideline is not available. The correct concept then, in theory, is to price transfers at their marginal costs, because under competitive conditions, prices should be equal to long-run marginal costs. However, it is not always possible for a firm to precisely determine the marginal costs of operations in a particular division. Hence, generally, transfer pricing is cost-related. Hopefully, the cost figure represents a measure relating to or approximating marginal costs.

For international transactions, three elements give rise to additional considerations. Because there are different rates of taxation in different foreign countries, there are incentives to transfer at relatively high prices and to take low profits in high taxation areas, and to transfer at low prices and to take high profits in low taxation areas.

Another variable is tariff rates. If the MNC is importing parts or components into a country with a high *ad valorem* tariff, it will have incentives to transfer at lower prices as compared with transfers into countries that have lower tariffs.

A third factor arises when foreign countries impose artificially low limits on the amount of dividends or cash flows that can be transferred back to the parent country. Such artificial restrictions may stimulate the MNC to transfer goods in at higher prices in order to achieve the level of dividends, or cash flow transfers back to the parent, necessary to make the foreign investment worthwhile.

There are two general principles which should also be recognized.
Regardless of the transfer price used by the MNC in moving goods to its subsidiaries in various foreign countries, the transfer price does not necessarily determine the price that will be charged in the foreign country where the goods are ultimately sold. Prices that are charged for final products in foreign countries will be determined by market demand and supply conditions for individual products in the individual foreign countries. It is market conditions in an individual country that determine the price that appropriately can be charged. Purely from an accounting standpoint, all that transfer pricing does is locate where, in the chain of manufacturing activities and transfers within the MNC, the profits are recorded.

The second general principle is that the individual MNC does not have complete freedom even within the general framework discussed above. The U.S. Internal Revenue Code, Section 482, and corresponding provisions of foreign tax systems, emphasize that the correct price is one which reflects an arms-length transaction. The U.S. Internal Revenue Service enforces these rules very energetically. Hence, whatever inclinations the MNC may have to minimize taxation, tariffs, or restrictions on profits imposed by foreign countries, what the MNC can do in the way of pricing ultimately is determined in part by the market; and it is subject to energetic supervision by the Internal Revenue Service with regard to improperly shifting the locus at which taxation will be levied.

REFERENCES

Two outstanding book-length treatments of organization aspects of the international enterprise have been published in recent years. They are:

Brooke, Michael Z., and H. Lee Remmers: *The Strategy of Multinational Enterprise: Organization and Finance,* American Elsevier, New York, 1970.

Stopford, John M., and Louis T. Wells: *Managing the Multinational Enterprise: Organization of the Firm and Ownership of Subsidiaries,* Basic Books, New York, 1972.

An excellent survey with case studies of organization patterns in international companies is found in:

Duerr, Michael G., and John M. Roach: *Organization and Control of International Operations,* The Conference Board, New York, 1973.

Chapter 4

The International Financial System

Theme: Because of the differences in economic and financial developments among the nations of the world, foreign exchange rates fluctuate and capital flows take place. The international adjustment processes introduce additional dimensions and new uncertainties to international business activities of the firm not encountered in domestic transactions. The nature of the international financial system must be understood to evaluate the effects of trends in the balance of payments and their relation to foreign-exchange-rate movements as well as the broader effects of both on national and international economic and financial trends.

I. The adjustment process in the balance of payments between nations.
   A. A formulation first set forth in the mid-eighteenth century is *the price-gold-flow mechanism*.
      1. Country A runs an export balance surplus (country B runs a deficit).
      2. Gold flows into country A (gold flows out of country B).
      3. Domestic prices in country A rise (the prices in country B fall).
      4. The foreign currency price of A's currency in B's currency rises (the foreign currency price of B's currency in A's currency falls).

5. A is an attractive market in which to increase sales from other countries (A's imports increase). A's goods are more expensive in other countries, so its export sales decrease. A's export surplus will be reduced or reversed until equilibrium between relative price relationships of the countries is restored.
6. Note that the flows of gold operate through prices to function as an adjustment mechanism for international balances of trade and payments as well as to regulate the price change relationships between countries.

B. While modern analysis takes additional factors into account, the task remains the same: to explain the interaction between national income, money supply, balance of payments (basic national accounting relationships) and prices, interest rates, forward exchange rates (representing price effects). The general pattern of relationships is set forth below (See Appendix 4A for a formal demonstration of these points).
1. An export surplus increases income and employment in the surplus country and decreases it in the deficit country.
2. If both countries were at full employment before the shift in the trade balances, prices would rise in country A and fall in country B; unemployment would develop in country B.
3. If prices rise in country A and fall in country B, the effects are similar to those described under the gold flow scenario and the process of readjustment would be as described under IA.
4. If country A was not at full employment before achieving the export surplus, the effects of the rise in income might be to increase employment as well as to increase prices. Country A might not be willing to passively accept a subsequent adjustment process that causes its national income and employment to decline, and it could take a number of measures to offset the effects of gold flows into or out of the country.

C. Basic issues are raised by the interaction of foreign trade balances and national income and employment policies.
1. Foreign trade entails transactions involving two currencies. A Volkswagon bought and produced in Germany and sold in the United States is ultimately paid for in German marks. This involves an exchange of U.S. dollars for German marks.
   a. U.S. exports are ultimately paid for in dollars.
   b. Exchanges of currencies give rise to the need for foreign exchange rates.
2. Foreign exchange rates are the prices of one currency in terms of another. A foreign exchange rate is the price of a foreign currency unit in terms of our own.
   a. Thus, the price of a British pound might be $2.00; the price of a German mark, $.25.
   b. Alternatively, the relation can be expressed in terms of the number of foreign currency units per $1. Thus, $2.00 per £ is equivalent to £.5 per $1, and $.25 per DM is equivalent to DM4 per $1.

THE INTERNATIONAL FINANCIAL SYSTEM

    3. Fundamental to an understanding of international financial management is a consideration of the economic principles that determine foreign exchange rates and underlie their movements. This requires a summary of alternative mechanisms of foreign exchange and trade. The leading alternative foreign exchange systems are:
       a. The gold standard.
       b. Gold exchange standard with fixed exchange rates.
       c. Floating exchange rates.
       d. Gliding bands of exchange-rate relationships.

II. Foreign exchange systems.
    A. The gold standard represents the ultimate fixed exchange-rate system.
       1. Under a pure gold standard, payment is made in gold at a price expressed in ounces of gold.
          a. Trade balances are settled by gold flows.
          b. Gold flows, through their effects on prices, bring about readjustments in trade imbalances.
       2. A gold standard has advantages.
          a. The rules of the game are known to all.
          b. The rules work without manipulation by political authorities.
       3. A gold standard has disadvantages.
          a. Domestic economies can be stimulated into strong expansions and painful recessions in response to gold flows.
          b. The supply of gold does not keep up with the rate of growth of international trade, causing periods of declines in price levels, disadvantageous to debtors, such as the farmers in the United States during the period from 1875 to 1890.
       4. Possible modifications in the operation of the gold standard are suggested.
          a. Government authorities might modify the impact of gold movements.
             (1) The impact might be magnified in that a gold outflow might be accompanied by a rise in the central bank discount rate, signaling a tightening of monetary policy by raising reserve requirements or open market sales of government securities.
             (2) Alternatively, the government might blunt the impact of a gold outflow by the reverse policies.
          b. A fractional reserve banking system could be used to magnify the effect of gold flows or to offset them. For example, if the required ratio of reserves to deposits is about 1/7, as in the United States, an increase in the monetary base (an increase in member bank free reserves) by an inflow of $2 billion of gold could potentially result in an expansion of commercial bank deposits (the major component of the money supply) by the reciprocal of the reserve requirement ratio, or 7 times $2 billion which equals $14 billion.

  c. Changing the number of units of the currency in relation to gold could economize on the use of gold and thereby increase its effective quantity.
    (1) If $25 equals 1 ounce of gold and the country owns one billion ounces of gold, it has $25 billion of gold.
    (2) If the price of gold is doubled, the dollar value of gold reserves is doubled. The relation can also go in the reverse direction.
B. The gold exchange standard exists with fixed exchange rates.
 1. In addition to gold, a nation holds claims on the currency of another country. Such currency is convertible into gold and is regarded as a strong currency.
 2. When a country suffers a balance-of-payments deficit, foreign exchange reserves and/or gold are used to settle balances.
 3. In addition to gold and foreign exchange reserves, a surplus or deficit on goods and services may be offset by government grants (if a surplus) or an increase of short-term or long-term liabilities (if a deficit).
 4. Thus, adjustments are made for an imbalance in the current account by a number of credit mechanisms in addition to the flows of foreign exchange reserves and gold.
C. Floating exchange rates are an alternate method.
 1. The adjustment mechanism, instead of flows of gold, foreign exchange reserves, and/or financial liabilities or claims, is movement of exchange rates.
 2. There are advantages.
  a. Adjustments in exchange value relationships (price movements) may be more prompt; they do not involve the lags of capital movements.
  b. Speculative movements based on the disparity between a country's balance on merchandise and services trade and the fixed exchange rates are avoided.
 3. There are disadvantages.
  a. Unless an efficient forward exchange market is functioning, buyers and sellers of goods may not know the actual price in a transaction until settlement actually takes place.
  b. It is also argued that speculative price movements may take place.
  c. Risks of competitive devaluation and lack of coordination of economic policies between nations may result in continued international instability.
D. Consider gliding bands of exchange-rate relationships.
 1. Exchange rates may fluctuate up or down by some specified percentage, such as 2.5%, on either side of a par rate of exchange. Both the par rate of exchange and the size of the peg may be adjusted periodically.
 2. There are pros and cons of the gliding band arrangement.
  a. It combines flexibility of floating rates with defined limits of exchange-rate fluctuations.
  b. Like other adjustment mechanisms it does not get at the fundamental factors that may be causing the imbalance between nations.

THE INTERNATIONAL FINANCIAL SYSTEM

- E. Foreign exchange systems that are currently in use.
    1. A combination of all of the mechanisms described above exist, in various degrees, except the pure gold standard.
    2. None of the above exchange systems have operated free of government intervention.
        a. Under the gold standard, government authorities could magnify or blunt the effects of gold flows.
        b. Under fixed exchange rates, government grants and loans are used to relieve pressures on exchange rates that would otherwise be required by shifting trade balances.
        c. Under floating exchange rates, government intervention may take place to moderate the effects that shifting trade balances would otherwise have on exchange rates—this is called a "dirty float" in contrast to a "clean float" in which no government intervention takes place.
    3. No exchange standard can make the adjustments required if major imbalances in trade and capital flows develop.
    4. With the trend toward wider use of floating exchange rates, competitive devaluations are a threat to world stability.
- F. Devaluation can be an adjustment device.
    1. If country A devalues, the prices of its goods in country B in the foreign currency are reduced, leaving them unchanged (other things being equal) in country A's currency price. Foreign goods are now more expensive for A to purchase in its own currency.
        a. A's exports will increase and its imports will decrease in physical volume.
        b. Whether A's devaluation reduces its trade deficit depends upon relative price changes which with volume changes determine the total values of imports and exports.
    2. The actual effects of devaluation, therefore, depend upon the price elasticities of demand for the products of country A and of the nations with which it trades.
        a. If the sum of the price elasticities of the goods traded equals 1, no change in the trade balance of country A will take place.
        b. If the sum of the price elasticities of the goods traded is greater than (less than) one, the trade balance of country A will improve (deteriorate further). (See Appendix 4B for a formal demonstration of these relationships.)
- G. The International Monetary Fund was created.
    1. The founding charter's main objective was to achieve relative stability of exchange rates for the nations of the free world.
        a. Almost all "free-world" nations, except Switzerland, are members.
        b. Each member country must supply capital to the fund on the basis of a quota which is determined by the country's
            (1) Monetary reserves.
            (2) Volume of foreign trade.

            (3) National income.
        c. Part of the quota, generally 25%, must be paid in gold. This is known as the country's *gold tranche* (*tranche* is French for slice or share). The remainder is contributed in the currency of the member.
    2. All countries agreed to maintain the value of their currencies within 1% of par by buying or selling foreign exchange or gold as needed.
        a. All countries set the foreign exchange value of their currencies in terms of the U.S. dollar and thus in terms of gold.
        b. The U.S. dollar was the only major currency readily convertible gold.
    3. Devaluation of up to 10% was allowed without formal approval by the International Monetary Fund (IMF).
    4. The IMF functions to relieve the strain on international financial relations.
        a. Short-term credit facilities are provided to help member nations meet *temporary* disequilibrium in their balance of payments.
            (1) The international short-term credit extended by the IMF provides foreign exchange funds.
            (2) A country may automatically purchase foreign currency from the IMF in an amount not exceeding the value of its gold tranche.
            (3) Additional foreign currency purchases require the approval of the IMF.
            (4) Upon the improvement of the foreign exchange reserve position of the country, it is supposed to reverse the transaction and buy back its own currency on deposit with the fund.
            (5) Thus, the IMF provides an international banking service for nations similar to the temporary or seasonal financing services which a commercial bank extends to business firms.
        b. Coordination of economic policies among nations is attempted through research studies and consultation.
            (1) The IMF monitors levels of indebtedness among countries.
            (2) It analyzes imbalances in the balance of payments of a nation and suggests methods of correction, such as removal of trade barriers or moderation of the rate of monetary expansion.

III. Factors leading to the international monetary crisis of August 1971.
    A. International developments taking place in the two decades following World War II.
        1. Full currency convertibility by major trading nations returned in 1959.
        2. Common markets and free trade areas developed.
        3. Trade and foreign direct investment rapidly increased.
        4. The need for an ever-increasing supply of international liquidity was met by the deficits of some reserve-currency countries.
        5. The United States began to run large deficits.

THE INTERNATIONAL FINANCIAL SYSTEM

      6. This raised doubts as to the convertibility of the reserve currencies into gold.
      7. A persistent drop in the foreign exchange reserves, particularly gold, of the United States occurred.
      8. Liquid short-term liabilities to foreigners on the part of the United States continued to increase.
  B. Several factors led to the decline in the value of the dollar.
      1. Exchange values of 1946 were unrealistic.
          a. Overwhelming strength of U.S. economy was expected.
          b. Concern over a possible dollar shortage affected rates.
          c. Rates established at the end of the war, in consideration of the devastated economies, failed to reflect the major economic advances later accomplished by other nations in relation to the U.S. economy.
      2. The United States launched a major program of foreign aid at the end of the war.
          a. Between 1945 and 1970, foreign aid expenditures totaled over $120 billion.
              (1) Economic and technical aid of $55 billion.
              (2) Net loans to foreign governments of $40 billion.
              (3) Net military grants of $25 billion.
          b. U.S. technical aid program (Point Four program) exported technological skills in order to increase economic progress among foreign nations.
          c. These foreign aid programs had dual effects on American business firms.
              (1) Certain firms benefited from the artificial stimulus of tied outlays—those in which foreign aid money had to be spent on U.S. goods and services.
              (2) Many other firms benefited from the generally increased spending power of foreign nations as a result of the program.
              (3) However, Point-Four-type programs which aided in the development of foreign industries also created increased competition for U.S. industries, such as steel and chemicals, and contributed to the deterioration of the U.S. balance-of-payments position.
      3. Development of the European Economic Community (EEC or the Common Market) caused massive outflows of investment funds.
          a. U.S. firms had opportunities to utilize their experience in mass-production and mass-distribution by:
              (1) Entering this market through acquisitions and mergers.
              (2) Establishing new business entities.
          b. The common tariff imposed against goods from outside the Common Market encouraged U.S. firms to increase the amount of their direct foreign investment in this area.

4. Military expenditures in Europe and the Far East, especially after 1966 with escalation in Vietnam, have had a major adverse impact on the U.S. balance-of-payments position.
C. Effects of inflation in the United States had a particularly unfavorable impact on the prices of export goods.
1. The relative price stability achieved in the United States between 1958 and 1965 was replaced by rapid inflation caused in part by large military expenditures for the war in Southeast Asia.
2. The relative prices of U.S. export goods increased between 1961 and 1971, so they were 8% higher than the prices of major competitor nations.
3. Thus, the United States began to experience foreign exchange difficulties.
 a. Inflation lowered the ability of the United States to compete for exports which contributed to the deficit in the merchandise and service accounts.
 b. Large government capital outflows were not offset by a surplus in goods and services.
 c. The resulting deficits in the balance of payments lowered the U.S. foreign exchange reserve position.
4. In 1968, a run on U.S. gold began.
D. The following events led up to the suspension of convertibility of the dollar.
1. November 1967: Pound sterling was devalued 14.3% from $2.80 to $2.40 to the pound. Other countries closely related to British trade also devalued their currencies.
2. March 1968: U.S. suspension of its support of the free-market price of gold established the two-tier gold price system.
 a. Ten leading nations agreed to suspend all gold contributions from official reserves to the free gold market.
  (1) All gold in official reserves was frozen.
  (2) Gold was used for settlements only among governments and only at official IMF parities.
 b. The private gold market was permitted to operate without government interference; consequently, supply and demand determined the price.
3. August 1969: French franc was devalued by 11.1%.
4. September 1969: German mark was permitted to float upward, parity rate subsequently raised 9.3%.
5. June 1970: Canadian dollar was permitted to float upward in response to large inflow of U.S. dollars.
6. May 1971: Swiss franc was revalued upward, German mark and the Dutch guilder were again permitted to float.

THE INTERNATIONAL FINANCIAL SYSTEM

E. The United States suspended convertibility of the dollar in August 1971.
   1. Balance-of-payments deficits continued to mount in 1971, and U.S. reserve assets declined rapidly.
      a. Reserves declined in spite of Federal Reserve use of foreign currencies under swap lines of credit with other central banks.
      b. The Federal Reserve used these currencies to buy dollars that foreign banks might otherwise have presented for conversion into gold.
   2. On August 15, 1971 the United States suspended convertibility of dollars into gold in order to protect its remaining reserves.
      a. The dollar began to float in terms of other major currencies.
      b. In addition, a 10% surcharge on imported goods was imposed.
      c. Foreign aid was reduced by 10%.

IV. Efforts to formulate a viable international financial system.
   A. The creation of Special Drawing Rights (SDRs) by the IMF in 1970 was unable to ward off the crisis of August 1971.
      1. SDRs are a form of reserve asset created by international agreement, and are used for official settlement of international imbalances.
         a. They cannot be used for private transactions.
         b. Between 1970 and 1972, 9.3 billion SDRs were allocated to IMF member countries.
      2. The value of SDR is set daily by the IMF according to a fixed formula which involves the exchange values of the sixteen "SDR-basket" currencies.
         a. The value of fixed amounts of the 16 basic currencies (i.e., 40 U.S. cents, 38 German pfennings, 4.5 British pence, 44 French centimes, 26 Japanese yen, etc.) determines the value of the SDR.
         b. The value can be translated with reference to individual currencies (i.e., at a point in time 1 SDR might equal 1.239 dollars, 361.9 yen, or 2.913 marks) and fluctuates as the basic currencies fluctuate.
      3. By pegging its currency to the SDR rather than the U.S. dollar, a country increases the stability of its currency in terms of nondollar currencies, even though reducing it in terms of the U.S. dollar.
      4. SDRs have been referred to as paper gold representing the creation of an international currency.
         a. This provides a leadership role for the IMF to achieve international agreements concerning the optimal rate of growth in reserves.
         b. Thus, the growth of international reserves need not be dependent upon increases in the price of gold or gold hoarding activity.

B. The Smithsonian Agreement was reached in December 1971 after four months of floating rates.
  1. New exchange rates were set to correct the relative overvaluation of the U.S. dollar.
    a. The U.S. dollar was devalued, in terms of gold, from $35 to $38 an ounce.
    b. Other currencies were revalued upward, in relation to the U.S. dollar.
  2. The agreement also widened the band of official support around the parity level of a currency.
    a. The original IMF agreement required a country to maintain the exchange value of its currency against gold or the U.S. dollar within 1%, plus or minus, of its official parity level.
    b. The Smithsonian Agreement widened this band to 2.25%, plus or minus, for a total spread of 4.5%.
  3. In spite of the agreement, many currency values moved to the upper limit of their parity levels within a very short time. This required governments
    a. To enter the foreign exchange markets to buy U.S. dollars to keep their own currencies within proper limits in relation to the U.S. dollar.
    b. Alternatively, to refuse intervention and in effect revalue their own currency in relation to the U.S. dollar.
C. U.S. policy following the Smithsonian Agreement continued to oppose attempts to restore convertibility of the dollar into gold or other currencies.
  1. The United States expected the surplus countries to defend the rate structure by accumulating more U.S. dollars. By the end of January 1972, foreign exchange reserves of IMF member central banks rose to over $100 billion, 90% of which were U.S. dollars. On February 12, 1973, the dollar devalued further, to $42.22 per ounce.
  2. The Common Market nations have sought to maintain a narrow band around parity relationships among their currencies. However, unless their economic and financial policies are coordinated, imbalances develop and changes in pegged rates are required as well as substantial capital flows.
D. There were subsequent events and further efforts at international financial coordination.
  1. Late 1973: Oil embargo and formation of the Organization of Petroleum Exporting Countries (OPEC) cartel lead to a quadrupling of the price of oil.
  2. January 1974: Programs for controlling capital outflows from the United States were eliminated.
  3. September 1975: Agreement among the finance ministers of the major industrial countries on International Monetary Fund rules governing the role of gold. In 1968, a two-tier price for gold had been established: an

official price of $35 per ounce, later $42 per ounce, was adopted for dealings between central banks; but a free-market price of gold for international transactions remained. However, central banks were reluctant to transfer gold at values below market prices, but agreed to transfer gold at market prices. Agreement provided for the eventual sales of one-sixth of the gold holdings of the IMF.
4. January 1976: Proposals of a committee (Jamaica meetings) representing the 128 member countries of the IMF.
   a. Greatly increased exchange-rate flexibility.
   b. Continued sanction of relatively fixed exchange rates for those countries preferring them.
   c. A code of good behavior and cooperation to achieve consistency between national exchange-rate policies.
5. March 1976: Merchandise trade balance of the United States for 1975 was announced as plus $9 billion, with a balance on current account of almost $12 billion. The U.S. net liquidity balance moved from a $19 billion deficit in 1974 to a $3 billion surplus in 1975, a swing of $22 billion.

V. Proposals for reform of the international financial system.
   A. Restoration of the gold standard has been a frequent proposal, and is one wrought with controversy.
      1. Attachment to gold as an international monetary standard is basically for two broad reasons.
         a. Psychological attachment to the gold standard stems from the fictional belief that economies were more stable in the past when the gold standard was used. However, it was the inability to function under a strict gold standard that forced countries to modify it or abandon it entirely.
         b. Gold has great speculative interest.
      2. The fundamental problem behind the unacceptability of the gold standard concerns the relationship of individual government economic policies to the policies of other nations.
         a. Individual countries will not accept the deterioration of their economies while following the hard and fast rules of an automatic gold standard.
         b. Proposals for a gold standard include a provision for periodically adjusting upward the price of gold to increase its supply as the need for international reserves grows faster than the physical output of gold.
         c. Under these proposals gold would not serve the economic disciplinary function intended.
   B. Since restoration of a gold standard is not feasible, the issues center on operating the international monetary mechanism with fixed or flexible exchange rates.
      1. Fixed exchange rates have long been the mechanism for conducting international financial relations.

      a. They encourage international trade by making it possible to transact business on the basis of pegged exchange rates. However, if there are major imbalances between nations, considerable uncertainty may arise about whether the fixed rates can be maintained.
      b. Fixed rates are undesirable because large capital outflows, at inflexible prices, may be required to achieve a balance in balance of payments.
      c. They may be adversely affected by speculative activity in anticipation of changes in pegged exchange rates.
2. Flexible rates are supported by the argument that free-market supply and demand conditions should determine the price of a currency.
      a. Flexible prices would prevent imbalances and disequilibrium from developing.
      b. A greater frequency of rate fluctuations would adjust for balance-of-payments differences, reducing the need for large capital flows and large international liquidity reserves.
      c. Uncertainties of price changes surrounding long-term international contracts would increase, but could be reduced by hedging in the forward market.
      d. Freely flexible rates would result in more active forward markets, thus increasing their efficiency and minimizing the cost of forward operations.
3. Disagreements regarding the effectiveness of using either system in international finance has resulted in compromise proposals.
      a. The provision for widening the band around currency parity levels from 1% to 2¼%, plus or minus, arrived at by the Smithsonian Agreement, increased the permissible range about the fixed level.
      b. Another proposal, the crawling or sliding peg, permits changes of currency parity levels by specified amounts such as 1% or 2% per year.
          (1) Coupled with the widened band, this would increase flexibility and slow down speculative pressures to move rates by larger amounts.
          (2) These continuous, moderate changes would reduce required amounts of capital flows and reduce potential gains from speculative activity.
4. Differences of opinion on the best international financial system still continue.
      a. The January 1975 Jamaica agreements provided for approval of floating exchange rates by countries that wish to use them.
      b. They also approved fixed exchange rates for countries which prefer them.
      c. The fundamental requirements for any effective international financial system are:

THE INTERNATIONAL FINANCIAL SYSTEM

     (1) Cordination between the economic policies of individual nations.
     (2) Consistency in exchange-rate policies between nations.
     (3) Achievement of fundamental, long-run solutions to economic imbalances between nations.
     [See problem 4-12]

PROBLEM 4-1

What is the principle of comparative advantage?

SOLUTION:

Trade will be mutually advantageous if one country is relatively more efficient in producing some products while other countries are relatively more efficient in producing other products.

PROBLEM 4-2

Discuss the events leading up to the international currency crisis which finally resulted in the suspension of convertibility into gold of U.S. dollars on August 15, 1971.

SOLUTION:

  A. The exchange rates of 1946, established at the Bretton Woods Conference, were too restrictive and as time went on, totally unrealistic.
  B. The grant and loan program of the United States to rebuild Europe resulted in a tremendous outflow of capital.
  C. The development of EEC increased direct investment in Europe.
     1. The opportunity for U.S. firms to utilize mass-production and mass-distribution techniques there was accomplished through mergers, acquisitions, and establishment of new companies.
     2. U.S. manufacturers feared that import duties and quotas would restrict export sales to Europe. Thus, heavy investment programs were deemed necessary.
  D. The maintenance of a large standing army to protect and preserve "democratic institutions" throughout Europe and the world resulted in heavy expenditures in foreign countries. Inflation resulted from the Vietnam war.
  E. These factors put unrelenting pressures on the U.S. balance-of-payments position. As the maintenance of the gold standard proved untenable, the $35/ounce gold price was suspended and a two-tier system was established in March 1968. Finally, in August 1971, convertibility of U.S. dollars was suspended.

PROBLEM 4-3

Discuss the advantages and disadvantages of a floating exchange rate, and a crawling peg exchange rate. What change seems appropriate for a practical gliding peg system? Would balance on goods and services equilibrate with floating rates?

SOLUTION:

A. The effects of a floating exchange rate are:
1. Exchange rates are the equilibrating mechanism instead of capital flows.
2. If a government budget deficit is inflationary or money supply growth is excessive, the floating rate will cause adjustments through price ratios.
3. Consumer price level will more accurately reflect a free-market position as imports and exports fluctuate in price.
4. The balance of goods and services may not equilibrate at floating rates (prices) because other money flows may be large compared to goods and services.
5. The central bank reserve positions should receive less long-run pressure from speculators.
6. There is increased risk and uncertainty as to actual dollar receipts when sales are paid for in foreign currency units.
7. Domestic monetary and fiscal policy can be pursued with a greater degree of independence as compared with a regime of fixed exchange rates.

B. The effects of a gliding peg exchange rate are:
1. Much the same as the floating exchange rate except slower. Slower rate may tend to dampen some of the possible speculative surges that have been common against a fixed exchange rate, and may not be as subject to temporary aberrations as is a floating rate.
2. A problem with the gliding peg is that it is a regulated rate, not a free-market rate, and may be subject to political pressures, as the fixed rate is today.

PROBLEM 4-4

The European Economic Community has become one of the most powerful economic blocs in the free world. What effect will this have on the position of the United States in world markets?

SOLUTION:

A. The European Economic Community is an agreement of ten European countries to establish initially a customs union, and to seek eventually a common economic policy and perhaps political unity.

THE INTERNATIONAL FINANCIAL SYSTEM

    B. Should the EEC succeed in uniting Europe it would put tremendous competitive pressure on the United States.
       1. It would eliminate much duplication in production capabilities of the individual countries.
       2. It would enable firms in EEC to gain the benefits of the economies of large scale production.
       3. It would allow each member to concentrate in areas where it has a comparative advantage.
       4. Sharing technological know-how among its members would close the "technology gap" between the United States and Europe.
       5. It would allow the EEC to concentrate on world markets.
    C. On balance, such a situation would be valuable to the economic development of the world.
       1. It would stimulate greater direct foreign investment.
       2. It would increase the supply of goods and services available for world consumption.

PROBLEM 4-5

Comment on the following statement: "When the less developed countries become industrialized, the opportunities for trade between the United States and the less developed countries will be decreased because they will no longer need the goods which we manufacture."

SOLUTION:

Mutually advantageous trade is based on the principle of comparative advantage. As a country develops, it can better employ the special social, environmental, and resource factors that it possesses in the production of goods where it holds a relative productive advantage. In so doing, it increases its ability to earn the foreign exchange necessary to trade with other developed and developing countries. Contrary to the above statement, trade will now increase as the developing country trades its expanded range of goods for those things other countries can produce at lower cost — thus reaping the cost saving. One need only observe the fact that the United States does by far the largest dollar volume of its foreign trade with other developed, industrialized countries.

PROBLEM 4-6

What was the significance of the agreement reached during September 1975 among the finance ministers of the major industrial countries concerning International Monetary Fund rules governing the role of gold?

SOLUTION:

The agreement ended four years of often acrimonious negotiations. The essential point of the agreement was to abolish the official price of gold which had been $42 an ounce. The practical effect of the agreement was to free central banks to transfer gold among themselves at the higher market-related prices. The agreement also provided for the eventual sale of one-sixth of the gold holdings of the International Monetary Fund. The difference between the sale price of the gold by the IMF and the official price could yield a profit of $3 billion, which would be distributed to the less developed countries. In addition, one-sixth of the IMF gold would be returned to the original contributors. The U.S. ratification of the agreement was made contingent on IMF legitimization of floating exchange rates; the previously existing IMF rules required fixed parities.

PROBLEM 4-7

How have international financial developments contributed to worldwide inflation in recent years?

SOLUTION:

It appears that there has been no effective control over the creation of international reserves—the raw material from which the world banking system manufactures money. The world reserves have more than doubled since 1970, and even during the worldwide recession of 1975, they were still increasing at a 10% annual rate—quadruple the rate of the 1960s. World reserves consist of gold plus the total stock of foreign currencies held or claims on foreign currencies.

Until the governments of the world in association with an international financial authority, such as the International Monetary Fund, come to grips with the need to control the broad problem of managing the world's liquidity, the international financial environment carries seeds of potential instability and inflation.

PROBLEM 4-8

What major problems remained for the major industrial countries after reaching an agreement in early September 1975 on the role of gold?

SOLUTION:

1. The broad problem of managing the world's liquidity remained. Especially important was the problem of the buildup of world reserves which continued to grow at an annual rate of 10%, and mostly in the holdings of reserve currencies, especially the U.S. dollar.

2. Another urgent problem has been the large deficits, estimated at $35 billion for 1975 alone, of the less developed countries. This big gap resulted from the oil price increase and the simultaneous decline in the value of their own commodity exports.
3. The problem of coordinating aid to the less developed countries existed. A special $5 billion oil facility had been created to help the less developed countries deal with increased deficits resulting from an increased price of oil. A new *development security facility* has been proposed, to be located in the IMF, to stabilize export earnings of less developed countries. This new facility would have the power to issue up to $10 billion in loans. This changes the IMF's central role of providing revolving credit. Long-term credits would normally be funded through the World Bank or Regional Development Banks. In addition, concern was expressed that the multiplication of special facilities encourages continued and increasing permanent debtor positions of the less developed countries.

PROBLEM 4-9

What are the problems of gold as a universal store of value?

SOLUTION:

1. Its supply is erratic.
2. Its price has fluctuated greatly in recent years.
3. The opportunity costs of resources used to produce gold simply for storage may be high in relation to the economic function performed by gold.
4. If the supply of international reserves is tied directly to gold, it is likely that world price levels would decline severely as they did in the latter part of the 1800s. For example, if real world GNP grows at 5% per annum, while the supply of gold grows at 1.5% per annum, prices on the average would fall 3.5% per annum. If there is a fractional gold reserve backing for currency, then this fraction could be changed to increase the money supply. However, the "iron discipline" of being tied to gold would then be lost and the situation is equivalent to a "managed" money supply.

PROBLEM 4-10

Why did the dollar essentially become the International Reserve Currency during the 1950s; and why can the dollar no longer hold that position during the 1970s?

SOLUTION:

Immediately after World War II, there was a large dollar gap and the dollar was in great demand as a store of value. The value of the dollar in international exchange markets was relatively stable and large capital movements were not required in order to preserve the stable value of the dollar. However, the persistent balance-of-payments deficits in the United States from the period of the late 1950s through all of the 1960s finally led to fundamental changes in August of 1971. Changes took place, and as a result the dollar was no longer convertible into gold. The dollar had been overvalued, the U.S. merchandise trade balance deteriorated, and persistent U.S. balance-of-payments deficits resulted. At first, the dollar inflow into foreign countries was welcomed. As an overhang growing to $100 billion in dollar holdings developed, pessimism toward the dollar ensued, and the foreign exchange value of the dollar in relation to other major currencies declined sharply. No currency in such excess supply could hope to function as a store of value with relative fixity in value in relation to the currencies of other countries.

PROBLEM 4-11

Explain Special Drawing Rights and discuss some aspects of the use of SDRs as a store of value in the world monetary system.

SOLUTION:

1. The International Monetary Fund has created a currency designated as Special Drawing Rights or SDRs. The SDR units represent a composite of sixteen currencies with the relative rate of each based on each country's share of world exports. The U.S. dollar represents 33% of the basic unit and the value of an SDR expressed in dollars in early 1975 was about $1.22. However, if SDRs continue to be held only by government treasuries and central banks in the absence of any other universally accepted store of value, the workings of the world monetary system will be subject to the constant threat of large masses of funds moving between countries.

2. It has been proposed that the SDRs could become a store of value if they could be privately held. If SDRs could be held by private individuals, the market price would be an indicator whether too few or too many were issued. Then central banks wishing to intervene in foreign exchange markets to push their exchange rates up or down would simply buy or sell their own currencies with SDRs.

PROBLEM 4-12

A. Outline the main characteristics of the Bretton Woods system.
B. Review recent developments in the efforts to deal with the three main requirements of an international monetary system:

THE INTERNATIONAL FINANCIAL SYSTEM

1. Liquidity requirements.
2. Confidence requirements.
3. The need for an effective adjustment mechanism.

SOLUTION:[1]

A. The Bretton Woods system and the problems that developed.
   1. The Bretton Woods agreement called for fixed rates of exchange between national currencies to foster international commerce.
      a. Fixed exchange rates were expressed in *par values* for their currencies in relation to the U.S. dollar.
      b. Nations bought or sold their currencies in exchange for dollars to prevent the dollar values of their currencies from departing from par values by more than 1% in either direction.
      c. The United States fixed the value of the dollar with reference to gold for transactions with foreign monetary authorities.
   2. A stock of international reserves in gold and/or dollars was held by each government to make this system work.
      a. It could draw on these reserves to purchase its currency when a decline in its foreign exchange value took place.
      b. A subsequent rise in the foreign exchange value of the currency would enable the country to accumulate other currencies with which it could repurchase its own currency and thus bring about a return inflow of its foreign exchange reserves.
      c. Fluctuating exchange rates reduce the need for international reserves of the magnitude required to maintain fixed exchange rates.
B. The three main requirements of an international monetary system.
   1. The problem of liquidity is one of having the right amount of international reserves.
      a. The correct amount of growth is necessary.
         (1) As the volume of international transactions increased, the magnitude of temporary deficits increased.
         (2) Hence, larger reserves were needed while working on long-run corrective measures.
         (3) If reserves were too small, harsher corrective actions would be required by governments to protect the exchange value of their currencies.
         (4) If reserves were too large, inflationary pressures would be created.

---

[1] Based on the article by N. S. Fieleke (Vice President of the Federal Reserve Bank of Boston), "International Monetary Reform: The Jamaica Composite," in the *New England Economic Review*, March/April 1976, pp. 57-62.

b. Because of limits on the growth of gold reserves, a country could add to its reserves in dollar form by running a balance-of-payments surplus with the United States.
   (1) Between 1970 and 1974, international reserves increased from $93 billion to $221 billion valuing the gold portion at official, rather than higher market prices.
   (2) Less reserves are required under floating exchange rates.
c. The need is not for more reserves, but for better international surveillance of international liquidity.

2. The problem of confidence is to avoid a flight from one reserve asset, such as the dollar, to another reserve asset, such as the German mark, the Swiss franc, or gold.
   a. This gave rise to the proposal for one reserve asset—the SDR. But the $9.3 million SDRs created during the period from 1970 to 1972 represent less than 5% of the total reserves of the member countries of the IMF.
   b. The Jamaica agreements took some actions to reduce the monetary role of gold.
      (1) The IMF is to dispose of one-third of its gold holdings by:
         (a) Refunding one-sixth to its member countries.
         (b) Selling another sixth over a 4-year period with the profits used to assist less developed countries.
      (2) Gold is no longer used as a medium of settlement with the IMF.
      (3) For a 2-year period, the ten largest industrial countries agreed that there would be no increase in the total stock of gold held by them; and that they would take no actions to fix the price of gold.
   c. Prospects for the role of gold in the three traditional functions of money:
      (1) Unit of account—not performed since no fixed price for gold.
      (2) Medium of exchange—with a fixed price below market, gold was not used to settle balances between central banks; but this use may increase at free-market prices.
      (3) Gold remains a store of value.
      (4) The total monetary gold stock of member countries is $130 billion (at early 1976 market prices) or 40% of their total reserves.
   d. Greater confidence can be attained. Flights from one reserve asset were stimulated when a divergence between the official price and market price developed. Without official prices, such divergences do not occur.

3. The problem of an effective adjustment mechanism is to avoid imbalances in international payments.
    a. Possible adjustment mechanisms did not function well under Bretton Woods rules.
        (1) Exchange-rate changes and government controls were discouraged.
        (2) A country could alter its monetary-fiscal policy in the effort to influence its exchange rates; but most countries placed a higher priority on the use of monetary-fiscal policy to achieve domestic full employment. Because of the lack of an adequate international adjustment mechanism, the balance-of-payments deficits of the United States continued without correction for a long period of time.
    b. Under floating exchanges, prices adjust so that cumulative imbalances requiring capital flows do not develop.
        (1) However, all governments intervene to some degree.
        (2) Thirty governments including the United States do not fix exchange rates, but are prepared to intervene.
        (3) As of July 31, 1975, there were 96 countries with fixed exchange rates.
            (a) Fifty-nine were fixed against the U.S. dollar.
            (b) Thirty-seven were fixed against currencies other than the dollar.
    c. The January 1976 Jamaica agreements sanction these diverse practices and include some general principles of good behavior. It is hoped that the diversity of the new system will provide flexibility for solving the three problems discussed above, while at the same time permitting countries to pursue desired domestic goals consistent with international coordination.

REFERENCES

Excellent interpretive presentations can be found in:

Aliber, Robert Z.: *The International Money Game*, Basic Books, New York, 1973.

Rolfe, Sidney E., and James L. Burtle: *The Great Wheel: The World Monetary System*, Quadrangle/The New York Times Book Company, New York, 1973.

Yeager, Leland B.: *International Monetary Mechanism*, Holt, Rinehart and Winston, New York, 1968.

Standard textbook treatments would include:

Caves, Richard E., and Ronald W. Jones: *World Trade and Payments: An Introduction*, Little, Brown, Boston, 1973.

Kindleberger, Charles P.: *International Economics*, 4th ed., Richard D. Irwin, Homewood, Ill., 1968.

Kreinin, Mordichai E.: *International Economics: A Policy Approach*, 2nd ed., Harcourt Brace Jovanovich, New York, 1975.

More general treatments of international business are found in:

Mason, R. Hal, Robert R. Miller, and Dale R. Weigel: *The Economics of International Business*, John Wiley & Sons, New York, 1975.

Salera, Virgil: *Multinational Business*, Houghton Mifflin, Boston, 1969.

Appendixes to Chapter 4

APPENDIX A
Interactions of National Income, the Money Supply, and the Balance of Payments

I. Some fundamental economic relationships are:
   A. The quantity equation.

   $$MV = PQ$$

   where:

   M = quantity of money
   V = its velocity or turnover
   P = price level
   Q = total quantity of goods transacted

   B. The national income equations.

$Y = C + I + G + X$	income creation
$Y = C + S + T + M$	income disposal
$Y = PQ$	definition

where:

- Y = gross national product
- C = consumption
- I = investment
- G = government spending
- X = exports
- M = imports

C. Both the quantity or monetarist approach and the national income or effective demand approach provide useful information on both domestic and international economic and financial developments. For some issues one framework may be used; for different issues the other framework may provide understanding more directly.

D. In either the quantity theory or national income equations framework, an increase in exports (X) from country A into country B (more imports (M) in country B) results in greater income in country A. If both countries were at full employment equilibrium before this shift, prices would rise in A and fall in B.

E. Table A4-1 illustrates how the income and price adjustment process might work using the national income equations.

Table A4-1 Exports and Imports in the National Income Accounts in Country A

	Income Generated					Income Disposal				
	C	I	G	X	Y	C	S	T	M	Y
Situation 1	750	100	100	50	1,000	750	100	100	50	1,000
Initial Change				+20						
Further Changes	+25					+25	+7	+9	+4	
Situation 2	775	100	100	70	1,045	775	107	109	54	1,045

Relations

$D = Y - T$ D = disposable personal income

$\Delta D = \Delta Y - \Delta T$

$c = \dfrac{\Delta C}{\Delta D}$ c = marginal propensity to consume out of disposable income

$s = \dfrac{\Delta S}{\Delta D}$ s = marginal propensity to save

$$m = \frac{\Delta M}{\Delta D} \qquad m = \text{marginal propensity to import}$$

$$r = \frac{\Delta T}{\Delta Y} \qquad r = \text{marginal tax rate}$$

$$\Delta Y = \frac{\Delta X}{1-c+cr} \qquad k = \frac{\Delta Y}{\Delta X} = \frac{1}{1-c+cr} = \text{income multiplier}$$

Assume: $c = .7 \qquad s = .2 \qquad m = .1 \qquad r = .2$

Then as a result of the increase in exports by 20, the new equilibrium, Y, is 1,045, an increase of 45.

This can be shown by the ΔY relation.

$$\Delta Y = \frac{\Delta X}{1-c+cr} = \frac{20}{1-.7+(.7)(.2)} = \frac{20}{1-.7+.14} = \frac{20}{.44} = 45.5$$

We can also quantify the other relations.

$\Delta D = \Delta Y - \Delta T$

$\Delta T = r \Delta Y$

$\qquad = .2 (45)$

$\qquad = 9$

$\Delta D = 45 - 9 = 36$

$\Delta C = c \Delta D$

$\qquad = .7 (36) = 25.2 \cong 25$

$\Delta S = s \Delta D$

$\qquad = .2 (36) = 7.2 \cong 7$

$\Delta M = m \Delta D$

$\qquad = .1 (36) = 3.6 \cong 4$

APPENDIX B

A Formal Analysis of the Effects of Devaluation

For the purpose of numerical illustration of the above points assume these facts. The value of the U.S. dollar declines from $1 = DM4 to $1 = DM3. The average price of goods exported to Germany from the United States is $50 or DM200 before the decline in value of the dollar. The average price of goods sold by Germany as imports into the United States is DM24 or $6 before the devaluation.

Case 1: The sum of elasticities is greater than one.
Symbols used: P = price, Q = quantity.
U.S. imports (See Figure A4-1.)
Before devaluation:
Demand for U.S. imports $Q = \$400 - 20P$.
Constant supply price = $6 which represents DM24/4 = $6.
Substitute $6 into the demand equation to obtain $Q = 400 - 120 = 280$.
After devaluation:
Have the same demand curve, but the price is now DM 24/3 = $8.
When $8 is substituted into the demand equation $Q = 400 - 160 = 240$ is obtained.
A decrease of U.S. imports from 280 to 240.
U.S. exports (See Figure 4-2.)
Before devaluation:
Demand for U.S. exports $Q = 85 - 1.2P$.
Constant supply price = $50 received by U.S. exporter.
Substitute $50 into the demand equation to obtain $Q = 85 - 60 = 25$.
After devaluation:
The supply price remains the same, but the demand for exports reflects the reduced price in DM that would be paid by the German importer. The new DM value of the dollar is 3/4 of the previous value. Hence, the slope of the new demand curve is (3/4) (1.2) = .9. The new demand curve is $Q = 85 - .9P$. Substitute the $50 into the demand equation $Q = 85 - 45 = 40$.
An increase of U.S. exports from 25 to 40.
We can now summarize the results.

	U.S. Imports (M)			U.S. Exports (X)			Balance of Trade (X–M)
	P	Q	Value	P	Q	Value	
Before Devaluation	$6 × 280		= 1680	$50 × 25		= 1250	–430
After Devaluation	$8 × 240		= 1920	$50 × 40		= 2000	+ 80
Sum of elasticities is $\frac{.43 + .67}{2} + \frac{2.4 + 1.13}{2}$ = .55 + 1.76 = 2.31 which is greater than 1							

Comments: This is the situation in which the sum of the price elasticities of demand for the product is greater than 1 as shown above. As a consequence, the trade balance of the United States, which was negative on these products, now becomes positive after devaluation. It moves from a –430 to a +80.

APPENDIXES TO CHAPTER 4

Case 2: The sum of elasticities is less than one.
U.S. imports (Same as Case 1, see Figure 4-1.)
U.S. exports (See Figure 4-3.)
Before devaluation:
Demand for U.S. exports $Q = 35 - .2P$.
Constant supply price = $50 received by U.S. exporter.
Substitute $50 into the demand equation to obtain $Q = 35 - 10 = 25$.
After devaluation:
The supply price remains the same, but the demand for exports reflects the price in DM that would be paid by the German importer. The new DM value of the dollar is 3 which is 3/4 of the previous value. Hence, the slope of the new demand curve is $(3/4)(.20) = .15$. The new demand curve is $Q = 35 - .15P$. Substitute the $50 into the demand equation $Q = 35 - 7.5 = 27.5$. We can now summarize the results.

	U.S. Imports (M)			U.S. Exports (X)			Balance of Trade (X–M)
	P	Q	Value	P	Q	Value	
Before Devaluation	$6 ×	280 =	1680	$50 ×	25 =	1250	–430
After Devaluation	$8 ×	240 =	1920	$50 ×	27.5 =	1375	–545
Sum of elasticities is	$\frac{.43 + .67}{2} + \frac{.4 + .27}{2}$ = .55 + .33 = .88 which is less than 1						

Comments: Thus, in the situation where the sum of the price elasticities of demand are less than 1, the negative trade balance of the United States is aggravated. It is not directly predictable what the effects of devaluation will be on the trade balance of a country.

However, the effect on prices in the devaluing country is more predictable. The dollar price of products imported into the United States becomes higher because of the lower value of the dollar. While initially the nominal dollar price of foreign exports may remain unchanged, the price has actually decreased when expressed in DM. Hence, given the more favorable demand conditions in the foreign country at the lower value of the dollar, an increase in the dollar price charged by the U.S. exporter may still represent a lower price when expressed in DMs. These relationships suggest that devaluation is to have further inflationary effects in the country which devalues. Recall also that the basic cause of devaluation may be associated with inflation in costs and prices in the devaluing country.

Figure A4-1   U.S. Imports

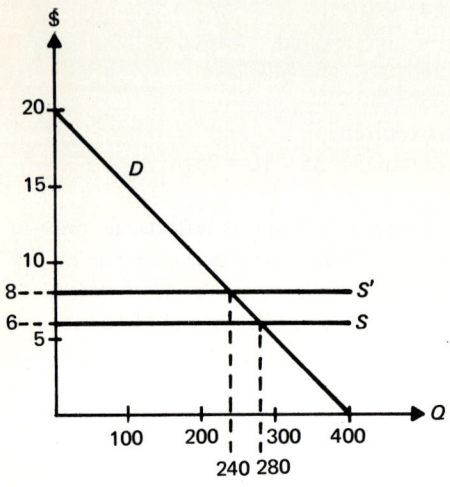

Figure A4-3   U.S. Exports

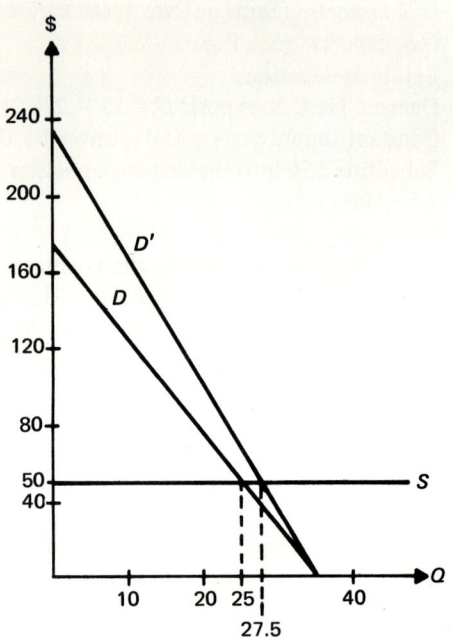

Figure A4-2   U.S. Exports

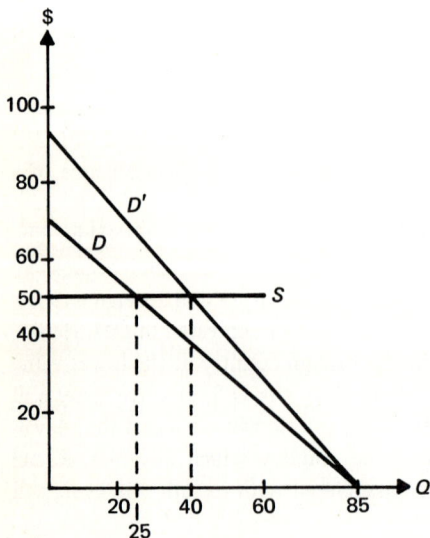

Chapter 5

The Balance of Payments and Forecasting Foreign Exchange Rates

Theme: The previous chapter has established the close relationships between the economic developments in individual countries, international economic and financial developments, and the consequent effects on other individual countries. In this chapter we examine the international adjustment processes in greater detail through analysis of the components of the balance-of-payments accounts. Recognizing the different ways in which adjustment processes may be transmitted, we are provided with a framework for analyzing the factors that will be transmitted through various elements of the adjustment mechanisms. This provides us with an apparatus for analyzing developments in the economic position of the United States, and what their implications are likely to be for exchange-rate movements. Exchange-rate movements will determine the actual prices received in the sales of goods and the dollar value of financial positions held in foreign currencies.

I. International transactions, financial flows, and the balance of payments.
    A. Under a strict gold standard a balance-of-payments analysis could consist of:
        1. The balance on goods and services.
        2. The gold outflow required to meet a negative balance or the gold inflow resulting from a positive balance.

B. With modern financial mechanisms, the number of accounts that may be involved in the balances between nations are numerous. The U.S. balance-of-payments accounts can be used to illustrate the elements that are involved.
II. Balance-of-payments statements.
   A. The balance of payments of a nation is a double-entry accounting statement of its economic transactions with the rest of the world during a specified time period—usually one quarter or one year.
      1. Inflows are recorded as a plus (credits):
         a. Exports of merchandise.
         b. Receipts for services (invisible exports).
         c. Decreases in foreign assets (liquidating a foreign security).
         d. Increases in foreign liabilities (borrowing abroad).
      2. Outflows are a minus (debits):
         a. Imports of merchandise.
         b. Payments for services (invisible imports).
         c. Increases in foreign assets (direct investments abroad).
         d. Decreases in liabilities (paying off a foreign loan).
         e. Unilateral payments, grants, and transfers.
         f. Government loans, private loans.
   B. The U.S. balance-of-payments accounts, until the changes announced in May 1976, followed the format shown in Table 5-1.
      1. Fifty individual items are shown including the four memoranda lines.
      2. Six measures of the balance of payments are set forth.
   C. The U.S. balance of payments is divided into ten major categories and six sub-balances.
      1. Merchandise exports and imports (tangible items such as machinery and foodstuffs).
      2. Services, net (intangible items such as airline travel).
      3. Investment income, net (+ return on investments abroad; − payments on foreign investment in the United States).
         Balance on goods and services (summation of lines 1-10 in Table 5-1).
      4. Remittances, pensions, and other transfers. } Unilateral payments for
         Balance on goods and services and } which nothing is immedi-
         remittances (summation of lines 11 and 12). } ately received in return.
      5. U.S. government grants.
         Balance on current account (summation of lines 13 and 14).
      6. Long-term private capital flows, net (− U.S. direct investment abroad; + foreign direct investment in United States).
         Balance on current account and long-term capital (basic balance summation of lines 15-25).
      7. Nonliquid short-term private capital flows, net.
         Net liquidity balance (summation of lines 26-32).
      8. Liquid private capital flows, net.
         Official reserve transactions balance (summation of lines 33-41; also lines 43-46).

9. Liabilities to foreign official agencies.
10. U.S. official reserve assets.
D. Transactions affecting the balance of payments can be classified as *primary* or *accommodating* (secondary) transactions.
 1. Primary transactions are initiated for their own purposes and constitute:
    a. Buying and selling of merchandise or services in the foreign sector.
    b. Unilateral flows, private or governmental, to or from foreigners.
    c. U.S. investments abroad and foreign investments in the United States.
 2. Accommodating transactions arise from the double-entry accounting process and must offset, or balance, the effect of primary transactions.
    a. An increase in United States claims on foreigners, debit –.
    b. A decrease in United States claims on foreigners, credit +.
    c. An increase in foreign claims on the United States, credit +.
    d. A decrease in foreign claims on the United States, debit –.
 3. These transactions are further classified as:
    a. Changes in U.S. claims on foreign banks.
    b. Changes in U.S. claims on foreign nonbanks.
    c. Changes in foreign claims on U.S. banks.
    d. Changes in foreign claims on U.S. nonbanks.
 4. The balancing transaction will increase and improve the U.S. foreign exchange reserve position if the net increase in U.S. claims on foreigners exceeds the net increase of foreign claims on the United States.
 5. The U.S. reserve position will be reduced when the increase of foreign claims on the United States exceeds the increase of U.S. claims on foreigners.
    a. This negative balance must be made up by U.S. official reserve transactions.
    b. The result will be reduction in the net worth position of the United States.
 6. Generally, the impact on the net position of the United States is determined by the primary transaction. Accommodating or compensating transactions simply alter the form of the U.S. claim (asset) or U.S. liability (foreign claim).
E. In summary, a good framework for thinking through the effects of every type of transaction on the U.S. balance of payments involves only four basic categories of items.

Effects on the Balance of Payments

Plus	Minus
Exports	Imports
Increase liabilities to foreigners	Decrease liabilities to foreigners
Decrease claims on foreigners	Increase claims on foreigners
Decrease in investments; sell assets	Increase investments; buy assets

Table 5-1 U.S. Balance-of-Payments Summary
(Millions of dollars, seasonally adjusted)

Line	(Credits +; debits −)	1974	1975	Change: 1974–75
1	Merchandise trade balance	−5,277	9,045	14,322
2	Exports	98,309	107,184	8,875
3	Imports	−103,586	−98,139	5,447
4	Military transactions, net	−2,158	−819	1,339
5	Travel and transportation, net	−2,692	−1,968	724
6	Investment income, net	10,121	6,030	−4,091
7	U.S. direct investments abroad	17,679	9,140	−8,539
8	Other U.S. investments abroad	8,389	8,735	346
9	Foreign investments in the United States	−15,946	−11,845	4,101
10	Other services, net	3,830	4,211	381
11	**Balance on goods and services**	**3,825**	**16,500**	**12,675**
12	Remittances, pensions and other transfers	−1,721	−1,763	−42
13	**Balance on goods, services and remittances**	**2,104**	**14,736**	**12,632**
14	U.S. Government grants (excluding military grants of goods and services).	−5,461	−2,820	2,641
15	**Balance on current account**	**−3,357**	**11,916**	**15,273**
16	U.S. Government capital flows excluding nonscheduled repayments, net	408	−3,500	−3,908
17	Nonscheduled repayments of U.S. Government assets	1		−1
18	U.S. Government nonliquid liabilities to other than foreign official reserve agencies.	710	1,774	1,064
19	Long-term private capital flows, net	−8,463	−8,789	−326
20	U.S. direct investments abroad	−7,455	−5,760	1,695
21	Foreign direct investments in the United States	2,224	1,934	−290
22	Foreign securities	−1,990	−6,328	−4,338
23	U.S. securities other than Treasury issues	672	3,899	3,227
24	Other, reported by U.S. banks	−1,166	−2,608	−1,442
25	Other, reported by U.S. nonbanking concerns	−748	74	822
26	**Balance on current account and long-term capital**	**−10,702**	**1,401**	**12,103**
27	Nonliquid short-term private capital flows, net	−12,936	−2,819	10,117
28	Claims reported by U.S. banks	−12,173	−1,913	10,260
29	Claims reported by U.S. nonbanking concerns	−2,603	−911	1,692
30	Liabilities reported by U.S. nonbanking concerns	1,840	5	−1,835
31	Allocations of special drawing rights (SDR)	......	......	......
32	Errors and omissions, net	4,698	4,556	−142
33	**Net liquidity balance**	**−18,940**	**3,138**	**22,078**

Source: Louis J. Moczar, "U.S. Balance of Payments Developments Fourth Quarter and Year 1975," *Survey of Current Business,* 56:30-52, March 1976.

Table 5-1 U.S. Balance-of-Payments Summary (Continued)

Line	(Credits +; debits —)	1974	1975	Change: 1974-75
34	Liquid private capital flows, net	10,543	−5,601	−16,144
35	Liquid claims	−6,267	−9,200	−2,933
36	Reported by U.S. banks	−6,134	−8,933	−2,799
37	Reported by U.S. nonbanking concerns	−133	−267	−134
38	Liquid liabilities	16,810	3,599	−13,211
39	To foreign commercial banks	12,621	−501	−13,122
40	To international and regional organizations	1,319	2,277	958
41	To other foreigners	2,870	1,823	−1,047
42	**Official reserve transactions balance**	**−8,397**	**−2,463**	**5,934**
	Financed by changes in:			
43	Liquid liabilities to foreign official agencies	8,503	1,007	−7,496
44	Other readily marketable liabilities to foreign official agencies	673	2,072	1,399
45	Nonliquid liabilities to foreign official reserve agencies reported by U.S. Government	655	−9	−664
46	U.S. official reserve assets, net	−1,434	−607	827
	Memoranda:			
47	Transfers under military grant programs (excluded from lines 2, 4, and 14).	1,811	2,287	476
48	Reinvested earnings of foreign incorporated affiliates of U.S. firms (excluded from lines 7 and 20).	7,508	n.a.	n.a.
49	Reinvested earnings of U.S. incorporated affiliates of foreign firms (excluded from lines 9 and 21).	1,554	n.a.	n.a.
50	Gross liquidity balance, excluding allocations of SDR.	−25,207	−6,062	19,145

III. Construction of the balance-of-payments accounts.

The following transactions are provided to illustrate the main categories of the balance-of-payments accounts. The transactions are recorded in the balance-of-payments form provided (Table 5-2, p. 87). The six balances in items 11, 13, 15, 17, 33, and 42 are calculated.

- A. Imports into the United States of $5,000 of merchandise are made. A time bill of exchange which matures in 30 days is used to pay for the import.
- B. The 30-day bill of exchange matures.
- C. Exports of $2,000 are made to a French importer and paid for by a check drawn on a Paris bank.
- D. A U.S. investor receives a dividend check of $2,000 on a German bank from his holdings of common stock in a German company.
- E. Jones, who now lives in Mexico, receives his social security check of $1,000, which he deposits in a bank in Mexico.

F. A grant of $10,000 is made to the government of Turkey to control poppy cultivation (not yet spent by the Turkish government).
G. A U.S. firm establishes a subsidiary in Mexico by buying machinery in Mexico paid for by a check of $5,000 on its U.S. bank.
H. A U.S. firm buys out a company in France and pays by drawing a $20,000 check on its U.S. bank.
I. An American buys a ticket from Lufthansa for a round-trip to Frankfort, Germany, paying by a $1,000 check on his U.S. bank; the check is deposited by Lufthansa in its New York bank account.
J. A French bank purchases French francs from the Central Bank of France, paying by an $8,000 check on its claims on U.S. banks.

IV. Balance-of-payments summary measures.
   A. In May 1976, the U.S. Department of Commerce announced a shift in the format of the balance-of-payments compilation and presentation.
      1. Of the six balances shown in Table 5-1, only the **Balance on current account** will be set forth.
      2. Items 1, 11, and 13 will be provided as memoranda information.
      3. The format of the new balance-of-payments summary is suggested by the organization of the material in Table 5-3 which reproduces a table from a discussion in the April 1976, *Federal Reserve Bulletin* on "Changing Patterns in U.S. International Transactions" (p. 284).
   B. Possible reasons for the shift to the new format of presenting balance-of-payments information are indicated.
      1. The thinking behind the new format of the balance-of-payments information is indicated by the following quotation.[1]

> The scale of net private and official capital transactions in the U.S. international accounts is by definition the mirror image of the balance on current transactions. To the extent that the current-account balance is largely predetermined in the short run by the levels of U.S. and foreign economic activity, the scale of net private and official capital transactions is also largely predetermined. Of course, interest rates and other financial market conditions, including exchange-rate expectations, respond jointly to the demand for current-account financing, thereby assuring the appropriate scale of net capital transactions. Many different combinations of financial conditions, and many different compositions of capital transactions, are consistent with any over-all scale of net capital flows.

      2. Another possible rationale may be related to the shift from fixed exchange rates to a floating exchange-rate system by the United States.

V. Significance of a balance-of-payments summary measure.
   A. When a country is on a system of fixed exchange rates, the most important balances are those reflecting the magnitude of capital movements required

---

[1] "Changing Patterns in U.S. International Transactions," *Federal Reserve Bulletin*, **62**:290, April 1976.

Table 5-2 Illustrative U.S. Balance of Payments

		+		−	
1.	Merchandise balance				(3,000)
2.	Exports	(C)	2,000		
3.	Imports			(A)	5,000
4.	Military transactions				
5.	Transportation and travel			(I)	1,000
6.	Investment income				
7.	Our investment abroad	(D)	2,000		
8.	Foreign investment in the United States				
9.	Other services				
11.	**Balance on goods and services**				(2,000)
12.	Remittances			(E)	1,000
13.	**Balance on goods, services, and remittances**				(3,000)
14.	U.S. government grants			(F)	10,000
15.	**Balance on current account**				(13,000)
16.	Long-term private investment			(G)	5,000
				(H)	20,000
26.	**Balance on current account and long-term capital** (basic balance)				(38,000)
	Nonliquid				
28.	Claims				
30.	Liabilities	(A)	5,000	(B)	5,000
33.	**Net liquidity balance**				(38,000)
	Liquid				
35.	Claims			(C)	2,000
38.	Liabilities			(D)	2,000
		(B)	5,000	(J)	8,000
		(E)	1,000		
		(G)	5,000		
		(H)	20,000		
		(I)	1,000		
42.	**Official reserve transactions balance**				(18,000)
43.	Liquid liabilities to official agencies	(F)	10,000		
46.	U.S. reserve assets	(J)	8,000		

to perform the adjustment processes. These are: balance on current account and long-term capital (basic balance), net liquidity balance, and official reserve transactions balance.

1. The balance on current account and long-term capital considers certain economic transactions as *basic* under fixed exchange rates.
    a. It excludes the influence of the more volatile items, such as short-term capital movements.
        (1) It places all current transactions and long-term capital movements above the "line" (which is itself subject to definition).

Table 5-3 U.S. International Transactions, 1973-75
(In billions of dollars; seasonally adjusted quarterly data.)

Item	1973	1974	1975
Merchandise exports	71.4	98.3	107.2
Merchandise imports	70.4	103.6	98.1
Trade balance	*1.0*	*−5.3*	*9.0*
Military transactions, net	−2.3	−2.2	−.8
Investment income, net	5.2	10.1	6.0
Other service transactions, net	.3	1.1	2.2
Official and private unilateral transfers[1]	−3.8	−4.0	−3.9
Balance on current account[1]	**.3**	**−.2**	**12.6**
U.S. Government capital flows[1]	**−1.5**	**−2.0**	**−2.4**
Private capital, net	**−1.7**	**−10.9**	**−17.2**
Reported by banks, net	−1.5	−2.7	−9.9
Claims on foreigners, increase (−)	−6.0	−19.5	−13.1
Liabilities to foreigners, increase (+)	4.5	16.8	3.2
Securities transactions, net[2]	3.3	−1.3	−2.4
U.S. purchases (−) of foreign securities	−.8	−2.0	−6.3
Of which: new bond issues	(−1.4)	(−2.4)	(−7.2)
Foreign purchases (+) of U.S. securities[2]	4.1	.7	3.9
Of which: stocks[2]	(2.8)	(.5)	(4.5)
Direct investment flows, net[2]	−2.3	−5.2	−3.8
U.S. investments abroad	−5.0	−7.5	−5.8
Foreign investment in U.S.[2]	2.7	2.2	1.9
Other corporate flows, net	−1.2	−1.6	−1.1
Liabilities to foreign official agencies, increase (+)	**5.1**	**9.8**	**3.1**
Of which: to OPEC countries[3]	.4	10.0	4.2
to other countries	4.7	−.2	−1.1
U.S. official reserve assets, increase (−)	**.2**	**−1.4**	**−.6**
Statistical discrepancy, inflow (+)	**−2.4**	**4.7**	**4.6**

[1] Data for 1974 and 1975 exclude certain special transactions with India, Israel, and Vietnam, which are recorded in Department of Commerce statistics as unilateral transfers matched by completely offsetting U.S. Government capital flows.
[2] Includes certain official transactions.
[3] Not seasonally adjusted.
*Absolute value less than $50 million.
Source: "Changing Patterns in U.S. International Transactions," *Federal Reserve Bulletin*, 62:284, April 1976.

(2) It places below the line all short-term capital movements, errors and omissions, and gold movements.
(3) Short-term capital movements are considered to be among the accommodating or compensating transactions, which have no real impact on the reserve position of the nation.

b. The basic balance measure has limitations.
   (1) Short-term capital movements may represent transactions initiated because of expectations of changes in relative interest rates or foreign exchange rates, and thus may not represent a simple accommodating entry.
   (2) With the existence of flexible exchange rates, long-term private movements perform less of a role as adjustment flows to maintain fixed exchange rates, but move more in response to prospects for returns from investments in different countries.
2. The net liquidity balance is intended to be a broad indicator of the magnitude of changes in liquidity claims or accommodations required to maintain the fixed exchange rates.
   a. Its purpose is to measure the amount of required *private* lending by the United States (if balance is positive) or the required *private* lending by foreigners (if balance is negative) before changes in reserves or official balances become necessary.
   b. It differs from the basic transactions balance by placing all movements of U.S. short-term capital and errors and omissions above the line. These items thereby affect the size of the surplus or deficit, not the *financing* of it.
   c. Below the line settling or financing transactions are:
      (1) Changes in U.S. liquid liabilities (bank deposits, commercial paper, government bonds) to *all* foreigners, officially or privately held by banks and nonbanks.
      (2) Changes in official U.S. reserves.
3. The balance of official reserve transactions considers only the changes in reserve assets and official balances.
   a. This indicates what type and how much official action must be taken to accommodate or settle the effects of all other transactions.
   b. This balance maintains that the key demarcation in international transactions is between those of the official agencies and all other transactors.

B. Under flexible exchange rates, greater emphasis is placed on the fundamental transactions which determine the probable direction of changes in the foreign exchange value of the dollar. These include: balance on merchandise trade; balance on goods and services; balance on goods, services, and remittances; and current account balance.
   1. These balances successively indicate the influence of the basic transactions and of government loan and grant policies affecting the supply and demand for the currency of a country and therefore its probable exchange-rate movements.
   2. The short-term or long-term private capital flows are not reflected since the prospects which give rise to their movements may change within relatively short periods, so that no fundamental, continuing effects on exchange rates may be involved.

3. The large dollar balances held by the oil-producing nations may be used for various investment purposes, changing the magnitude of short-term liabilities or claims, without affecting the more basic economic position of the United States.
   C. Significance of the new balance-of-payments format may depend on the point of view.
      1. One view of the reason for the shift is that the changes reflect the different information relevant for a nation on fixed versus flexible exchange rates.
      2. Another possibility is that the United States is seeking to moderate the possibly destabilizing effects of information that may simply represent short-term temporary flows.
      3. Our view is that the significance of balance-of-payments measures depends on particular international economic developments and the circumstances of an individual country. We would therefore urge that information continue to be provided so that analysis can be made of the many economic and financial developments that at different times are reflected in changes in balance-of-payments items. Such changes may have significance for the adjustment processes resulting in changes in foreign exchange rates.

VI. Exchange Rates.
   A. International business transactions are conducted in many different currencies.
      1. A U.S. exporter, selling to a French importer, expects to be paid in dollars.
      2. A French importer, buying from an American exporter, desires to pay in francs.
   B. Existence of the foreign exchange market allows buyer and seller to deal separately in the currency of their preference.
      1. The participants in the foreign exchange market are individual brokers, a few large international money banks, and many commercial banks that facilitate transactions on behalf of their customers. Payment may be made in one currency by an importer and received in another by the exporter.
      2. The foreign exchange rate represents the conversion relationship between currencies and depends on demand and supply relationships between two currencies.
      3. The foreign exchange rate is the price of one currency in terms of another.
   C. Exchange-rate fluctuations expose a firm to the risk of loss in the value of the currency in which it may be transacting business. Exposure to this risk may be measured by the net asset or net liability position of the firm in a foreign currency, taking into account prospective future flows as well as current holdings.
      1. A "long position," where net assets exceed liabilities in the foreign currency, will benefit from an increase in value of the foreign currency.

THE BALANCE OF PAYMENTS AND FORECASTING FOREIGN EXCHANGE RATES

      2. A "short position," a net debtor in the foreign currency, will benefit from a decline in value of the foreign currency.
- D. In order to hedge against the risk of exchange-rate fluctuations, a firm may participate in the forward market for foreign exchange.
  1. Forward contracts are usually written for 30, 60, or 90 days; longer maturities can be negotiated.
  2. The forward market also allows speculators to participate on the basis of their expectations.
     a. If speculators expect the value of a currency to rise (i.e., the "spot" price of the currency will be higher in 90 days than the "current futures" price) they will immediately enter into a 90-day forward contract to purchase that currency at the current futures price. This current futures price is established by the rate currently charged on 90-day forward contracts.
     b. If the dollar value of the foreign currency is expected to fall, the speculator (or business firm) will sell the currency short on a 90-day contract. Then he will be able to make a profit by purchasing the currency in 90 days at a lower price than when he sold it.
- E. The exchange rate may be expressed in dollars-per-foreign currency or units of foreign currency-per-dollar.
  1. An exchange rate of $.50 to LC1 shows the value of one foreign currency unit in terms of the dollar; one foreign currency unit equals fifty cents.
  2. An exchange rate of LC2 to $1 shows the value of the dollar in terms of the number of foreign currency units it will purchase; one dollar equals two foreign currency units.
- F. *Arbitrage* is the free-market process which works to equate exchange-rate quotations on a worldwide basis and also ties interest rates in national markets closer together.
  1. Specialists buy and sell currencies across geographic lines to make profits on differences in cross rates of exchange (discussed in VII below), causing the interest rate quotations to move toward equality throughout the international markets.
  2. Arbitragers use interest rate differentials of various national markets in conjunction with foreign exchange transactions.
     a. *Covered interest arbitrage* is an opportunity for making a profit by taking a position in an arbitrage outflow or inflow. This provides higher interest return with no loss on foreign exchange.
     b. An arbitrage outflow takes place when the interest rate differential favoring the foreign country is positive and exceeds the forward exchange discount, or the interest rate differential is negative but offset by a greater forward exchange premium.
     c. An arbitrage inflow takes place when the interest rate differential favoring the foreign country is negative and not offset by a forward exchange premium, or the interest rate differential is positive and is offset by a larger forward exchange discount.

        d. This process moves toward equilibrium of differential national interest rates and forward exchange rates, creating the *interest rate parity line.*
- 3. The theoretical equilibrium position may not be reached in practice because of a variety of artificial barriers and governmental interference.

VII. Exchange-rate adjustment processes.
- A. Equilibrating transactions take place when exchange rates are not in proper relationship with one another. This will be illustrated by some examples (unrealistic numbers will be used to make the arithmatic easy).
- B. Arbitragers follow the general maxim for profitable trading—"sell high, buy low." Three categories will be illustrated: spot rates in different countries, consistent cross rates requirements, and covered interest arbitrage.
  1. Spot rates.
     - a. Suppose the dollar value of the pound is $2.00 in New York City and $1.50 in London. The following adjustment actions would take place.
     - b. In New York City, sell £150 for $300 (£ high).
     - c. In London, sell $300 for £200 ($ high).
     - d. Thus, £150 sold in New York City buys $300 which can be used to buy £200 in London at a gain of £50.
     - e. The pound declines in New York City and rises in London until no arbitrage opportunities remain: the same price (assuming no transportation costs) would have to obtain in both locations.
  2. Consistent cross rates.
     - a. Assume that the equilibrium relation between the dollar and the pound is $2 to £1 and that it is $.25 to fr. 1. Now, suppose that in New York City £.10 = fr. 1. The following adjustment process would take place.
     - b. Sell $200 for £100 used to obtain fr. 1,000. The fr. 1,000 will buy $250. This is a $50 profit over the initial $200.
     - c. Sell dollars for pounds and pounds for francs since the pound is overvalued with respect to the dollar to pound and dollar to franc relationships. Dollars will fall in relation to the pound and the pound will fall in relation to the franc until consistent cross rates obtain.
     - d. If the relation were fr. 1 = £.125, consistent cross rates would obtain. Check using the following relation:

          $1 = £.5
          £1 = fr. 8.00
          fr. 1 = $.25

       The product of the right hand side of each relationship must equal 1. *Check:* .5 × 8 × .25 = 1.

3. Covered interest arbitrage.
   a. Overall perspective. Figure 5-1 provides a visual method for determining opportunities for covered interest arbitrage.
   b. In the arbitrage outflow area, the net differential in favor of the foreign country is positive, resulting in an outflow of funds.
   c. In the arbitrage inflow area, the net differential in favor of the foreign country is negative, resulting in an inflow of funds.

Figure 5-1 Interest Rate Arbitrage

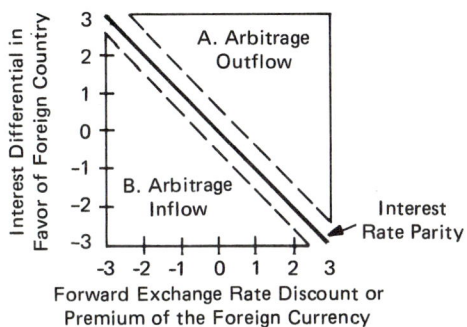

VIII. Illustration of arbitrage outflow—situation A.
   A. Basic facts.
      1. U.S. interest rate 5%.
      2. German interest rate 7%.
      3. Spot exchange rate $1 = DM4.
      4. Forward exchange rate discount 1%.
   B. Arbitrage transaction.
      1. In New York, borrow $100,000 for 90 days (¼ year) at 5%.
         Loan repayment at the end of 90 days is
         $100,000 [1 + (5% × ¼)] = $101,250.
      2. At the spot exchange rate, convert the $100,000 loan into DM400,000.
      3. In Germany, invest the DM400,000 for 90 days at 7%.
         Receive at the end of 90 days
         DM400,000 [1 + (7% × ¼)] = DM407,000.
   C. Covering transaction.
      1. To insure against adverse changes in the spot rate during the 90-day investment period, sell investment proceeds forward.
      2. Since the forward exchange rate discount is 1%,
         then 4[1 + (1% × ¼)] = DM4.01 is required to exchange for $1, in 90 days (forward).
      3. Sell investment proceeds forward, i.e., contract to receive DM407,000 ÷ 4.01 = $101,496.
   D. Arbitrage profits = investment receipts − loan payments
                        = $101,496 − 101,250
                        = $246

E. Equilibrating forces.
1. The arbitrage transaction increases the *demand* for currency in New York and increases the *supply* of funds in Germany. This raises the interest rate in New York and lowers it in Germany, thus narrowing the differential.
2. The covering transaction increases the supply of German forward exchange while the arbitrage investment action increases the demand for spot funds. Both forces tend to increase the forward exchange discount.
3. The interest rate differential decreases and the forward rate discount increases until both are equalized.

IX. Illustration of arbitrage outflow—situation B.
A. Basic facts.
1. U.S. interest rate 5%.
2. German interest rate 6%.
3. Spot exchange rate DM4 = $1.
4. Forward exchange rate discount 2%.
B. Arbitrage transaction.
1. In Germany, borrow DM400,000 for 90 days at 6%.
Loan repayment at the end of 90 days is
DM400,000 $[1 + (6\% \times 1/4)]$ = DM406,000.
2. At the spot exchange rate, convert the DM400,000 loan into $100,000.
3. In New York, invest the $100,000 for 90 days at 5%.
Receive at the end of 90 days
$100,000 $[1 + (5\% \times 1/4)]$ =$101,250.
C. Covering transaction.
1. To insure coverage for the loan repayment, buy DM406,000 forward.
2. At a 2% forward exchange rate discount, it costs
DM4$[1 + (2\% \times 1/4)]$ = DM4.02 to buy $1 forward.
Thus, to repay DM400,000 requires DM406,000 ÷ 4.02 = $100,995.
D. Arbitrage profits = investment receipts − loan repayments.
= $101,250 − $100,995
= $255
E. Equilibrating forces.
1. The arbitrage transaction increases the *demand* for DM and increases the supply of dollars. The U.S. interest rate decreases and the German rate rises, thus the differential increases.
2. Covering transactions increase the spot supply of DM, thus decreasing the premium on forward DM.
3. The interest rate differential and the forward exchange rate discount decrease until both rates are equalized.

X. Historical examples of covered interest arbitrage opportunities.
A. The Pound Sterling: 1960 to 1961.
1. June 1960: The British bank rate increased from 5% to 6%. The U.S. Federal Reserve lowered interest rates from 4% to 3%. This caused an

interest differential of 3%. Since the forward sterling rate was at a discount of 1.8%, a type-A situation was created.
2. This produced a covered differential of about 1.2% in favor of London.
3. Heavy funds flowed into London.
4. October and December 1960: British monetary authorities lowered interest rates to 5% in response to inflows of funds.
5. Gradually money inflows declined, until March 1961.
6. March 1961: German and Dutch currency revaluations caused short-term funds to leave London in favor of the continent.
7. The sale of forward sterling in order to speculate in continental funds drove the forward discount in sterling to 4%. This, when coupled with the 5% interest rate, created a type-B situation. A positive interest differential in favor of New York was created. This caused an accentuated outflow of funds from London.
8. The London interest rate was raised to 7%, thus restoring a small covered arbitrage position in favor of London.
9. Funds again flowed into London.
10. End of 1961: The bank rate was reduced to 6% in London and approximate interest parity between New York and London prevailed.

B. The Canadian Dollar: June to December 1962.
1. June 1962: Stringent monetary, fiscal, and tariff restraints were adopted in response to uncertainty and speculative attacks on the Canadian dollar arising from the reestablishment of a fixed currency par value.
2. July 1962: The Canadian treasury bill rate reached a peak of 5¾%, while speculation drove the forward rate to a discount, but still offered type-A arbitrage opportunities.
3. The resulting covered differential in favor of Canada failed to result in inflows of funds until the stabilization program had taken hold.
4. Late July and early August 1962: Funds began to flow into Canada as confidence developed.
5. September to November 1962: The interest rate was reduced in steps to 4%. Speculative positions in forward currency were liquidated as stability was achieved. The forward discount rate declined, approaching parity with the interest rate.
6. This example shows that covered arbitrage positions should be taken only in conjunction with other factors. Specifically, investors must have:
   a. Confidence in currency par values.
   b. Freedom in exchange transactions.
   c. Confidence that exchange controls will not be imposed.

XI. Equilibrium market relationships.
A. Several market relationships are implied by the economic processes discussed in the preceding materials. They are summarized here as a framework for

guidance in formulating judgments based not only on these idealized relationships, but qualitative factors, such as changes in governmental policies as well.
B. Fisher effect.
1. It is named after the great American economist Irving Fisher who developed the concept.
2. Nominal interest rates rise to reflect the anticipated rate of inflation.
3. Formal statement.

$$\frac{P_o}{P_1} = \frac{1+r}{1+R_n}$$

$$1+r = (1+R_n)\frac{P_o}{P_1}$$

$$r = [(1+R_n)\frac{P_o}{P_1}] - 1$$

$$R_n = [(1+r)(\frac{P_1}{P_o})] - 1$$

where:

P_o = initial price level
P_1 = subsequent price level
$\frac{P_1}{P_o}$ = rate of inflation
$\frac{P_o}{P_1}$ = relative purchasing power of the currency unit
r = real rate of interest
R_n = nominal rate of interest

4. Illustrations.
   a. Over a given time period, if the price index is expected to rise by 10% and the real interest rate is 8%, then the current nominal rate of interest is:

   $$R_n = [(1.08)(1.10)] - 1$$
   $$= 18.8\%$$

   b. If the nominal rate of interest is 12% and the price index is expected to rise by 8% over a given time period, the current real rate of interest is:

   $$r = [(1.12)(\frac{100}{108})] - 1$$
   $$= 1.037 - 1 = .037 = 3.7\%$$

THE BALANCE OF PAYMENTS AND FORECASTING FOREIGN EXCHANGE RATES

C. The Interest Rate Parity Theorem (IRPT).
 1. This is an extension of the Fisher effect to the international markets.
 2. The ratio of the forward and spot exchange rates will equal the ratio of foreign and domestic gross interest relationship.
 3. Formal statement.

$$\frac{X_f}{X_o} = \frac{1 + R_{fo}}{1 + R_{do}} = \frac{E_o}{E_f}$$

where:

X_f = current forward exchange rate expressed as LC units per \$1
E_f = current forward exchange rate expressed as dollars per LC1
X_o = current spot exchange rate expressed as LC units per \$1
E_o = current spot exchange rate expressed as dollars per LC1
R_{fo} = current foreign interest rate
R_{do} = current domestic interest rate

 4. Illustration.
  a. The foreign interest rate is 12% while the domestic interest rate is 8%. The spot exchange rate between the two currencies is LC10 per \$1. What is the current forward exchange rate (under the idealized equilibrium relations assumed)?

$$X_f = \frac{1 + R_{fo}}{1 + R_{do}} (X_o)$$

$$= \frac{(1.12)}{(1.08)} (10)$$

$$= (1.037)(10) = 10.37$$

  b. *Implications:* This result indicates that the foreign forward rate is at a discount of 3.7% on an annual basis. If the time period is 90 days, the discount on the 90-day forward rate would be .925%. The 90-day forward rate would be 10.0925.
 5. If the foreign exchange rate is expected to rise over a period of time, relative interest rates will reflect the change in the foreign exchange rate. After the foreign exchange rate has stabilized at a new level, the relative interest rates will return to their former relationship, if no other influences have intruded (See Figure 5-2).
 6. *Comments on Figure 5-2:* The movement in the foreign exchange rate in the upper panel is shown to first increase at an increasing rate and then at a decreasing rate. The foreign interest rate, therefore, peaks at the inflexion point of the rising segment of the line of the exchange-rate movement in the upper panel. When the line in the upper panel levels out at the new plateau, the foreign interest rate again coincides with the domestic interest rate (under the idealized conditions assumed).

Figure 5-2 Illustration of the Interest Rate Parity Theorem

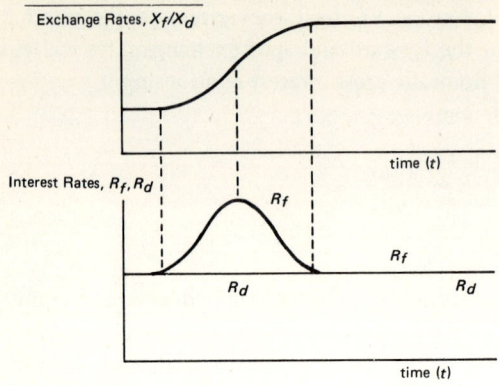

D. The Purchasing Power Parity Theorem (PPPT).
1. Changes in exchange rates reflect changes in the relative prices between two countries.
2. Formal statement.

$$(CX) = \frac{X_1}{X_o} = \frac{P_{f1}/P_{fo}}{P_{d1}/P_{do}} = (RPC)$$

where:

$$\frac{X_1}{X_o} = \frac{E_o}{E_1}$$

X_o = LCs per \$ now
X_1 = LCs per \$ one period later

$$E_o = \frac{1}{X_o} = \text{\$'s per LC now}$$

$$E_1 = \frac{1}{X_1} = \text{\$'s per LC one period later}$$

$$(CX) = \frac{X_1}{X_o} = \text{change in exchange rate}$$

$$(RPC) = \frac{P_{f1}/P_{fo}}{P_{d1}/P_{do}} = \text{change in relative prices}$$

P_{fo} = initial price level in the foreign country
P_{f1} = foreign country price level one period later
P_{do} = initial domestic price level
P_{d1} = domestic price level one period later

3. Graphic presentation.

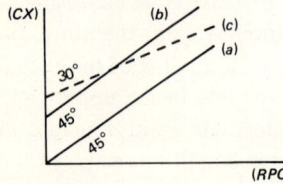

Line *a* implies that both the average and marginal relations are one to one. Line *b* implies that the marginal relation is one to one, but not the average relation. Line *c* implies a relationship, but not a one to one relationship. This discussion will reflect the line *a* relation.

4. Illustration. Foreign prices have risen 20%, while domestic prices have risen 10%. If the initial exchange rate is LC10 to $1, the subsequent new exchange rate will be:

$$\frac{1.20}{1.10} = \frac{X_1}{10}$$

$$X_1 = 1.09(10)$$
$$= 10.9$$

5. The actual relation may reflect the line *b* or *c* relation because of:
   a. Differences in endowments between the two countries.
   b. Changes in government policies.
   c. Lags in market responses.
   d. Differences in the price ratios of internationally traded goods to domestically traded goods between the two countries.
   e. Whether the changes are anticipated or uncertain.
   f. Additions of a risk premium influence.

E. Implied full set of equilibrium relationships.
   1. Linking the relations.

   $$\frac{P_{f1}/P_{fo}}{P_{d1}/P_{do}} = \frac{X_1}{X_o} \text{ and } \frac{1 + R_{fo}}{1 + R_{fd}} = \frac{X_f}{X_o}$$

   2. Hence the windfall real gain or loss from holding assets in foreign currency units is: $r_1 = [(E_1/E_o)(P_o/P_1)/(1+r_d)] - 1$. Using the Fisher effect and the interest rate parity relation, this reduces to: $r_1 = (E_1/E_f) - 1$.

XII. Checklist of factors for forecasting foreign exchange rates.
   A. Political and social factors.
      1. Decisions to stimulate the economy or to control inflation.
      2. Stability of government, and economic position of various social groups.
      3. Government deficits or surpluses.
      4. Rate of growth in population in relation to the rate of growth in real GNP.
   B. Fundamental economic forces.
      1. Trends in productivity.
      2. Ratio of capital investment to GNP.
      3. Level and rate of economic development.
   C. Leading economic indicators.
      1. Rate of growth in money supply and in government deficits or surpluses.
      2. Trends in prices; purchasing power parity.

3. Foreign exchange reserve position.
    a. In relation to net imports.
    b. In relation to money supply changes.
    c. Exchange controls.
D. Balance-of-payments analysis.
    1. Balance on goods and services.
    2. Balance on current account.
    3. Basic balance.
    4. Liquidity balance.
    5. Official reserve transactions balances.
E. Graphic or chartist methods.
F. Overall evaluation.
G. Probability forecast

Probability Distribution of Spot Rate Dollar Value of Mark and Pound, May 1, 1976
(The blanks are to be filled in with forecasts as illustrated in Problem 5-6.)

From Standpoint of U.S.	German Mark		British Pound	
	Actual 12/75	Probability 5/76	Actual 12/75	Probability 5/76
Adverse				
Most likely	.3820		2.0262	
Favorable				

[See Problem 5-6]

PROBLEM 5-1

Several transactions are described below.

1. American individuals purchased $10 million worth of bonds issued by a foreign company operating in France:
    a. $5 million in checks drawn on U.S. banks
    b. $5 million in deposits in foreign banks.
2. A U.S. parent company loans $20 million to a subsidiary in Mexico from bonds sold in the United States.
3. A U.S. parent company loans $10 million to a foreign subsidiary by drawing a check on its U.S. bank. The subsidiary uses the $10 million to purchase equipment manufactured in Mexico.
4. An American parent company borrows $50 million in the Eurodollar market for 9 months and uses these funds to establish a subsidiary in Brazil. It plans to raise the money on a more permanent basis later.

THE BALANCE OF PAYMENTS AND FORECASTING FOREIGN EXCHANGE RATES

A. Make the appropriate debit and credit entries in the U.S. balance-of-payments accounts. How does this affect the balance-of-payments position?
B. Indicate the effect on the U.S. investment position.

SOLUTION:

A.

	Debit	Credit
1.		
a.	Increase in private direct investments	Increase in short-term liquid claims of foreigners on United States.
b.	Same	Decrease in U.S. private short-term liquid claims on foreigners.
2.	Same	Increase in short-term liquid claims of foreigners on United States.
3.	Same	Same
4.	Same	Same

Refer to the balance-of-payments statement on page 102 for the entries.

B. All four entries cause a deterioration in the balance-of-payments position. On the other hand, they all improve the U.S. investment position.

PROBLEM 5-2

For balance-of-payments purposes, assume that the following transactions have taken place during an accounting period.
A. Exports were $1,000 of which
  1. $250 were paid for in dollars.
  2. $250 in foreign currency was deposited in a foreign bank by the exporter.
  3. $250 was sold on an open account basis.
  4. $250 were goods that had been prepaid by the foreign buyer.
B. Imports were $1,600 of which
  1. $1,200 were paid for in dollars which the foreign exporter deposited with his bank.
  2. $200 were paid with foreign currency.
  3. $200 were obtained on an open account basis.
C. Direct investment income of $400 was received from a foreign subsidiary which acquired the dollars from its bank in the foreign country.

Balance-of-Payments Statement

Line	Item	Credit +	Debit −
2	Exports		
3	Imports		
7	U.S. direct investment income		
10	Other services, net		
11	Balance on goods and services		
12	Remittances		
13	Balance on goods, services, and remittances		
14	U.S. government grants		
15	Balance on current account		
20	U.S. direct investment abroad		1a,b 10 2 20 3 10 4 50
21	Foreign direct investment in United States		
26	Balance on current account and long-term capital		
29	Nonliquid claims by U.S. nonbanks		
30	Nonliquid liabilities by U.S. nonbanks		
32	Errors and omissions		
33	Net liquidity balance		
36	Liquid private claims by U.S. banks		
37	Liquid private claims by U.S. nonbanks	1b 5	
39	Liquid private liabilities to foreign banks	1a 5 2 20 3 10 4 50	
42	Official reserve transaction balance		
43	Liquid liabilities to foreign official agencies		

D. Travel accounts netted out at a $100 outflow which was paid for in dollars.

E. The U.S. government made a grant of $1,000 to a foreign country. (The funds have not yet been spent by the foreign government.)

F. A citizen made a $100 gift to a foreign friend who deposited the check with his bank.

G. A multinational firm made an investment of $500 on a direct basis in dollars in one of its foreign subsidiaries. The funds were converted into foreign currency in its country by the subsidiary.

THE BALANCE OF PAYMENTS AND FORECASTING FOREIGN EXCHANGE RATES

H. If the official reserve transaction balance is less than zero, the central bank will settle the problems by increasing its debt to official foreign agencies.

To do:
1. Record the transactions under the appropriate plus or minus columns on the table below, keyed by the transaction letter, and fill in the dollar amounts.
2. Calculate the balance-of-payments measures as indicated by rows 11, 13, 15, 26, 33, and 42.

SOLUTION:

Balance-of-Payments Statement

Account Number		Credit +		Debit −		Balance
2	Exports	A	1,000			
3	Imports			B	1,600	
7	U.S. direct investment income	C	400			
10	Other services, net			D	100	
11	Balance on goods and services					(300)
12	Remittances			F	100	
13	Balance on goods, services, and remittances					(400)
14	U.S. government grants			E	1,000	
15	Balance on current account					(1,400)
20	U.S. direct investment abroad			G	500	
21	Foreign direct investment in United States					
26	Balance on current account and long-term capital					(1,900)
29	Nonliquid claims by U.S. nonbanks			A_3	250	
30	Nonliquid liabilities by U.S. nonbanks	B_3	200	A_4	250	
32	Errors and omissions					
33	Net liquidity balance					(2,200)

(Table continued on next page)

Balance-of-Payments Statement (Continued)

Account Number		Credit +		Debit -		Balance
36	Liquid private claims by U.S. banks					
37	Liquid private claims by U.S. nonbanks	B_2	200	A_2	250	
39	Liquid private liabilities to foreign banks	B_1 D	1,200 100	A_1	250,	
42	Official reserve transaction balance	F G	100 500	C	400	(1,000)
43	Liquid liabilities to foreign official agencies	E	1,000			

PROBLEM 5-3

The interest rate in the United States is 7%, while the interest rate in Germany is 5%. In the current spot foreign exchange market, the exchange ratio is 4 German marks to 1 U.S. dollar. The German mark is selling at a 1% premium on an annualized basis for a 90-day contract in the forward exchange market. On a covered interest arbitrage, will funds flow into the United States or out of the United States? Explain the process and determine the gain from such.

SOLUTION:

Since the interest rate differential favors the United States (by 2% per annum), and this is not offset by the cost of buying forward exchange cover (1%), the arbitrager would buy U.S. securities with foreign currency (inflow of funds into the United States) and cover the repayment of the foreign currency by buying forward. He loses 1% on the purchase of foreign currency, but gains 2% on the U.S. investment. On a 90-day basis, he has a net gain of 1/4 of 1%. A detailed analysis of the process is presented below.

Step 1: *Borrow* 400,000 *German* marks at 5%.
Pay back 400,000 + (400,000 × 5% × 1/4) = DM405,000 after 90 days.

Step 2: Convert at spot rate DM4 to $1 = $100,000 to *invest* in U.S. securities at 7%.
Receive $100,000 + (100,000 × 7% × 1/4) = *$101,750* after 90 days.

Step 3: Cover repayment of loan in DM by *buying forward* exchange DM405,000 to be delivered at 1/4 of 1% premium after 90 days, or at a conversion rate of DM3.99 to $1.
Require DM405,000 ÷ [(4) (1 − .01/4)] = *$101,504* to pay off the loan.

Analysis.

Receive	$101,750
Pay	101,504
Net Gain	$246

Therefore, there will be an *inflow* of funds into the United States.

PROBLEM 5-4

The interest rate in the United States is 6%, while the interest rate in Germany is 5%. The exchange ratio is 2.5 German marks to 1 dollar in the current spot foreign exchange market. The German mark is selling at a 2% premium per annum in the current 90-day forward exchange market. On covered interest arbitrage, will funds flow into the United States or out of the United States? Explain the process and determine the gain.

SOLUTION:

Although the interest rate favors the United States by 1% (per annum), the arbitrager can buy forward exchange cover at the 2% premium. The arbitrager would invest in foreign securities and sell the foreign currency he would obtain upon the maturity of the securities, at the premium. He loses 1% on the investment but gains 2% on the forward sale of the foreign currency. On a 90-day basis, he nets a gain of 1/4 of 1%. A detailed analysis of the process is presented below.

Step 1: *Borrow* $100,000 in United States at 6%.
Pay back $100,000 [1 + (6% × 1/4)] = *$101,500* after 90 days.
Step 2: Convert at spot rate of DM2.5 to $1 = DM250,000
to *invest* in *German* securities at 5%.
Receive DM250,000 [1 + (5% × 1/4)] = DM253,125 after 90 days.
Step 3: Sell 90-day forward exchange contract for the maturing amount DM253,125 at 1/4 the 2% premium or at a conversion rate of DM2.4875 to $1.
Receive DM253,125 ÷ [(2.5) (1 − .02/4)] = *$101,759* after 90 days.

Analysis.

Receive	$101,759
Pay	101,500
Net Gain	$259

Therefore, there will be an *outflow* of funds from the United States.

PROBLEM 5-5

Consider the following situation. The interest rate in Germany is 10%; at the same time in the United States the interest rate level is 7%. The spot rate is 4 marks per $ which is $.25 per mark.

What must be the relation between the spot exchange rate and the 90-day forward exchange rate for neither covered interest arbitrage outflow or inflow to occur between the two countries? (Assume zero transactions costs). Be explicit in referring to the spot and future exchange rate whether it is in marks per dollar or dollars per mark. Perform the calculations on the basis that $100 is involved.

SOLUTION:

1. Borrow in U.S. at 7%.
2. Invest in Germany at 10%.
3. Repay loan in United States in dollars in 90 days.
4. Buy a forward contract in dollars agreeing to pay marks for the future dollars.
5. The forward mark must sell at a discount as shown below.

The quotation on the forward mark would be on a 90-day basis.

Alternative #1: express in DM/$.

Cost in United States   Returns in Germany

$$\$100\,[1+(.07/4)] = \frac{\$100\,(4)\,[1+(.10/4)]}{X_f}$$

$$100\,(1+.0175)\,X_f = 100\,(4)\,(1+.025)$$

$$101.75\,X_f = 410$$

$$X_f = 4.02948$$

$$\frac{.02948}{4.00} = .00737 = .737\% \text{ for 90 days, discount}$$

$$4\,(.737) = 2.948\% \text{ on an annual basis}$$

Alternative #2: express in $/DM.

Cost in United States	Returns in Germany

$$100 (1.0175) = \frac{\$100 (1.025) E_f}{.25}$$

$$101.75 = 400 (1.025) E_f$$

$$E_f = .248171$$

$$.001829/.25 = .007316 \times 4 = 2.9264\% \text{ on an annual basis}$$

Regardless of whether the analysis is made in $ per DM or DM per $, a discount in the forward market of the currency of the high interest rate country is required for covered interest arbitrage parity to obtain. The discount is slightly over .7% on a 90-day basis, and somewhat under 3% on an annual basis.

PROBLEM 5-6

Briefly outline the factors to be used in forecasting the strength of the U.S. dollar in relation to the German mark and the British pound over the 6-month period, December 1975 to May 1976. Use the checklist in part XII of this chapter.

SOLUTION:

Most of the data required for the analysis is available in data for individual countries set forth in the International Monetary Fund monthly publication, *International Financial Statistics*. This information can be supplemented from other financial publications that may be available to the reader.

    A. Political and social factors — United States.
        1. Economy on trend toward strong, sustained recovery.
        2. Election year and tendency toward stimulation.
        3. Projected federal deficits of $50 billion per year; estimated in real terms 1976, GNP $1674 billion; 3% growth.
        4. Slow population growth rate; less thán 1%.
    B. Fundamental economic forces — United States.
        1. Productivity improvement good, but not as high as the best of the other developed nations.
        2. Lower than the West German and Japanese ratio of capital investment to GNP; 15% in United States versus 20% in Germany and Japan.
        3. Economic growth in strong cyclical upturn; but recent secular movement only moderately strong.

C. Leading economic indicators – United States.
   1. Growth in money supply recently has been below target 6%; government deficit 3% of GNP.
   2. Recent record of price movements is the best of developing countries, except Germany.
   3. Relative export price trends are favorable.
   4. The large favorable balance on exports of foodstuffs may be temporary.
   5. Foreign exchange reserve position $16 billion near end of 1975.
      a. Reserves to basic balance, 1974 $16/(-5) = 3.2X$ (neg.); estimated 1975, $16/10 = 1.6X$ (plus). A plus multiple is very favorable. Much concern if a negative multiple drops below 1. This would indicate either credit extension from foreigners or depletion of the foreign exchange reserves of the nation.
      b. *Monetary base change* is defined as the monetary base (the currency in circulation plus member bank reserves at the central bank) divided by the money supply as measured by M_1 (the currency in circulation plus private demand deposits). For 1975, estimate is: (+ $3 bil.)/ (+ $300 bil.) = 10%. If the percentage is greater than 10, this indicates future upward pressure on the money supply of inflationary dimensions. The 10% calculated is therefore somewhat unfavorable, but mitigated by a consideration that this reflected a strong monetary policy to reverse the 1974 recession in the United States.
D. Balance-of-payments trends between 1974 and 1975.
   1. Merchandise trade negative $5 billion in 1974 to plus $10 billion forecast for 1975.
   2. Basic balance negative $10 billion to forecast of plus $2 billion.
   3. Liquidity balance from negative $19 billion to forecast of plus $4 billion.
   4. Official reserve transactions balance from negative $8 billion to zero.
   5. All the above represents a strong turn around giving strength to the dollar.
E. Graphic method. The chart below shows recovery of the value of the dollar in relation to 22 other currencies from a 20% decline between 1971 and 1973 with a subsequent recovery of almost one-half of the previous drop.
F. *General comments:* Relative price stability has returned. A very favorable influence is the large food and grain exports from the United States which shifted the merchandise trade balance from –$5 billion to an estimated +$10 billion between 1974 and 1975, despite the large payments for oil to OPEC. Only Germany seems to be doing a better job than the United States in controlling price level increases in the short run. So the

THE BALANCE OF PAYMENTS AND FORECASTING FOREIGN EXCHANGE RATES

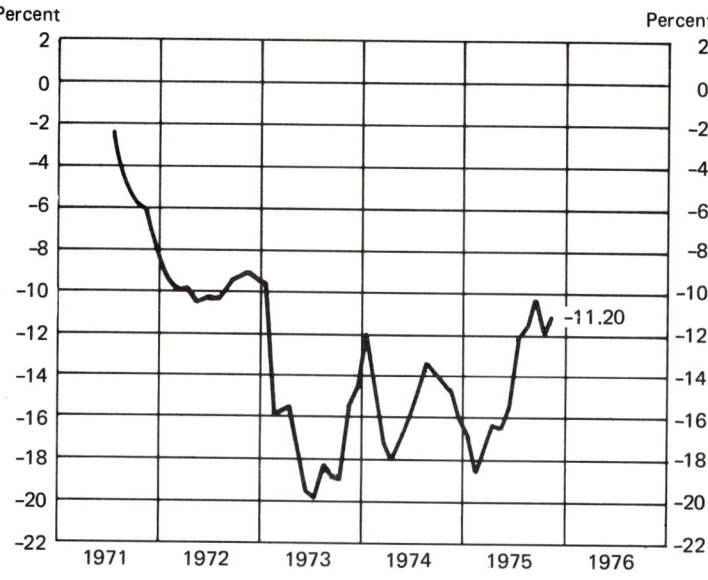

Effective Dollar Devaluation

Source: U.S. Treasury
Note: Effective devaluation is measured by the appreciation of the twenty-two currencies of DECD countries relative to the par values which prevailed as of May 1970. The appreciation is then weighted by separate export and import shares with the United States based on 1972 trade data.
Latest Data Plotted: November

Prepared by Federal Reserve Bank of St. Louis

United States should improve versus the United Kingdom. But the U.S. dollar will deteriorate somewhat against the DM. In the longer run, the United States needs to increase its ratio of investment to GNP for an improved sustained growth in productivity.

G. Probability forecast.

Probability Distribution of Spot Rate Dollar Values of Mark and Pound for May 1976

From Standpoint of United States	German Mark			British Pound		
	Actual 12/75	Probability 5/76		Actual 12/75	Probability 5/76	
Adverse		.1	$.380		.4	$1.70
Most likely	.3820	.6	.390	2.0262	.5	1.80
More favorable		.3	.395		.1	1.90

(The probability figures represent the best judgment of the decision maker responsible for the analysis. See Chapter 14 for further discussion of assessing future risks.)

The above forecast is for a strengthening of the mark in relation to the dollar, and a high probability of a weakening of the pound in relation to the dollar. The forecast of revaluation of the mark upward and further devaluation of the pound would have implications for other decisions of a firm as discussed in subsequent chapters.

PROBLEM 5-7

Comment on the major developments in the U.S. balance of payments as indicated by the changes that took place between 1974 and 1975 shown in Table 5-1 in Part II of this chapter.

SOLUTION:

A major turnabout took place in the merchandise trade balance, representing a swing of over $14 billion, with a shift from a $5 billion deficit to a $9 billion surplus. This resulted in part from the recession during the early part of 1975 which caused sharp inventory liquidation in the United States. The decline in the income from U.S. direct investments abroad was over $8 billion. This resulted primarily from the lower earnings of U.S. petroleum companies reflecting the sharp increase in tax and royalty payments to producing countries and the recession-induced decrease in petroleum demand, with sharp production cutbacks of about 10% in OPEC as a group.

Large private flotation of securities took place in the United States resulting in negative factor of over $4 billion. Purchases of already issued U.S. company securities by OPEC countries was a $3 billion plus factor.

The balance on current account improved by $15 billion. The net liquidity balance went from a $19 billion negative figure into a $3 billion positive figure, a swing of $22 billion. Thus, the need to increase liabilities to foreigners or to decrease claims on foreigners was reduced. Liquid liabilities to foreigners was reduced by $13 billion. The official reserve transactions balance was reduced to a negative $2.5 billion, a $6 billion improvement over 1974. Liquid liabilities to foreign official agencies were reduced by $7.5 billion.

Thus, 1975 represented a year of a major turnabout in the merchandise trade balance of the United States, a substantial reduction in liquid liabilities and a strengthening of the position of the dollar.

PROBLEM 5-8

What is the monetary view of the balance of payments?

SOLUTION:[3]

The MBOP (the monetary balance-of-payments approach) may be summarized by the proposition that the transactions recorded in balance-of-payments (BOP) statistics reflect aggregate portfolio decisions by both foreign and domestic economic units. Under a system of fixed exchange rates, such as the gold standard or the type of arrangement set up in 1944 at Bretton Woods, overall net surpluses (deficits) in the trade and capital accounts are viewed as flows associated with either an excess demand for money on the part of domestic (foreign) economic units or an excess supply of money in foreign economies (the domestic economy). That is, a BOP flow is one of the mechanisms by which actual money balances are adjusted to their desired levels.

The MBOP maintains that the transactions recorded in the balance of payments are essentially a reflection of monetary phenomena. It places emphasis on the direct influence of an excess demand for or supply of money on the BOP.

The crucial BOP concept is that which captures all transactions reflecting the adjustment of actual money balances to their desired levels. That is, the only transactions considered below the line are those which have an influence on domestic and foreign monetary bases and thus on domestic and foreign money supplies.

The analysis presented here does not attempt to provide a theory of the individual subaccounts; it merely lumps the individual components (goods, services, transfers, short- and long-term capital) into a single category—"items above the line." This approach recognizes that an excess supply of or demand for money may be cleared through the markets for either goods, services, or securities.

The MBOP is a theory of an automatic adjustment process. According to this theory, any BOP disequilibrium or exchange-rate movement reflects a disparity between actual and desired money balances and will automatically correct itself. While the adjustment process is different under different exchange-rate regimes, the implication is that the process is automatic and that its effects cannot be neutralized in the long run.

An implication of this theory is that, under a system of fixed exchange rates, domestic monetary policy does not control a country's money supply. Excessive monetary expansion (contraction), via expansion (contraction) of some controllable component of the monetary base, will result in an outflow (inflow) of international reserves (an uncontrollable component of the monetary base) and a tendency for the money supply to return to its former level.

Under a system of freely floating exchange rates, the domestic monetary authorities retain dominant control over the money supply, while the

---

[3] This summary is taken from Donald S. Kemp, "A Monetary View of the Balance of Payments," *Monthly Review*, Federal Reserve Bank of St. Louis, April 1975, pp. 14-22.

interaction of domestic and foreign monetary policies determines the exchange rate rather than the BOP (which is now zero by definition). In this case, a country neither imports nor exports international reserves. As a result, the domestic economy is subjected to the full consequences of inflationary or deflationary domestic monetary policies and is insulated from the effects of monetary actions taken in other countries.

Another feature of the MBOP is that it provides a framework within which one is able to assess the differential impact of monetary disturbances which occur in a world in which there is at least one reserve currency country (RCC) as opposed to those occurring in a world with no RCCs. An RCC is a country whose currency is held by others as a form of international reserves.

An expansionary (contractionary) monetary policy in the RCC may have no effect on its BOP as defined in this article. However, the RCC's trading partners will always experience a BOP surplus (deficit) and an inflow (outflow) of international reserves as a result of such RCC policies. The reason for this is that the RCC currency is held by foreign central banks as a form of international reserves. While non-RCC monetary authorities are not willing to accumulate large balances denominated in other non-RCC currencies, they are willing to accumulate large balances denominated in the RCC currency.

The exchange value of country J's currency in terms of foreign currencies is determined by the rate of growth of the money supply and real income in country J relative to the rate of growth of the money supply and real income respectively in the rest of the world.

Finally, if the balance of payments is viewed within the MBOP framework, the pitfalls of placing emphasis on any particular BOP subaccount are obvious. A deficit (surplus) in any one account need not have any effect on domestic aggregate economic activity if its impact on money balances is offset by a surplus (deficit) in another account.

Comment: As in domestic economic models, we do not regard the national income and monetarist approaches to balance-of-payments analysis as mutually exclusive. We feel that each has some important elements of analysis that are useful. Real demand and relative price elasticities perform a role in the adjustment process. The quantity theory equation will also be satisfied after the fact. The relative strength of effective demand, relative price elasticities, and the supply of money as causal variables is still in dispute.

PROBLEM 5-9

Why can the U.S.S.R. maintain a value for the ruble at arbitrary levels?

SOLUTION:

Basically, the U.S.S.R. does not permit transactions in the ruble to take place at free-market prices. Transactions in the ruble at other than official rates in the U.S.S.R. or a country controlled by the U.S.S.R. are subject to severe punishment. Some brief background materials are provided in the following outline.[4]

A. Since buyers and sellers are not free to exchange the ruble for other currencies at market-determined rates, the U.S.S.R. must peg the ruble to a convertible currency or gold.
    1. In 1937, the ruble was pegged to the U.S. dollar at 4 rubles to the dollar.
    2. In 1950, the ruble was pegged to gold at 140 rubles per ounce of gold. Since the U.S. gold parity was $35 per ounce, the implied relation to the dollar was still 4 rubles to the dollar.
B. In 1961, a currency reform occurred in the U.S.S.R.
    1. Outstanding ruble notes had to be exchanged for new notes at the rate of one new ruble for 10 old rubles.
    2. The gold parity for the new ruble was set at 32 rubles per ounce. The implied relation to the dollar was 1 ruble = $1.10. The ruble was now "worth more" than the dollar.
    3. Note that since 1 new ruble was made equal to 10 old rubles, the implied gold parity should have been 14 rubles per ounce of gold and the new ruble would have been worth $2.50. But in terms of actual purchasing power value, the ruble was still overvalued at $1.10. So devaluation was necessary to reduce the disparity between purchasing values to reduce incentives for black market transactions, exchanging the ruble for other currencies.
C. The exchange rate structure for the ruble, between the U.S.S.R. and other Eastern-bloc countries, is pegged to be favorable to the U.S.S.R.
    1. Example. The parity of the Polish zloty to the dollar is z4 = $1. The ruble parity is r1 = $1.10. Hence, the ruble should be equal to 4.4 zlotys, but the pegged rate is about 14 zlotys to the ruble. As a consequence, when Poland must make up a deficit in the barter balance of trade with the U.S.S.R., more zlotys are required than the parity relation would indicate. Also, the costs of the Russian troops stationed in the Eastern European countries are lower because their pay in rubles is higher than it otherwise would be in local purchasing power.
    2. This is economic as well as political imperialism.

REFERENCES

Aliber, Robert Z.: *The International Money Game,* Basic Books, New York, 1973.

Bowditch, Richard L., and James L. Burtle: "The Corporate Treasurer in a World of Floating Exchange Rates," in J. Fred Weston and Maurice B. Goudzwaard (eds.), *Treasurer's Handbook*, Dow Jones-Irwin, Homewood, Ill., 1976, pp. 84-110.

[4] Robert Z. Aliber, *The International Money Game*, Basic Books, New York: 1973, pp. 207-14.

Committee for Economic Development: *Toward a New International Economic System: A Joint Japanese-American View*, Committee for Economic Development, New York, 1974.

Dufey, Gunter: "Corporate Finance and Exchange Rate Variations," *Financial Management*, **1**:51-58, Summer 1972.

Duwendag, Dieter: "The Postwar Economic System in Germany: Creation, Evolution, and Reappraisal," *Review*, Federal Reserve Bank of St. Louis, **57**:16-22, October 1975.

Fieleke, Norman S.: "International Monetary Reform: The Jamaica Composite," *New England Economic Review*, Federal Reserve Bank of Boston, March/April 1976, pp. 57-62.

Fleming, J. M.: "On Exchange Rate Unification," *The Economic Journal*, pp. 467-488, September 1971.

Folks, William R., Jr.: "Decision Analysis for Exchange Risk Management," *Financial Management*, **1**:101-112, Winter 1972.

―――, and Stanley R. Stansell, "The Use of Discriminant Analysis in Forecasting Exchange Rate Movements," *Journal of International Business Studies*, **6**:33-50, Spring 1975.

Giddy, Ian H., and Gunter Dufey: "The Random Behavior of Flexible Exchange Rates: Implications for Forecasting," *Journal of International Business Studies*, **6**:1-32, Spring 1975.

Kemp, Donald S.: "A Monetary View of the Balance of Payments," *Review*, Federal Reserve Bank of St. Louis, April 1975, pp. 14-22.

Kohlhagen, Steven W.: "The Performance of the Foreign Exchange Markets: 1971-1974," *Journal of International Business Studies*, **6**:33-39, Fall 1975.

Krueger, Anne O.: "Balance-of-Payments Theory," *Journal of Economic Literature*, **7**:1-26, March 1969.

―――, "The Impact of Alternative Government Policies under Varying Exchange Systems," *Quarterly Journal of Economics*, **79**:195-208, May 1965.

Stoll, Hans R.: "An Empirical Study of the Forward Exchange Market under Fixed and Flexible Exchange Rate Systems," *The Canadian Journal of Economics*, **1**:55-78, February 1968.

Chapter 6

The Accounting Treatment of Foreign Operations and Transactions

Theme: Accounting principles and practices for business are not the same all over the world. Of lesser importance are procedural facts such as: South American countries place long-term items at the top of the balance sheet and accountants in India place liability and capital items on the left side and short-term items on the lower part of the balance sheet. Of greater importance to multinational firms is the fact that generally accepted accounting principles and practices vary considerably even among developed countries. Numerous complications arise when accounting is performed in several national currencies. When one currency changes in value in relation to others, this may affect the parent organization's financial statements denominated in its home currency.

I. Accounting systems are based on four alternative points of view.
    A. A macroeconomic point of view demands that accounting data be prepared in such a way as to aid the government in directing overall economic policy.
    B. A microeconomic point of view requires that accounting be done to further the welfare of the individual firm by optimizing the return from its operations.
    C. An independent discipline approach recognizes that judgment and estimation are part of the art of managing a business. Evaluations to be meaningful must

be similar and consistent with generally accepted accounting principles. These principles have been developed based on past experience and are changed as the need arises.
- D. A uniform accounting system defines accounting terms and account classifications uniformly for all business entities. Such a system has advantages as well as disadvantages.
  1. Advantages.
     a. Training of accounting personnel is made simpler.
     b. Comparisons between firms are more meaningful.
     c. Data from many firms can be readily assembled and used.
     d. Requirements for accounting jobs do not differ from firm to firm.
  2. Disadvantages.
     a. All businesses are not the same. Uniform systems can not serve all needs.
     b. Uniform data may not give meaningful information for firms that are greatly different.
     c. Managerial accounting to provide improved management information may not be possible.
     d. Improvements in methods are less likely due to the difficulty of effecting overall changes.

II. There are two basic problems in accounting for international operations: differences in accounting principles and practices between countries and the requirement to translate financial statements from one currency into another.
- A. Differences in accounting principles and practices between countries of the world are many. Particular practices that are required in some countries are prohibited in other countries. Between these extremes are many countries in which these same practices are used in varying degrees. These differences are illustrated by reference to selected accounting items.[1]
  1. Variations in accounting treatment of long-term assets.
     a. Fixed assets are required to be carried at cost of acquisition or construction cost minus accumulated depreciation.
        (1) The United States, Germany, Greece, Japan, Spain, and Venezuela require this practice.
        (2) Chile does not permit this practice and in Argentina, Bolivia, Peru, and Zaire only a small minority of firms observe this practice (due to a continuing high degree of price-level changes).
     b. The cost of construction of fixed assets includes only direct costs of labor and materials while all other costs are charged to current income.
        (1) The United States and Japan prohibit this practice.

---

[1] The materials in this section are taken from Price Waterhouse, *Survey of Accounting Principles and Reporting Practices in 46 Countries*, Price Waterhouse International, October 1975.

THE ACCOUNTING TREATMENT OF FOREIGN OPERATIONS AND TRANSACTIONS 117

      (2) The majority of firms in Belgium, Chile, Denmark, Norway, and Switzerland use this definition of cost.
- c. Items no longer in service are removed from the fixed asset and accumulated depreciation accounts.
  - (1) The United States and a number of other countries require this practice.
  - (2) In Australia, Denmark, Greece, Italy, and New Zealand only a minority of firms follow this practice.
- d. The amount of an asset to be depreciated is equal to the cost of the asset minus its estimated salvage value.
  - (1) The United States is joined by Canada, Japan, Mexico, and Ireland in requiring this.
  - (2) In contrast, in three times as many countries, including Belgium, Denmark, Germany, and Switzerland, a minority of firms follow this practice.
- e. Overconservatism is practiced through excessive depreciation charges on fixed assets in many countries. (See Table 6-1A.)

2. Inventories.
   - a. Inventories are generally carried at cost or market, whichever is lower, but in one country this is not permitted and is followed by only a minority of firms in other countries. (See Table 6-1B.)
   - b. A breakdown of inventories into raw materials, goods in process, and finished goods is shown in financial statements or footnotes.
     - (1) The United States, Australia, France, Germany, Japan, and other countries require this.
     - (2) Only a minority of firms in Belgium, Denmark, Italy, Ireland, Switzerland, the United Kingdom, and elsewhere follow this practice.
   - c. Payments received on account of work in progress are deducted from inventory in most countries, but are not permitted in Japan and West Germany. (See Table 6-2A.)
   - d. Undisclosed undervaluation of inventories is practiced.
     - (1) In the United States a minority of firms follow this practice.
     - (2) A majority of firms follow this practice in Denmark, Italy, Spain, and Switzerland.
     - (3) A large number of countries including Belgium, France, Germany, and Japan do not permit this practice.

3. Investments.
   - a. Investments in 50% owned companies are carried on the firm's books on an equity basis.
     - (1) This is required by the United States, the United Kingdom, Rhodesia, Nigeria, and Ireland.
     - (2) It is prohibited by Columbia, Germany, Sweden, and Switzerland.

Table 6-1 Accounting Principles and Practices

A. Depreciation	B. Inventories
Overconservatism is practiced through excessive charges for depreciation of fixed assets.	Inventories are carried at cost or market, whichever is lower.

Required	Majority	About half	Minority	Not found in practice	Not permitted	No application	Country	Required	Majority	About half	Minority	Not found in practice	Not permitted	No application
			*				Argentina		*					
			*				Australia		*					
		*					Bahamas		*					
*							Belgium		*					
			*				Bermuda	*						
		*					Bolivia		*					
*							Brazil					*		
			*				Canada	*						
		*					Chile						*	
		*					Colombia					*		
*							Denmark		*					
			*				Ethiopia		*					
		*					Fiji		*					
*							France		*					
	*						Germany	*						
		*					Greece	*						
		*					India	*						
		*					Iran				*			
		*					Italy	*						
			*				Jamaica	*						
		*					Japan		*					
		*					Kenya		*					
			*				Malaysia	*						
			*				Mexico	*						
			*				Netherlands		*					
		*					New Zealand		*					
				*			Nigeria		*					
			*				Norway	*						
			*				Pakistan		*					
			*				Panama		*					
			*		*		Paraguay		*					
*							Peru		*					
			*				Philippines	*						
			*				Rep. of Ireland	*						
		*					Rhodesia		*					
		*					Singapore		*					
		*					South Africa		*					
			*				Spain						*	
	*						Sweden		*					
	*						Switzerland						*	
		*					Trinidad		*					
			*				United Kingdom	*						
		*					United States	*						
			*				Uruguay		*					
		*					Venezuela	*						
		*					Zaire		*					

Table 6-2 Accounting Principles and Practices

A. Inventories	B. Consolidations
Payments received on account of work-in-progress are deducted from inventories.	Amount of share capital of a holding company held by subsidiary companies is disclosed.

Required	Majority	About half	Minority	Not found in practice	Not permitted	No application	Country	Required	Majority	About half	Minority	Not found in practice	Not permitted	No application
	*						Argentina	*						
	*						Australia						*	
	*						Bahamas		*					
	*						Belgium					*		
	*						Bermuda		*					
			*				Bolivia					*		
		*					Brazil				*			
*							Canada	*						
		*					Chile				*			
		*					Colombia					*		
	*						Denmark	*						
	*						Ethiopia			*				
	*						Fiji					*		
			*				France					*		
				*			Germany	*						
					*		Greece							*
		*					India					*		
*							Iran				*			
			*				Italy					*		
	*						Jamaica	*						
				*			Japan	*						
	*						Kenya					*		
	*						Malaysia					*		
	*						Mexico					*		
		*					Netherlands		*					
	*						New Zealand						*	
	*						Nigeria						*	
		*					Norway					*		
	*						Pakistan							*
	*						Panama					*		
		*					Paraguay					*		
		*					Peru	*						
		*					Philippines		*					
*							Rep. of Ireland	*						
	*						Rhodesia					*		
	*						Singapore					*		
	*						South Africa	*						
		*					Spain				*			
			*				Sweden	*						
			*				Switzerland							*
	*						Trinidad				*			
	*						United Kingdom	*						
*							United States	*						
	*						Uruguay				*			
		*					Venezuela				*			
	*						Zaire					*		

b. Where the market value of quoted investments is below book value, the market value is disclosed.
   - **(1)** This is required by the United States and a majority of countries.
   - **(2)** In Germany, Greece, Japan, Paraguay, and Zaire this is seldom done.
4. Liabilities. Where a liability is secured by a company's assets, disclosure is made.
   - **a.** Most countries including the United States require this disclosure.
   - **b.** A few firms in France, Italy, Spain, and Switzerland also do.
5. Long-term debt. Discounts on the rate of long-term debt are written off in the year of issue.
   - **a.** The United States, Greece, Mexico, Philippines, and Spain prohibit this.
   - **b.** The majority of firms in Ethiopia, Ireland, Rhodesia, Sweden, and the United Kingdom follow this practice.
6. Shareholders equity.
   - **a.** Capital. Treasury stock, shares reacquired by a firm, is recorded at cost and shown as a deduction from shareholders equity.
     - **(1)** This is required by some South American countries, Canada, Denmark, and Norway.
     - **(2)** The majority of firms in the United States follow this practice.
     - **(3)** In the majority of countries including Germany, Japan, and Mexico this practice is not permitted.
   - **b.** Reserves. Reserves are increased or decreased without disclosing the amounts charged or credited or the reasons for the change.
     - **(1)** Most countries including the United States do not permit this.
     - **(2)** The majority of firms in Brazil, Italy, Paraguay, Spain, and Switzerland practice this.
   - **c.** Earnings per share. Fully diluted earnings are disclosed in the financial statements.
     - **(1)** The United States, Canada, Ireland, and the United Kingdom require this.
     - **(2)** Firms in most other countries do not make this disclosure.
7. Consolidations. Disclosure of the amount of share capital of a holding company held by subsidiary companies is required in the United States but is not the predominant practice. (See Table 6-2B.)
8. Income taxes. For variations in the measurement of taxable income, taxation rules, and practices see Chapter 7. In general, the tax treatment of multinational corporations is less favorable in the United States than in the other major trading nations.

B. The introduction of price-level accounting has taken place in many countries with a high rate of inflation. Price-level accounting in foreign countries includes the following practices.

1. *Net* plant and equipment assets are written up annually by a percentage equal to the percentage of price-level changes during the preceding year. Assuming a rate of inflation of 10% during 1975, the following adjustments would be made.

	Dec. 31, 1975	January 1976
Gross plant and equipment	LC1,000,000	LC1,060,000
Reserve for depreciation	400,000	400,000
Net plant and equipment	LC 600,000	LC 660,000

The increase in the gross plant and equipment account is depreciated over the remaining life of the asset. What happens later to this increase in the revaluation account depends on the tax laws of the particular country involved. Some variations are:
  a. The reserve is kept to be applied to future revaluation losses, if any.
  b. Some countries require that the increase in the revaluation account be eliminated by the declaration of a common stock dividend of equal magnitude in order to avoid the requirement of paying income taxes on the amount of the asset write-up. This adjustment results in the following entries:

  Debit revaluation reserve   LC60,000
  Credit common stock   LC60,000

2. Investments are increased by the percentage of inflation during the preceding year. If the investment is not amortized, the increase merely increases the original cost. If the investment is amortized, the written-up amount can be included in future amortization.
3. Plant and equipment assets purchased on credit in a foreign currency can be written up each year by the amount which the foreign denominated debt increases due to devaluation of the local currency in relation to the currency of the creditor.

PROBLEM 6-1

Assume a firm in an LDC incurs a foreign debt of DM100,000. The spot rate at the beginning of 1976 is LC100 per DM. A 20% devaluation in the LC per DM takes place during 1976. Make the proper adjustments for the accounts presented below.

	Dec. 31, 1976		
Foreign purchased assets	LC20,000,000	Foreign debt	LC10,000,000
Reserve for depreciation	8,000,000		
Net foreign purchased assets	12,000,000		

SOLUTION:

	January 1977		
Foreign purchased assets	LC22,000,000	Foreign debt	LC12,000,000
Reserve for depreciation	8,000,000		
Net foreign purchased assets	14,000,000		

Note that the increase in the value of the foreign purchased assets is equal to the increase in the local currency denominated foreign debt. The write-up is depreciable.

    4. In some countries capital accounts are permitted to be revalued by the percentage of inflation during the preceding year. This increased amount can then be used to balance the increases in the normal plant and equipment assets and investments.

    5. At the initiation of price-level accounting, governments usually issue tables of price-level change indicators so that the book value of capital assets purchased in prior years can be increased in value by an amount which is related to the magnitude of price-level changes which have occurred since the original purchase of the asset and the present. The coefficient for asset value change for equipment purchased during the year of initiation of price-level accounting is usually 1.0. The value of the coefficient for prior years increases from this to much larger values depending on the rate of price-level changes that have taken place in the past.

C. The United States during the last few years has moved toward price-level accounting.
    1. A large number of firms in 1974 shifted from first-in-first-out (FIFO) accounting for inventories to the last-in-first-out (LIFO) method.
        a. Under this latter method charge-outs from inventory to in-process inventories are made at a level closer to present costs rather than prior costs which prevailed when the oldest units of particular inventory items were purchased.
        b. The use of present costs rather than prior costs has reduced reported operating incomes.
    2. Accelerated depreciation methods have been employed to speed up the recovery of funds spent following the purchase of capital assets.
        a. Accelerated depreciation causes larger charges against income during the early years of the economic life of an asset and lower charges later on when compared with straight-line depreciation.
        b. This results in a lowering or saving of taxes during the early years and an increase in the later years.
        c. Accelerated depreciation, however, does not change the total funds recovered during the economic life of an asset as long as the depreciation method is based on original cost.

3. Actions by the Financial Accounting Standards Board (FASB).
   a. On February 15, 1974, the FASB issued a discussion memorandum on an analysis of issues related to "Reporting the Effects of General Price Level Changes in Financial Statements."
   b. On December 31, 1974, an exposure draft of a proposed statement of financial accounting standards entitled "Financial Reporting in Units of General Purchasing Power" was published.
   c. In its Status Report, No. 37 of June 4, 1976, the FASB stated that it had decided to defer further consideration of general purchasing power accounting. The FASB stated that "general purchasing power information is not now sufficiently well understood by preparers and users and the need for it is not now sufficiently well demonstrated to justify imposing the cost of implementation upon all preparers of financial statements at this time." It also referred to current efforts to provide current replacement cost data required by SEC Accounting Series, Release No. 190.
4. In March 1976, the Security Exchange Commission issued a notice of adoption of amendments to Regulation S-X. This requires firms that have inventories, gross property, and plant and equipment of more than $100 million to:
   a. Disclose the current replacement cost of inventories and productive assets at the end of each year.
   b. Disclose the approximate value of cost of sales and depreciation based on replacement cost.
   c. Present the above required information in a footnote to financial statements or in a separate section following the footnotes.
5. These are some effects of the lack of price-level accounting in the United States.
   a. Original cost depreciation rather than replacement cost depreciation creates two problems.
      (1) The excess of the replacement cost over the original cost must be provided from earnings or from additional financing.
      (2) Not setting aside sufficient replacement funds via depreciation charges causes the overstatement of income from operations, and thus results in higher than normal income taxes.
   b. In the process of accounting for operations, material costs are continuously understated without price-level accounting. This causes reported operating profits to be greater than they should be, resulting in higher income taxes.

III. The financial translation of accounting statements—historical background.
   A. The proper translation of financial statements from a foreign currency into the home currency takes on the greatest importance when the parent consolidates the financial results of its subsidiaries with its own.

1. Consolidation occurs if any of the following obtains.
    a. The parent's ownership of the subsidiary exceeds 50%.
    b. The parent wishes to give complete information about its overall operating results to outsiders.
    c. The contribution of the subsidiary is substantial in relation to that of the parent.
2. Consolidation does not occur if one of the following obtains.
    a. The ownership interest of the parent in a subsidiary is less than 50%.
    b. The contribution of the subsidiary is small in relation to that of the rest of the organization.
    c. If the risks and uncertainties affecting the financial performance of the subsidiary are great.
3. These accounting practices are prevalent.
    a. If the results of a subsidiary are consolidated, the ownership interest of the minority shareholders is shown in the capital section of the parent's balance sheet.
    b. If the subsidiary's income is not consolidated, the parent's investment in the subsidiary is shown as an investment at cost.
        (1) Dividends, if any, are reported as investment income.
        (2) If no dividends are paid, the percentage of the amount of earnings accruing to the parent that are retained in the business are added to the cost of the investment.
4. The consolidated statements are of interest to:
    a. Shareholders of the parent firm.
    b. Shareholders of the subsidiary, if the parent plays an important part in the management and financing of the subsidiary.
    c. Creditors of the subsidiary, when the parent firm has guaranteed the payment of interest and principal of loans of the subsidiary.
    d. Management of the parent firm.
5. Regardless of whether or not a foreign subsidiary's financial results are consolidated, the subsidiary must prepare and publish financial reports in its host country following locally accepted accounting principles and practices and in terms of the local currency. These are of interest to:
    a. Other shareholders of the subsidiary.
    b. Management of the subsidiary.
    c. Creditors of the subsidiary.
    d. Management of the parent because the statement gives operating results without the effects of translation.

B. Alternative principles of translation of financial statements from one currency into another exist.
1. The current-noncurrent approach is based on *Accounting Research Bulletin*, no. 43, Chapter 12, issued in 1953. In accordance with this concept
    a. All current assets and liabilities are translated by the spot rate in effect on the statement date.

THE ACCOUNTING TREATMENT OF FOREIGN OPERATIONS AND TRANSACTIONS

    b. All noncurrent items are translated by the exchange rate in effect on the day of acquisition.
    c. The above means that:
       (1) Inventory is treated as a monetary asset.
       (2) Long-term receivables and monetary liabilities are treated as real assets.

2. The modification of the current-noncurrent approach by the *Accounting Principles Board Opinion, No. 6* in 1965 approved the use of the rate of exchange in effect on the statement day when translating long-term monetary receivables and liabilities. This opinion continued to ignore that inventories are not monetary assets.
3. The monetary-nonmonetary approach to financial translation is stated in the *National Association of Accountants Research Paper, No. 36* published in 1960.
    a. Definition of monetary and nonmonetary assets and liabilities.
       (1) Monetary items are those assets and liabilities which are denominated in a currency and which will not change in units of that currency over time. Among these are:

Monetary Assets	Monetary Liabilities
Cash	Accounts payable
Marketable securities	Notes payable
Accounts receivable	Tax liability reserves
Tax refunds receivable	Bonds
Notes receivable	Preferred stock
Prepaid insurance	

       (2) Real items, or nonmonetary items, are those assets and liabilities that have real value, whose money value changes with changes in the purchasing power of the currency in use. Among these are:

Real Assets	Real Liabilities
Inventories	Liabilities in a stronger foreign currency
Prepaid assets	
Plant and equipment	Common stock
Land	Paid-in capital
	Retained earnings

    b. In accordance with this concept:
       (1) All monetary items are translated using the exchange rate on the statement date.
       (2) All nonmonetary assets, including inventories, are translated by the exchange rate in effect on the date of their acquisition.
4. The temporal principles of translation were presented in *Accounting Research, Study No. 12* of the American Institute of Certified Public

Accountants, in 1972. This concept is very similar to the monetary-nonmonetary approach. It includes the following principles.
- a. A translation process should only change the unit of measure and cannot be used to change the attribute measured.
- b. Translation is similar to general price-level accounting in two important respects.
  - (1) The unit of measure in financial statements is changed in both translation and general price-level accounting.
  - (2) Both translation and general price-level accounting change no other accounting principle used in preparing financial statements.
- c. Exchange rates to be used in the translation process.
  - (1) Money, receivables, and payables measured at the amounts promised should be translated at the foreign exchange rate in effect on the balance sheet date.
  - (2) Assets and liabilities measured at money prices should be translated at the foreign exchange rate in effect at the dates to which the money prices pertain.
5. Translation practices on which there was general agreement.
   - a. All short-term monetary assets and liabilities are translated using the exchange rate in effect on the statement date.
   - b. All long-term real assets are translated using the exchange rate in effect on the date of their acquisition. When they are later sold or disposed of, the value received is translated using the exchange rate in effect on the date of sale or disposal. The difference between the translated sale or disposal price and translated book value determines whether the transaction has resulted in a profit or loss.
6. Translation practices on which there was no general agreement.
   - a. Inventory.
     - (1) According to the current-noncurrent approach, inventory is treated as a monetary asset.
     - (2) According to the monetary-nonmonetary approach, inventory is treated as a real asset.
     - (3) Unless inventory costs and charge-outs or sales are converted into the home currency at the time they happen and that figure is used on the parent balance sheet, it is difficult to develop a proper historical exchange rate. The charge-ins and charge-outs are a continuing process. Also in many inventories there are a minority of parts that are high-cost items but slow-moving.
   - b. Long-term liabilities.
     - (1) Prior to 1972, American firms were quite content to treat long-term monetary liabilities as such because usually this resulted in reduction in dollar liability and a credit to the revaluation account.

(2) Since then many currencies have been revalued in relation to the dollar. This results in dollar losses if a subsidiary in a revaluating country has an excess of monetary liabilities over monetary assets. FASB Statement No. 8, discussed below, requires that any losses be charged against income during the period incurred.

PROBLEM 6-2

The Easton Company, S.A., a subsidiary of the Easton Company, a U.S. firm, is operating in an inflationary country. A year ago the exchange rate of the host country's currency was LC4 per $1. It is now LC5 per $1. The host government permits write-up of assets on an annual basis. This is accomplished every January in line with the rate of inflation during the prior year. For this reason, the proper historical exchange rate is the one in effect at the beginning of the year. For the sake of simplicity, it is assumed that the firm uses an average rate of LC4.5 per $1 for profit and loss statement purposes. Translate:

1. The balance sheet using both the current-noncurrent and the monetary-nonmonetary approach.
2. The profit and loss statement.

SOLUTION:

Easton Company, S.A. Balance Sheet as of December 31, 1974 (in thousands)			Translation			
			Current-noncurrent		Monetary-nonmonetary	
			x_i	Amount	x_i	Amount
Current assets						
Cash	LC	400	5	$ 80	5	$ 80
Accounts receivable		600	5	120	5	120
Inventory*		2,000	5	400	4	500
Total current assets	LC	3,000		$ 600		$ 700
Investments, nonmonetary	LC	1,000	4	$ 250	4	$ 250
Plant and equipment		10,000	4	2,500	4	2,500
Reserve for depreciation		4,000	4	1,000	4	1,000
Net plant and equipment		6,000	4	1,500	4	1,500
Total assets	LC	10,000		$2,350		$2,450
Current liabilities						
Accounts payable	LC	400	5	$ 80	5	$ 80
Notes payable		600	5	120	5	120
Other payables		400	5	80	5	80
Total current liabilities		1,400		280		280
Bonds		1,600	4	400	5	320
Revaluation account		–		(80)		100
Common stock		4,000	4	1,000	4	1,000
Retained earnings		3,000	4	750	4	750
Total liabilities and capital	LC	10,000		$2,350		$2,450

*Assuming the LIFO method of inventory accounting.

Easton Company, S.A.

Profit and Loss Statement Ending December 31, 1974
(in thousands)

			X_i	Amount
Sales, net		LC6,000	4.5	$1,333
Cost of sales				
Inventory charge-outs*	LC 400		5	80
Depreciation	600		4	150
Other costs	2,000		4.5	444
Gross operating profit		3,000		659
Selling, general and administrative expenses		800	4.5	178
Net operating profit		2,200		481
Interest expense		200	5	40
Earnings before taxes		2,000		441
Income taxes, 30%		600	5	120
Earnings after taxes		LC1,400		$ 321

*Assuming the LIFO method of inventory accounting.

Comments: Note that the revaluation account serves as the balancing figure. It can be derived as follows:

Under the monetary-nonmonetary approach, the net monetary position (NMP) of the firm is equal to monetary assets (MA) − monetary liabilities (ML).

$$NMP = MA - ML$$
$$= 400 + 600 - (400 + 600 + 400 + 1,600)$$
$$= 1,000 - 3,000 = -2,000$$

This net monetary liability position is favorable under the existing conditions of devaluation. The change of the monetary assets and liabilities in terms of the U.S. dollar due to translation is therefore calculated as:

$$\text{Change} = NMP\left(\frac{1}{X_1} - \frac{1}{X_0}\right)$$
$$= -2,000 \left(\frac{1}{5} - \frac{1}{4}\right)$$
$$= -2,000 \left(-\frac{1}{20}\right) = +100$$

This represents a net gain of $100 thousand in net worth dollar value due to the decrease in the dollar value of the monetary liabilities and results in this amount being added to the revaluation reserve. The revaluation account can likewise be determined for the current-noncurrent approach.

$$\text{Net current position} = CA - CL$$
$$= 3,000 - 1,400$$

$$\text{Change} = NCP\left(\frac{1}{X_1} - \frac{1}{X_0}\right)$$
$$= 1{,}600\left(\frac{1}{5} - \frac{1}{4}\right) = -80$$

IV. FASB Statement No. 8 is now the governing guideline for U.S. based multinational firms as they translate the financial statements of foreign subsidiaries denominated in foreign currencies into U.S. dollars. This statement became effective for all fiscal years beginning on or after January 1, 1976. It defines the objective of translation to be to measure and express (a) in dollars and (b) in conformity with U.S. generally accepted accounting principles the assets, liabilities, revenues, or expenses that are measured or denominated in a foreign currency.
   A. Accounting for foreign currency transactions.
      1. Remeasuring in dollars items measured or denominated in a foreign currency should not affect either the measurement bases for assets and liabilities or the timing of revenue and expense recognition.
      2. At the transaction day, each asset, liability, revenue, or expense arising from the transaction shall be translated into (that is measured in) dollars by the use of the exchange rate in effect on that date, and shall be recorded at that dollar amount.
      3. At each balance sheet date, recorded dollar balances representing cash and amounts owed by or to the enterprise that are denominated in a foreign currency shall be adjusted to reflect the current rate.

PROBLEM 6-3

Zorbacorp, whose fiscal year corresponds to the calendar year, makes a LC100,000 sale of capital goods to a firm in country X on June 30, 1976. The equipment is sold under the conditions of a 20% down payment, 40% on December 31, 1976, and 40% on June 30, 1977. The foreign firm makes a 10% interest payment on the unpaid foreign currency balances when the installment payments on the principal are made. These are the exchange rates:

	E_t ($/LC)
June 30, 1976	.250
December 31, 1976	.245
June 30, 1977	.235

Zorbacorp receives LC in country X, and the overseas branch of its U.S. bank converts the amount to dollars at the current exchange rate and sends it to the United States. Make the journal entries to record this transaction if a forward contract is not used to hedge the LC receipts.

SOLUTION:

According to FASB No. 8, the amount of the sale and the interest income are determined by the exchange rate at the time of the initial transaction.

They are not adjusted for subsequent exchange-rate changes. Only the asset or liability accounts involved will be adjusted for subsequent exchange-rate changes.

June 30, 1976	Amount of the sale LC100,000×.25 = $25,000
December 31, 1976	Interest income [.25(.5)(.10)(80,000)] = $1,000
June 30, 1977	Interest income [.25(.5)(.10)(40,000)] = $500

Journal Entries and Effect of New Exchange Rates

1. 6/1/76 (Date of sale)

Cash	$ 5,000	
Notes receivable 80,000(.25)	20,000	
Sales		$25,000

2. 12/31/76 (First installment payment)

Cash .245[40,000+(80,000)(.10)(.5)]	10,780	
Exchange loss (See below.)	420	
Notes receivable [20,000−.245(40,000)]		10,200
Interest income (per above)		1,000

In this transaction the loss on the principal and the loss on the currency received interest is recognized. The components of the exchange loss are:

Gain (loss) on unpaid balances = $P_1(E_1-E_0)$ = (80,000)(.245−.25) = $ (400)
Gain (loss) on interest = $(P_1)(r)(E_1-E_0)$ = (80,000)(.10)(.5)(.245−.25) = (20)
 Total loss = $ (420)

where P_t = amount of unpaid balance outstanding
 r = annual interest rate
 E_0 = exchange rate on day of the sale transaction
 E_1 = exchange rate on the date of the first installment

3. 6/30/77 (Second installment payment)

Cash .235[40,000+(40,000)(.10)(.5)]	$ 9,870	
Exchange loss	430	
Interest income (per above)		$ 500
Notes receivable (remaining balance)		9,800

The exchange loss is:

Gain (loss) on unpaid balance = $(P_2)(E_2-E_1)$ = (40,000)(.235−.245) = $ (400)
Gain (loss) on interest = $(P_2)(r)(E_2-E_0)$ = (40,000)(.10)(.5)(.235−.25) = (30)
 Total loss = $ 430

where E_2 is the exchange rate on the date of the second installment payment.

B. Forward contracts. There are two components of the forward contract to account for, the gain or loss and the discount or premium. Accounting for each depends on the use of the forward contract.
  1. If the contract is for an identifiable foreign currency commitment, then the gain or loss and the discount or premium is deferred. A forward contract used to hedge a definite commitment will not result in book entries until the sale occurs. To qualify, the transaction must satisfy *all* of the following requirements.

a. The life of the forward contract is equal to or greater than the life of the commitment involved.
b. The contract is for the currency of commitment.
c. The commitment has been finalized and cannot be cancelled.
2. If the contract is to hedge an exposed asset or liability position, the gain or loss is recognized as of the balance sheet date while the discount or premium is amortized over the life of the contract.

Premium (discount).

Let F_O be the amount of the contract in LC.

E_O be the spot rate at the time of the contract.

E_f be the forward rate.

Then the premium (discount) = $F_O(E_f - E_O)$.

Gain (loss).

Let E_1 be the spot rate at the first date a statement is prepared.

Gain (loss) = $F_O(E_O - E_1)$.

Let E_2 be the spot rate at the end of the forward contract.

Gain (loss) = $F_O(E_1 - E_2)$.

3. If the forward contract is for speculation then gain (loss) is recognized currently with the premium (discount) included in the gain (loss).

PROBLEM 6-4

Contract Used to Cover an Identifiable Foreign Currency Commitment

U.S. based Magnum Engineering is building a plant for a U.S. firm and buys components from a manufacturer in England. The price is £400,000 on the delivery date, January 31, 1976. To hedge possible exchange-rate fluctuations of the pound sterling, Magnum buys a 90-day forward contract on November 1, 1975, for £400,000 at the rate £1 = $2. Magnum's fiscal year ends December 31, 1976.

1. Assume the spot exchange rates shown below. Make the journal entries to record the transaction. What is the cost of the components to be added to the cost of the plant?

November 1, 1975   £1 = $2.10
December 31, 1975   £1 = $2.00
January 31, 1976   £1 = $1.95

2. Assume these are the spot rates. Rework part 1.

November 1, 1975   £1 = $2.10
December 31, 1975   £1 = $2.10
January 31, 1976   £1 = $2.15

SOLUTION:

Under FASB No. 8, the forward contract is a hedge against a specific identifiable commitment.

1. 11/1/75, 12/31/75 no entry

    1/31/76   Cost of equipment inventory $800,000
          Cash to complete the forward
            contract $800,000

    Equipment inventory
      Cash payment to
       English firm $780,000
      Loss on forward
       contract   20,000
        Cost of equipment
         inventory $800,000

    If the firm had not purchased a forward contract, the £400,000 could have been purchased at £1 = $1.95 or $780,000 instead of $800,000 under the forward contract.

2. 11/1/75, 12/31/75 no entry

    1/31/76   Cost of equipment inventory $800,000
          Cash to complete the forward
            contract $800,000

    Equipment inventory account:
      Cash payment to English firm $860,000
      Gain on forward contract   (60,000)
       Cost of equipment inventory $800,000

    For this type of transaction the effect is to fix the cost of the equipment at the time of purchase of the forward contract regardless of subsequent fluctuations in exchange rates.

PROBLEM 6-5

Contract Used with an Exposed Net Asset or Net Liability Position

U.S. based Globalcorp's subsidiary in country X is in a net monetary position of LC300,000. High inflation in country X is putting devaluation pressure on the LC in terms of the dollar and Globalcorp sells a 90-day forward contract of LC300,000 on 11/1/75 at the forward rate of LC1 = $.09.

THE ACCOUNTING TREATMENT OF FOREIGN OPERATIONS AND TRANSACTIONS

Globalcorp's fiscal year corresponds to the calendar year. These are the relevant foreign exchange rates:

		Assumptions				
		A	B	C	D	E
November 1, 1975						
Spot rate	E_O = LC1 =	$.11	$.11	$.11	$.11	$.11
90-day forward rate	E_f = LC1 =	.09	.09	.09	.09	.09
December 31, 1975						
Spot rate	E_1 = LC1 =	.10	.11	.10	.12	.05
January 31, 1976						
Spot rate	E_2 = LC1 =	.09	.15	.05	.10	.11

Determine the exchange gain or loss to be recognized at year end and at January 31, 1976, under each set of assumptions of exchange-rate values.

SOLUTION:

The premium (discount) to be amortized over the life of the contract is:

$$\text{Premium (discount)} = F_O(E_f - E_O) = 300{,}000\,(.09 - .11)$$
$$= (\$6{,}000)$$

The gain or loss recognized at year end includes the amortized portion of the discount and the change in dollar value from the change in spot rates.

(1)	(2)	(3)	(4)	(5)	(6)	(7)	(8)
Assumptions	Amortized Portion of Forward Contract Premium (Discount) (2/3) $F_O(E_f-E_O)$	Gain (Loss) on 12/31/75 $F_O(E_O-E_1)$	Total Gain (Loss) on 12/31/75 (2)+(3)	Remainder of Forward Contract Premium (Discount) (1/3) $F_O(E_f-E_O)$	Gain (Loss) 1/31/76 $F_O(E_1-E_2)$	Total Gain (Loss) on 1/31/76 (5)+(6)	Overall Gain (Loss) 11/1/75-1/31/76 (4)+(7)
A	($4,000)	$3,000	($1,000)	($2,000)	$3,000	$1,000	$0
B	(4,000)	0	(4,000)	(2,000)	(12,000)	(14,000)	(18,000)
C	(4,000)	3,000	(1,000)	(2,000)	15,000	13,000	12,000
D	(4,000)	(3,000)	(7,000)	(2,000)	6,000	4,000	(3,000)
E	(4,000)	18,000	14,000	(2,000)	(18,000)	(20,000)	(6,000)

We can describe what the net gains or losses at each reporting point would be. At 12/31/75, the amortized amount of the forward contract discount of $4,000 is added to the gain or loss due to the change in the spot foreign exchange rates between 11/1/75 and 12/31/75. At 1/31/76, when the forward contract expires, the net gain or loss will be the remainder of the forward contract discount, a gain of $2,000 plus or minus the gain or loss on the change in the spot foreign exchange rates between 12/31/75 and 1/31/76. Overall, the gain or loss recorded will be a gain of $6,000 plus or minus the gain or loss on the changes in the spot foreign exchange rates between 11/1/75 and 1/31/76.

The procedure discussed in 6-5 treats only the gain or loss from the use of the forward contract to hedge the exposed position. The gain (loss) on the net monetary position (from translation of the financial statements) is equal to $F_O(E_2-E_O)$, which added to column (8) will give the net final gain (loss) of ($6,000). This demonstrates that the use of the hedge fixes the net final cost of the exposed position, to the discount between the current spot rate and the current forward rate.

Business firms have complained (see *Forbes*, June 15, 1976, pp. 37, 40) that FASB No. 8, paragraph 25, introduces unreal fluctuations into income statement results. These comments fail to take into consideration the gains or losses from translation of the financial statements. When combined with gains or losses on the forward contract, the net results, are columns (2) and (5), representing the amortization of the cost of hedging. However, if hedging is not used by the firm, gains or losses at each interim period, (3) and (6), simply record the reality to that point. Future changes could go in either direction.

PROBLEM 6-6

Contract Used in Speculation

Transcorp's chief of economics and planning, on June 1, 1976, predicts the LC of country Y will devalue to LC1 = $.22 by August 1, 1976. The spot rate on June 1, 1976, is LC1 = $.25 and the 90-day forward rate is LC1 = $.23. Based on this prediction, Transcorp sells a forward contract of LC1,000,000 at LC1 = $.23. The fiscal year of Transcorp ends on July 31. Determine the initial discount or premium and the exchange gain or loss on 7/31/76 and 8/31/76 if the exchange rate falls to LC1 = $.24 on 7/31/76 and to LC1 = $.22 on 8/31/76. To summarize the current and expected exchange rates:

$$E_O = .25$$
$$E_1 = .24$$
$$E_2 = .22$$
$$E_f = .23$$

SOLUTION:

This forward contract is for speculation and there is no initial discount or premium taken into account.

7/31/76 Recognized gain (loss) on forward contract = $F_O(E_f-E_1)$
$$= LC1,000,000(.23-.24)$$
$$= (\$10,000)$$

8/31/76 Recognized gain (loss) on forward contract = $F_O(E_1-E_2)$
$$= LC1,000,000(.24-.22)$$
$$= \$20,000$$

The net gain for the contract is $10,000. On 8/31/76 Transcorp covers the forward contract at LC1 = $.22 while LC1 had been sold at $.23 under the forward contract. Hence, the net gain is $10,000 as shown.

C. Foreign operations. Financial statements for foreign operations represent the aggregate of the foreign currency transactions performed by a subsidiary. Although FASB No. 8 distinguishes transactions from operations, the underlying principles are the same, and the discussions under A, foreign transactions, as well as under B, forward contracts, are reflected in the procedures described in this section on translation of the results of foreign operations.
1. General principles.
   a. The general principle in translating foreign statements is that the exchange rate should match the way the transaction is carried on the books.
   b. Exchange-rate gains or losses are to be included as part of current operating gains or losses and they are not to be deferred.
2. Balance sheet items.
   a. Balance sheet items are translated at the historical exchange rate if carried at the historical rate and at the current rate if carried on the books at market value.
   b. Prepaid expenses are translated at the historical rate.
   c. Future monetary liabilities and assets are translated at the current exchange rate.
   d. Inventories are translated according to their makeup as discussed below.
3. Sales revenue is translated at an average exchange rate for the accounting period.
4. The translation of cost of goods sold depends on the makeup of the value of the component parts of those costs.
   a. Inventory items.
      (1) If LIFO is used, charge-outs are made at a level near current prices. Therefore the balance sheet value of an inventory at the end of an accounting period is determined by the items longest in inventory. A study can develop the proper historical rate to use for translation into the home currency.
      (2) If FIFO is used, charge-outs are made on the basis of the value of the oldest items in inventory. Therefore the balance sheet

value of the inventory is derived from near present prices. However, a study should still be made to determine the proper translation rate.
- (3) Convert the purchase price of inventory into dollars at the time of purchase and do the same when it is sold. In this way inventory records are kept on a dollar basis. In strongly inflationary countries this may even be done in the country of the subsidiary. Inventory charge-outs or sale prices are then determined by multiplying the dollar value by the spot rate. In some instances this method may not be possible due to the complexity and rapid turnover of the inventory.

5. Depreciation.
   a. Use the information from the dollar denominated long-term asset records.
   b. Determine a proper translation rate from a study of the years in which the assets were purchased.
   c. If the country permits the annual write-up in value of long-term assets in line with price-level changes during the preceding year, a year-old translation rate may be appropriate.
6. Other current costs are translated at the average rate for the accounting period.
7. Selling and general and administrative expenses are translated at an average rate for the accounting period.
8. Interest payable is translated by the exchange ratio existing on the balance sheet date. Interest charges are translated at the average rate for the period.
9. Other income and expenses are usually translated at the end of the period exchange ratio. The same holds true for taxes, and income before and after taxes.
10. The determination of the average exchange rate for an accounting period. How the average exchange rate is determined for the accounting period depends on the magnitude at the time of the rate of devaluation.
    a. Under conditions of mild devaluation the same rate may be used for 3 months or 6 months.
    b. For conditions of more rapid devaluation an average monthly rate may be determined.
    c. Under conditions of rapid devaluation a weekly average may be used.
    d. Daily rates may be required under circumstances such as existed under the German inflation and devaluation of 1919 to 1923.
11. Exchange gains or losses shall be included in determining net income for the period in which the exchange rate changed.

a. An aggregate exchange gain or loss shall be disclosed in financial statements or a note thereto.
b. Income from certain foreign operations are not taxable until returned in the form of dividends to the U.S. parent. Therefore translation gains or losses resulting from such operations are shown as deferred taxes payable or deferred tax credits. At the present time, rulings from the Internal Revenue Service have not appeared to clarify the conditions under which these deferred taxes or credits would become payable or could be used as a credit.

V. *Illustrative translation example.* The Emerson Manufacturing Corporation, a U.S. based firm, is operating manufacturing plants in the United States, in a number of developed countries, and in a few developing countries. The firm initiated a manufacturing subsidiary in Elceland at the beginning of 1975. The Emerson Manufacturing Company, S.A., was capitalized at 100,000 shares of par value LC10 at a price of LC36 per share. In addition, LC1 million was borrowed on a 15-year basis at 10%. The firm also arranged a short-term line of credit at a rate of 10%. This was not used until the end of the year.

Prior to the initiation of operations in January 1975, LC4 million of equipment was purchased for cash. It purchased an additional LC1 million of equipment at the end of 1975. It was planned to depreciate the equipment on a straight-line basis over a 10-year period. Salvage value at the end of that period was considered to be equal to removal costs.

LC400,000 of inventory was purchased prior to the opening and further amounts of LC100,000 were purchased each month during 1975. In addition, of course, inventory replacement purchases were charged to manufacturing. There are no finished goods inventories because finished goods are immediately sold to a financing subsidiary. General insurance of LC100,000 was purchased at the end of 1974 for a 2-year period.

Income taxes in Elceland are 30% and are payable in the early months of the following year. The exchange ratio between the local currency and the U.S. dollar was LC8=$1 and, at the end of 1975, LC10=$1 with the rate of devaluation in relation to the U.S. dollar on a uniform basis during 1975. These exchange ratios can also be stated as $1=LC0.125 at the beginning of 1975 and $1=LC0.100 at the end of 1975.

Net income from sales for 1975 was estimated as LC5 million, cost of goods sold as depreciation plus 60% of sales, selling expenses as LC50,000 plus 5% of sales, and general and administrative expenses as LC100,000 plus 6% of sales. It was estimated that accounts receivable would be 10% of annual net sales. Dividends are paid on 12/31. The balance sheet of the firm prior to the beginning of operations is shown on the following page.

Emerson Manufacturing Company, S.A.
Balance Sheet as of January 1, 1975
(in thousands of LC)

Current assets		Current liabilities	
Cash	LC 300	Accounts payable	LC 200
Accounts receivable	–	Notes payable	–
Inventory	400	Other payables	–
Prepaid items	100	Taxes payable	–
Total current assets	600	Total current liabilities	200
Plant & equipment	4,000	Long-term debt	1,000
Reserve for depreciation	–	Common stock	1,000
Net plant and equipment	4,000	Paid in capital	2,600
Total assets	LC4,800	Retained earnings	–
		Total liabilities & capital	LC4,800

The translation of the subsidiary's profit and loss statement for 1975 and the 12/31/75 balance sheet for the subsidiary are shown below.

Emerson Manufacturing Company, S.A.
Profit and Loss Statement, year ending 12/31/75

	Amount in thousands of LC		Translation Factor		Amount in U.S. Dollars
Net sales		LC5,000	.111		$555,000
Inventory charge-outs	1,200		.111	133,200	
Prepaid items	50		.125	6,250	
Depreciation	400		.125	50,000	
Other costs	1,750		.111	194,250	
Gross operating profit		1,600			171,300
Selling expenses		300	.111		33,300
General and administrative expenses		400	.111		44,400
Net operating profit		900			93,600
Interest		100	.111		11,100
Earnings before taxes		800			82,500
Provision for income taxes $t = .3$		240	.111		26,640
Earnings after taxes		560			55,860
Dividends paid		100			10,000
Retained earnings		LC 460			$ 45,860

In the translation above, for the beginning of the year, 1/8 or 0.125 was used and 1/10 or 0.100 was used for the end of the year. The average exchange rate for the year was 1/9 or 0.111. Sales, inventory charge-outs, other costs, selling expenses, and general and administrative expenses are assumed to be evenly distributed throughout the year.

Emerson Manufacturing Company, S.A.
Balance Sheet as of December 31, 1975 in LC and Translated into $

	Amount in thousands of LC	Translation Factor	Amount in U.S. Dollars
Current assets			
Cash	LC 500	.100	$ 50,000
Accounts receivable	500	.100	50,000
*Inventory	400	.125	50,000
Prepaid items	50	.125	6,250
Total current assets	1,450		156,250
Plant and equipment	5,000	Schedule A	600,000
Reserve for depreciation	400	.125	50,000
Net plant and equipment	4,600		550,000
Total assets	LC6,050		$706,250
Current liabilities			
Accounts payable	400	.100	40,000
Notes payable	300	.100	30,000
Other payables	250	.100	25,000
Income taxes payable	240	.100	24,000
Total current liabilities	1,190		119,000
Long-term debt	1,000	.100	100,000
Common stock, par value LC10	1,000	.125	125,000
Paid in capital	2,400	.125	300,000
Retained earnings	460		62,250
Total liabilities and capital	LC6,050		$706,250

Schedule A — equipment translation

Purchase of 12/31/74	LC4 million	.125		$500,000
Purchase of 12/31/75	1 million	.100		100,000
			Total	$600,000

*The LIFO method of inventory accounting is used.

Comments: The retained earnings of $62,250 shown in the balance sheet of 12/31/75 is composed of three elements: (1) operating earnings, (2) translation gains or losses from operations as reflected in the translation adjustments shown on the income statement, and (3) gains or losses from translation of the changes in the balance sheet items.

PROBLEM 6-7

The Miller Company, S.A., a subsidiary of the U.S. based Miller Company, is operating in a country in which after a period of relative price-level stability, exchange rates moved from LC4 to $1 to LC5 to $1 in one year. Following are the balance sheets for the fiscal years ending in 1975 and 1976 and the income statement for the fiscal year ending June 30, 1976.

Balance Sheet
Miller Company, S.A.
(000)

	6/30/76	6/30/75
Current assets		
Cash	LC 600	LC 400
Accounts receivable	700	600
Notes receivable	800	700
Inventory	2,200	2,000
Prepaid expenses	100	100
Total current assets	4,400	3,800
Property, plant and equipment		
Land	2,200	2,200
Buildings and equipment	12,000	10,000
Less allowance for depreciation	5,200	4,000
Net property, plant and equipment	9,000	8,200
Investments, nonmonetary	800	1,000
	LC14,200	LC13,000
Current liabilities		
Accounts payable	LC 600	LC 400
Accrued expenses	700	600
Income taxes payable	400	400
Total current liabilities	1,700	1,400
Long-term debt	3,310	3,600
Stockholder's equity		
Common stock	6,000	6,000
Retained earnings	3,190	2,000
Total equity	9,190	8,000
	LC14,200	LC13,000

Statement of Income and Retained Earnings
Miller Company
Year Ended June 30, 1976
(000)

Sales, net		LC8,000
Cost of goods sold:		
Inventory, 6/30/75	LC2,000	
Cost of production	3,700	
	5,700	
Less inventory, 6/30/76	LC2,200	
Cost of goods sold		3,500
Depreciation		1,200
Other costs		800
Gross operating profit		2,500
Selling, general and administrative expenses		500
Net operating profit		2,000
Interest expense		300
Earnings before taxes		1,700
Income taxes (30%)		510
Net income		1,190
Retained earnings 6/30/75		2,000
Retained earnings		LC3,190

Notes:

1. Miller Company bought equipment for LC2,000 on December 31, 1975. The useful life of the equipment is 5 years and straight-line depreciation is used.
2. Inventory turns over 4 times a year and Miller, S.A., uses FIFO.
3. The nonmonetary investments, which had been carried at historical cost, were written down on 12/31/75 to reflect a decline in their market price.
4. Buildings and equipment had an original life of 10 years, and as of 6/30/75 had 6 years remaining useful life. Depreciation is straight-line.
5. There were no changes in the prepaid items during the year.
6. The prepaid items and the nonmonetary investments were acquired on 6/30/75.
7. The revenue, costs of production, selling, interest, and general and administrative expenses are evenly spread throughout the year.
8. The company was established and the common stock was issued on 6/30/71.

These are the applicable exchange rates.

		(LC/$)
1.	6/30/71	3.0
2.	6/30/74-6/30/75	4.0
3.	Average for the period 6/30/75-6/30/76	4.5
4.	Average for the period 3/31/76-6/30/76 (4th fiscal quarter)	4.75
5.	12/31/75	4.5
6.	6/30/76	5.0

Translate the financial statements for consolidation with the financial statements of Miller U.S. which adopted FASB No. 8 one year before the mandatory adoption date.

SOLUTION:

Balance Sheet
Miller Company, S.A.

	6/30/76 (000)	Exch. Rate (LC/$)	6/30/76 (000)	6/30/75 (000)	Exch. Rate (LC/$)	6/30/75 (000)
Current assets						
Cash	LC 600	5	$ 120	LC 400	4	$ 100
Accounts receivable	700	5	140	600	4	150
Notes receivable	800	5	160	700	4	175
Inventory	2,200	4.75	463	2,000	4	500
Prepaid expenses	100	4	25	100	4	25
Total current assets	4,400		908	3,800		950
Property, plant and equipment						
Land	2,200	3	733	2,200	3	733
Building and equipment	12,000	Sched. 1	3,777	10,000	3	3,333
Less allowance for depreciation	5,200	Sched. 1	1,710	4,000	3	1,333
	9,000		2,800	8,200		2,733
Other assets						
Investments, nonmonetary	800	4.5	178	1,000	4	250
	LC14,200		$3,886	LC13,000		$3,933
Current liabilities						
Accounts payable	LC 600	5	$ 120	LC 400	4	100
Accrued expenses	700	5	140	600	4	150
Income taxes payable	400	5	80	400	4	100
Total current liabilities	1,700		340	1,400		350
Long-term debt	3,310	5	662	3,600	4	900
Stockholder's equity						
Common stock	6,000	3	2,000	6,000	3	2,000
Retained earnings	3,190		884	2,000		683
	9,190		2,884	8,000		2,683
	LC14,200		$3,886	LC13,000		$3,933

THE ACCOUNTING TREATMENT OF FOREIGN OPERATIONS AND TRANSACTIONS

Statement of Income and Retained Earnings
Miller Company
Year Ended June 30, 1976

			Exch. Rate (LC/$)	Translated Amount (000)
Sales, net		LC 8,000	4.5	$1,778
Cost of goods sold:				
Inventory, 6/30/75	LC2,000		4.0	500
Cost of production	3,700		4.5	822
	5,700			1,322
Less inventory, 6/30/76	2,200		4.75	463
Cost of goods sold		3,500		859
Depreciation		1,200	Sched. 1	377
Other costs		800	4.5	178
Gross operating profit		2,500		364
Selling, general and administrative expenses		500	4.5	112
Net operating profit		2,000		252
Interest expense		300	4.5	67
Earnings before taxes		1,700		185
Income taxes (30%)		510	4.5	113
Net income		1,190		72
Retained earnings 6/30/75		2,000		
		LC 3,190		

Schedule 1

	Foreign Currency Amount (000)	Exch. Rate (LC/$)	Translated Amount (000)
1. Buildings and equipment (purchased 6/30/71)	LC10,000	3	$3,333
2. Equipment (purchased 12/31/75)	2,000	4.5	444
	LC12,000		$3,777
3. Depreciation allowance (6/30/75)	4,000	3	1,333
4. Depreciation expense on 1 above [LC10,000/10]	1,000	3	333
5. Depreciation expense on 2 above [LC(2,000/5).5]	200	4.5	44
6. Depreciation allowance	LC 5,200		$1,710

Comments:

1. In translating the balance sheet for 6/30/75, a period of unchanged exchange rates encompassed all balance sheet items except the fixed assets and common stock which had been purchased when the exchange rate was LC3 to $1. Hence, the exchange rate used to translate all items is 4, except for the fixed assets and common stock which are translated at an exchange rate of 3.
2. The translation of the income statement for the fiscal year ending 6/30/76 illustrates the application of FASB No. 8. Sales, costs of production, selling, general and administrative expenses, interest expenses, and income taxes, assumed to be distributed uniformly throughout the year, are translated at the average exchange rate for the year at 4.5.

    In the income statement, beginning inventory is translated at the applicable exchange rate of 4; the ending inventory is translated at 4.75, the average for the 4th fiscal quarter during which the inventory was produced.

    Depreciation as shown in Schedule 1 is translated at the rates applicable to the assets to which each component of inventory expense relates. Net income is composed of the results of operations plus or minus the gains or losses from translation.

    In translating the balance sheet for 6/30/76, the temporal method of FASB No. 8 is applied. Monetary assets and liabilities are translated at the current exchange rates. Real assets, except inventories, are translated at the applicable historical rates. With regard to inventory, since FIFO is used to determine inventory expenses in the income statement, the balance sheet inventory represents inventory purchased or manufactured most recently, in this example during the most recent quarterly period.

    The retained earnings account includes the addition to retained earnings which reflects both the results of operations and translation of the income statement as well as the gains or losses from translation of the balance sheet.

REFERENCES

Ernst & Ernst: "Accounting for Foreign Currency Translations, FASB Statement No. 8," *Financial Reporting Developments*, February 1976.

Financial Accounting Standards Board, Statement No. 1, *Disclosure of Foreign Currency Translation Information*, Stamford, Conn., December 1973.

Mueller, Gerhard G.: *International Accounting*, Macmillan, New York, 1967.

Price Waterhouse & Co.: *Guide for the Reader of Foreign Financial Statements*, New York, June 1971.

———: *Survey of Accounting Principles and Reporting Practices in 46 Countries*, New York, 1975.

Chapter 7

Government Rules and Policies Affecting International Business

Theme: Governments exert an ever stronger influence on the activities of businesses. This influence is even greater in international business transactions due to the international balance-of-payments problem. The transfer of funds on an international basis and particularly the taxation of foreign earned income of U.S. persons are strongly influenced by the actions of the United States and many foreign governments. This chapter particularly emphasizes the problems of a U.S. person (remember that U.S. law treats a corporation as a person) deriving profit from operations in foreign countries.

I. The preservation of foreign exchange reserves.
    A. Measures to husband the foreign exchange reserves of a nation become necessary when the quantity of these reserves is reduced to a level that is considered dangerous by the government of the country. These shortages usually arise from the following events.
        1. Internal inflation raises the level of prices.
        2. The higher prices make the exports of the country less competitive.
        3. A drop in exports results.
        4. At the same time, the high level of internal prices makes lower priced foreign goods more desirable, thus increasing imports.

5. A decrease in exports of goods and services and an increase in imports of the same causes a trade deficit which creates an imbalance in the international balance of payments of the country unless offset by other international transactions.
6. The continuing deficit in the foreign balance of payments of a country causes a heavy drain on the nation's foreign exchange reserves since these are normally used to settle international accounts.

B. The effort to slow the outflow of foreign exchange reserves usually calls for these measures.
1. Strict limitations are placed on all imports.
2. Reduction or complete prohibition of the outflow of funds is demanded for the purpose of:
    a. Payment of interest due foreigners.
    b. Dividend payments to foreigners.
    c. Principal reduction payments on foreign loans.
    d. Foreign travel expenses for business or pleasure.

C. The efforts to control and reduce this outflow are not always successful.
1. The level of vitally needed imports is too large.
2. The country requires additional foreign investment funds to develop the local economy, therefore it cannot reduce the outflow of funds for interest and loan payments to a small enough level.

D. Devaluation of the local currency is the remedy most often applied under these circumstances.
1. It reduces the price level of export goods in terms of foreign currencies.
2. It causes an increase of the local prices of import goods thereby reducing imports.
3. It aids a strong government promoted effort to increase exports to the rest of the world.

E. Other efforts to increase exports may be required.
1. Provide subsidies to exporters in the form of reduction or refund of taxes on exported goods.
2. Provide financial aid in planning assistance to develop additional foreign markets for exports.
3. Furnish commercial and political risk insurance for exports to improve the financing of these exports.
4. As an incentive, permit exporters to keep a small percentage of the foreign funds earned from increased exports.
5. Permit the formation of export sales companies with reduced taxation as an inducement to greater export efforts.
6. Grant special import permits to export industries so they may increase the volume of export goods manufactured and sold.
7. Grant special favorable foreign exchange rates to export industries so they may derive a larger number of local currency units from their foreign currency export receipts.

8. Offer special incentives to foreign investors in export oriented or import replacement industries.
   a. Tax holidays for a specified number of years.
   b. Reduced income taxes following the tax holiday.
   c. Special favors for obtaining import permits for capital goods and raw materials and supplies needed to manufacture exports.

   The only problem with all the above is that all countries are always attempting to increase exports and yet on a worldwide basis the overall volume of exports must equal imports.

II. Alternative taxes and tax theories.
   A. A business operating in a number of countries may find each has its own tax laws. These are some of the types of taxes levied.
      1. Income taxes.
      2. Capital taxes based on the value of real assets.
         a. Real estate property taxes.
         b. Personal property taxes.
         c. Taxes on investment assets.
            (1) Cash in bank accounts.
            (2) Stocks and bonds.
            (3) Net book value of investments.
      3. Business taxes and license fees.
      4. Dividend withholding taxes.
      5. Excise taxes.
      6. Import and export duties.
      7. Sales taxes.
      8. Value added taxes.
      9. Turnover taxes.
   B. The basic theories of taxation are not the same in all countries. Some countries tax income:
      1. At the source of the income in the country where earned.
      2. At the location of control of the business enterprise.
      3. No matter where earned.
      4. See the detailed description and comparison of U.S. tax treatment with the tax treatment of other countries on the foreign earnings of their companies in Sections V and VI.
   C. In order to minimize the tax difficulties of businesses operating on an international basis, the U.S. government has taken the lead since the latter part of the nineteenth century in negotiating bilateral tax treaties with the governments of the major trading nations.
      1. Most of the tax treaties include provisions for:
         a. The taxation of income earned by citizens and residents of both countries.
         b. The rates of withholding taxes on dividends, interest, and royalties.

c. Credit for income taxes paid in one country which may reduce double taxation.
d. Prohibition of discrimination against residents of the other country.
e. Exchange of information.
f. Exemptions from tax for activities not conducted through a permanent establishment.
2. Most of the tax treaties define the terms of
   a. Residence.
   b. Permanent establishment.
   c. Taxes covered.
   d. The contracting states.
   e. Control.
3. Most of the treaties define the taxes payable on unearned income such as
   a. Dividends.
   b. Interest.
   c. Royalties.
4. Most of the treaties determine when income from sales transactions between the countries is taxable.

III. United States taxation of international operations.
  A. The United States taxes the income of its citizens, corporations, and resident aliens no matter where earned. All income is taxable.
  B. Some income, resulting from income in a foreign country or profits resulting from transactions with foreign countries, is treated as an exception to the general tax rules.
     1. Taxation of the earned income of a U.S. citizen living abroad is an exception. Any citizen who has been living outside of the United States in excess of 510 "full" days within an 18-month period enjoys an exclusion of $20,000 annually for the first 3 years and $25,000 per year thereafter. His unearned income, however, is taxed in a normal manner.

PROBLEM 7-1

Edward Johnson, a U.S. citizen, has been working on a contract basis for the Consolidated Aviation Service Company in Venezuela for the last 3 years. In his third year his salary income was $35,000. He is married and files a joint return. He has had dividend income of $750 and a long-term capital gain of $3,000 which did not result from the sale of an equity interest in a controlled foreign corporation. What would be his taxable income before deductions?

SOLUTION:

His taxable income before deductions would be as follows:

Earned Income	$35,000	
Less exclusion	20,000	$15,000
Dividend income	750	
Less dividend credit	200	550
50% of long-term capital gain	1,500	1,500
Taxable income before deductions		$17,050

2. Income on investments in Puerto Rico and U.S. possessions are exceptions to the general rules. The taxation of this income is deferred from U.S. taxation until it is returned in the form of dividends or liquidating distribution.
    a. However, a U.S. Corporation must derive more than 80% of its income from Puerto Rico or a U.S. possession for a 3-year period.
    b. Furthermore, 50% or more of such income must be derived from the active conduct of a trade or business within a possession of the United States.
3. A Western Hemisphere Trade Corporation is also an exception. This business entity was created by the Revenue Act of 1942 to encourage U.S. business to do business with other Western Hemisphere nations. The taxable income of such a domestic corporation is allowed a special deduction computed by a fraction — the numerator is 14% and the denominator is 48%. This makes the effective tax rate $(1 - .14/.48).48 = (.7083).48 = .34$, or 34% at present.
    a. However, it must conduct all of its business in the Western Hemisphere.
    b. Furthermore, 95% of its income must be derived from sources outside of the United States. Generally, the source of income is where title passes.
    c. Lastly it must obtain 90% or more of its gross income from the active conduct of a trade or business venture.
4. Another exception is a Domestic International Sales Corporation (DISC). The Revenue Act of 1971 permits the creation of these corporations to encourage the expansion of U.S. exports. As the result of the Tax Reduction Act of 1975, exports of natural resources and energy no longer participate in the benefits offered by exporting through a DISC. While the income of the DISC itself is not taxed, one-half of its taxable income is deemed to have been received by its shareholders and thus is taxable as part of their income. Taxes on the other half of the income are deferred provided these earnings are reinvested in export promoting activities.
    a. A corporation incorporated in one of the 50 states can qualify as a DISC providing:
        (1) 95% of its gross receipts consist of qualified export receipts.

(2) Its qualified export assets are 95% of total assets.
(3) That during the year in which it is treated as a DISC it has only one class of stock, with a stated value of at least $2,500.
(4) The corporation has elected to be treated as a DISC.
b. The deferral of DISC income is reduced to the extent of an increase in foreign investments. A DISC's foreign investments in connection with export promoting activities are limited to:
(1) The amount of depreciation of the previous foreign investment.
(2) The amount of capital raised abroad.
(3) 50% of the profits from foreign operations.
(4) 50% of the royalty payments received from foreign sources.
c. The so-called producer's loans are further limited.
(1) A loan plus the unpaid balances of all previous loans may not exceed the accumulated DISC income at the beginning of the month in which the loan is made.
(2) The loan must be evidenced by a note or other evidence of indebtedness with a maturity not to exceed 5 years from the date of the loan.
(3) The loan may be made only to a person who is engaged in the United States in manufacturing, production, growing, or extraction of export property.
(4) The total of all unpaid loans may not exceed the borrower's investment in plant, machinery, and equipment plus the amount of property held for sale, lease, or rental plus the aggregate research and experimental expenditures which sum total is multiplied by the proportion of export sales to total sales during a prior 3-year period.
(5) If profits are not so invested, they are taxed on a regular basis instead of 50% of normal.
d. The profits of a DISC are limited.
(1) Profits may be equal to 4% of qualified export sales plus 10% of the DISC's and parent's export promotional expenditures.
(2) DISC profits may be 50% of the profits of both the DISC and its parent that are export-related plus 10% of the export promotional expenses.
(3) DISCs may claim all of the profits on export sales of goods that have been transferred to it on an arm's length basis.

PROBLEM 7-2

Assume that a firm has overall sales of $100 million and foreign sales of $40 million, the overall profit is $25 million, and the profit on foreign sales is $12 million before income taxes. The firm's export promotion expenses were $2 million during the last year. The normal income tax rate is 50%. The firm's

GOVERNMENT RULES AND POLICIES AFFECTING INTERNATIONAL BUSINESS

DISC did all of the foreign selling and purchased the goods sold from the parent at an actual cost of $23 million. The overhead expenses of the DISC were $5 million. Should a DISC have been used? If so, which of the three alternative tax computation methods would be most advantageous?

SOLUTION:

A. Calculations without a DISC.

Total net sales	$100,000,000
Profits before taxes	25,000,000
Income taxes at 50%	12,500,000
Earnings after taxes	$ 12,500,000

B. Calculations with a DISC.

1. Alternative 1

Permissible profit of DISC = .04(40,000,000) + .10(2,000,000)
       = 1,600,000 + 200,000 = $1,800,000

	DISC	Parent
Earnings before taxes	$1,800,000	$23,200,000
Income taxes at 25%	450,000	
Income taxes at 50%		11,600,000
Earnings after taxes	$1,350,000	$11,600,000
Total income after taxes		$12,950,000
Earnings after taxes before DISC		12,500,000
Deferred taxes due to DISC		$ 450,000

2. Alternative 2

50% of foreign before-tax profits = $6,000,000
10% of export promotion expenses = 200,000
Total before-tax earnings of DISC = $6,200,000

	DISC	Parent
Earnings before taxes	$6,200,000	$18,800,000
Taxes at 25%	1,550,000	
Taxes at 50%		9,400,000
Earnings after taxes	$4,650,000	$ 9,400,000
Total earnings after taxes		$14,050,000
Earnings after taxes before DISC		12,500,000
Deferred income taxes		$ 1,550,000

3. Alternative 3

DISC sales	=	$40,000,000
DISC cost of goods sold	=	23,000,000
Other costs	=	5,000,000
Earnings before taxes	=	$12,000,000

	DISC	Parent
Earnings before taxes	$12,000,000	$13,000,000
Income taxes at 25%	3,000,000	
Income taxes at 50%		6,500,000
Earnings after taxes	$ 9,000,000	$ 6,500,000
Total earnings after taxes		$15,500,000
Earnings after taxes before DISC		12,500,000
Deferred income taxes		$ 3,000,000

It can be seen that the use of a DISC results in higher total earnings after taxes. This is because part of the taxable income is deferred with a DISC. Under the facts assumed, alternative 3 provides the most advantageous tax computation method.

5. Export trade corporation is an exception to the general rules. A corporation may be defined as an export trade corporation if:
   a. It had for a prescribed period 90% or more of its gross income from foreign operations, income derived from the sale, installation, servicing, and leasing of U.S. goods to unrelated persons outside of the United States.
   b. 75% or more of its income resulted from export trade,
   c. 50% or more of its income resulted from the sale of U.S. grown agricultural products.
   d. The limit on the amount of such export trade income that may be excluded is equal to:
      (1) 150% of export promotional expenses.
      (2) 10% of gross receipts.
      (3) The proportion of the increase in investments and total export trade assets for the particular year. This means in effect that export trade income must be reinvested in export operations if it is not to be taxed in a particular year.
6. International financing subsidiaries are also considered exceptions to the general rules. These subsidiaries are formed by multinational firms to facilitate the raising of funds in the Eurodollar or Eurobond markets.
   a. The functions of these subsidiaries are:
      (1) To avoid withholding taxes on interest payments made to foreign bondholders which would increase the cost of borrowing.
      (2) To minimize the taxation of dividends and/or interest payments made by the parts of the multinational firm that made use of the borrowed funds.
   b. The subsidiaries formed are so-called "80-20" corporations that cannot have a greater debt than 5 times their equity funds.
      (1) They can make interest payments to foreign bondholders without a withholding tax on these payments.
      (2) They must be located in countries whose tax treaties with other nations minimize taxes on dividends and/or interest received.

(3) They should have income slightly in excess of the magnitude of the required interest payments to the foreign creditor.

c. The country of incorporation of these financing subsidiaries depends on who will use the funds borrowed from European dollar lenders. Rosenberg and Singer (1969) have suggested the following arrangements which may have to be modified with changes in rules and regulations.

(1) When funds are to be used by foreign subsidiaries of a U.S. parent, locate the financing subsidiary in the U.S.
  (a) Since the financing subsidiary is owned 100% by the parent, the parent can make payments to it without taxation.
  (b) Since less than 20% of the income is from U.S. sources, this subsidiary can make payments to foreign lenders without withholding taxes being required.
  (c) Interest received from foreign subsidiaries is minimized by tax treaties between the United States and the countries of the location of the foreign subsidiaries.
  (d) Should the financing subsidiary make any dividend payments to the parent, these may be 100% excluded from the parent's U.S. tax liability if:
    i. A consolidated return is filed.
    ii. A 100% dividend exclusion is elected when separate returns are filed.
    iii. Otherwise 85% of the dividend income may be excluded when separate returns are filed and multiple surtax exemptions are still available under sections 243 (a) (3) and (b).

(2) When the funds are to be used by the parent, locate the financing subsidiary in the Netherland Antilles.
  (a) A tax treaty with this country specifically exempts interest payments by the financing subsidiary from U.S. withholding taxes even if all of the income of the subsidiary is derived from U.S. sources.
  (b) The 5:1 debt to equity ratio must be observed.
  (c) It is advisable to obtain a section 367 ruling from the U.S. Internal Revenue Service. In the summer of 1976 there were numerous bills before Congress designed to curtail privileges presently enjoyed by U.S. multinational firms. Adoptions of any of these proposed bills would alter the operations of these financing subsidiaries.

(3) When the funds are to be used in the United States and by foreign subsidiaries, it is suggested that two financing subsidiaries be formed: one in the United States and the other in the U.S. Virgin Islands.

(a) If the Virgin Islands subsidiary borrows the Eurobond funds, its interest payments will not be subject to Virgin Islands or U.S. withholding taxes as long as less than 20% of the income of the subsidiary is derived from Virgin Islands sources.
(b) Less than half of the Eurobond funds are loaned to the parent and the remainder is loaned to the U.S. located financing subsidiary to be reloaned to foreign subsidiaries.
(c) No withholding taxes apply when the parent or the U.S. financing subsidiary make interest payments to the Virgin Islands financing subsidiary.
(d) When the foreign subsidiaries pay interest or dividends to the U.S. located financing subsidiary, the tax on these payments will be minimized by tax treaties.

IV. Tax aspects of the selection of the operating form of foreign organizations.
  A. Branch of parent is one possible form.
    1. Advantages.
      a. Income is readily consolidated.
      b. Losses and normal expenses are fully deductible from other income of the parent.
    2. Disadvantages.
      a. Financial disclosures of the parent are required to be made to the host government.
      b. Potential tax difficulties exist in the host country due to the fact that worldwide income of the parent may get involved in income tax considerations.
      c. Problems may arise over disallowance of allotted overhead expenses by the parent.
  B. Foreign subsidiary either 100% owned, majority owned, or minority owned, is another possible form.
    1. Advantages.
      a. It may more readily be able to borrow money in the host country.
      b. It may be entitled to tax incentives and other benefits designed to promote certain lines of activity.
      c. In the instance of a manufacturing subsidiary, profits are not taxed by the United States until returned in the form of dividends.
      d. No financial disclosures of the parent's worldwide operating results are required to be made to the host country.
    2. Disadvantages.
      a. It may be more difficult to dissolve if the venture is unprofitable, thus causing additional financial losses.
      b. The subsidiary, being a citizen of the country of its incorporation, may be more closely regulated than a branch.

GOVERNMENT RULES AND POLICIES AFFECTING INTERNATIONAL BUSINESS 155

V. Items that influence the before-tax earnings of a foreign subsidiary.
   A. Any contact with foreign taxing authorities complicates the profit planning of the multinational firm because each country is primarily interested in maximizing its tax revenues.
   B. The following items are most often questioned.
      1. Transfer pricing.
      2. Allocation of overhead charges.
      3. Levying of license fees and research and engineering development costs.
      4. Payments of dividends.
      5. Loans challenged as being in reality equity investments.
   C. These are possible remedies for the above items.
      1. Use transfer prices equal to those charged by third parties.
      2. Allocate overhead on a defensible basis and apply it worldwide.
      3. Develop a defensible basis for these charges.
      4. Use a worldwide dividend payout ratio, then, if less is paid out occasionally in a particular country, no foreign taxing authority is likely to challenge it.
      5. Be able to clearly distinguish between loans and equity funds; always charge and collect a rate of interest on all loans.
   D. Use these general guides.
      1. Be honest.
      2. Be consistent.
      3. Be a patient and persistent negotiator.

VI. The U.S. Revenue Act of 1962. This act drastically changed the ways in which U.S. firms operate on an international basis.
   A. Overview.
      1. Sought to prevent tax avoidance by the use of a foreign subsidiary to record profits which were not remitted and therefore not subject to U.S. taxes.
      2. Defined a controlled foreign corporation (CFC) and types of income (subpart F) characteristically involved in such tax avoidance.
         a. A CFC's subpart F income is subject to U.S. tax whether or not remitted.
         b. A CFC's non-subpart F income is subject to U.S. tax when remitted.
      3. Methods of calculating the U.S. tax.
         a. Generally, a new method, the gross-up method (explained below) is applicable to income subject to the U.S. tax.
         b. However, non-subpart F income from a subsidiary in a developing country may continue to use the old ("normal") method.
   B. The concept of a Controlled Foreign Corporation (CFC).
      1. For a first tier or direct subsidiary a foreign corporation is a CFC if 50% or more of its common stock is held by U.S. persons (including corporations) each owning 10% or more of this common stock.

2. For a second and later tier or farther removed subsidiary such corporation is a CFC if 50% or more of its equity values are held by U.S. persons each holding 10% or more of such values. Equity value in this instance includes preferred stock in addition to common stock.
3. If a foreign corporation whose equity values are 60% owned by U.S. persons each owning 10% or more of such values, and if such corporation owns a 40% interest in another foreign corporation, the qualifying U.S. interest is deemed to be 60% of 40%, or 24%.

PROBLEM 7-3

Multinat owns 40% of the common stock and 90% of the preferred stock of a joint venture South African subsidiary. The book value of the common stock is $20,000 and the preferred stock is $80,000. The partners are all non-U.S. persons. The South African company in turn owns a 60% interest in a Kenyan company in which the other 40% is owned by non-U.S. persons.
1. Is the South African firm a controlled foreign corporation?
2. Is the Kenyan firm a CFC?
3. Now assume that a 20% interest in the Kenyan firm is owned by a related firm in which Multinat has a 20% equity interest. The other 80% of the related firm is foreign owned as is the remaining 20% of the Kenyan firm. Is the Kenyan firm now a CFC?
4. What is the maximum ownership interest percentage that Multinat can have in the related firm without making the Kenyan firm a CFC?
5. What is the maximum equity interest that Multinat could own of the related firm if that company's interest in the Kenyan firm was only 5%? All other ownership interests are held by foreign persons.

SOLUTION:

1. The firm is not a CFC because 60% of its common stock is held by non-U.S. persons.
2. The Kenyan firm is not a CFC because the percentage of ownership in the South African firm = 40% (20K) + 90% (80K) = 80K, or 80%. Percentage of ownership in Kenyan firm = 80% (60%) = 48% < 50%.
3. U.S. person's ownership interest = 80% (60%) + 20% (20%) = 48% + 4% = 52%. Now the Kenyan firm is a CFC.
4. 80% (60%) + x%(20%) must be less than 50%. Therefore,
   x%(20%) must be less than 2%, or x less than 10%.
5. 80% (60%) + x%(5%) must be less than 50%. Therefore,
   x%(5%) must be less than 2%, or x less than 40%.

C. Shareholders of CFCs holding more than 10% of such shares must declare their portion of subpart F income on their own tax returns regardless of whether or not this income has been received by them in the form of a dividend.

1. Definition of subpart F income.
   a. Foreign personal holding company income under subpart F consists of dividends, interest, oil lease rents, gains from the sale and exchange of securities, and gains from trades in commodity futures.
   b. Foreign based company sales income is derived from the purchase of personal property from a related person and its sale to any other person.
   c. Foreign based company service income is derived from the performance of technical, managerial, engineering, scientific, commercial, or similar services, which are performed for or on behalf of a related person in a country outside of a CFC country of incorporation.
2. Exclusions from subpart F income.
   a. Shipping income received by a foreign subsidiary of a U.S. corporation to the extent such income is reinvested in shipping operations.
   b. Subpart F income which does not equal or exceed 10% of the subsidiary's gross income.
   c. The sale of goods produced or manufactured in the country of incorporation.
   d. The sales of goods acquired from nonrelated persons sold to nonrelated persons.
   e. The sales of services connected with U.S. produced property providing the CFC can qualify as an export trade corporation, i.e., a foreign corporation 90% or more of whose income is foreign income, 75% or more of which results from export trade, or 50% of which is derived from U.S. grown agricultural products. However, the exclusion is limited to 150% of export promoting expenses or the proportion of income reinvested in export operations.
   f. Certain items of income received from nonrelated persons such as rents, royalties, interest, dividends, and gain of those in the banking and finance business.

PROBLEM 7-4

One of Gensler's 100% owned manufacturing and sales subsidiaries is located in a developed country. This subsidiary reports LC1,000,000 total income of which LC50,000 is subpart F income. Must Gensler pay U.S. income taxes regardless of whether dividends have been received? The local tax rate in the foreign country is 30%.

SOLUTION:

No, Gensler does not need to pay any U.S. taxes prior to receiving dividends from the subsidiary. Since the subpart F income is less than 10%, all of the income is treated as non-subpart F income.

D. Tax calculations of the foreign source income of U.S. corporations.
   1. Follow these steps in the instance of income from a subsidiary organized in a developed country or subpart F income from any country (gross-up basis). Note that the line numbers referred to below are keyed to the solution to problem 7-5.
      a. Report the net dividends received. **(1b)**
      b. Add to the above the foreign income taxes that apply to the dividend received. **(2)**
      c. Add to this any dividend withholding tax that may have been deducted by the foreign government. **(3)**
      d. The above items represent the gross-up income or foreign income before taxes. **(4)**
      e. Apply the U.S. corporate income tax rate to the gross-up income. **(5)**
      f. Deduct from this tax the applicable foreign income tax, and foreign dividend withholding tax. **(2,3)**
      g. This will give the net U.S. tax due. **(9 = 5 − 8)**
      h. Total taxes. **(10)**
         (1) The applicable foreign income tax. **(6a)**
         (2) The foreign dividend withholding tax. **(3)**
         (3) The net U.S. income tax. **(9)**
      i. Net income after all taxes is then equal to the part of the foreign before-tax income that applies to the dividend received less the taxes enumerated in (h) above. **(11 = 4 − 10)** This is also equal to the net dividend received less the net U.S. tax paid. **(11 = 1b − 9)**
   2. In the instance of non-subpart F income received from a developing country (normal basis), refer to Problem 7-5. Note that the line numbers are keyed to the solution to Problem 7-5.
      a. Report the actual dividend received. **(1b)**
      b. Add to this the amount of the dividend withholding tax. **(3)**
      c. Apply the U.S. income tax rate to this amount. **(5)**
      d. Subtract from the U.S. tax due:
         (1) The foreign income tax credit that applies to the dividend received. **(6b)**
         (2) The dividend withholding tax. **(7)**
         This will result in the net U.S. income tax. **(9)**
      e. Total taxes. **(10)**
         (1) The applicable foreign income tax. **(6b)**
         (2) The dividend withholding tax. **(7)**
         (3) The net U.S. income tax. **(9)**
      f. Earnings after all taxes are equal to the net dividend received less the net U.S. tax paid. **(11 = 1b − 9)** Note that the foreign tax credit is used only to calculate the net U.S. tax. **(9)**

PROBLEM 7-5

The MNC Company has foreign earnings before taxes of $10,000. The foreign income tax rate is 30%. Assuming a 50% dividend payout and a 10% dividend withholding tax, calculate the applicable U.S. income tax in the instance where the company's foreign income qualifies for (a) subpart F income, gross-up basis; (b) non-subpart F income, normal basis.

SOLUTION:

			U.S. Income Tax Calculations	
			a. Gross-up Basis	b. Normal Basis
A.		Foreign earnings before taxes	$10,000	$10,000
B.		Foreign income tax, 30%	3,000	3,000
C.		Foreign earnings after taxes	7,000	7,000
	1.	50% dividend to parent	$ 3,500	$ 3,500
		less a. 10% dividend withholding tax	350	350
		b. net dividend received by parent	3,150	3,150
	2.	Add: applicable foreign taxes (1/2 of 3,000)	1,500	
	3.	Add: dividend withholding tax	350	350
	4.	Taxable income	5,000	3,500
	5.	U.S. income tax (50% × 4)	2,500	1,750
	6.	Credit: applicable foreign income tax:		
		a. line 2	1,500	
		b. 30% × 1		1,050
	7.	Credit: dividend withholding tax	350	350
	8.	Total foreign tax credits (6 + 7)	1,850	1,400
	9.	Net U.S. tax (5 - 8)	650	350
	10.	Total of all taxes (.5B + 1a + 9)	2,500	2,200
	11.	Earnings after all taxes (1b - 9)	$ 2,500	$ 2,800

E. Taxation on the disposal of an equity interest in a controlled foreign corporation by a controlling shareholder.
  1. Gross profit equals sales price minus cost.
  2. The portion of the profit taxed as ordinary income is equal to the accumulated earnings and profits after taxes during the period of ownership multiplied by the percentage of ownership of the selling shareholder. The remainder of the gross profit on the sale in excess of the accumulated earnings and profits is taxed as capital gains.

PROBLEM 7-6

Gensler has a subsidiary in a developed country that earns LC500,000 of which LC400,000 is subpart F income. All (100%) of its earnings are paid to the parent. The local tax rate is 40%. The exchange rate is LC5 per U.S. dollar. Calculate the earnings after taxes that accrue to the parent.

SOLUTION:

Since 80% of the income is subpart F income, 100% is treated as subpart F income.

Earnings before foreign taxes	$100,000
Foreign taxes, 40%	40,000
Foreign income paid to parent	60,000
Gross-up income	100,000
U.S. tax, 50%	50,000
Less foreign tax credit	40,000
Net U.S. tax due	10,000
Total taxes	50,000
Earnings after all taxes	$ 50,000

PROBLEM 7-7

A 30% ownership in a CFC was sold for $20,000. The original cost of the investment was $10,000. Profits earned during the period of ownership were $5,000. The seller's marginal tax rate is 40%. What are the taxes due on the sale?

SOLUTION:

Sale price	$20,000
Cost	10,000
Gross profit	10,000
Amount taxed on a straight tax basis	
$5,000 (.30)	1,500
To be taxed on a capital gains basis	$ 8,500

Taxes due on the sale = $1,500(.4) + $8,500(.4/2) = $600 + $1,700 = $2,300. Without this provision of the Revenue Act of 1962, the complete tax on this sale would have been $10,000(.4/2) = $2,000.

VII. Taxation of international business by major trading nations. All countries tax earnings at the location where earned. However, considerable differences exist in the taxation of domestic firms that have income resulting from operations in foreign countries either on their own part or that of their foreign subsidiaries. These differences are due to a variety of views as to the appropriate government policies in regard to the taxation of the foreign income of domestic firms.

A. The income of a corporation should be taxed at the same rate whether it is earned domestically or in a foreign country.
   1. An argument for this view is that the incentives for locating operations should not be distorted by taxation.
   2. Some hold the view (e.g., labor union leaders) that foreign operations should be subject to punitive taxation to keep production at home.
   3. However, punitive taxation against the foreign operations of domestic firms may not result in an increase of domestic operations, but rather result in the domestic firm losing out in international competition completely.
B. The foreign income of domestic firms should be taxed as much as possible on the same basis as other governments treat the foreign income of their domestic firms.
   1. The main argument for this principle is that the competitive opportunities of multinational firms of one nation should be equal to that of similar firms of all other nations.
   2. If domestic firms of one nation lose out in international competition because of the tax treatment by their home government of their international income, which is unfavorable as compared with that of multinational firms of other nations, the net amount of home country operations and jobs will be decreased.

The table below gives a summary of the differences discussed above for the major trading nations.

Taxation of International Business

Does Country Tax Profit of Foreign Subsidiary:

Home Country	When Unremitted?	When Available as Dividends?	Earnings of Foreign Branch?	Is Foreign Tax Credit Given?	Are Earnings Taxed as a Practical Matter?
Belgium	No	No	No	Not Needed	No
France*	No	No	No	Not Needed	No
Germany*	No [1]	Yes	No	Yes	No
Italy* [2]	No	Yes	No	Partially	Partially
Japan*	No	Yes	Yes	Yes	No
The Netherlands*	No	No	Yes	Yes	No
United Kingdom	No	Yes	Yes	Yes	No
United States	No	Yes	Yes	Yes	Yes
U.S. CFC-subpart F	Yes	—	Yes	Yes	Yes

*In addition to the general pattern of not effectively taxing foreign subsidiary and branch profits, five countries allow special deductions based on investments in or losses of the foreign operations.

Notes:
[1] Germany has limited subpart F type of provisions.
[2] Italy only taxes foreign branches which do not have separate management and accounting. It allows foreign tax credits for taxes paid on branch income and for withholding taxes, but not indirect credits, on dividends.

Source: Arthur Andersen, (statement, 1976).

VIII. This section presents information taken from a report of Arthur Anderson and Company on April 20, 1976, to the Committee on Finance of the United States Senate. Presented first are the assumptions made that led to the results of Exhibits I to III. These exhibits show the effect on profitability of identical investments made in Brazil, Japan, and the United Kingdom by U.S., German, and Japanese owned subsidiaries in those countries. The calculations were made according to present tax statutes of the three countries.

Exhibits IV to VI show similar results for the Japanese and German subsidiaries, but for the U.S. owned subsidiary calculations were made in accordance with the presently proposed tax law changes.

Finally, Exhibit VII shows the present and the proposed overall tax rates, both foreign and domestic, that would be imposed on U.S. multinational firms if Congress adopted the proposal to eliminate the foreign tax credit which would make foreign taxes paid deductible from income instead of U.S. taxes due.

A. Assumptions relating to investments in Brazil and Japan (Exhibits I, II, IV and V).
1. A German company, a Japanese company, and a U.S. company each own 100% of the stock of a foreign corporation which owns identical manufacturing operations in Brazil and Japan.
2. The investment earns $500,000 annually before tax.
3. There are no adjustments between book income and taxable income in the local country or in the United States.
4. All profits after tax in the country of operation are reinvested in the business each year.
5. The United States currently taxes unremitted earnings on a gross-up basis. Germany and Japan do not tax unremitted earnings.
6. The income tax rates are:
   a. Brazil – 30%
   b. Japan – 52.6% (an effective rate)
7. The target rate of return on equity invested in the manufacturing business sought by each investor is 16% for Brazil and 22% for Japan. Profits after local tax, but before any tax on unremitted earnings, attain that objective. These rates of return represent the average return on capital investment of U.S. owned manufacturing business in those countries in 1973 from statistics compiled by the U.S. Department of Commerce.
8. The results of the differences in tax treatment for a German, Japanese, and U.S. investor are computed for only one year, for purposes of illustrating rates of return. Unless profits increase in subsequent years commensurate with the additional capital provided from reinvested earnings, the rate of return will drop below the desired standard (16% or 22%).

B. Assumptions relating to investments in the United Kingdom (Exhibits III and VI).
1. A German company, a Japanese company, and a U.S. company each own 100% of the stock of a foreign corporation which owns identical manufacturing operations in the United Kingdom.

2. The target rate of return on equity invested in the business is 14%. Profits after U.K. taxes (but before any tax on unremitted earnings) accomplish that objective. This rate of return represents the average return on capital investment of U.S. owned manufacturing businesses in the United Kingdom in 1973 from statistics compiled by the U.S. Department of Commerce.
3. Cumulative profits after U.K. taxes paid are reinvested in the business each year and generate a pretax profit of 28% of the equity investment.
4. The United States currently taxes unremitted earnings on a gross-up basis. Japan and Germany do not tax unremitted earnings.
5. The business invests $5,000,000 in new machinery as an addition to an already profitable business. This machinery qualifies as an investment which is entirely deductible in the United Kingdom in the year of acquisition. No U.K. tax depreciation is allowed in subsequent years on the $5,000,000 cost deducted as an incentive allowance. The normal depreciable life of the machinery is 10 years. The existing U.K. business produces enough income to utilize the entire $4,500,000 extra depreciation deduction in the first year.
6. The funds necessary to pay the U.S. tax on the unremitted earnings are borrowed at a 10% interest cost by the U.S. investor. The interest cost is reduced by the applicable U.S. tax benefit (48% rate) which results.
7. The U.K. corporate income tax rate is estimated to be 52%.
8. The excess of the U.K. tax available as a U.S. foreign tax credit in a particular year can only be utilized by the U.S. investor against the foreign income from the U.K. investment. The investor has no other foreign-source income. (Exhibit III only.)
9. Reinvested earnings increase the business's capital at the beginning of the year following the year of the earnings. The business then earns additional profits in each subsequent year in the United Kingdom sufficient to keep the rate of return at the average rate of 14% on the capital available during the year in the United Kingdom. This 14% return does not consider interest costs referred to in No. 6 above or U.S. taxes. Calculations were made for the 10-year period over which the machinery is used. The average of the 10-year results is shown in the exhibits.

Exhibit I Investment in Brazil Assuming Current United States Taxation of Unremitted Earnings and a Deemed Foreign Tax Credit for Foreign Taxes Paid

Line No.		Investment by Company Incorporated in		
		United States	Germany	Japan
(1)	Annual income in Brazil	$ 500,000	$ 500,000	$ 500,000
(2)	Brazilian income tax—30%	(150,000)	(150,000)	(150,000)
(3)	Net income in Brazil (1) - (2)	$ 350,000	$ 350,000	$ 350,000
	Tax on unremitted earnings —			
(4)	Taxable income (1)	$ 500,000	$ —	$ —
(5)	Tax before credit—48%	$ (240,000)	$ —	$ —
(6)	Less—foreign tax credit	150,000	—	—
(7)	Additional tax due (5) - (6)	$ (90,000)	$ —	$ —
(8)	Total taxes (2) + (7)	$ (240,000)	$ (150,000)	$ (150,000)
(9)	Net income after all taxes (1) - (8)	$ 260,000	$ 350,000	$ 350,000
(10)	Effective rate of tax (8) ÷ (1)	48%	30%	30%
	Rate of return on equity investment	12%	16%	16%

Exhibit II Investment in Japan Assuming Current United States Taxation of Unremitted Earnings and a Deemed Foreign Tax Credit for Foreign Taxes Paid

Line No		Investment by Company Incorporated in		
		United States	Germany	Japan
(1)	Annual income in Japan	$ 500,000	$ 500,000	$ 500,000
(2)	Japanese income tax—52.6%	(263,000)	(263,000)	(263,000)
(3)	Net income in Japan (1) - (2)	$ 237,000	$ 237,000	$ 237,000
	Tax on unremitted earnings—			
(4)	Taxable income	$ 500,000	$ —	$ —
(5)	Tax before credit—48%	$ (240,000)	$ —	$ —
(6)	Less—foreign tax credit	263,000	—	—
(7)	Additional tax due (5) - (6)	$ —	$ —	$ —
(8)	Total taxes (2) + (7)	$ (263,000)	$ (263,000)	$ (263,000)
(9)	Net income after all taxes (1) - (8)	$ 237,000	$ 237,000	$ 237,000
(10)	Effective rate of tax (8) ÷ (1)	52.6%	52.6%	52.6%
	Rate of return on equity investment	22%	22%	22%

Exhibit III Investment in United Kingdom Assuming Current United States Taxation of Unremitted Earnings and a Deemed Foreign Tax Credit For Foreign Taxes Paid

Line No.		Investment by Company Incorporated in		
		United States	Germany	Japan
(1)	Annual income in United Kingdom	$ 714,000[1]	$ 714,000	$ 714,000
(2)	United Kingdom income tax — 52% (a)	(371,000)	(371,000)	(371,000)
(3)	Net income in United Kingdom (1) – (2)	$ 343,000[1]	$ 343,000	$ 343,000
	Tax on unremitted earnings—			
(4)	Taxable income	$1,164,000	—	—
(5)	Tax before credit — 48%	$ (559,000)	$ —	$ —
(6)	Less—foreign tax credit (a)	343,000	—	—
(7)	Additional tax due (5) – (6)	$ (216,000)	$ —	$ —
(8)	Interest cost of additional tax (less U.S. tax effect)	(11,000)	—	—
(9)	Total costs in U.S. (7) + (8)	$ (227,000)	$ —	$ —
(10)	Total taxes plus interest cost (2) + (9)	$ (598,000)	$ (371,000)	$ (371,000)
(11)	Net income after all taxes and interest cost (1) – (10)	$ 116,000	$ 343,000	$ 343,000
(12)	Effective rate of tax (10) ÷ (1)	83.75%	52%	52%
	Rate of return on equity investment	4.73%	14%	14%

[1] U.S. taxable income exceeds U.K. pretax income because the excess of the $5,000,000 special allowance in the first year over normal depreciation ($500,000) is taxable for U.S. purposes. We have assumed the special allowance offsets U.K. taxable income from the existing U.K. business (see assumptions).

Exhibit IV   Investment in Brazil Assuming Current United States Taxation of Unremitted Earnings and a Deduction For Foreign Taxes Paid

Line No.		Investment by Company Incorporated in		
		United States	Germany	Japan
(1)	Annual income in Brazil	$ 500,000	$ 500,000	$ 500,000
(2)	Brazilian tax—30%	(150,000)	(150,000)	(150,000)
(3)	Net income in Brazil (1) - (2)	$ 350,000	$ 350,000	$ 350,000
	Tax on unremitted earnings—			
(4)	Taxable income (3)	$ 350,000	$ —	$ —
(5)	Tax on unremitted earnings—48%	$ (168,000)	$ —	$ —
(6)	Total taxes (2) + (5)	$ (318,000)	$ (150,000)	$ (150,000)
(7)	Net income after all taxes (1) - (6)	$ 182,000	$ 350,000	$ 350,000
(8)	Effective rate of tax (6) ÷ (1)	63.6%	30%	30%
	Rate of return on equity investment	8%	16%	16%

Exhibit V   Investment in Japan Assuming Current United States Taxation of Unremitted Earnings and a Deduction For Foreign Taxes Paid

Line No.		Investment by Company Incorporated in		
		United States	Germany	Japan
(1)	Annual income in Japan	$ 500,000	$ 500,000	$ 500,000
(2)	Japanese tax — 52.6%	(263,000)	(263,000)	(263,000)
(3)	Net income in Japan (1) - (2)	$ 237,000	$ 237,000	$ 237,000
	Tax on unremitted earnings—			
(4)	Taxable income	$ 237,000	$ —	$ —
(5)	Tax on unremitted earnings—48%	$ (113,760)	$ —	$ —
(6)	Total taxes (2) + (5)	$ (376,760)	$ (263,000)	$ (263,000)
(7)	Net income after all taxes (1) - (6)	$ 123,240	$ 237,000	$ 237,000
(8)	Effective rate of tax (6) ÷ (1)	75.35%	52.6%	52.6%
	Rate of return on equity investment	11%	22%	22%

Exhibit VI Investment in United Kingdom Assuming Current United States Taxation of Unremitted Earnings and a Deduction For Foreign Taxes Paid

Line No.		Investment by Company Incorporated in		
		United States	Germany	Japan
(1)	Annual income in United Kingdom	$ 714,000	$ 714,000	$ 714,000
(2)	United Kingdom income tax—52% (a)	(371,000)	(371,000)	(371,000)
(3)	Net income in United Kingdom (1) − (2)	$ 343,000	$ 343,000	$ 343,000
	Tax on unremitted earnings —			
(4)	Taxable income	$ 558,000	$ —	$ —
(5)	Tax on unremitted earnings — 48%	$ (268,000)	$ —	$ —
(6)	Interest cost of additional tax (less U.S. tax benefit)	(14,000)	—	—
(7)	Total costs in U.S. (5) + (6)	$ (282,000)	$ —	$ —
(8)	Total taxes plus interest cost (2) + (5) + (6)	$ (653,000)	$ (371,000)	$ (371,000)
(9)	Net income after all taxes and interest cost (1) − (8)	$ 61,000	$ 343,000	$ 343,000
(10)	Effective rate of tax plus interest cost (8) ÷ (1)	91.46%	52%	52%
	Rate of return on equity investment	2.49%	14%	14%

[1] U.S. taxable income exceeds U.K. net income because the excess of the $5,000,000 special allowance in the first year over normal depreciation ($500,000), less the deduction for U.K. taxes thereon, is taxable in the U.S. We have assumed the special allowance offsets U.K. taxable income from the existing U.K. business (see assumptions).

Exhibit VII Statutory Tax Rates in Foreign Countries (Accounting for 82% of 1973 Overseas Earnings of U.S. Companies)

	Country	Statutory Profits Tax Rate	Dividend Withholding Tax Rate	Combined Foreign Statutory Rate	Total Statutory Tax Rates (Foreign and U.S.) With Foreign Taxes Credited Against U.S. Tax		Total Statutory Tax Rates (Foreign and U.S.) With Foreign Taxes Taken as a U.S. Deduction		
					U.S. Taxes	Total Taxes	U.S. Taxes	Total Taxes	
1	Canada —								1
1a	Manufacturing	40.00%	15%	49.00%	–%	49.00%	24.48%	73.48%	1a
1b	Other	48.00	15	55.80	—	55.80	21.22	77.02	1b
2	United Kingdom	52.00	15	59.20	—	59.20	19.58	78.78	2
3	Belgium	42.00	15	50.70	—	50.70	23.66	74.36	3
4	Luxembourg	45.00	15	53.25	—	53.25	22.44	75.69	4
5	France	50.00	5	52.50	—	52.50	22.80	75.30	5
6	Germany	50.47	15	57.90	—	57.90	20.21	78.11	6
7	Italy	35.00	5	38.25	9.75	48.00	29.64	67.89	7
8	The Netherlands	48.00	5	50.60	—	50.60	23.71	74.31	8
9	Norway	49.50	10	54.55	—	54.55	21.82	76.37	9
10	Spain	32.80	15	42.88	5.12	48.00	27.42	70.30	10
11	Sweden	54.40	5	56.68	—	56.68	20.79	77.47	11
12	Switzerland	17.00–32.00	5	21.15–35.40	26.85–12.60	48.00	37.85–31.01	59.00–66.41	12
13	Japan	52.60	10	57.34	—	57.34	20.48	77.82	13
14	Australia	45.00	15	53.25	—	53.25	22.44	75.69	14
15	New Zealand	45.00	15	53.25	—	53.25	22.44	75.69	15
16	South Africa	41.00	15	49.85	—	49.85	24.07	73.92	16
17	Mexico	42.00	20	53.60	—	53.60	22.27	75.87	17
18	Argentina	45.00	35	64.25	—	64.25	17.16	81.41	18
19	Brazil	30.00	25	47.50	.50	48.00	25.20	72.70	19
20	Chile	19.55	40	51.73	—	51.73	23.17	74.90	20
21	Colombia	52.64	12	58.32	—	58.32	20.01	78.33	21
22	Venezuela	50.00	15	57.50	—	57.50	20.40	77.90	22
23	Libya	60.00	13	65.20	—	65.20	16.70	81.90	23
24	India	55.00	25	66.25	—	66.25	16.20	82.45	24
25	Philippines	35.00	35	57.75	—	57.75	20.28	78.03	25
26	Middle East*	49.94	—	49.94	—	49.94	24.03	73.97	26

Note: The rates listed for those countries with graduated income tax rates are those for the highest level of income.

*The rate shown is an average of the rates for the following Middle Eastern countries: Iran, Iraq, Israel, Kuwait, Lebanon, Saudi Arabia, and Syria. The dividend withholding rates varied with the country and in most cases were very low or zero.

Source: Tax rates — latest available published statutory rates.

PROBLEM 7-8

Discuss the Revenue Act of 1962. What are the important effect of the act on international operations of foreign corporations controlled by U.S. companies?

SOLUTION:

A. Prior to 1962, income earned by U.S. companies was not taxable to its U.S. owners until the income was repatriated in the form of dividends. The Revenue Act of 1962 provided that most income of the CFC is taxable even if not yet received in the form of dividends.
B. The text of the act specifies the definition of a CFC and sets forth the nature of the foreign income to be taxed.
   1. Subpart F income includes:
      a. Foreign personal holding company income (e.g., dividends, interests, oil lease, rents).
      b. Foreign-based company sales income (e.g. profits, commission in connection with purchase of personal property).
      c. Foreign-based company service income (e.g., technical, managerial, engineering, scientific fees).
   2. Exclusions from subpart F income:
      a. Income from investments in LDCs. When remitted, they become taxable.
      b. Shipping income in connection with use or chartering or leasing of ships or aircraft in foreign commerce providing this revenue is reinvested in the same activity.
      c. Export trade income derived from the sale of services connected with U.S. produced property., etc.
C. The Revenue Act of 1962 generally requires use of the gross-up method in reporting foreign earned income thus increasing the total tax liability.
D. It provides that capital gains in part be treated as ordinary income.

PROBLEM 7-9

The following information applies to a U.S. parent corporation (subject to a U.S. income tax rate of 50%) with ownership patterns in a number of subsidiaries.
A. Fully owned foreign subsidiary in a Western European developed country.
B. Fully owned foreign subsidiary in England.
C. Fully owned foreign subsidiary with 100% of its income and assets in Brazil (a less developed country).
D. Fully owned foreign controlled corporation in France.
E. Fully owned Western Hemisphere Trading Corporation (WHTC).

Selected Financial Information on Each of the Subsidiaries ($ millions)

	A	B	C	D	E
Earnings before taxes	$100	$100	$100	$100	$100
Foreign income taxes	40	60	40	40	
Earnings after taxes	60	40	60	60	
Dividends payable to parent	30	10	30	0	
Withholding tax − 10%	3	1	3	0	

1. What taxes would be owed by the parent on each subsidiary?
2. What would be the total amount of tax payable by the parent, assuming that it does not have any other foreign subsidiaries?

SOLUTION:

Tax Calculations ($ millions)

		A	B	C	D	E
1.	Dividends received Gross-up	27	9	27	0	
2.	Withholding tax	3	1	3	—	
3.	Tax credit	$(\frac{30}{60})(40)=\underline{20}$	$(\frac{10}{40})(60)=\underline{15}$	$(\frac{30}{100})(40)=\underline{12}$	40	$(\frac{14}{48})(100)=\underline{29}$
4.	Total foreign tax credit	23	16	15	40	
5.	Parent taxable income	50	25	30	100	71
6.	U.S. taxes	25	12.5	15	50	35
7.	Less tax credits	23	16.0	15	40	
8.	Taxes owed (credit)	2	(3.5)	0	10	35

Comments: The gross-up method is used for subsidiaries A and B. When the foreign tax rate is less than the U.S. tax rate, U.S. taxes are owed and conversely. For C, located in an LDC, the normal method is used. Note that the taxes owed are lowest in C versus A and B. For D, the foreign controlled corporation, all earnings are considered received, so the taxes owed are greatest as compared with A and C, with the same income and the same foreign tax rate. The WHTC receives special tax treatment. The total tax owed on subsidiaries A, B, C, and D is $8.5 (credits can be netted against amounts owed). The $35 million tax owed on the WHTC could not be netted against the others if they had totaled to a credit.

IX. Value added tax (VAT).
    A. Historical development
        1. It was adopted at the end of World War II by the six original members of the European Economic Union (EEU)–Germany, France, Italy, Nether-

GOVERNMENT RULES AND POLICIES AFFECTING INTERNATIONAL BUSINESS 171

lands, Belgium, and Luxembourg—plus Britain and the Scandinavian countries.
   2. VAT is a tax that is presently not being used in the United States. It is similar to a turnover tax based on volume of business rather than profits.
   3. Rates vary from 10% to 20% on standard items and from 25% to 33 1/3% on luxury items such as cars and furs, with France the highest.
   4. Eventually the VAT rates are planned to be equalized within the EEU, thus eliminating the need for border adjustments.
B. Definition.
   1. It is a tax applied at each successive transfer stage of a commodity or service only on the value added in an accounting sense.
   2. The destination principle is applied under which the sale is presumed to have taken place and is therefore taxable in the country of destination, rather than at the origin.
      a. If a French exporter sells to a New York buyer, he is presumed to have made the sale in New York so that the VAT is not applicable to the French export. Under the origin principle, the sale would be treated as having been made in France.
      b. If a New York exporter sells to a Paris importer, the sale is presumed to take place at the destination and therefore the French VAT would apply to the import and would be payable by the New York exporter. Under the origin principle the sale would have taken place in New York.
C. Computation of the value added tax.
   1. Invoices for all sales show a line computing the tax on the sale. A credit is allowed for the VATs paid on purchases of goods or services that became part of the goods or services being sold.
   2. The taxes are paid on the purchase of capital goods such as plant, land, equipment, and machinery, and on consumption goods. When purchases of capital goods exceed sales in the year of purchase, the buyer of capital goods may build up a VAT credit to be carried over as a credit to be applied to VAT obligations due in subsequent years.
   3. On exports from France, for example, the exporter would receive a credit for value added taxes paid on purchases, but would not be obligated for a value added tax on the sale. Credits so developed are rebated so that the exporter does not have to wait until VAT liabilities are developed in future years.
D. Problems illustrating the computations of the VAT.
   1. Assume primary producer P sells DM100 of raw materials to manufacturer M. M sells DM200 of finished goods to wholesaler W. The wholesaler sells the goods to retailer R for DM250, and finally the retailer sells the goods to a domestic consumer for DM300. All prices given exclude the VAT. Germany has a value added tax of 10%. Let us compute:
      a. The VAT due for each firm.

b. The VAT due if all the firms were subunits of a parent company.
   c. Instead of the VAT apply a 5% sales tax, and compute the tax for each firm.
   d. Compute the tax if the firms were subunits of a parent company.
2. Solutions.
   a. VAT, separate companies (10% rate) in DM.

(1)	(2)	(3)	(4)	(5)	(6)	(7)	(8)	(9)
Value Added	Transaction	Purchase Price excl. VAT [Col. (5) of previous stage]	Purchase Price incl. VAT [Col. (7) of previous stage]	Selling Price excl. VAT [(1)+(3)]	VAT Liability [(1)(5)]	Selling Price incl. VAT [(5)+(6)]	VAT Credit [Col. (6) of previous stage]	VAT Due [(6)−(8)]
100	P sells to M	0	—	DM 100	DM 10	DM 110	0	DM 10
100	M sells to W	100	110	200	20	220	10	10
50	W sells to R	200	220	250	25	275	20	5
50	R sells to consumer	250	275	300	30	330	25	5
300								

   b. VAT, same company.

	P sells to consumer	0	0	300	30	330	0	30

   c. Sales tax, different companies.

(DM)	Selling Price excl. Sales Tax	Selling Price with Sales Tax	Tax Due
P sells to M	100	105	0
M sells to W	200	210	0
W sells to R	250	265.50	0
R sells to consumer	300	315	15
			Total DM 15

   d. Sales tax, same company.

R sells to consumer	DM 300	DM 315	DM 15

The total sales tax for the individual companies was DM15 because all sellers have resale certificates which exempt their purchases from sales taxes. As a result there is no difference between c and d. The seller receives credits for the VAT paid on his previous purchases.

E. Operation of the VAT in international trade.
   1. Assume firm P, a primary producer, sells fr. 100 of raw materials to manufacturers M_d and M_x. Firm M_d sells fr. 200 of finished goods to domestic consumers while firm M_x exports fr. 200 of finished goods to a

New York importer. M_c purchases fr. 100 of raw materials from U.S. suppliers and sells fr. 200 of goods to domestic consumers. All amounts are before the application of the VAT. The VAT rate is 10%. What is the VAT liability or credit for each firm?

2. Solutions.

	Value Added	(tr) Transactions	Purchase Price excl. VAT	Purchase Price incl. VAT	Selling Price excl. VAT	VAT Liability	Sales Price incl. VAT	VAT Credit	VAT Due
(1)	100	P sells to M_d			100	10	110		10
(2)	100	P sells to M_x			100	10	110		10
(3)	100	M_d sells to domestic consumer	100	110	200	20	220	10	10
(4)	100	M_x exports to United States	100	110	200		200	10	(10)
(5)	100	M_c imports from United States and sells to a domestic consumer	100	110	200	20	220	10	10

3. *Comments:* In line (1) the primary producer sells to a domestic manufacturer who subsequently sells on a domestic basis. In line (2) he sells to an exporter who includes the raw materials in the goods to be sold on an export basis. The VAT due on both transactions is the same from the standpoint of the primary producer. The firm that sells the product domestically incurs a fr. 20 liability, but receives a fr. 10 credit and has a VAT due of fr. 10. The exporter on the basis of the destination principle does not incur a VAT liability, but receives the VAT credit on his purchases. He is also able to sell the merchandise to the foreign importer at a price which excludes the 10% VAT. This gives the French manufacturers a strong inducement to sell in export markets.

In line (5) is shown the situation of the French manufacturer who imports from the United States and sells to a domestic consumer. This is no different than the experience of the manufacturer in line (3) who made his purchase in France and sold to a domestic consumer. However, there is a difference between a German who seeks to export to France and a U.S. producer attempting to do the same. Assuming the same VAT rate in Germany, the German exporter will receive a VAT credit equal to the VAT paid on his purchases. By comparison the U.S. firm seeking to export to France does not receive such a credit and is therefore at a disadvantage as compared with the German exporter. Thus, the use of the VAT in Europe and the heavier use of the corporate income tax in the United States gives an advantage to the producers in countries using the VAT that desire to export to countries within the EEU.

Exporters from the EEU also have an advantage in attempting to sell to United States in that they pay no tax on the goods they thus sell. The U.S. exporter is not so fortunate. He has to pay an income tax on his profits of the export sale, a disadvantage which he can minimize by exporting via a Domestic International Sales Corporation (DISC). In spite of the above, the EEU countries have criticized the United States strongly for permitting exporters to export via DISCs.

REFERENCES

International taxation is, of course, a very complex subject. Our summary treatment has been designed primarily to provide the central concepts and to alert business managers to the need for the use of expert guidance for international taxation issues. Our discussion also was aimed to provide a basis for sound public policy on somewhat basic issues with respect to the taxation of multinational corporations. We feel that the report of Arthur Andersen and Company of April 20, 1976, entitled "Statement on U.S. Companies in International Markets—the Competitive Factor in Tax Policy," before the Committee on Finance of the United States Senate, in *Public Hearing on H. R. 10612, Extension of Expiring Tax Provisions and Other Tax Reform Proposals* provides important factual materials on the comparative tax treatment among the major trading nations.

For details on technical aspects of international taxation, useful reference sources are provided by a number of accounting firms and tax service firms. These include the following:

Arthur Andersen and Company, *Tax and Trade Guides*. Separate booklets, New York, various dates.

Chown, John F.: *Taxation and Multinational Enterprise*, Longman Group Ltd., 1974.

Commerce Clearing House, *Common Market Reporter*. Two vols., loose-leaf, Chicago, 1962.

Commerce Clearing House, *World Tax Series*. Chicago, various issues.

Coopers and Lybrand, *International Tax Summaries*. Loose-leaf, New York, various dates.

Haskins and Sells, *International Tax and Business Service*. Two vols., loose-leaf, New York.

Price Waterhouse and Company, *Information Guide Series*. Separate booklets, New York, various dates.

Rosenberg, Herbert C., and Stuart R. Singer: "Selecting an International Finance Subsidiary: Review of Available Methods," *The Journal of Taxation*, **30**: 296-298, May 1969.

Chapter 8

The Risks of International Financial Management

Theme: The risks of international financial management are both similar and different from those of domestic financial management. Similarities are differential impacts of inflation on costs, prices, and investments. The impact of governmental, political, and economic policies must be considered for both domestic and international operations. However, foreign-exchange-rate fluctuations represent an additional dimension in the analysis of the risks of international financial management. Furthermore, political instability, restrictions, and expropriation represent new and increased risks. Commercial risks may be increased by political instability, different commercial practices, and different legal rules. The potentials of the use of diversification as one method for dealing with international financial risks are introduced.

I. The risks of foreign operations differ in degree and kind from domestic operation risks.
    A. Risks particular to foreign operations include:
        1. Impact of differential rates of inflation on costs and prices of goods manufactured in one country and sold in other countries.
        2. Changes in foreign exchange rates, devaluations, and revaluations.

3. Restrictions on currency and investment transfers.
4. Expropriation of foreign investments by host governments.
5. Adjustment to different institutions and laws.
B. Categories of risk in international operations are:
1. Exchange-rate risks.
   a. Changes in foreign exchange rates.
   b. Most directly encountered in international operations.
   c. The indirect impacts on a firm in domestic operations may sometimes be substantial also.
2. Political risks.
   a. Most directly observed in international operations.
   b. Are also a factor in domestic operations as the rules of the game are changed.
3. Commercial risks.
   a. Basic ideas are the same as for sales to domestic customers.
   b. Problems of lack of information and distance when dealing with foreign customers.

II. Discussion of risks associated with foreign activity.
A. Exchange-rate risks affect selling transactions and investments made in terms of a foreign currency.
1. Value of the receipts is uncertain until the foreign currency is converted into the home currency.
   a. Devaluation of a foreign currency results in a loss in purchasing power of the receipts in terms of the home currency.
   b. Revaluation of a foreign currency, on the other hand, increases the value of the foreign receipts.
2. Portfolio and direct investments are affected in varying degrees.
   a. Debt instruments which return a fixed number of foreign currency units are highly sensitive.
   b. Risk exposure of portfolio type equity and direct investments is not as high since the value of the underlying real assets increases as the currency is devalued.
3. Profits from foreign operations are always affected by exchange-rate changes.

PROBLEM 8-1

There are two kinds of exposed positions to which a company engaged in international transactions may be subject: long positions and short positions. Explain the meaning of each and the nature of the risks involved.

SOLUTION:

In long positions, the prospective net monetary net position of a firm, taking its future cash inflows and cash outflows into account, is positive. Thus, a company will lose from foreign currency devaluation because its net positive foreign currency claims position will be worth less in dollars. If there is a revaluation upward of the foreign currency, the company will gain because its positive net holdings of the foreign claims expressed in the foreign currency, translated into dollars will be worth more.

In short positions, the prospective net monetary position of a firm, taking its future cash receipts and outflows into account, is negative. In a short position, the company gains from devaluation because it can discharge its obligations with depreciated currency. If there is a revaluation upward, the company will lose because it will have to pay off its obligations expressed in the foreign currency at a higher exchange value.

B. Political risks affect all foreign business actions.
  1. Governmental interference may cause losses due to:
     a. Restrictions on transfer of funds from the foreign country to the United States.
     b. Quotas, embargoes, or increases in tariff rates.
     c. Cancellation of export or import licenses.
     d. Requisition, expropriation, or confiscation of property.
     e. War, civil strife, etc.
  2. Insurance against political risks is provided by government and quasi-governmental sources.
     a. Foreign Credit Insurance Association (FCIA).
     b. Export-Import Bank (Eximbank).
        (1) Directly.
        (2) Via the Foreign Credit Insurance Association by reinsurance.
     c. Overseas Private Investment Corporation (OPIC).
        (1) Successor to Agency for International Development (AID).
        (2) Provides investment insurance and investment guarantees.
C. Commercial risks are encountered when selling to foreign buyers on a credit basis.
  1. The sources of commercial risks are as follows:
     a. There are delays in receiving payment.
     b. Buyers may refuse to accept and pay for goods and services.
     c. Insolvency of the buyer.
  2. Commercial risk insurance is provided by
     a. FCIA for a basic minimum amount per policy; excess is reinsured by the Eximbank.
     b. Eximbank additionally through its lender guarantee program and directly for larger projects.

III. Environmental factors, political, social, and economic in nature, directly influence the risk exposure of a firm doing business in a foreign country.
   A. Awareness of factors leading to foreign currency devaluations can decrease the firm's foreign-exchange-rate risk exposure. Critical factors involved in exchange-rate fluctuations include:
      1. Sound money supply growth.
         a. Price-level stability depends on a balance between growth rate of the money supply and growth rate of real economic output.
         b. Excessive growth of the money supply creates an increase in the price level (inflation).
      2. Appropriate fiscal policy.
         a. Government surplus or deficit should reflect the needs of the economy.
         b. Below full employment, deficit spending stimulates economic activity.
         c. Near full employment, a government surplus, or decrease in deficit will reduce excess demand.
      3. Effective coordination of national economic policies.
         a. Relation of monetary and fiscal policies to the needs of the balance-of-payments position.
         b. A surplus in the balance of payments should be offset by tight fiscal policy (surplus) and loose monetary policy. This would lower interest rates and prevent inflow of funds.
         c. A deficit in the balance of payments should be offset by expansionary fiscal policy and moderate monetary policy. Interest rates should be maintained to prevent an outflow of funds.
      4. Upward trends in price levels and costs of production
         a. Create a loss of competitive position in international markets for domestic products.
         b. Aggravate balance-of-payments difficulties.
         c. Build pressures on exchange-rate movements.
      5. Labor union strength and aggressiveness.
         a. Strong unions may force excessive wage increases.
         b. Excessive wage increases may aggravate inflation and balance-of-payments problems.
      6. Size and growth rate of welfare expenditures not matched by productivity increases. This will create inflationary pressures.
      7. Character of foreign diplomatic and military commitments.
         a. Large foreign expenditures represent outflows in the balance of payments.
         b. These expenditures may cause domestic fiscal deficit trends.
      8. Balance-of-payments position
         a. Indicates potential movements in currency value.
         b. Reflects policies pursued in other areas discussed above.

9. Foreign-exchange-reserve position.
    a. Large foreign exchange surpluses can absorb balance-of-payments deficits for awhile.
    b. Declining reserve position will indicate increasing pressures for foreign exchange adjustments.
    c. Declining reserves and rising liquid liabilities to foreigners are likely to result in devaluation of the currency of the country.
10. Investment versus liquidity in balance-of-payments position.
    a. Foreign direct investments improve long-term asset position.
    b. On the other hand, foreign direct investments increase short-term liabilities which are liquid claims on the currency of the investor. These potential claims thus put pressure on the exchange value of the currency and cause balance-of-payments problems.

PROBLEM 8-2

Indicators were set forth in the chapter that would provide barometers giving advance indications to financial managers of prospective depreciation or appreciation of a nation's currency. Using the list of indicators given below, discuss how these factors provide signals as to the need for currency realignments as they apply to Argentina and Mexico for the years 1968 to 1974.

1. Government surplus or deficit.
2. Money supply.
3. Consumer price index.
4. Balance on goods, services, and transfers plus long-term capital.
5. International reserve position.

The single best source of data here would be *International Financial Statistics* published by the IMF.

SOLUTION:

See Tables 8-1 and 8-2 on pages 180 and 181.

B. Political risks are directly related to the stability of the local government.
   1. Political risks arise from the actions of national governments.
      a. Interference with or prevention of business transactions.
      b. Changing terms of increases.
      c. Confiscation of foreign-owned property.
   2. A government with a stable political base is less likely to create interruptions in international business.
   3. Investors need to consider the short-term and long-term political stability of the country based on the following factors:
      a. Length and quality of experience in self-government; appropriate concern needed when evaluating a former colony.

Table 8-1 Indicators of Increased Pressure on the Argentine Peso, 1968–1974

	(1) Government Surplus or (Deficit) (Millions of Pesos)	(2) Money Supply (Billions of Pesos)	(3) Consumer Price Index (1970=100)	(4) Basic Balances Current Account ($Millions)	(5) Basic Balances Long-Term Capital ($Millions)	International Reserve Position ($Millions)
1968	(840)	13.64	82	(49)	(66)	760
1969	(970)	15.08	88	(226)	(18)	538
1970	(1,149)	17.96	100	(159)	97	673
1971	(3,425)	23.61	135	(390)	341	290
1972	(6,052)	33.60	214	(223)	220	465
1973 I		38.53				645
II		46.90				817
III		56.31				1,213
IV	(19,574)	67.95	344	717	29	1,323
1974 I		72.53				1,461
II		83.68				1,844
III		95.35				1,519
IV	(31,004)	112.20	425	245	198	1,315

Source: IMF, 8/1975

Notes

Pressures on the country's currency resulted mainly from the excessive growth of its money supply which grew 8-fold over the 7-year period, particularly the last 2 years when the money supply almost doubled annually. Compounding this was the increasing expansionary fiscal policy also excessive in the last 2 years. These excesses were reflected in an abnormally high inflation rate. The resulting deteriorating competitive position of the country's goods in the international market was reflected in a substantial balance-of-trade deficit through 1972 and the consequent dwindling of foreign exchange reserves.

Although an official rate of 5 pesos to the dollar was kept from 1971 through 1974, the free-market rate doubled between 1971 and 1972 and consistently floated upward until it stabilized in 1973. Here we observe a turnaround in the country's balance-of-payments position and a consequent buildup of its international reserve position. However, as indications in 1974 seemed weak, there would likely be continued pressure for readjustments of the currency in the future.

Table 8-2 Indicators Related to the Value of the Mexican Peso, 1968–1974

	(1)	(2)	(3)	(4)		(5)
	Government Surplus or (Deficit) (Millions of Pesos)	Money Supply (Billions of Pesos)	Consumer Price Index (1970=100)	Basic Balances		International Reserve Position ($Millions)
				Current Account ($Millions)	Long-Term Capital ($Millions)	
1968	(5,296)	42.26	91.6	(743)	547	657
1969	(9,143)	48.59	95.0	(596)	732	662
1970	(6,082)	53.80	100.0	(1,076)	626	744
1971	(4,280)	57.89	105.7	(849)	767	952
1972	(16,726)	68.24	111.1	(911)	827	1,164
1973 I		65.14				1,282
II		67.17				1,233
III		69.02				1,093
IV	(27,415)	83.52	123.5	(1,490)	1,855	1,356
1974 I		78.54				1,540
II		81.91				1,547
III		81.74				1,354
IV	(27,216)	100.77	151.3	(2,895)	3,218	1,395

Source: IMF, 8/1975

Notes

Although money supply more than doubled over the period and there were large fiscal deficits, these were moderate compared to the excesses in Argentina. Nevertheless, upward pressure on price levels was high enough to result in consistently large trade deficits even though these were offset by increasingly larger long-term capital inflows. Some risks of exchange adjustments exist but prospective oil exports by Mexico may improve its balance-of-payments position.

        b. Length of time as an independent nation.
        c. Strength of tribal and regional ties vis-à-vis allegiance to the national government.
        d. Degree of unemployment.
        e. Equality of income distribution.
        f. Relative levels of industrialization and agriculture in the economy.
        g. Political and social constraints that limit upward movement and vertical mobility of an individual within social, economic, or political hierarchies.
        h. Degree of splintering of political parties.
    4. The individual firm or investor can to some degree manage and control the political risk exposure.
        a. The items discussed under (2) and (3) above provide some basis for forecasting the probability and kinds of political intervention.
        b. As discussed in Chapter 2, by the choice of products involved in the transactions with the foreign market, the firm or investor can influence the probability of foreign government intervention.
            (1) A product that generally contributes to the economic development and foreign exchange position of a foreign government is likely to be encouraged, rather than penalized, by the foreign government.
            (2) Foreign governments have characteristically encouraged investments in the production of products that substitute for imports.
  C. Commercial risk is inversely related to the growth and prosperity of an economy.
    1. Prosperous businesses are not likely to default on agreements.
    2. Governments supported by a prospering economy are not likely to restrict the availability of foreign currency to local importers.
    3. The analysis of commercial risks is basically the same as credit analysis for a domestic sale, but the interactions with political and economic conditions in the foreign country must be taken into account.
        a. Adverse foreign government actions may change a good credit risk into a bad one.
        b. Unanticipated economic and political developments may adversely affect the foreign firm.
    4. The usual problems of credit analysis are complicated by distance, lack of familiarity, and different commercial rules and business practices.

PROBLEM 8-3

The Martel Corporation

What are the risks to which the following transactions are subject?

1. The firm sells on a 90-day credit basis in German marks to an importer in West Germany whose credit rating is AAA.

2. The firm sells in U.S. dollars a shipment of capital goods on a 3-year basis to a manufacturer in the Philippines.
3. The firm is contemplating a further investment in an Argentine subsidiary.
4. It has been demanded of the firm that it establish a subsidiary in Uganda in order to be able to continue to sell supplies to its customers in that country.
5. To avoid the effects of inflation in the United States, the firm is considering placing some of this temporarily idle cash with a Swiss bank.
6. The firm is considering the sale of a large capital goods order in U.S. dollars on a 5-year basis to a customer in Italy. The customer has offered to pay 10% down at the time of shipment, but also insists that he will not pay more than 8% interest on the unpaid balance. The firm's opportunity cost of capital is 12%.

SOLUTION:

(Some answers serve to introduce materials further developed in Chapter 9.)

1. The political, commercial, and exchange-rate risks are all negligible. Since the forward mark is likely to be selling at a premium, the firm can lock up this premium by selling marks by a forward contract. Our decision rule is: stay with strong currencies as long as possible. On this basis the firm would do nothing further. But many managers would prefer to lock up the forward rate premium rather than run the risk that it might be smaller in 90 days. With regard to insurance, West Germany is an A-rated country and the firm has a AAA rating. The cost of a comprehensive policy would be quite low, so a firm might buy it although its need is quite small. This illustrates that even when the risks are small, managerial decisions must be made.
2. The political and exchange-rate risks are high; this may also cause commercial risks to be high. Buy a comprehensive policy if available and if the costs are not excessive in relation to the estimates of risk.
3. The political and exchange risks are high; political risks might cause commercial difficulties for the subsidiary. A swap contract might be negotiated for the exchange risk. Insurance from OPIC may be sought for the political risks.
4. First the firm must determine whether the profits from its sales make it worthwhile to expose itself to the high political and foreign exchange risks. A swap arrangement is not likely to be available, so the firm should attempt to put itself in a net monetary debtor position. Investment insurance through OPIC should be sought for 180% of the amount of the investment to include future profits as well.
5. This may be sound if the negative rate of interest charged by the Swiss bank does not exceed the expected decline in the foreign exchange value

of the dollar. There are no political, commercial, or foreign exchange risks. However, since the firm will have a claim on Swiss francs, it might sell forward contracts in the Swiss franc to lock up the premium. (Cf. discussion under 1.)
6. The political and foreign exchange risks are high; these instabilities may also create commercial risks. A comprehensive FCIA policy should be obtained. Although the Italian firm is willing to pay only a small interest rate, the firm should compare the interest rate paid by the Italian firm plus its profitability rate on the sale in relation to the costs of funds and the risks associated with the sale.

IV. The risks affecting the returns from a foreign subsidiary are more complex than changes in foreign exchange rates.
   A. Consider the possibilities when a high rate of inflation is also reflected in deterioration over time in the country's foreign exchange rates.
   B. A number of factors will influence the profitability of the subsidiary.
      1. Will the sales prices of the products sold increase at a rate that is faster, slower, or equal to the rate of increase in costs?
      2. What if labor costs are a high percentage of total costs and wages rise in anticipation of further inflation? Or wages may be indexed to the rate of inflation that is experienced.
      3. If the firm has a fixed price contract for raw materials or owns the source, it has achieved a windfall gain.
      4. If raw materials are purchased from another country, the exchange-rate movements may result in higher raw material costs than the rate of inflation.
      5. Does volume increase with the inflation? If so, is the firm operating with decreasing or increasing costs to scale?
      6. What happens to relative prices? How do the firm's prices change in relation to prices of other goods in the country and in other countries.
         a. If relative prices have increased, is the price elasticity of demand greater than or less than 1?
         b. If relative prices have fallen, what will be the influence of the size of demand price elasticity?
      7. Is the subsidiary in a line of activity that is likely to be adversely affected or helped by government policies to deal with inflation or alternatively, unemployment?
   C. *Conclusion:* The influence of inflation and related foreign-exchange-rate movements may be offset or aggravated by other effects on the profit margins of the subsidiary.

PROBLEM 8-4

"Whenever a company faces a foreign exchange risk, it should always obtain foreign exchange forward market cover." Evaluate this statement.

THE RISKS OF INTERNATIONAL FINANCIAL MANAGEMENT

SOLUTION:

This statement is false. Whether forward market cover should be obtained depends upon the risk exposure in relation to the cost of the forward market cover.

Sometimes the costs of cover may be greater than a reasonable expectation of losses from a currency value change. For example, in the summer of 1970 there was perhaps a 25% probability that the Italian lira would be devalued by 10%. But this would not have justified a "cover" operation of selling lira forward at the then prevailing discount of 6.0% on one-year contracts. (25% of 10%, or 2½%—the expectation of loss from devaluation—was less than 6%). Likewise, through most of the 1960s, Mexican pesos sold forward at discounts often as high as 4.0%. In retrospect, it seems clear that the possibilities of a Mexican peso devaluation were not great enough to justify paying such high "insurance."

But there have been numerous cases when there was strong justification for paying the costs of protection against foreign-exchange-rate risks. On September 16, 1968, French francs could have been sold forward for one year at a 1.72% discount. This cost was a reasonable insurance rate against the August 1969 devaluation of the French franc by 11.1%. On April 7, 1972, forward sterling sold at a 0.02% discount. Subsequently, it was allowed to float and depreciated about 10%, between April 7, 1972 and November 7, 1972.

PROBLEM 8-5

In the following table, indicate whether or not to cover a foreign exchange position.

	(1) Forecast Devaluation or Revaluation	(2) Probability of Devaluation or Revaluation	(3) Mathematical Expectation of Devaluation or Revaluation (1) × (2)	(4) % Cost of Cover Against Currency Change
A	10%	50%	5%	7%
B	10%	30%	3%	1%
C	4%	50%	2%	5%
D	10%	50%	5%	2%
E	10%	60%	6%	10%
F	20%	25%	5%	2%
G	15%	66-2/3%	10%	5%

SOLUTION:

Cover: If (3) exceeds (4).
Do not cover: If (4) exceeds (3).

A. Do not cover.
B. Cover.
C. Do not cover.
D. Cover.
E. Do not cover.
F. Cover.
G. Cover.

PROBLEM 8-6

The organization of the foreign exchange market, mainly through large banks, (a) discourages equilibrating speculation in forward markets of major currencies and (b) does not provide forward markets in minor, but nevertheless important, currencies. Explain.

SOLUTION:

The banks appear not to want speculation because, at least against the background of current methods of personalized country-store-type exchange trading, managing speculative accounts would be too much of an administrative bother. Unlike the big hedgers, who are usually corporations with established credit rating backed up by deposit balances, many speculators are "little guys" who could not always guarantee meeting potential obligations. In security markets or commodity markets this problem has been handled by margin requirements. Banks appear to view margin requirements as a nuisance that would not be worth the time. This may be so, under current trading arrangements, but commodity exchanges can handle small contracts involving only hundreds of dollars and still make money.

Another reason why banks tend to avoid speculators is that the banks tend to fix contracts for specific periods and like to have their customers stick to them. Speculators have an "in and out" image and are feared to be troublesome, for example, in wanting to sell a 3-month contract after 6 weeks of it are gone.

The Chicago Mercantile Exchange has set up a foreign currency exchange market, the International Monetary Market (IMM). As yet, the IMM accounts for a small fraction of foreign exchange trading. One difficulty is that most IMM brokers are also commodity brokers and, since this has been a prosperous field in recent years, they have given relatively little attention to currencies. Perhaps this will change in the years ahead.

V. Anticipated inflation and exchange risk versus uncertain inflation and exchange risk is considered.
   A. Anticipated inflation and exchange risk are already reflected in prices, spot and forward exchange rates, and in interest rates.
      1. To the extent that the markets are efficient, it will make no difference whether the firm uses the forward market to hedge or whether it borrows in the United States or foreign country.
      2. However, the expected degree of inflation and exchange risk as reflected in market relationships may also change over time.
      3. The view of the firm may differ from the average expectations reflected in the market relationships, but over a period of time a firm is not likely to be able to "beat the international financial markets."
   B. Uncertain inflation and uncertain exchange risks have a different influence than anticipated inflation and exchange risk.
      1. By hedging and diversification a part of the total risk can be diversified away or removed by entering into protective contracts. The returns will not reflect a premium for this unsystematic risk which can be eliminated by protective appropriate actions of the firm.
      2. However, some risk cannot be diversified away or eliminated. This is *systematic risk*.
         a. Systematic risk is the response of the return on the project or firm to movements in the returns on the world market as a whole.
         b. The nature of these relations is spelled out in greater detail and illustrated in Chapter 14, "Return on Investment and Cost of Capital."
VI. Risk analysis concerns probabilities of unfavorable developments in relation to the position of the firm or investor.
   A. The use of probability distributions is sometimes considered artificial.
      1. However, it is unrealistic to assign only one value to a future event—this is equivalent to assigning a probability of 1.
      2. It is natural to think in terms of a number of alternative possibilities.
         a. One formulation is in terms of most probable, optimistic, and pessimistic.
         b. A variation on this is in terms of the most probable, the best that can happen, and the worst that can happen—technically this would represent the modal return and the range of possible returns.
   B. At this point, risk will be analyzed in terms of expected values and their degree of dispersion.
      1. The benefits of diversification in improving the return to a risk relationship will be illustrated.
      2. The nature of risk that cannot be reduced or eliminated by diversification is discussed in connection with the concept of "covariance" explained more fully in Chapter 14, "Return on Investment and Cost of Capital."

PROBLEM 8-7

A U.S. exporter is contemplating the sale of goods to customers in two countries. The possible exchange-rate changes with relation to the U.S. dollar and the associated probabilities for each country are given below. If the exporter sells 50% in each country, what is the expected exchange-rate gain or loss and standard deviation of the returns? What sales weights will minimize the standard deviation and what is the expected exchange-rate gain or loss with these weights?

		Expected Exchange-Rate Changes (%)	
(1)	(2)	(3)	(4)
States	Probabilities	Country A (R_A)	Country B (R_B)
1	.2	−40	10
2	.3	−20	5
3	.5	−12	0

SOLUTION:

States	Probabilities	R_A	$R_A - \bar{R}_A$	$[R_A - \bar{R}_A]^2$	$p[R_A - \bar{R}_A]^2$
1	.2	−.40	−.20	.04	.008
2	.3	−.20	0	0	0
3	.5	−.12	.08	.0064	.0032
		$\bar{R}_A = -.20$		$\sigma_A^2 = .0112$	
				$\sigma_A = .1058$	

States	Probabilities	R_B	$R_B - \bar{R}_B$	$[R_B - \bar{R}_B]^2$	$p[R_B - \bar{R}_B]^2$
1	.2	.10	.065	.004225	.000845
2	.3	.05	.015	.000225	.0000675
3	.5	0	−.035	.001225	.0006125
		$\bar{R}_B = .035$		$\sigma_B^2 = .001525$	
				$\sigma_B = .03905$	

States	Probabilities	$[R_A - \bar{R}_A]$	$[R_B - \bar{R}_B]$	$p[R_A - \bar{R}_A][R_B - \bar{R}_B]$
1	.2	−.20	.065	−.0026
2	.3	0	.015	0
3	.5	.08	−.035	−.0014
			$Cov(R_A, R_B) =$	−.004

Consider the portfolio $R_p = aR_A + (1-a)R_B$, $VAR(R_p) = \sigma_p^2$. Then $\sigma_p^2 = a^2\sigma_A^2 + 2a(1-a)\,Cov_{AB} + (1-a)^2\,\sigma_B^2$.

If $a = (1-a) = .5$ then

$$\sigma_p^2 = (.5)^2\,(.0112) - 2(.5)^2\,(.004) + (.5)^2\,(.001525)$$
$$= .00118125$$

$\sigma_p = .03437 \qquad \bar{R}_p = .5(-.20) + .5(.035) = -.0825$

The minimum variance portfolio R_{p*} occurs when

$$a = \frac{\sigma_B^2 - Cov_{AB}}{\sigma_A^2 + \sigma_B^2 - 2Cov_{AB}} = \frac{.001525 + .004}{.0112 + .001525 + .008} = .2666$$

$(1-a) = .7334$

$$\sigma_{p*}^2 = (.2666)^2(.0112) - 2(.2666)(.7334)(.004) + (.7334)^2(.001525)$$
$$= .00005211$$

$\sigma_{p*} = .007219$

$\bar{R}_{p*} = (.2666)(-.20) + (.7334)(.035) = -.02765 \cong -3\%$

This example illustrates that by diversifying across countries in which devaluation may take place as well as countries in which revaluation may take place the combined portfolio of activities has a lower risk as measured by the variance or standard deviation of exchange-rate movements. By placing about one-fourth of the firm's activities in the country subject to devaluation and about three-fourths of the activities in the country with prospective revaluation, the variance of the combined activities is reduced to almost zero. The portfolio exchange-rate fluctuation has an expected value of about a 3% devaluation. Of course, by conducting its activities only in the country where revaluation upward is expected, the firm can attain an expected revaluation upward of 3½%. However, the risks of exchange-rate fluctuations will be greater than under the minimum variance portfolio in which one-fourth of the activity is in country A and three-fourths of the activity is in country B.

We would emphasize also that the market is reflecting a similar kind of probability assessment of the outlook for devaluation and for revaluation in the two countries. The spot and forward exchange rates will reflect the kinds of probability assessments that have been set forth in this problem. Also, at any particular point in time it is possible that the market is overoptimistic about the country in which revaluation is expected to take place and overpessimistic about the country in which devaluation is expected to take place. If so, there may be a possibility of better results in the weak currency country than in the strong currency country.

It should be noted also that in the formula for the variance of the portfolio, one of the terms is the covariance between the exchange-rate fluctuations in country A and exchange-rate fluctuations in country B. In the example this covariance relationship is negative. One of the terms in the variance formula is negative which reduces the resulting variance of the portfolio. An important aspect of assessing the extent to which activity should be carried on in an individual country is the covariance of possible exchange-rate fluctuations in that country with exchange-rate fluctuations in all of the other countries in which the firm may potentially conduct its activities. Thus, the pattern of fluctuations in exchange rates in one country in relation to other countries, or its covariance, is an important aspect in evaluating the effect on the overall risks of a firm's operations attributable to its activities in a particular country.

REFERENCES

A number of articles deal with various aspects of the subjects included in this chapter.

deVries, M.: "Exchange Depreciation in Developing Countries," *IMF Staff Papers*, November 1968, p. 560.

Folks, William R., Jr.: "The Optimal Level of Forward Exchange Transactions," *Journal of Financial and Quantitative Analysis*, January 1973, pp. 105-110.

Heckerman, Donald: "The Exchange Risk of Foreign Operations," *Journal of Business*, January 1972, pp. 42-48.

Hoyt, Newton H., Jr.: "The Management of Currency Exchange Risk by the Singer Company," *Financial Management*, Spring 1972, pp. 13-20.

Lietaer, Bernard A.: *Financial Management of Foreign Exchange Risk: An Operational Technique to Reduce Risk*, M.I.T., Cambridge, Mass., 1971.

Rutenberg, David P.: "Maneuvering Liquid Assets in a Multinational Company," *Management Science*, June 1970, pp. B671-B684.

Shapiro, A. C.: "Exchange Rate Changes, Inflation, and the Value of the Multinational Corporation," *Journal of Finance*, May 1975, pp. 485-502.

_____, and David P. Rutenberg: "When to Hedge Against Devaluation," *Management Science*, August 1974, pp. 1514-1520.

Chapter 9

Insurance and Guarantee Programs for Foreign Operations

Theme: Doing business on an international basis exposes a firm to commercial and political risks which may cause severe financial losses. Political risks, particularly in developing countries, are difficult to predict with certainty. Only a few firms, due to favorable location of their foreign sales and/or operations, are in a position to self-insure these risks. Fortunately, insurance protection against these risks is available from FCIA and Eximbank for commercial foreign sales, and from OPIC and AID for portfolio and direct investments in foreign countries. With this protection a firm can exchange an uncertain and potentially large loss for the finite and smaller cost of an insurance premium. Even though insurance may not be needed for transactions with firms in some countries, a spreading of risks for insurance writers requires that a high percentage of the activities of an insured firm be covered by a policy. For commercial and political risk insurance offered by FCIA and Eximbank, the premium for comprehensive coverage may be substantially reduced by lower financing costs made possible by the elimination of risks.

I. Insurance and guarantee programs involving foreign operations.
   A. Insurers.
      1. Export sales.
         a. Foreign Credit Insurance Association.
         b. Export-Import Bank of the United States.

2. Investments.
   a. Overseas Private Investment Corporation
   b. Agency for International Development
B. Insured against
   1. Commercial risks.
   2. Political risks.
C. Advantages.
   1. Eliminates the covered risks.
   2. Facilitates the financing of export sales, usually at a lower cost.
   3. Facilitates U.S. private capital investments abroad consistent with the development assistance objectives of the United States.

II. Foreign Credit Insurance Association.
   A. Premiums
      1. Are paid at the initiation of the policy.
      2. Vary with the risk of the customer's country. There are four risk classes designated by base rates: .53 (safest), .78, 1.17, and 1.37 (riskiest).
      3. Vary with the length of the credit period.
   B. Programs.
      1. Short-term policy, for consumer goods and credits of less than 6 months.
         a. It is a blanket-type policy.
         b. It must include essentially all of an exporter's short-term transactions or a reasonable spread of risk.
         c. No down payment is required.
         d. Goods covered must be at least 50% of U.S. origin.
         e. Eligible insured must be a U.S. corporation or a foreign corporation doing business in the United States.
         f. Coverage available:
            (1) 90% of commercial risk.
            (2) 95% of political risk.
            (3) 98% for both risks in the case of agricultural goods and a possible 1-year credit period.
         g. Protection available:
            (1) Comprehensive, commercial and political risks.
            (2) Political risk only.
         h. Special policy provisions:
            (1) Policy may contain a first-dollar-loss-cumulative-per-year deductible provision on commercial risks. FCIA pays any losses above the deductible by standard coverage percentages during the policy year.
            (2) With the deductible provision, exporter is given a discretionary limit up to which a new transaction may be insured without prior FCIA approval.

i. Rates.

FCIA Comprehensive Coverage, Short-term

Type of Transaction	Range of Average Fees per $100 of Gross Invoice Value			
	Country Classification by Base Rate			
	0.53	0.78	1.17	1.37
30-day confirmed irrevocable letter of credit	0.17	0.25	0.40	0.45
180-day open account	0.65	1.00	1.60	1.80

j. Fees are payable upon shipment.

2. Medium-term policy, for capital equipment and credit terms usually from 6 months to 5 years.
   a. It is available on a case-by-case basis or for repetitive sales to a customer.
   b. It is available on a comprehensive basis or for political risk only.
   c. It requires that the customer make a down payment of at least 10%.[1]
   d. The exporter must carry for his own account at least 10% of the financed portion's risk. For countries in the riskier classes, the exporter may be required to assume a risk higher than 10%.
   e. Amounts payable after the down payment must be covered by specified monthly, quarterly, or semiannual notes.
   f. Rates.

FCIA Comprehensive Coverage, Medium-term

Credit Period in Years	Approximate Fees Paid per $100 of Financed Portion			
	Country Classification by Base Rate			
	0.53	0.78	1.17	1.37
1	0.70	1.00	1.60	1.80
3	1.60	2.40	3.60	4.20
5	2.50	3.80	5.70	6.60

(1) Fees are payable in advance of policy issuance.
(2) For all risk classes except the safest (.53), the above fees would be reduced by approximately 12% or 29% depending on whether the exporter carries 20% or 30% of the risk for his own account.

[1] In view of FCIA's relationship with Eximbank it was announced that effective July 1, 1976, the down-payment requirements for insured medium-term transactions would be raised from 10% to 15%. For details see the Eximbank announcement in section III of this chapter.

3. Master policy.
    a. It is a blanket-type policy and must include all the exporter's sales.
    b. It usually covers short-term as well as medium-term transactions.
    c. The policy may be obtained on a short-term and/or medium-term transaction basis.
    d. It is usually written to cover both commercial and political risk.
    e. It may be obtained on a political risk coverage basis only.
    f. It is written on a year-to-year basis and includes:
        (1) An aggregate amount, the maximum risk to FCIA.
        (2) A discretionary credit limit per buyer permitting an exporter to insure a transaction without prior FCIA approval.
        (3) A special buyer's credit limit above the discretionary amount is available subject to confirmation by FCIA.
        (4) A first-dollar-loss-deductible-per-year provision for commercial risks requiring the exporter to absorb this first loss, after which FCIA will cover any further losses in accordance with standard coverage percentages. The greater the deductible, the lower the premium.
4. Combination.
    a. Covers short-term and intermediate-term transactions with overseas franchised dealers and distributors. It is designed to cover
        (1) Parts and accessories up to 180 days.
        (2) Inventory financing on a consignment or floor-plan basis up to 270 days with no down payment required.
        (3) Receivable financing up to 3 years following a minimum down payment upon sale by the dealer or the end of the inventory period.
    b. Coverage is usually up to 90% for commercial risks and 95% for political risks.
5. Small exporter policy.
    a. It is available only to exporters that have exported less than $200,000 annually over the previous 3 years.
    b. The maximum length of the policy is 2 years or until the exporter has reached an export volume of $500,000, whichever occurs first.
    c. The advantage of this policy is the simplicity of paperwork required.
6. Service policy. This policy is designed to cover the foreign business of consulting and engineering firms through which the services of U.S. based individuals are sold and are paid for in U.S. dollars.

PROBLEM 9-1

The Smith Company sells a $5,000 order to a buyer in a base rate 0.53 country on a 30-day confirmed irrevocable letter of credit basis. The FCIA comprehensive premium on this transaction is $0.17 per $100 insured amount.

INSURANCE AND GUARANTEE PROGRAMS FOR FOREIGN OPERATIONS

What is the cost of the policy in dollars and on a percentage basis?
What is the net cost since the policy will lower financing costs by 1.0%?

SOLUTION:

On a dollar basis: The cost of the policy is $\frac{\$5{,}000}{100}$ (0.17), or $8.50.
The net cost of the policy equals the premium cost minus the interest savings.

$$\text{Net cost} = \text{premium} - \$5{,}000(.01)/12$$
$$= 8.50 - 4.17 = \$4.33$$

On an annual percentage basis: Percentage cost = (0.17/100)(12) = 2.04%

$$\text{Net cost} = 2.04\% - 1.0\% = 1.04\%$$

PROBLEM 9-2

The Johnson Company sells to buyers in base rates 1.17 and 1.37 countries on a 6-month open account basis. The rate of the FCIA comprehensive policy is $2.34 per $100 insured amount. The financing cost is lowered by 1.0% due to the FCIA guarantee.

For a $10,000 transaction, calculate in dollars and on a percentage basis:

A. The net cost of a comprehensive policy.
B. The cost of a political-risk-only policy. A political-risk-only policy has a premium of 75% of a comprehensive policy.

SOLUTION:

A. 1. The dollar cost of the policy = 10,000(2.34)/100 = $234
   The interest cost saving = 10,000(.01)6/12 = $50
   The net cost of the policy = 234 - 50 = $184
   2. The percentage cost = 2.34(12)/6 = 4.68%
   Less financing savings   1.00
   Net percentage cost =   3.68%
B. 1. The premium for a political-risk-only policy is approximately 75% of that for a comprehensive policy. The dollar cost of the policy = 10,000 (.0234)(.75) = $175.50.
   There is no saving in interest since financial institutions will not finance transactions that are covered for political risk only.
   2. The percentage costs of the policy = 4.68 (.75) = 3.51%. Thus, there is very little additional cost for a comprehensive policy.

PROBLEM 9-3

The Kord Company makes a $10,000 sale to a firm in a country on a 2-year confirmed letter of credit basis. The comprehensive premium on this transaction is $1.00 per $100 insured value. The customer is required to make a 10% down payment and the company must carry 10% of the financed portion of the sale at its own risk. After the down payment, the customer will make 50% payments at the end of each year. The customer is charged 14% on his unpaid balance. The seller pays 8% on insured and 10% on uninsured sales. The cost of the sale is $8000 incurred 2 months before the sale. As funds are received from the customer, they are turned over to the bank to reduce the balance on the firm's loans. Take the time value of money into account by discounting receipts and disbursements at a cost of capital of 14% and assume that interest payments are made at the end of the year.
A. Should the policy be purchased?
B. Does Kord gain or lose from the financing arrangements?

SOLUTION:

Total sales	$10,000
Less 10% down payment	1,000
Financed portion	9,000
10% at risk of the seller	900
Insured portion	$ 8,100

Insurance premium = 8,100(0.01) = $81

In the following, $P_{1,14\%}$ is the present value factor for the first year at 14%. $P_{2,14\%}$ is for the second year.

A. A way to evaluate this project from an overall point of view is to calculate an investment schedule for the project on a net present value basis.

Item		Investment Schedule		
	$	Time	PVF	PV
Merchandise shipped 8000 [1+(0.14)(1/6)]	8,186.67	0	1.0	−8,186.67
Down payment received	1,000	0	1.0	1,000
Bank loans received	9,000	0	1.0	9,000
Cost of policy	81	0	1.0	− 81
First payment received	4,500	1	.877	3,946.50
Payment to bank	4,500	1	.877	−3,946.50
Interest received [9000(.14)]	1,260	1	.877	1,105.02
Interest paid [(900(.10) + 8100 (.08)]	738	1	.877	− 647.23
Second payment received	4,500	2	.769	3,460.50
Second payment made	4,500	2	.769	−3,460.50
Interest received [4500 (.14)]	630	2	.769	484.47
Interest paid [450(.10) + 4050(.08)]	369	2	.769	− 283.76
			Net present value =	$2,390.83

Proposal is acceptable because net present value is greater than zero.

B. 1. Insure if there is a net benefit to insurance.

$$\text{Cost if insured} = [900(.10) + 8{,}100(.08)]P_{1,14\%} + [450(.10) + 4050(.08)]P_{2,14\%} + \text{cost of policy.}$$
$$= (90+648)(.877) + (45+324)(.769) + 81$$
$$= 647.23 + 283.76 + 81.00 = \$1{,}011.99$$
$$\text{Cost if not insured} = 9{,}000(.10)P_{1,14\%} + 4500(.10)P_{2,14\%}$$
$$= 900(.877) + 450(.769) = \$1{,}135.35$$
$$\text{Benefit of insurance} = \text{cost if not insured} - \text{cost if insured}$$
$$= 1{,}135.35 - 1{,}011.99 = \$123.36$$

Therefore, insure. The benefit is derived from interest savings from insuring.

2. Insure if interest savings from insuring exceed the cost of the policy.

$$\text{Net cost of policy} = \text{cost less financing saving}$$
$$= 81.00 - [8{,}100(.02)P_{1,14\%} + 4{,}050(.02)P_{2,14\%}]$$
$$= 81.00 - [162.00(.877) + 81.00(.769)]$$
$$= 81.00 - (142.07 + 62.29)$$
$$= 81.00 - 204.36$$
$$= -\$123.36$$

Therefore, insure.

PROBLEM 9-4

A $200,000 sale is made to a base rate 1.17 country on a 5-year open account basis. The required down payment is 10% and the firm will have to carry 20% of the financed portion at its own risk. The selling firm's cost of capital is 14%. The seller saves 1½% on his financing cost due to FCIA insurance coverage. The FCIA premium on this transaction is $4.00 per $100 of insured amount.

1. The buyer will make equal payments plus interest at the end of each year. Take into account the time value of money.
2. After making the above determinations, assume that the customer pays interest only at the end of each of the first 4 years and pays the principal with interest at the end of the 5th year. What are costs or benefits of each version?

SOLUTION:

Total transaction	$200,000
Less down payment	20,000
Balance	180,000
Less risk of seller, 20%	36,000
Insured part	144,000

Insurance premium = 144,000(.04) = $5,760
Interest saving = 0.015%

1. Buyer's annual principal payment = 180,000/5 = 36,000
   Annual reduction of insured loan = 144,000/5 = $28,800
   Interest savings = 144,000(.015)(.877) + 115,200(.015)(.769)
   $\qquad\qquad\qquad$ + 86,400(.015)(.675) + 57,600(.015)(.592)
   $\qquad\qquad\qquad$ + 28,800(.015)(.519)
   $\qquad\qquad$ = $4,833.65

   Net cost of insurance = premium − interest saving
   $\qquad\qquad\qquad\qquad$ = 5,760.00 − 4,833.65 = $926.35

   Note that the original insured loan is reduced annually on a pro rata basis on which the 1½% interest savings apply. This results in a net cost of insurance of $926.35.
   Therefore, insure if the protection is worth $926.35.

2. In the following, $A_{\overline{5}|,14\%}$ is the present value of an annuity factor for 5 years at 14%.

   Net cost of insurance = premium − interest savings
   $\qquad\qquad\qquad\qquad$ = 5,760.00 − 144,000 (.015)$A_{\overline{5}|,14\%}$
   $\qquad\qquad\qquad\qquad$ = 5,760.00 − 2,160(3.433) = 5,760.00 − 7,415.28
   $\qquad\qquad\qquad\qquad$ = −$1,655.28

   Note that interest savings here apply on the original amount over the entire 5-year period. Consequently, interest savings are greater than the premium. Therefore, the insurance should be obtained.

III. The Export-Import Bank of the United States. The Eximbank was established in 1934. Presently it is charged with the responsibility of facilitating the export of U.S. goods and services. It accomplishes this in several ways.
   A. Through an agency and reinsurance agreement with the FCIA, it is the principal insurer for all of the policies issued by FCIA for political risks and a

INSURANCE AND GUARANTEE PROGRAMS FOR FOREIGN OPERATIONS

reinsurer for commercial risks above agreed upon amounts, per buyers, per policy, per annum, etc. (See section II.)

B. It makes loans that are used to purchase U.S. goods and services for large foreign projects. These funds must be repaid on a regular payment basis. The loans usually have long-term maturities. See Chapter 13 for further details.

C. On these same projects, Eximbank provides loan guarantees to intermediate-term lenders such as Private Export Funding Corporation (PEFCO) or other private lenders.
1. PEFCO is owned by 55 commercial banks, 7 industrial corporations, and one investment banking firm. It finances the intermediate-term funds by the sale of notes or bonds to purchase debt obligations issued by the foreign buyers of U.S. exports.
2. Cooperative financing facilities, private foreign credit institutions.
    a. Eximbank makes available to these credit institutions one-half of the funds needed to finance exports of U.S. goods and services, and permits them to charge the borrower 2.5% above the rate charged by Eximbank on its half of the funds.
    b. A financial guarantee may be granted if a credit institution has to borrow the other half of the funds required by the project from private sources.
        (1) A guarantee fee of 0.5% per year is charged.
        (2) A commitment fee of 0.5% is charged the credit institution on any undisbursed balance of Eximbank's one-half of the loan to the buyer beginning 60 days from final approval of each specific export loan.
        (3) The credit institution may charge the buyer 2.5% above its borrowing rate on its half of the funds if the Eximbank guarantee is utilized.

D. Eximbank operates a commercial bank exporter guarantee program. It will guarantee repayment of medium-term (181 days to 5 years) export debt obligations acquired by U.S. banking institutions from U.S. exporters.
1. Under this program
    a. It holds the bank harmless from commercial and political risks.
    b. It requires the bank involved to buy without recourse to the exporter, except for the normal exporter retention, notes or debt instruments from the exporter. If the transaction is guaranteed for political risks only, Eximbank will then permit the bank to buy the papers on a full recourse basis for commercial risks.
2. The general terms that apply are:
    a. A 10% cash payment is required on or before delivery of the product.[2]

---

[2]The June 10, 1976 issue of the *Wall Street Journal* carried a story of a press conference of Mr. Stephen Dubrul, Jr., president of Eximbank, in which it was announced that effective July 1,

b. The remainder must be evidenced by promissory notes or other acceptable debt instruments payable in equal installments of principal over the period of the loan.
c. The exporter must retain at least 10% of the risk of the financed portion of the transaction.
3. Eximbank offers the commercial bank several plans.
   a. Plan I requires the commercial bank to take for its own account all commercial risk on the first half of the payments, but not to exceed a duration of 18 months on longer credits. Eximbank will then assume all commercial risks on the later payments and political risks for the entire term.
   b. Plan II requires the commercial bank to take for its own account 15% of the commercial risk on all installments. Eximbank will guarantee 85% of each installment for commercial risk and all the political risk. If Eximbank at the halfway point is satisfied that the foreign buyer will meet the remainder of his installments, it will consider guaranteeing the commercial bank at 100% for the comprehensive coverage on the remaining payments.
   c. Under both plans I and II a fully comprehensive guarantee of 100% may be provided if the sale is to an acceptable public (governmental) buyer.
   d. Political-risk-only coverage. Under both plans I and II it is possible to cover political risks only at a slightly lower rate.
4. Premiums.
   a. The basis for guarantee charges vary with the
      (1) Length of the credit period.
      (2) Country of the buyer.
      (3) Amount of exporter participations.
   b. Fees are one-time charges based on actual shipments.

PROBLEM 9-5

A sale of $100,000 is made to a customer in country Y on credit terms of 3 years. A 10% down payment is required, and the firm must carry 10% of the financed portion at its own risk. The Eximbank medium-term guarantee rate is 2.61%. What is the premium on the policy?

1976, down-payment requirements for medium-term transactions would be raised from 10% to 15%. This change is being made on a one-year trial basis after consultation with similar agencies of other nations. The purpose of this change, providing that others will do likewise, is to decrease competition among major trading nations in export financing. Exempt from this change are agricultural commodities, aircraft, steel mills, communication satellite ground stations, and nuclear and conventional power plants. Due to the trial basis of this change and the fact that at this time only Germany, Japan, and the United Kingdom have agreed to do the same, we will continue to utilize the traditional 10% down payments in this text.

SOLUTION:

Sale	$100,000
Less down payment	10,000
Balance	90,000
Less exporter's risk, 10%	9,000
Insured portion	81,000
Premium or fee = 81,000(0.0261) =	$ 2,114.10

IV. OPIC offers three programs: an investment insurance program, an investment guarantee program, and a financing program using its own funds.
   A. OPIC's guiding policies.
      1. It aims to become eventually a reinsurer of privately owned insurers against political risks for U.S. investors. In 1975 an Overseas Investment Insurance Group was formed consisting of 13 insurance companies and OPIC.
         a. This group insures and reinsures U.S. private investments abroad against the political risks of convertibility and expropriation.
         b. In addition to insuring new investments, it will share a portion of the risks of OPIC's existing insurance portfolios.
      2. OPIC continues to cover all political risks due to war, revolution, and insurrection. It expects to share these risks with investors or private insurers through some form of mutual or reciprocal arrangement.
      3. OPIC reinsures the excess losses of the Overseas Investment Insurance Group.
      4. OPIC is required by stature to conduct its financing and insurance on a self-sustaining basis and conduct its insurance operations with due regard to risk management.
         a. It must avoid overconcentration in particular countries or in certain industries in any one country.
         b. It must charge variable premiums for expropriation insurance, depending on the degree of risk.
         c. It must insist that the insured carry at least 10% of the risk for his own account, more in the case of high risk investments or overconcentration on OPIC's part of investments in countries or industries. For investments in mineral extractive industries in high risk countries, the share of risk of the insured may be as high as 50%.
   B. Investment insurance.
      1. Premiums or fees.
         a. Risk of inconvertibility: the inability of the investor to convert into dollars the currency received as profits or earnings or return of the original investment, 0.3%.
         b. Risk of expropriation ranges from 0.4% to 0.8% or more depending on risk-increasing or risk-decreasing factors.

c. Risk of war, revolution, or civil upheaval, 0.6%.
   d. Stand-by coverage, 0.25% per coverage.
2. Percentage of normal coverage.
   a. Investments in average projects, 90%.
   b. Large equity investments, particularly in extractive industries, 75% or even as low as 50%.
   c. A doubling of normal coverage is permitted to cover the reinvestment of earnings.
3. Terms used in OPIC's policies.
   a. The current insured amount is the value of the actual risk covered in the contract year beginning at the date of execution of the insurance contract by OPIC.
   b. Maximum amount is the highest possible insurance coverage under the policy, ordinarily 180% on a standard equity or loan investment.
   c. Stand-by amount is the difference between the maximum amount and the insured amount.
4. Requirements.
   a. Investments must be located in developing countries.
   b. An investment agreement must have been finalized between the foreign government and the U.S. government.
   c. A specified agency in the foreign country must attest to the fact that the proposed investment is desirable and is in the interest of the local economy and provide specific approval for the issuance of insurance by OPIC.
   d. The maximum insured amount must be determined at the initiation of the policy.
   e. Insurance premiums must be paid annually by the contract anniversary date.
   f. For expropriation and war risk, the insured amount must be equal to the amount of the insured investment at risk.
   g. The investment must be a new investment or a substantial expansion of an existing investment.
   h. The investment must not have been irrevocably committed at the time of preliminary application. An OPIC registration letter must have been obtained previously.
   i. The term of investment coverage is from 3 to 20 years.
5. Eligible investors.
   a. A citizen of the United States.
   b. A corporation, partnership, or other association created under the laws of the United States, any state or territory of the United States which is substantially and beneficially owned by U.S. citizens.

c. A foreign business at least 95% of which is owned by investors listed in parts (a) and (b).
6. Eligible investments.
    a. Cash.
    b. Retained earnings.
    c. Materials and equipment, both new and used.
    d. Patents, processes, and techniques.
    e. Service.
    f. Loans and loan guarantees.
7. Ineligible investments.
    a. Short-term investments.
    b. Foreign-government-owned projects.
    c. Manufacturing of ammunitions.
    d. Gambling facilities.
    e. Production of alcoholic beverages.
    f. Sports stadiums, amusement parks, or golf courses, etc.
    g. Investments which are adverse to U.S. interests or host country interests.

PROBLEM 9-6

Assume that the transaction of problem 9-4 is an investment in a subsidiary with a before-tax profitability of 30% per year. The investment is insured with OPIC against convertibility, expropriation, and war risk. Annual profits will also be insured to the maximum permitted. What is the present value of the cost of this protection for a 5-year period? What, if any, are the advantages or disadvantages over problem 9-4? Assume that the local tax rate is 30%. Since all after-tax earnings are reinvested each year, earnings growth is on a compounded basis. The applicable fee is 1.5% on the insured amount and 0.75% for standby coverage.

SOLUTION:

At the beginning of the policy, the insured must decide on the amount of maximum coverage which may not exceed 180% of the investment since, according to the latest rules, the insured must carry 10% of the risk himself. Therefore, the maximum insured amount here can be 180% ($200,000) = $360,000. It is not necessary, however, to insure for convertibility in the same amount as for expropriation and war risk. Coverage for convertibility may be governed by the actual exposure to that risk. In this example, the same coverage for all three risks is assumed for the sake of simplicity.

Year	Maximum Amount	Insured Amount $	Fee (1.5%)	Stand-by Amount $	Fee (.75%)	Total Fee	PVF	Present Value
1	360,000	180,000	2,700	180,000	1,350	4,050	1.000	4,050.00
2	360,000	217,800	3,267	142,200	1,066	4,332	.877	3,800.04
3	360,000	263,538	3,953	96,462	723	4,676	.769	3,595.84
4	360,000	318,881	4,783	41,119	308	5,091	.675	3,436.43
5	360,000	360,000	5,400	–	–	5,400	.592	3,196.80

Net present value of costs until received amount reaches maximum = $18,079.11

The original insured amount of $180,000 (90% of $200,000) increases by the yearly insurable portion of the annual profit. At the same time, the stand-by amount decreases by the same amount. A schedule of the annual profit and its insurable portion is presented below.

End of Year	Annual Profit ($) (a)	Insurable ($) 90% of (a)
1	200,000(.3)(1-.3) = 42,000	37,800
2	242,000(.3)(1-.3) = 50,820	45,738
3	292,820(.3)(1-.3) = 61,492	55,343
4	354,312(.3)(1-.3) = 74,405.5	41,119

The annual profit after taxes is equal to 200,000(.30)(1-.3) or $42,000 for the first year of which 90% is insurable. Therefore, the insured amount increases by $37,800 to $217,800 in year 2. The stand-by amount decreases by the same amount to $142,200. Note that in year 4, however, only $41,119 is additionally insurable as that increases the insured amount to the maximum value of $360,000.

The applicable fee of 1½% on the insured amount is made up of .3% for inconvertibility risk and .6% each for expropriation and war risks. The fee for stand-by coverage is 0.25% for each, or a total applicable fee of 0.75%.

For all following years, the coverage and costs would be the same as in year 4 to the end of the economic life of the investment. Whether this cost is acceptable for the protection offered depends on many factors, among which are the firm's opportunity cost for funds, the risks of the investment, and the firm's attitude towards risks. The advantage over problem 9-4 is that profits are also insured. One of the disadvantages is that financing costs are not reduced by this protection.

C. Investment guarantees and direct investment fund loans.
   1. Nature.
      a. Investment guarantees cover repayment of 100% of the principal and interest on medium-term and long-term loans made by U.S. lenders to the project.
      b. Direct investment fund loans are medium-term and long-term loans made to the project by OPIC.

2. OPIC requirements for participation.
    a. Normally there must be a U.S. sponsor who owns at least 25% or more of the outstanding common stock of the project borrower. The U.S. sponsor must have a proven record of success in the industry, and have a continuing role in project management.
    b. The investment must be in a developing country.
    c. Project considerations include:
        (1) Soundness and financial viability.
        (2) Local development benefits.
        (3) Effect on the host country's balance of payments.
        (4) Effect on the local ecology.
        (5) Source of needed raw materials and supplies.
            (a) The availability of proper import licenses.
            (b) The existence of supply contracts.
        (6) Adequate demand for the project's output.
    d. Funds must be spent substantially in:
        (1) The United States.
        (2) The host country.
        (3) Other developing countries.
    e. Equipment from developed countries must be financed in the country of manufacture.
    f. Sponsor considerations include:
        (1) Record of successful operation in a similar venture.
        (2) Required depth of management.
        (3) Competence in setting up and operating the proposed project.
        (4) Ability to make and follow through with an *overrun commitment*, that is, a commitment to make available as needed additional funds beyond project estimates.
3. Unacceptable projects.
    a. "Runaway plants" that replace existing U.S. facilities and export a substantial portion of their products to the United States.
    b. Production of munitions.
    c. Facilities for gambling.
    d. Production of agricultural commodities which are in surplus in the United States.
    e. Those involving unreasonable restrictions on trade.
    f. Those creating a monopoly not in the interest of the United States or the host country.
    g. Those with agreements unreasonably disadvantageous to the host country or its citizens.
    h. Service projects where the equipment and other physical assets are a small part of the total project.
    i. Projects wholly in the public sector.
4. Investment guarantee provisions.
    a. Funds may be on-shore or off-shore dollars.

b. Interest rates on loans must be representative of market rates.
c. Interest rates must be fixed, if possible.
d. The length of the loan period generally ranges from 5 to 15 years.
e. The guarantee charge by OPIC varies between 1.75% and 3% annually, depending on risk.
f. OPIC has established a guarantee reserve of 25% of guaranteed loans.
g. OPIC payment to the U.S. lender will occur
   (1) No later than 60 days after first notice of default.
   (2) No later than 10 days after subsequent notices of default.

V. Investment guarantees offered by the Agency for International Development.
   A. AID operates under the Foreign Assistance Act of 1969 which has the following objectives:
      1. To facilitate and increase the participation of private enterprise in furthering the development of the economic resources and productive capacities of less developed, friendly countries and areas.
      2. To promote the development of thrift and credit institutions engaged in programs of mobilizing local savings for financing of self-liquidating housing projects and related community facilities.
   B. Eligible investments.
      1. Those that make a material contribution to the solution of existing housing and urban development programs.
      2. Those that aid or make possible the participation of private enterprise in the development of the economic resources and productive capabilities of the developing, friendly countries.
      3. Loans to thrift and credit institutions that are engaged in the financing of the construction of homes and housing projects.
      4. Preferred projects are those in American republics which are of a self-liquidating nature and aid the local housing problem.
   C. Requirements of AID.
      1. A minimum of 25% of the financing must be from local sources. The greater the local participation the more favorable the evaluation of the project.
      2. Project sponsor must be a host country citizen or firm at least 50% beneficially owned by host country persons.
      3. Project must be a bona fide joint venture between the host country sponsor and the U.S. participant who must be a U.S. citizen or entity more than 50% beneficially owned by U.S. persons.
      4. The investment must be in the form of long-term, 15- to 20-year dollar loans, to provide mortgage financing.
      5. The interest on these loans must not exceed normal market rates considering the risk involved.
      6. Present guarantee limits are
         a. A maximum of $3,000,000 per project.
         b. A minimum of $1,000,000, unless the host country has established other limits.

INSURANCE AND GUARANTEE PROGRAMS FOR FOREIGN OPERATIONS

D. AID fees and charges.
 1. Application fee of $1,000.
 2. Acceptance fee of $2 per $1,000 of guarantee.
 3. Guarantee fees are as follows:
    a. 0.5% per annum where the repayment of the loan in U.S. dollars has been guaranteed by the government of the host country.
    b. 1% per annum where the mortgages are insured in local currency by a government mortgage insurance institution, housing agency, or other public or private institution acceptable to AID.
    c. 2% per annum in all other cases where AID has decided to extend a loan guarantee.
    d. A fee for the risk of devaluation insurance to be determined for each project. Protection against the risk of devaluation is available only if it has not been offered by the host government. This represents a distinct departure from previous practice. This is the only source, to our knowledge, of insurance against devaluation except for the use of the forward foreign exchange market as described in the following chapter.

PROBLEM 9-7

Compare the Eximbank, the FCIA, OPIC, and AID with respect to insurance and guarantee services offered and their comparative advantages and disadvantages with nongovernment services, if available. (Distill Chapter 9 to one page or less.)

SOLUTION:

Eximbank	FCIA	OPIC	AID
Term:			
Large commercial risk reinsurance of FCIA accounts, and medium-term comprehensive and political risk only policies. Guarantees banks up to 12 years.	Short-term credit sales up to 6 mo. for consumer goods; 181 days to 5 years for capital or producer goods. Exception basis, 7-year terms available on some capital goods.	3 years or more up to 20 years. Must be privately owned or managed, and *not* manufacturer of ammunition, gambling, alcoholic beverages, sports stadiums, or producer of surplus items.	15- to 20-year dollar loans to provide mortgage financing.
Cost:			
By country, length of credit and security.	By destination country class, length of credit and the security.	3/10% to 1.5% plus ¼% for stand-by.	25% of financing must be local.

Eximbank	FCIA	OPIC	AID

Coverage:

10%–20% down payment for medium-term. None for short-term. Seller carries 10% of commercial risk, 5% of political risk.		Currency inconvertability. Expropriation, war, revolution, etc. Commercial risk, loans and counseling. Must be new or expansions, competitive and welcome in the foreign country. Does *not* cover devaluation of foreign currency, or other business risks. For economic and social progress. Investment guarantees against commercial and political risk for portfolio investment guarantee agreements with the U.S. government.	Country must have investment guarantee agreement with U.S. government. Self-liquidating, housing, or community facilities projects. Must be sponsored by host country persons *and* U.S. citizen or firm. $1 million to $3 million. Devaluation insurance available.
Covers goods consigned, leased, or exhibited abroad. Guarantees engineering, planning, and feasibility studies and technical, constructional services performed abroad.	Catastrophe policy for high-volume low-profit exporters (who carry 30% of risk and 9 mo. wait on inconvertability (political risk only). Comprehensive policy (90% coverage). Small Business policy ($200,000). Comprehensive Master—covers all exports but may have discretionary credit policy limit. Agriculture—covers up to 98%.		

Eligible investments:

Loans and guarantees to promote exports.	Credit sales to foreigners.	Equity, cash, retained earnings, materials and equipment, patents, processes and techniques, services, loans, construction contracts, l.t. supplier's credit, lender's contract, branch bank contracts.	Pilot housing projects and development of housing financial institutions.

Other services available; foreign and forward exchange markets; self insurance by the parent corporation, or by the exporter, or group of exporters.

REFERENCES

Export-Import Bank of the United States, *Annual Reports.*

_____, Act of 1945 as amended through January 4, 1975.

Foreign Credit Insurance Association, *Annual Reports of Operations.*

_____, *Export Credit Insurance: The Competitive Edge* (n.d.).

International Credits Institute, *Insurance Systems in International Finance, 1970-71.*

Overseas Private Investment Corporation (Washington, D.C.), *Annual Reports.*

―――, *An Introduction to OPIC*, July 1971.

―――, *General Terms and Conditions, Contract of Insurance* (n.d.).

―――, *Guaranties of Loans*, June 1971.

―――, *Incentive Handbook for Cooperatives*, July 1971.

―――, *Incentive Handbook for Financial Institutions*, July 1971.

―――, *Incentive Handbook – Investment Financing*, July 1971.

―――, *Incentive Handbook – Investment Insurance*, January 1973.

―――, *Incentive Programs for Small Business in Developing Nations* (n.d.).

―――, *U.S. Private Investment in International Development*, July 1971.

Private Export Financing Corporation, *Annual Reports.*

U.S. Department of Commerce, *Guide to Financing Exports.*

Chapter 10

Exchange-Rate Risk Protection in Foreign Operations

Theme: Methods of dealing with exchange-rate risks must take into account that the foreign exchange markets are essentially efficient. New information is rapidly reflected in foreign exchange market relationships so that the foreign exchange markets are either at or moving toward equilibrium. If a firm has receipts that will be received or commitments that must be paid in the future, it can determine the amounts of foreign currencies it will receive or will be required to use in payment. The forward market can be used to fix the amount of these payments in dollars. If the forward market is at a discount or a premium, this will involve gains or losses with respect to the nominal price quoted for international transactions.

Similarly, if a firm is in a net monetary asset or liability position, it is exposed to gains or losses from exchange-rate fluctuations. The firm can seek protection by borrowing or lending to offset the exposed position, but again some costs will be involved. This illustrates the general proposition that a firm can avoid exchange-rate risk fluctuations only by planning its balance sheet position and future cash flows so that at any point in time it will be in a neutral net monetary asset or liability position. Otherwise, the firm will be exposed to exchange-rate fluctuations. If the firm is in an exposed position, it cannot avoid some costs of limiting risks of losses from exchange-rate fluctuations. However, there are policies and procedures that will help to minimize these costs.

I. The equilibrium relationships in the foreign exchange markets provide the framework for decision making to minimize the costs of exchange-rate fluctuations.
   A. Theoretical expansion of these relationships.
      1. Fisher Effect—nominal interest rates rise to reflect the anticipated rate of inflation.

$$\frac{P_1}{P_o} = \frac{1 + R_n}{1 + R_o}$$

where:

P_1 = price level one period later
P_o = current price level
R_n = nominal interest rate
R_r = real interest rate

      2. The Purchasing Power Parity Theorem (PPPT)—changes in exchange rates reflect changes in the relative prices between two countries.

$$(CX) = \frac{X_1}{X_o} = \frac{P_{f1}/P_{fo}}{P_{d1}/P_{do}} = (CRP)$$

where:

$$\frac{X_1}{X_o} = \frac{E_o}{E_1}$$

(*Recall:* LC = local or foreign currency.)

X_o = LCs per $ now
X_1 = LCs per $ one period later
$E_o = \frac{1}{X_1}$ = $s per LC now
$E_1 = \frac{1}{X_1}$ = $s per LC one period later
$(CX) = \frac{X_1}{X_o}$ = change in exchange rate
$(CRP) = \frac{P_{f1}/P_{fo}}{P_{d1}/P_{do}}$ = change in relative prices

P_{fo} = initial price level in the foreign country

P_{f1} = foreign country price level one period later

P_{do} = initial domestic price level

P_{d1} = domestic price level one period later

3. The Interest Rate Parity Theorem (IRPT)—interest rate levels in two countries will reflect the ratio of their expected exchange-rate movements.

$$\frac{1 + R_{fo}}{1 + R_{do}} = \frac{X_f}{X_o}$$

where:

R_{fo} = current foreign interest rate

R_{do} = current domestic interest rate

X_f = forward exchange rate (LC/$1)

X_o = spot exchange rate (LC/$1)

B. Movements toward equilibrium.
1. Interest rate levels in a country will represent the real rate of interest plus a factor reflecting the anticipated rate of inflation.
2. The relative rates of anticipated inflation in two countries will also be reflected in the relative movements in their exchange rates.
3. Current relative interest rate levels between two countries will reflect their expected exchange-rate movements.
4. Thus, relative price movements, relative exchange-rate movements, and relative interest rate levels between two countries will move together in a consistent fashion.

C. Covered interest arbitrage is one of the important processes by which these consistent equilibrium relationships are brought about.
1. This represents another form of the Interest Rate Parity Theorem.

$$R_{fo} - R_{do} = \frac{X_f - X_o}{X_o}$$

This equation states that the interest rate differential between two countries must be equal to the expected rate of devaluation or revaluation of the foreign currency in relation to the domestic currency.

2. This expression can also be written as:

$$(R_{fo} - R_{do}) - \left(\frac{X_f - X_o}{X_o}\right) = 0$$

If a currency revalues upward, the second term has a negative sign so it becomes positive. Therefore, the first term must be negative in order for the sum to equal zero.

3. Illustrations.

Assumptions (1)	Assumptions (2)
R_{fo} = 10%	R_{fo} = 7%
R_{do} = 7%	R_{do} = 10%
X_o = LC10/$1	X_o = LC10/$1
X_f = LC10.3/$1	X_f = LC9.7/$1

Covered interest arbitrage relationships:

$$(.10 - .07) - \frac{10.3 - 10}{10}\qquad\qquad (.07 - .10) - \frac{9.7 - 10}{10} = 0$$

$$= .03 - (.03) = 0 \qquad\qquad -(.03) - (-.03) = 0$$

D. Other factors that influence the size of the interest rate differential between two countries (in addition to the relation between the forward and spot exchange rates).
  1. The general pattern of the flow of funds. When there is a net flow of funds into a country, it will tend to make exchange rates stronger in that country. For a net flow of funds out of the country, the reverse is true.
  2. An imbalance in the flow of orders to either buy or sell a currency in a forward market. This may make it difficult for banks to achieve a neutral position in a currency. For being in a "speculative" exposed position, the banks will require compensation. For example, if banks were required to be net sellers of forward dollars, they would probably raise the price of forward dollars. Conversely, if banks find that they are required to be net buyers of dollars, they will reduce the price they will pay.
  3. Thus, fund flow factors of the two types described will cause the interest rate differences between two countries to be greater or less than the differential between the forward and spot exchange rates. Because little work has been done on quantifying these influences, and we are concentrating on the main, directly measurable factors, we will not take into account the additional adjustment term in the analysis which follows.

EXCHANGE-RATE RISK PROTECTION IN FOREIGN OPERATIONS

II. The use of the forward exchange market protects future commitments or receipts.
   A. The forward contract.
      1. It is an agreement for an exchange of two currencies: A into B or B into A
         a. At a specified exchange rate.
         b. At a specified future date.
      2. The basis on which forward contracts are offered.
         a. There are two types of quotations.
            (1) On a discount basis in relation to the present spot rate.
            (2) On a premium basis in relation to the present spot rate.
         b. Which of the two prevails depends on the forward expectations of those in the particular market. Other things being equal:
            (1) If A is expected to decline in value in relation to B by 5% in a specified time period, the quoted discount will be greater than 5% for a contract that calls for an exchange of A into B.
            (2) If A is expected to increase in value by 5% in relation to B during a specified time period, the premium quoted in a forward contract will be less than the expected revaluation. The opposite will prevail if the contract agrees to exchange B into A.
         c. When the expected value change between two currencies is greater than 20% per year it becomes very difficult to obtain forward contract protection.
   B. Measuring the percentage of devaluation or revaluation. Assume that there has been a devaluation of the French franc from 3 per U.S. dollar to 4 per U.S. dollar.
      1. This can be expressed as the percentage change in the number of French francs required to purchase 1 U.S. dollar ($=D_{fd}$).

      For example, where $X_o = 3$ and $X_1 = 4$,

      % change = $(X_1 - X_o)/X_o = (4 - 3)/3 = 1/3$, or $33\ 1/3\% = D_{fd}$.

      There has been an increase of 33 1/3% in the number of French francs required to equal 1 U.S. dollar.
      2. To show the percentage change in the dollar value of the franc ($=D_{df}$),

      $$E_o = \frac{1}{X_o} = \frac{1}{3} \text{ and } E_1 = \frac{1}{X_1} = \frac{1}{4}$$

      Now the percentage change is given by

      $$\% \text{ change} = (E_o - E_1)/E_o = \left(\frac{1}{X_o} - \frac{1}{X_1}\right) / \frac{1}{X_o}$$
      $$= (1/3 - 1/4)/(1/3) = [(4 - 3)/12]/(1/3) = 1/4 = 25\% = D_{df}.$$

      There has been a 25% decrease in the value of the franc in terms of the U.S. dollar.

3. Summary of exchange-rate relationships.
D_{fd} is the change in value in terms of LC/$.
D_{df} is the change in value in terms of $/LC.

$$D_{fd} = \frac{X_1 - X_o}{X_o} = \frac{\frac{1}{E_1} - \frac{1}{E_o}}{\frac{1}{E_o}} = \frac{E_o}{E_1} - 1 = \frac{E_o - E_1}{E_1}$$

$$D_{df} = \frac{E_o - E_1}{E_o} = \frac{\frac{1}{X_o} - \frac{1}{X_1}}{\frac{1}{X_o}} = \frac{X_o}{X_o} - \frac{X_o}{X_1} = \frac{X_1 - X_o}{X_1}$$

C. The following two problems illustrate that by the use of a forward market the dollars that will be received for future receipts in a foreign currency, or the dollars that will have to be paid under a future commitment in foreign currency, can be fixed in amount by the use of the forward market. It will be demonstrated that the gains or losses reflected in the forward rate to current spot rate relationship cannot be avoided without incurring the risk of additional losses of an uncertain amount.

PROBLEM 10-1

The XYZ Company is expecting a payment of LC110,000 in 90 days. The current spot rate on April 1 is LC10/$1. The current forward rate is LC11/$1.
a. If the firm enters the forward market to gain protection from unanticipated changes in the LC rate, will it buy or sell the LC currency?
b. What will it cost the firm to use the forward market?
c. Compare the position of the firm when it does or does not use the forward market. Assume that the future spot rate is equal
   1. to 12
   2. to 8.
d. Comment on the implications of the above.

SOLUTION:

a. The firm will enter the forward market to sell LCs for dollars. This determines the exact number of dollars it will receive in the future.

b.
$$C_f = \frac{F_o}{X_o} - \frac{F_o}{X_f} = E_o F_o - E_f F_o \qquad (10\text{-}1)$$

where:

C_f = cost of the use of the forward market for protection against foreign-exchange-rate fluctuations in the value of future receipts

F_o = current LC amount of future receipts

X_o = spot exchange rate in LC/$1

E_o = spot exchange rate in dollars/LC1

X_f = forward exchange rate in LC/$1

E_f = forward exchange rate in dollars/LC1

$C_f = \frac{110,000}{10} - \frac{110,000}{11} = \$1,000 = (.10)110,000 - (.0909)111,000$.

The cost is $1,000 as compared with the number of dollars that could be received if the LC were received today.

c.
$$A_1 = \frac{F_o}{X_1} = E_1 F_o \qquad (10\text{-}2)$$

where:

A_1 = future dollar value of the LC amount of future receipts

X_1 = future spot exchange rate in LC/$1

E_1 = future spot exchange rate in dollars/LC1

1. $A_1 = \frac{110,000}{12} = \$9,167 = .0933(110,000)$

2. $A_1 = \frac{110,000}{8} = \$13,750 = .125(110,000)$

Thus, without the use of a forward contract the firm could receive much less than $10,000 or much more than $10,000.

d. The use of the forward contract fixes the exact amount of dollars the firm is to receive. This can be taken into account in negotiating the sales price or, if the sales price is given, to determine whether the firm can profitably make a sale at the given nominal price. Note that the use of a forward market does not avoid the decline in the value of the LC anticipated by the forward market. It simply limits the loss to the present decline in the LC value anticipated by the market plus a risk premium.

PROBLEM 10-2

The ABC Company has made a purchase of LC110,000 of merchandise on terms of net 90 days. The current spot rate on April 1 is LC10/$1. The current forward rate is LC11/$1.
A. If the firm enters the forward market to gain protection from unanticipated changes in the LC rate, will it buy or sell LC currency?
B. What will it cost the firm to use the forward market?
C. Compare the position of the firm when it does or does not use the forward market. Assume the future spot rate is equal
  1. to 12.
  2. to 8.
D. Comment upon the implications of the above.

SOLUTION:

A. The ABC Company should enter a 90-day forward contract to buy the LC currency because it will be required to have the LC currency in 90 days.
B. If LC are bought now, the dollar cost would be $\frac{110{,}000}{10} = \$11{,}000$. If LC are bought in a forward contract, the dollar cost would be $\frac{110{,}000}{11} = \$10{,}000$. So net *gain* is $1,000. In other words, because ABC is permitted to delay its payment, it benefits from the expected future decline in the value of the LC currency.
C. Dollars paid in 90 days if no forward contract is used at $X_{1a} = \frac{110{,}000}{12} = \$9{,}167$; at $X_{1b} = \frac{110{,}000}{8} = \$13{,}750$. Thus, without the use of a forward market the firm could pay much less than $10,000 or much more than $10,000.
D. ABC Company could gain even more if the LC devalued to 12, but if the LC should strengthen, ABC would be paying more than the $10,000 it can fix with certainty by buying an LC forward contract. While ABC gains $1,000 by being permitted to delay its payment 3 months, this factor may also be reflected in the price that it pays for the merchandise.

III. The currency swap.
  A. What is a currency swap?
    1. A parent U.S. firm enters into a contract with a foreign central bank to deposit a fixed number of dollars for a specified number of LC currency units of country B.
    2. The foreign central bank makes an LC loan to the parent firm's foreign subsidiary, which pays an interest rate even though no interest is paid on the dollars deposited by the parent with the foreign central bank.
    3. To make the transaction more advantageous to the foreign bank, the swap rate is usually lower than the spot rate. This means that the business firm must use a greater number of dollars in order to obtain a given number of foreign currency units.

B. The purpose of a currency swap.
   1. Official currency swaps have been made between central banks of various major trading nations since the early part of this century. This practice is actively continuing as central banks attempt to intervene in foreign exchange markets for purposes of stabilization.
   2. Swaps between central banks and business firms became prevalent in parts of the world following World War II due to an extreme shortage of convertible foreign exchange by some countries and due to the absence of a forward market for some currencies.
   3. Swaps are used for protection in connection with future receipts and commitments.
C. The types of currency swaps.
   1. Official swaps involve the use of government central banks, while private swaps utilize commercial banks.
   2. Credit swaps. A credit in one currency is exchanged for a credit in another.
   3. Financial swaps. A convertible currency is sold to a central bank on a time basis. At the initiation of the swap, the local currency received is equal in value to the convertible currency sold. At the end of the contract period, additional local currency is paid the seller to make the total amount of local currency received equal to the value of the convertible currency at the end of the contract period.
   4. Export swaps are similar to financial swaps except that the convertible currency is earned from export sales and then sold to the government bank.
D. The cost of a swap.
   1. The cost of a swap is the cost that the parent must pay for the dollars loaned to the bank (or the opportunity cost of these funds) and the interest cost on the local currency paid when the swap matures. Thus, the after-tax cost of a swap is

$$C_s = E_s F_o R_{us} (1-t_{us}) + E_1 F_o R_s (1-t_f) \qquad (10\text{-}3)$$

$$C_s = E_s F_o k_p + E_1 F_o R_s (1-t_f) \qquad (10\text{-}4)$$

where:

C_s = cost of swap

F_o = the amount in foreign currency units to be protected by the swap arrangement

X_o = the spot rate of exchange = $1/E_o$

X_1 = the future spot rate of exchange = $1/E_1$

S_o = the swap rate of exchange = $1/E_s$

k_p = parent company opportunity cost of funds or cost of capital

R_s = the interest rate paid for the local currency obtained via a swap

R_{us} = the cost of debt funds in the United States to the parent

D_{fd} = the rate of devaluation of the LC per \$1 value which is equal to $(X_1 - X_o)/X_o$

D_s = the swap discount which equals $(X_o - S_o)/X_o$

A_o^s = the number of dollars required to obtain F_o foreign currency units using the swap rate S_o for conversion = $E_s F_o = F_o/S_o$

t_f = income tax rate in the foreign country

t_{us} = U.S. income tax rate and tax rate on foreign exchange gains or losses

2. Discussion of the reasons for the use of two equations.
   a. When the cost of a swap is calculated to compare its cost with the cost of an alternative method of obtaining debt funds for the foreign subsidiary, the cost of funds deposited by the parent with the foreign bank to make funds available for the foreign subsidiary is a debt cost. This is measured by the cost of debt funds obtained by the U.S. parent.
   b. When the cost of a swap is involved in the determination of the profitability of a project, the parent firm's cost of capital or opportunity cost of capital is used. Since this is calculated on an after-tax basis, the $(1-t_{us})$ term drops out. Later in this chapter, when the profitability of a project with and without the use of a swap is calculated, equation (10-4) is used. Whenever equation (10-3) is used, it is used to calculate the cost of obtaining debt in one form as compared with alternative forms and sources. For use in making investment decisions, the cost of debt must be weighted with the appropriate proportion and the cost of equity must be combined in appropriate proportions to determine the firm's applicable cost of capital as discussed in Chapter 15.
   c. Initially, it will be assumed that the cost of a swap is calculated for use in comparisons of the cost of alternative forms of debt financing. Hence, equation (10-3). In section (F) below, equation (10-4) is used to determine the profitability of an investment in which a comparison is made between using a swap and not using a swap.
3. *Example:* Assume that the PDQ Corporation will receive LC100,000 in 6 months. No forward market exists for this particular LC, but a swap

EXCHANGE-RATE RISK PROTECTION IN FOREIGN OPERATIONS

arrangement can be obtained from a foreign commercial bank under the following conditions:

$E_o = .10$	$S_o = 5$
$X_o = 10$	$E_s = .20$
$F_o = LC100{,}000$	$t_{us} = .5$
$R_{us} = .12$	$t_f = .4$
$\bar{E}_1 = \$.08$	$R_s = .20$
$\bar{X}_1 = 12.5$	The bar denotes expected value.

What would be the cost of a swap, compared with the loss if no protective position were taken, with respect to the future receipts?

Answer: (The annual interest rate is divided by 2 because the swap period is 6 months.)

$$\bar{C}_s = E_s F_o R_{us}(1-t_{us}) + \bar{E}_1 F_o R_s (1-t_f)$$

$$\bar{C}_s = .20(100{,}000)(\tfrac{.12}{2})(.5) + .08(100{,}000)(\tfrac{.20}{2})(.6)$$

$$= \$600 + \$480$$

$$= \$1{,}080$$

The expected loss without the swap is:

$$(E_o - \bar{E}_1)F_o(1-t_{us}) = (.10-.08)(100{,}000)(.5) = \$1{,}000 \quad (10\text{-}5)$$

a. Hence, the loss would be less than the cost of the swap. However, the swap reduces the risk of loss from further devaluation.
b. For example, if E_1 actually turned out to be \$.06, the comparison would be:

$$C_s = \$600 + .06(100{,}000)(\tfrac{.20}{2})(.6)$$

$$= \$600 + 360$$

$$= \$960$$

The loss without the swap is

$$(.10-.06)(100{,}000)(.5) = \$2{,}000$$

c. Hence, the swap may:
      (1) Reduce the cost of a decline in the future LC value.
      (2) Reduce the risk of uncertain future LC values.
E. The use of a swap in an investment project.
   1. A swap is advisable whenever the overall profitability of an investment is greater than the sum of the U.S. opportunity cost (R_p) and the swap costs to protect against exposure of the funds employed.
   2. Additional symbols used.

   A_o = number of dollars required to obtain F_o foreign currency units used to spot rate X_o for conversion = $E_o F_o = F_o/X_o$

   g_f = annual growth rate of an investment in a foreign country or its annual rate of profitability

   $\bar{R}_g^n$ = the annual expected rate of profitability of an investment not using swap protection

   $\bar{R}_g^s$ = the annual expected rate of profitability of an investment making use of a currency swap

   Since the spot rate is usually greater than the swap rate, $A_o^s = (F_o/S_o)$ is usually greater than $A_o = (F_o/X_o)$, because it takes a greater number of dollars at a lower exchange rate to obtain a specified number of local currency units.
   3. Comparison of swap versus no-swap for investments.
      a. The expected rate of profitability of a no-swap investment is

      $$\bar{R}_g^n = \left(\frac{X_o}{\bar{X}_1}\right)[1+g_f(1-t_f)] - (1+k_p) \qquad (10\text{-}6)$$

      b. The rate of profitability of the same investment *with* the swap is

      $$\bar{R}_g^s = \left(\frac{S_o}{\bar{X}_1}\right)(g_f-R_s)(1-t_f) - k_p \qquad (10\text{-}7)$$

      c. The swap is advisable whenever

      $$\bar{R}_g^s > \bar{R}_g^n, \text{ or}$$

      $$\left(\frac{S_o}{\bar{X}_1}\right)(g_f-R_s)(1-t_f) - k_p > \left(\frac{X_o}{\bar{X}_1}\right)[1+g_f(1-t_f)] - (1+k_p)$$

From this relationship, one can derive that the swap is beneficial when the following relationship holds:

$$\frac{\bar{D}_{fd}}{(1-t_f)} > R_s + D_s(g_f - R_s) \tag{10-8}$$

4. *Example:* Firm A in country X approaches the U.S. based Interglobal Corporation (IGC) about installing and setting up a factory in country X. The project would take 1 year to complete and would cost IGC LC100 million. Firm A will pay LC180 million to IGC for the installation, so the gross return would be 80%. The current spot rate is LC100 = $1. IGC's planning group predicts that the exchange rate at year end will be LC150 = $1. There is no forward contract market for the LC and IGC could not borrow locally. A swap arrangement is available with the country X central bank such that the swap rate is equal to LC50 = $1, with a swap interest rate of 10%. IGC's opportunity cost for projects of equivalent risk is 12%. The U.S. tax rate is 50%, and the local tax rate is 40%. What is IGC's profit percentage
   a. if no swap is used?
   b. if a swap is used?

Answer:

a. The profitability when no swap is used.

$$\bar{R}_g^n = \left(\frac{X_o}{\bar{X}_1}\right)[1+g_f(1-t_f)] - (1+k_p)$$

$$= \left(\frac{100}{150}\right)[1+(.8)(.6)] - (1+.12)$$

$$= -.133$$

$$= -13.3\%$$

b. The profitability when the swap is used.

$$\bar{R}_g^s = \left(\frac{S_o}{\bar{X}_1}\right)(g_f - R_s)(1-t_f) - k_p$$

$$= \left(\frac{50}{150}\right)(.8-.1)(.6) - (.12)$$

$$= .02$$

$$= 2\%$$

c. The swap is preferable. Note that even with a nominal profit of 80% on the project, when swap costs and the opportunity cost of funds are taken into account, there is a net incremental return of only 2% over the U.S. opportunity cost of capital.

PROBLEM 10-3

The U.S. based GYA Corporation's subsidiary in country N needs a LC100,000 working capital loan. The current exchange rate is LC1 = $.25. GYA expects the exchange rate to fall to LC1 = $.20 by the time of repayment. A swap is available with a swap rate of LC1 = $.50 and a swap interest rate of 15%. GYA's cost of borrowing the funds is 10%, the marginal tax rate in country N is 40%, and the marginal tax rate in the United States is 50%. What is the dollar cost and percentage cost of the swap? What is the expected loss without using the swap?

SOLUTION:

The cost is given by

$$\bar{C}_s = E_s F_o R_{us}(1-t_{us}) + \bar{E}_1 F_o R_s(1-t_f)$$

$E_s = \$.50$; $E_o = \$.25$; $\bar{E}_1 = \$.20$;
$F_o = \text{LC}100{,}000$; $t_f = .4$; $t_{us} = .5$

$$\bar{C}_s = (.50)(100{,}000)(.10)(.5) + (.20)(100{,}000)(.15)(.6)$$
$$= \$2{,}500 + \$1{,}800$$
$$= \$4{,}300$$

The dollar amount of funds required for the swap is

$$A_s^o = E_s F_o = (.50)(100{,}000) = \$50{,}000$$

Hence the percentage cost is

$$\bar{c} = \left(\frac{\bar{C}_s}{A_s^o}\right) = \frac{\$4{,}300}{50{,}000} = 8.6\%.$$

The expected loss without the swap is

$$(E_o - \bar{E}_1) F_o (1-t_{us}) = (.25-.20)100{,}000(.5)$$
$$= \$2{,}500$$

The expected percentage loss is

$$\frac{\$2,500}{E_o F_o} = \frac{\$2,500}{25,000} = 10\%$$

Here the swap reduces the risk and costs less than the expected loss, so it should be used.

PROBLEM 10-4

The Dennison Pump Company's South American subsidiary has requested an additional LC1 million to expand its manufacturing facilities, and the funds would be repaid at year end. The funds needed cannot be borrowed locally or from any other alternative source. The annual rate of return on the investment is expected to be 25%. The local currency is expected to continue its downward trend in relation to the U.S. dollar at an annual rate of 20%.

The present spot rate is LC50 per $1. A currency swap is available from the country's central bank with a swap rate of LC45 per $, and an interest rate on the local funds thus obtained at 10%. The firm's opportunity rate in the United States is .12%. The marginal tax rates in the foreign country and the United States are 40% and 50% respectively. How will the use of a swap or non-use of a swap influence the firm's investment decision?

SOLUTION:

$$g_f = .25;\ S_o = 45;\ X_o = 50;\ \bar{D}_{fd} = .20;$$
$$k_p = .12;\ R_s = .10;\ t_f = .40;\ t_{us} = .50$$

Without the swap, the profitability is

$$\bar{R}_g^n = \left(\frac{X_o}{\bar{X}_1}\right)(1+g_f(1-t_f)) - (1+k_p)$$

To compute $\bar{X}_1$, $X_o \bar{D}_{fd} = \bar{X}_1 - X_o$, so $\bar{X}_1 = X_o(1+\bar{D}_{fd}) = 50(1+.2) = 60$

$$\bar{R}_g^n = \left(\frac{50}{60}\right)[1+.25(.6)] - (1+.12)$$
$$= .9583 - 1.12$$
$$= -.1617$$
$$= -16.17\%$$

With the swap, the profitability is

$$\bar{R}_g^s = \left(\frac{S_o}{\bar{X}_1}\right)(g_f - R_s)(1-t_f) - k_p$$

$$= \left(\frac{45}{60}\right)(.25-.10)(.6) - .12$$

$$= .0675 - .12$$

$$= -.0525$$

$$= -5.25\%$$

The firm should not make the investment since it would not earn its cost of capital on the project.

PROBLEM 10-5

The BMC Corporation is contemplating an investment of LC150,000 in its foreign subsidiary. Its expected rate of return on the investment is 70%. The current exchange rate is LC15 to the $. The expected exchange rate at the end of the 1-year investment period is LC20. The opportunity cost of money in the United States is 12% for projects of similar risk. The firm can buy a swap at LC10 per $1 and would be required to pay an interest rate of 20%. The local marginal income tax rate is 40% while the marginal income tax rate in the United States is 50%.

Under the assumptions, calculate the return
1. Without a swap.
2. With a swap.
3. Would you advise the BMC Corporation to make the investment and, if so, should it use a swap?

SOLUTION:

$$g_f = .70;\ X_o = 15,\ \bar{X}_1 = 20,\ S_o = 10,$$
$$R_s = .2;\ k_p = .12;\ t_f = .40;\ t_{us} = .50$$

1. Without the swap, the rate of profitability is

$$\bar{R}_g^n = \left(\frac{X_o}{\bar{X}_1}\right)[1+g_f(1-t_f)] - (1+k_p)$$

$$= \left(\frac{15}{20}\right)[1+.70(.6)] - (1+.12)$$

$$= 1.065 - 1.12$$

$= -.055$

$= -5.5\%$

2. With the swap, the rate of profitability is

$$\bar{R}_g^s = \left(\frac{S_o}{\bar{X}_1}\right)(g_f - R_s)(1 - t_f) - k_p$$

$$= \left(\frac{10}{20}\right)(.70 - .20)(.6) - (.12)$$

$$= .15 - .12$$

$$= .03$$

$$= 3\%$$

3. If the opportunity cost is for projects of equivalent risk, then the investment should be made and BMC should use the swap.

IV. The concept of monetary balance.
   A. Effects of price-level changes.
      1. Effects of price-level inflation.
         a. Firms or persons in a net monetary liability position gain purchasing power at the expense of their creditors.
         b. Firms or persons in a net monetary asset position lose purchasing power to the advantage of their debtors.
      2. Effects of falling prices.
         a. Creditors gain at the expense of debtors.
         b. Debtors lose to the benefit of creditors.
   B. Monetary assets (MA) versus monetary liabilities (ML).
      1. Monetary assets are those assets denominated in a fixed number of units of money. Among monetary assets are:
         a. Cash.
         b. Marketable securities.
         c. Accounts receivable.
         d. Tax refunds receivable.
         e. Notes receivable.
         f. Prepaid insurance.
      2. Monetary liabilities are those liabilities expressed in fixed monetary terms. They include:
         a. Accounts payable.
         b. Notes payable.
         c. Tax liability reserves.
         d. Bonds.
         e. Preferred stock.

C. A net monetary position results in gains or losses from exchange-rate fluctuations. Net monetary position $(NMP) = (MA-ML)$. Note that when monetary liabilities exceed monetary assets, NMP has a negative value.

1. $C_p = [(MA-ML)/X_o - (MA-ML)/X_1](1-t_{us})$
   $= (E_o-E_1)(MA-ML)(1-t_{us})$
   $= (E_o-E_1)(NMP)(1-t_{us})$

   where:

   C_p = cost of a NMP due to exchange-rate changes
   MA = monetary assets
   ML = monetary liabilities
   X_o = exchange rate at the beginning = $1/E_o$
   X_1 = exchange rate a period later = $1/E_1$
   t_{us} = tax rate in the United States

2. Effects of a decline in LC value.
   a. Net monetary debtor gains.
   b. Net monetary creditor losses.
   c. Examples.

   MA = LC200,000; X_o = 4; t_{us} = .5;
   ML = LC100,000; X_1 = 5

   (1) $NMP = MA - ML = 200{,}000 - 100{,}000 = 100{,}000$

   $C_p = NMP(E_o-E_1)(1-t_{us}) = 100{,}000(.25-.20)(.5)$
   $= \$5{,}000(.5) = \$2{,}500$ \hfill (10-9)

   Decrease in dollar value of asset position = loss = $2,500

   (2) Let ML = LC300,000

   $NMP = MA - ML = 200{,}000 - 300{,}000 = -100{,}000$
   $C_p = NMP(E_o-E_1)(1-t_{us}) = -100{,}000(.25-.20)(.5)$
   $= -\$2{,}500$

   The net amount owed is decreased by $2,500, representing a gain.

3. Effects of an increase in LC value.
   a. Net monetary debtor losses.
   b. Net monetary creditor gains.
   c. Examples.

   (1) MA = LC10 million X_o = 5
         ML = LC8 million X_1 = 4

   NMP = 10,000,000 − 8,000,000 = 2,000,000

   C_p = $NMP(E_o - E_1)$ = 2,000,000(.20−.25) = −$100,000

   The cost is a negative $100,000, representing a gain in the value of the net monetary position with revaluation upward in the LC currency.

   (2) Let MA = LC6 million

   NMP = 6,000,000 − 8,000,000 = −2,000,000

   C_p = $NMP(E_o - E_1)$ = −2,000,000(.20−.25) = +$100,000

   Both terms are negative, so their product is positive, indicating that revaluation upward results in a positive cost (or a *loss*) to a firm in a negative net monetary position (monetary liabilities exceed monetary assets). The LC values of its net obligations have increased.

D. Protection against an exposed net monetary position.
   1. A foreign subsidiary is usually in a positive net monetary position because its cash and accounts receivable are greater than its monetary liabilities. How can the exposed position be protected? Should the exposed position be protected?
      a. If the foreign currency revalues upward, the NMP provides a gain, so revaluation is not a risk of a positive NMP. Devaluation is the unfavorable event against which protective action is required by an exposed NMP.
      b. The exposed position can be protected (neutralized) by borrowing in the foreign currency in which the subsidiary is in a positive net monetary asset position and investing in a strong currency or real assets.
      c. The cost of neutralizing the exposed position can be compared with the expected loss from the exposed position. However, this does not provide a basis for a decision, because the risk position under the neutral net monetary position must be compared with the risk position of the firm when it is in an exposed position, as will be discussed below.

2. The first step in the comparison is to determine the expected loss from the exposed position. The expected loss from the exposed position is the after-tax loss due to devaluation of the local currency.
   a. The amount of the expected loss is calculated using a slight modification of equation (10-9), in which F_o is used for NMP and $\bar{E}_1$ is the expected value of E_1.

   $$\bar{C}_p = (E_o - \bar{E}_1)(1 - t_{us}) \qquad (10\text{-}10)$$

   b. To illustrate the application of equation (10-10), assume the following:

   $$E_o = .25;\ \bar{E}_1 = .20;\ t_{us} = .50;\ R_f = .25$$
   $$t_f = .40;\ NMP = F_o = LC100{,}000;\ R_{us} = .10$$

   The dollar amount of expected loss from the net monetary position exposure is:

   $$C_p = 100{,}000\,(.25 - .20)\,(.5) = \$2{,}500$$

   c. The expected percentage loss is obtained by dividing C_p by the current dollar value of the exposed position, $F_o E_o$, as shown in equation (10-11), where $\bar{R}_e$ = expected percentage loss from the exposed NMP.

   $$\bar{R}_e = \frac{F_o(E_o - \bar{E}_1)(1-t_{us})}{F_o E_o} = \frac{E_o - \bar{E}_1(1-t_{us})}{E_o} = \bar{D}_{df}(1-t_{us}) \qquad (10\text{-}11)$$

   For the data given, the percentage loss would be:

   $$\bar{R}_e = \frac{E_o - \bar{E}_1}{E_o}(1-t_{us}) = \frac{.25 - .20}{.25}(.5) = 10\%$$

   The expected percentage loss from the exposed NMP is therefore the after-tax expected percent devaluation of the dollar value of the foreign currency.

3. Next, the cost of neutralizing the exposed NMP by borrowing in the foreign currency in which the subsidiary is in a positive NMP should be calculated and compared with the expected percentage loss from the exposed NMP. Therefore, we must next calculate the net after-tax cost of borrowing in the local currency. F_o is borrowed at $R_f(1-t_f)$. The interest is paid at the end of the period, and the interest that can be earned by the use of the funds must also be taken into account as shown in equation (10-12).

EXCHANGE-RATE RISK PROTECTION IN FOREIGN OPERATIONS

a. The net after-tax cost of borrowing in the foreign currency will be:

$$k_b = \frac{E_1 F_o R_f(1-t_f)}{E_o F_o} - \frac{E_o F_o R_{us}(1-t_{us})}{E_o F_o}$$

$$= \frac{\bar{E}_1}{E_o} R_f(1-t_f) - R_{us}(1-t_{us})$$

(10-12)

b. Given the values assumed above, we can calculate k_b by solving equation (10-12).

$$k_b = \frac{.20}{.25}(.25)(.6) - .10(.5) = .12 - .05 = .07 = 7\%$$

c. It will cost 7% to avoid an expected 10% loss. This clearly is advantageous. Furthermore, if the actual E_1 is lower than the expected E_1, a greater actual loss is avoided. Thus, the maximum cost can be limited by borrowing in the foreign currency of the exposed position.

4. The next question is what can the nominal R_f be and still represent a cost no greater than the expected loss?

   a. In general terms, the relation required to make it worthwhile to borrow in the foreign country to neutralize an exposed net monetary asset position is:

$$E_1 R_f(1-t_f) - E_o R_{us}(1-t_{us}) < (E_o - E_1)(1-t_{us})$$

(10-13)

This reduces to:

$$R_f \leq \left(\frac{1-t_{us}}{1-t_f}\right)[R_{us}(1+D_{fd}) + D_{fd}]$$

(10-13a)

   b. Inserting all parameters except R_f, we obtain:

$$R_f \leq \left(\frac{1-.5}{1-.4}\right)[.10(1.25)+.25]$$

$$\leq \frac{.5}{.6}(.375)$$

$$\leq .3125$$

   c. Thus, the nominal R_f could be as high as 31.25% and enable the firm to fix the percentage cost of the exposed NMP at a level no greater than the expected loss.

5. Or we can solve for the minimum rate of devaluation for borrowing foreign to be profitable, if the R_f is given at 35%, for example.
   a. We solve equation (10-13a) for D_{fd} as shown in equation (10-13b).

   $$D_{fd} \geq \frac{(1-t_f)}{(1-t_{us})} R_f \left(\frac{1}{1+R_{us}}\right) - \frac{R_{us}}{(1+R_{us})} \qquad (10\text{-}13b)$$

   $$\geq \frac{1-.4}{1-.5}(.35)\frac{1}{1.10} - \frac{.10}{1.10}$$

   $$\geq \frac{.42-.10}{1.10}$$

   $$\bar{D}_{fd} \geq .291$$

   b. Given the $E_o = .25$, we can also solve for the E_1 value which would represent a devaluation of 29.1%.

   $$\frac{E_o - E_1}{E_1} = D_{fd} = .291$$

   $$\frac{E_o}{E_1} = 1.291$$

   $$1.291\, E_1 = .25$$

   $$E_1 = .1936$$

6. It is sometimes assumed that the subsidiary can profitably employ the funds required to establish a neutral monetary net asset position.
   a. In this case, replace $R_{us}(1-t_{us})$ in equation (10-13) with k_s which represents the subsidiary's after-tax foreign opportunity return.

   $$\bar{E}_1 R_f(1-t_f) - E_o k_s < (E_o - E_1)(1-t_{us}) \qquad (10\text{-}13c)$$

   b. The result is equation (10-14)

   $$R_f \leq \frac{(1-t_{us})}{(1-t_f)} \bar{D}_{fd} + \frac{(1+\bar{D}_{fd})}{(1-t_f)} k_s \qquad (10\text{-}14)$$

   c. If $k_s = .12$, the breakeven R_f becomes

   $$R_f \leq \frac{(.5)}{(.6)}(.25) + \frac{(1.25)}{(.6)}(.12)$$

   $$R_f \leq .458$$

d. But this mixes a profit-making opportunity with protecting an exposed position. Therefore, equation (10-12) is the most relevant equation to employ. As shown in equation (10-13c), the opportunity return from the funds is an offset to the R_f term. Hence, the foreign borrowing rate can now be higher because the after-tax opportunity return from the funds is higher.
E. An exposed net debtor position in a strong currency.
1. A strong currency such as the German mark at any point in time may be overvalued and decline in value in any future 2- to 3-month period.
2. However, firms would be concerned about being in a negative net monetary position (debtor position) in a strong currency country because of the loss if revaluation takes place.
3. Protective devices to deal with a net debtor position in a currency likely to revalue. Let R be a currency likely to revalue and N be a currency most likely to remain unchanged in its foreign exchange value.
a. Borrow in currency N and use the funds to buy government bonds denominated in currency R so that the net monetary position of the firm is neutralized. The interest earned on the R bonds is likely to be relatively low reflecting the probable premium in the forward rate on currency R.
b. Borrow in currency N not likely to revalue and pay off the debt in currency R likely to revalue. The cost will also reflect an interest rate differential.

V. Centralization and an overview of the firm's position and its alternatives.
A. Centralization and covering net flows or net exposure.
1. Since protecting against exposure is expensive, it is important not to duplicate protective actions.
2. If one subsidiary of the MNC firm is in a positive net monetary position in currency D (likely to devalue) while other subsidiaries are in a negative net monetary position, the overall position of the MNC firm may net out to a neutral position or only a small net monetary asset or liability position remain to be covered, currency by currency.
3. If feasible, firms are therefore likely to centralize analysis of the company exposure on receipts versus commitments and on financial positions in the individual segments of its account.
B. Use of the forward market versus the money market.
1. A future net position in a currency will reflect the current balance sheet position plus future receipts and commitments.
a. Exposure may therefore result from a financial position plus future flows.
b. Protection against exposure involves a number of alternative transactions.

2. Alternative methods of "going short" in currency D (likely to devalue).
   a. Developing a net monetary debtor position in currency D.
   b. Borrowing in currency D is going short in currency D–a firm will gain if currency D declines in value.
   c. Selling currency D in the forward market is going short in currency D–if the future spot rate of currency D is below the current forward rate, the firm will gain when it purchases currency D in the future to cover its forward sale.
3. Alternative methods of "going long" in currency R (likely to revalue upward).
   a. Developing a net monetary asset position in currency R.
   b. Developing receivables or buying the bonds of a country or firms in currency R represents a long position–a firm will gain when these monetary assets are paid off in a higher valued currency.
   c. Buying currency R in the forward market is going long in currency R–if the future spot rate of currency R is above the current forward rate, the firm will gain when it receives currency R in the future under its forward purchase.

C. Since borrowing or lending in a currency is similar to selling or buying the currency in the forward market, it is useful to consider both alternatives when considering possible actions in relation to balance sheet exposure or from future receipts and commitments.

PROBLEM 10-6

On January 1, 1976, U.S. parent expects to receive LC100,000 on December 31, 1976, from its subsidiary in Elsie-land (whose currency is the LC). The spot and forward rates for January and the expected values for December of the given year are:

January 1, 1976

Spot rate	LC10/$
One-year forward rate	LC12/$
Expected December 31, 1976 spot rate	LC11/$

December 31, 1976

Actual spot rate	LC14/$

Consider the following alternatives.

Alternative 1: Enter a December 31 forward contract to sell LC100,000. Cover by receipt of LC100,000 on December 31.

Alternative 2: Have the subsidiary borrow LC100,000, buy spot dollars and remit to parent. Funds in the United States earn 10%. On December 31, the subsidiary repays loan plus interest on loan at 30%. The applicable tax rate in Elsie-land is 40%; in the United States it is 50%.

EXCHANGE-RATE RISK PROTECTION IN FOREIGN OPERATIONS

Alternative 3: Accept the exchange-rate risk. The parent is paid at the spot rate on December 31, 1976.

A. What are the expected receipts under the three alternatives?
B. If X_1 is actually 14, what would the receipts be under each alternative?
C. What factors would the parent consider in selecting among the three alternatives?

SOLUTION:

A. **Alternative 1:**

$$F_o/X_f = 100,000/12 = \$8,333$$

Alternative 2:

Expected receipts $= (F_o/X_o) + (F_o/X_o)R_{us}(1-t_{us}) - (F_o/X_1)(R_f)(1-t_f)$

$(F_o/X_o) = 100,000/10 = \$10,000$

$(F_o/X_o)[R_{us}(1-t_{us})] = 10,000(.05) = 500$

$(F_o/\bar{X}_1)[R_f(1-t_f)] = \dfrac{100,000}{11}[(.30)(.6)] = \$1,640$

Expected receipts $= 10,000 + 500 - 1,640$
$= \$8,860$

Alternative 3:

$$F_o/\bar{X}_1 = 100,000/11 = \$9,090$$

B. **Alternative 1:**

$$F_o/X_f = 100,000/12 = \$8,333$$

Alternative 2:

The foreign interest cost becomes $\dfrac{100,000}{14}(.18) = \$1,290$, so receive $\$9,210$.

Alternative 3:

$100,000/14 = \$7,140$

C. Evaluation.
   1. Note that the use of alternative 1 eliminates all risk at a cost, but is never the best of the alternatives in terms of expected receipts.
   2. Alternative 2 eliminates all risk except the risk on the interest to be paid on the local borrowing. This interest cost could also be protected by the use of the forward market, but would add to the costs of alternative 2 which provides the greatest expected receipts when $X_1 = 14$.

3. Alternative 3 is best if the future spot exchange value of the foreign currency does not deviate from expectations under (a) of LC11/$1. However, it involves the greatest risk exposure.

Comments: Clearly, there is a trade-off between the degree of remaining risk exposure and costs. Some managements are willing to incur costs to reduce risks. Others avoid the costs, but are required to report substantial losses periodically.

Over the long run, if a firm were well diversified across currencies and balanced with regard to its NMP and future receipts, its losses (if no protection were used) would approximate the costs of obtaining protection in efficient foreign exchange and money markets. So in a sense, the purchase of protection is a cost required when the conditions for diversification of foreign exchange risks are not available to the firm.

PROBLEM 10-7

U.S. based Worldmotors purchased LC100,000 of machine equipment at the beginning of the year from firm A in country X. Country X's currency has been revaluing for the past 2 years and Worldmotors predicts the LC will revalue from the current spot rate of LC5=$1 to LC4.80=$1 by year end, when payment for the equipment will be due. The applicable tax rate in country X is 40%; in the United States the rate is 50%. The forward rate for 1-year contract is LC4.9=$1. Worldmotor's opportunity cost in the United States for the funds to pay the debt is 10%, and it can buy 1-year country X government bonds with a yield of 5.0%. Consider the following alternatives.

Alternative 1: Enter into a 1-year forward contract to buy LC and use the funds in the United States until year end. Then use the forward contract to pay the commitment.

Alternative 2: Convert the funds to country X currency at the spot rate and invest in government bonds. Convert only enough so that the principal plus interest at year end will equal the commitment of LC100,000.

Alternative 3: Convert the funds to country X currency and pay the commitment off immediately.

Alternative 4: Use the funds in the United States and convert at the spot rate at year end to pay the obligation.

SOLUTION:

Alternative 1:

$$C_f = F_o/X_f = 100{,}000/4.9 = \$20{,}410$$

EXCHANGE-RATE RISK PROTECTION IN FOREIGN OPERATIONS

Alternative 2:

Let A be the amount of dollars needed at the beginning of the year, so that A plus the interest on A will equal the commitment.

Convert to LC. $X_o A[1+R_f(1-t_f)] = F_o$

$$5A[1+.05(1-.40)] = LC100,000$$
$$5(1.03)A = LC100,000$$
$$5.15A = LC100,000$$
$$A = \$19,417$$

The cost of borrowed dollars converted at the beginning of the year is:

$$= A[1+R_{us}(1-t_{us})]$$
$$= A[1+(.1)(.5)]$$
$$= 19,417(1.05)$$
$$= \$20,390$$

Alternative 3:

$$F_o/X_o = 100,000/5 = \$20,000$$

Opportunity value of prepayment:

$$F_o/X_o[1+(.1)(.5)] = 20,000(1.05) = \$21,000$$

Alternative 4:

$$F_o/\bar{X}_1 = 100,000/4.80 = \$20,833$$

Comments: Since the currency in X is likely to revalue, we seek to cover the exposed liability position by investing in government bonds of country X or use the forward market to go long in the X country currency to offset our short position represented by the liability. Both eliminate uncertainty, but the interest rate relations make the use of the money market in X somewhat less costly than the use of the forward market.

Alternative 3 involves the loss of earnings that could have been achieved on the funds. Alternative 4 involves the greatest risk exposure. In addition, the expected strengthening of X currency means that the liability will require a larger number of dollars at year end.

PROBLEM 10-8

The MNC Company has a net monetary asset position of LC200,000 in country X. The following parameters are used as the basis for making a decision.

$E_o = .25$; $t_{us} = .50$; $R_{us} = .10$;
$\bar{E}_1 = .20$; $t_f = .40$; $R_f = .25$; $E_f = .21$

MNC is considering these alternatives to protect its exposed position:
Alternative 1: Borrow LC200,000, convert to dollars, and invest at U.S. rates; repay at the end of 1 year.
Alternative 2: Enter into a contract to sell LC200,000 in the forward market.
Alternative 3 Do nothing.
Which alternative will involve the least cost?

SOLUTION:

Alternative 1:

$$\text{Cost} = E_1 F_o R_f (1-t_f) - E_o F_o R_{us}(1-t_{us})$$
$$= .20(200,000)(.25)(.6) - .25(200,000)(.10)(.5)$$
$$= \$6,000 - 2,500$$
$$= \$3,500$$

Alternative 2:

$$\text{Cost} = F_o(E_f - E_o)(1 - t_{us})$$
$$= 200,000(.25 - .21)(1-t_{us})$$
$$= \$4,000$$

Alternative 3:

$$\text{Cost} = F_o(E_o - \bar{E}_1)(1 - t_{us})$$
$$= (200,000).05(.5)$$
$$= \$5,000$$

Comments: Alternative 1 involves the use of borrowing in the local currency, so the net monetary asset position of MNC is neutralized. The cost reflects the higher interest rates in country X as compared with the opportunity earning rate of the funds.

The use of the forward market does not neutralize the net monetary asset position of MNC. It simply fixes the amount of loss to the difference between the forward rate and the spot rate.

Alternative 3 provides no protection for the exposed position. It therefore involves the greatest risk. Even if it were less costly under the assumptions, this alternative might be avoided because of the uncertainty remaining.

PROBLEM 10-9

The methods of seeking protection against foreign-exchange-rate fluctuations discussed in this chapter emphasize alternative strategies for dealing with the risks involved in an individual transaction. Discuss how the analysis should be extended to take the point of view of the firm as a whole, viewing the totality of its balance sheet positions as well as the total pattern of receipts and outflows on its many transactions involving all of the countries with which it does business in its international operations.

SOLUTION:

The basic principles for exchange-rate risk protection that we emphasize throughout this book may be restated here. It is not the intuitively appealing method. An apparently practical commonsense method would recommend: "Forecast foreign exchange rates in all the countries in which the firm does business. Where foreign exchange rates are expected to decline, the firm should take a position that benefits from a decline in foreign exchange rates. Conversely, if foreign exchange rates are expected to rise, the firm should take a position which enables it to benefit from a rise in foreign exchange rates."

If a firm were to follow the recommendation quoted above, it would have to devote considerable resources to efforts to achieve forecasts superior to the forecasts implicit in the set of foreign exchange rates observed in the international financial markets. However, our position is that international foreign exchange markets are sufficiently efficient so that attempts to "beat the international foreign exchange markets" are likely to be either unsuccessful or yield no more than normal compensation for such efforts.

An alternative approach is to attempt to avoid exposure to fluctuations in foreign exchange rates. A firm, taking its current balance sheet position and prospective receipts and outflows into account, will be in either a net monetary asset or a net monetary liability position. So it will be exposed to foreign-exchange-rate fluctuation risks. Quotations in the forward exchange markets have already taken anticipated exchange-rate fluctuations into account so they will involve costs if used in the effort to limit risks. Thus, the only method of avoiding the costs of exchange-rate fluctuations is to avoid being in an exposed position. This, too, involves transactions costs which must be taken into account. The firm must compare the costs of attempting to forecast exchange-rate fluctuations and taking appropriate positions in relation thereto versus the costs of seeking to avoid exposure to foreign-exchange-rate fluctuations.

In seeking to set forth in a relatively simple fashion alternative methods of achieving exchange-rate risk protection, we have necessarily emphasized individual transactions. In this setting, the impact of alternative methods of seeking exchange-rate risk protection are seen most clearly. However, we recognize that the task of the firm is to seek to deal with exchange-rate risk protection and the other needs of international financial management as an ongoing firm involved in a series of investments and a continuous series of transactions on a worldwide basis. To adequately deal with these requirements in a quantitative way requires a financial planning model. The complexity of such models is beyond the scope of this overview of international financial management. The problem in its broader setting is discussed by Sidney M. Robbins and Robert B. Stobaugh in their book, *Money in the Multinational Enterprise: A Study of Financial Policy*. See particularly the presentation of a "simulation model of a multinational enterprise" developed by Daniel M. Schydlowsky and presented in Appendix B of their book.

REFERENCES

Aliber, Robert Z., and Clyde P. Stickney: "Accounting Measures of Foreign Exchange Exposure: The Long and Short of It," *The Accounting Review*, **50**:44-57, January 1975.

Balassa, Bela: "The Purchasing Power Parity Doctrine: A Reappraisal," *Journal of Political Economy*, **72**:584-596, December 1964.

Dufey, Gunter: "Corporate Finance and Exchange Rate Variations," *Financial Management*, **1**:51-57, Summer 1972.

Gailliot, Henry J.: "Purchasing Power Parity as an Explanation of Long-Term Changes in Exchange Rates," *Journal of Money, Credit and Banking*, **2**:348-375, August 1970.

Giddy, Ian H., and Gunter Dufey: "The Random Behavior of Flexible Exchange Rates: Implications for Forecasting," *Journal of International Business Studies*, **6**:1-32, Spring 1975.

Heckerman, Donald: "The Exchange Risks of Foreign Operations," *The Journal of Business*, **45**:42-48, January 1972.

Horst, Thomas: "The Theory of the Multinational Firm: Optimal Behavior under Different Tariff and Tax Rates," *Journal of Political Economy*, **79**:1059-1072, September/October 1971.

May, L. Chester: "Managing the Multinationals' International Exchange Risks," *The Conference Board Record*, October 1975, pp. 45-48.

Robbins, Sidney M., and Robert B. Stobaugh: *Money in the Multinational Enterprise: A Study in Financial Policy*, Basic Books, New York, 1972.

Shapiro, Alan C.: "Exchange Rate Changes, Inflation, and the Value of the Multinational Corporation," *The Journal of Finance*, **30**:485-500, May 1975.

Solnik, Bruno H.: "An Equilibrium Model of the International Capital Market," *Journal of Economic Theory,* 8:500-524, 1974.

———: *European Capital Markets,* Lexington Books, Lexington, Mass., 1973.

Stein, Jerome L.: "The Forward Rate and the Interest Parity," *The Review of Economic Studies,* 32:113-126, April 1965.

Stoll, Hans: "An Empirical Study of the Foreign Exchange Market under Fixed and Flexible Exchange Rate Systems," *The Canadian Journal of Economics,* 1:55-78, February 1968.

Chapter 11

International Working Capital Management

Theme: On an international basis, working capital management has become one of the most important financial activities in multinational firms. The development of fluctuating exchange rates since August 1971 has added a new dimension to the management of working capital, the management of the net monetary position for all parts of an international organization. International banks, after heavy losses in recent years, seek to operate on a nonexposed basis in all foreign currencies. Similarly, the working capital manager of a multinational firm must make every effort to avoid seriously exposed positions either on the asset or liability side of the balance sheet. If found in an exposed position unexpectedly, he must make every effort to change it and undertake measures that would ease the exposure of his firm. The advent of the Financial Accounting Standards Board (FASB) Statement No. 8 in November 1975 has greatly increased the need for action. Foreign exchange translation, gains or losses, can no longer be charged or credited to a valuation reserve account. They must now be taken into account when determining gains or losses for the period in which foreign-exchange-rate changes took place. This chapter discusses some possible solutions to this important problem.

  I. Working capital management. In general, working capital includes all current assets and current liabilities, funds which even on a normal domestic basis require a large percentage of the time of financial personnel.

A. Current assets.
   1. Cash must be available in sufficient quantities to meet normal needs as well as those unforeseen events for which a firm must have a precautionary balance on hand.
   2. The collection of receivables must be accelerated so funds due will be available for reassignment as soon as possible.
   3. Inventories must be on hand in ample quantities to meet the needs of the firm and its customers. Yet excess quantities must be avoided.
B. Current liabilities. Payables should be deferred until the due date. The firm gains nothing by paying its bills ahead of time.
C. Foreign-exchange-rate risk.
   1. This risk occurs as a result of value changes of one currency in relation to another.
   2. This requires that the multinational firm, on an overall basis, not be exposed from a monetary asset or monetary liability point of view.
   3. In order to be informed of impending value changes, continuing studies need to be made in an attempt to predict the occurrence of these value changes so that preventative actions may be taken.
D. Float.
   1. Transfer times are considerably longer for international transfers. This results in an unnecessary tying up of funds that could be gainfully employed if available.
   2. International banks have been quite successful in reducing transfer times and can be of assistance to the working capital manager.

PROBLEM 11-1

A. Compare the techniques of cash management employed by domestic (U.S.) companies and international or multinational corporations.
B. Comment on the respective policies for investing these temporary excess funds. Specifically, what types of money market investments are likely to be used by domestic and multinational companies?

SOLUTION:

A. Comparison of the techniques of cash management—domestic versus international corporations.
   1. The general principles are very similar.
      a. Speeding up the collection of cash by:
         (1) Having special bank accounts in each country.
         (2) Using a "giro" account in the postal banking system of each country.
      b. Using telegraphic transfers to send funds to strategic centers.
      c. Using the banking system on a worldwide basis.

INTERNATIONAL WORKING CAPITAL MANAGEMENT

2. Dissimilarities:
   a. Lockboxes are available only in the United States.
   b. U.S. corporations use funds denominated in the same currency; international firms must deal with numerous currencies.
   c. The problem of float differs.
      (1) Float from a domestic point of view involves only the temporary loss of income from the funds that are tied up.
      (2) Float from an international point of view is twofold:
         (a) Transfer process is longer, and loss of income is greater.
         (b) Funds are exposed to foreign-exchange-rate risk during the transfer period.
   d. Multinational companies must deal with many foreign governments; domestic firms deal only with one national government. In the United States as well as foreign countries there are many political subdivisions. Each city, county, or state will have many laws that affect business operating in the area. Usually the laws of these entities are strongly influenced by the national laws.
   e. Multinational companies are required to do their part in providing domestic funds for the host countries.
B. Investment media. Given that the obstacles above can be overcome, the full range of money market securities are available to both domestic and multinational firms. They are:
   1. Treasury bills (United States, United Kingdom, Canada, etc.).
   2. Commercial paper (United States, multinational and foreign issues).
   3. Negotiable certificates of deposit and Eurodollar deposits.
   4. Eurocurrency deposits and paper.
   5. Bankers' acceptances.
   6. Short-term tax exempt securities.

PROBLEM 11-2

Contrast the effects of using FIFO and LIFO to value inventory
A. When price levels are rising.
B. When price levels are falling.
C. Which would the manager of a subsidiary want to use in his reports to the home office?

SOLUTION:

A. When price levels are rising.
   1. FIFO tends to undervalue charges from inventory since they are based on the earliest prices. This understates actual costs thus overstating profits. The value of goods remaining in inventory is stated near present market values.

2. LIFO tends to value charges from inventory near current levels since the charges are based on the latest inventory purchases. This states costs fairly and limits holding gains or inflation profits. Remaining goods in inventory are priced at historical costs based on the earliest purchases.
  B. When price levels are falling.
   1. FIFO tends to overvalue charge-outs from inventory. This overstates costs and reduces reported profits. The remaining inventory is thus fairly priced near present prices.
   2. LIFO values charge-outs from inventory at latest prices which keep costs down in line with a dropping price level. This improves profit over what it would be if FIFO were used. The remaining inventory value would be overstated in relation to latest prices since the earliest purchases were made at higher than present prices.
  C. The manager of the subsidiary would prefer to use A1 or B2 when reporting profits. He would prefer to use A2 or B2 when reporting an increase in net worth. If he is dealing with a knowledgeable staff at the home office, he would use A2 or B1 since this would minimize the taxes of his subsidiary.

II. The problem of foreign-exchange-rate risk. Since the advent of FASB Statement No. 8, U.S. firms are required to determine translation gains or losses that occur when financial statements are translated from a foreign currency into the home currency. This requirement became effective for all fiscal years beginning January 1, 1976. These translation gains or losses must now be taken into account in computing consolidated gains or losses for each accounting period.
  A. The translation effect.
   1. Translation gains result largely from:
      a. An exposed net monetary asset position when the local currency revalues in relation to the home currency.
      b. Real assets being translated at historically higher rates.
   2. Translation losses result largely from:
      a. Exposed net monetary asset positions in the face of a local currency devaluation in relation to the home currency.
      b. The existence of a net monetary liability position in the face of local currency revaluation.
  B. Avoidance of translation losses.
   1. This requires a knowledge of impending foreign-exchange-rate movements, as well as expert forecasting ability.
   2. It also requires the ability to quickly adjust monetary accounts, up or down, in the financial structure of any subsidiary. These moves must be consistent with the firm's need for funds on a worldwide basis.

C. The difficulties of implementation.
   1. A considerable staff is required to perform the task of forecasting foreign-exchange-rate changes for all countries with or within which a firm is executing business transactions.
      a. It is difficult to predict in advance the generally expected exchange-rate movements.
      b. It is impossible, by definition, to predict the unanticipated changes in foreign exchange rates triggered by randomly occurring events such as war, revolution, and sudden cancellation or granting of large currency loans to a country by other nations.
   2. It requires the development and maintenance of a worldwide monetary asset and liabilities relationship model that not only indicates present magnitudes but can be used to predict what monetary asset and liability relationships will be in future periods.
   3. The limitations of foreign-exchange-rate risk protection.
      a. The forward market.
         (1) If a forward contract is purchased on the basis of the existing forward rate, it means that the loss will be fixed on that basis instead of on an unknown future exchange rate at the end of the contract period.
         (2) The writers of forward contracts adjust forward rates in line with their expectations. Therefore, losses can only be frozen in line with what these writers expect to happen.
         (3) It does not offer complete protection against anticipated foreign-exchange-rate losses.
      b. The lending or borrowing of local currencies to avoid exposed net monetary asset or liability positions involves
         (1) A knowledge of the present exposed monetary position and of what this position might be at several time periods in the future.
         (2) Consideration of present interest rates as well as the expected trends of these rates not only in the country in which a problem exists but also worldwide.
      c. The replacement of local currency cash with local currency cash obtained by means of a credit swap. This requires that the freed cash be exchanged and moved to the home country from which the readily convertible currency desired by the local swap partner was made available. The following must be considered.
         (1) The rate of interest charged on the local currency obtained.
         (2) The interest rate on the home country funds made available to the swap partner.
         (3) The relationship of the swap rate to the spot rate.
         (4) The income tax rates in both countries. See Chapters 10 and 13 for the solution to such a problem.

D. The claim is sometimes made that losses from an exposed monetary asset position in the face of devaluation are not always meaningful. Particular firms may benefit from an increase in volume of business and profits caused by local currency devaluation. The increase in profits will offset, in varying degrees, the loss from the exposed asset position. If, however, the exposed net monetary asset position was not required by the operations of the subsidiary but existed as a result of an historical accident, then an increase in volume and profit following devaluation should not be used to excuse an exposed net monetary asset position that need not have been there.
   1. An increase in profits under devaluation occurs only under particularly fortunate circumstances to firms whose
      a. Volume of export sales rise due to lower prices and rise more than proportionally to the price reductions as the result of devaluation.
      b. Sales prices will eventually rise above predevaluation levels.
      c. Raw material and labor costs will rise only slowly following devaluation.
   2. It is useful for the firm to analyze the possibility of devaluation in an individual country in relation to its operations in that country in terms of its effects on prices, volume of sales, cost levels, etc. But the firm should still seek to minimize the cost of protection against forward commitments or receipts and from its net monetary position exposure.
E. A possible solution to the problem of foreign-exchange-rate risk.
   1. Conduct a study of monthly, seasonal, or annual cash flow trends for all subsidiaries and divisions of a firm on a worldwide basis.
   2. Develop models of relationships between volume of sales for the same subparts on a yearly basis.
   3. Attempt to establish the normal relationships between the net monetary position and volume of sales for each group.
   4. Try to use this information to predict the net monetary position, over a period of time, for each part of the organization. The practice of operating on a near zero net monetary position is presently used by all international banks. They have learned the advisability of this as a result of some rather substantial losses in connection with their operations in the international foreign exchange market. When financial experts like large international banks cannot forecast exchange-rate movements with sufficient accuracy to prevent losses, what chance does a business have to do this in addition to all its other operating problems?
   5. Remove excess cash to the home country from all foreign locations except countries where revaluation is a strong near-term possibility due to present strong undervaluation of the local currency.
   6. Place these idle cash funds temporarily in any foreign country where covered arbitrage will assure a gain. See Chapter 5 for an example of these temporary short-term investments.

7. In addition to steps under (5) and (6) above, move funds, or loan or borrow funds, in all locations where it is possible as required to approach monetary neutrality.
8. Do not move cash for temporary investment into an inflationary country, poorly managed, for the sake of seeking a higher interest yield. Business organizations do best when they do what they know best—manufacturing, sales, service, or whatever their principal business might be. They are well advised to leave efforts to profit from foreign exchange speculation to those who are more knowledgeable and can afford those risks.

PROBLEM 11-3

One of Allen International's 100% owned subsidiaries operates in a country with an extreme shortage of foreign exchange. The exchange of funds into convertible foreign currencies for the payment of imports, interest, and loan principal reduction payments is largely impossible. Dividend payments are not permitted to be made to foreign owners. In order to promote exports, the government offers business firms the opportunity to retain 20% of foreign currency received from new exports. Otherwise all foreign currency earned must be turned into the country's central bank for conversion into local currency. The subsidiary is presently operating at 70% of capacity; 100% capacity operations at sales value is LC5 million per year. Goods used by subsidiaries in other countries can be manufactured by the subsidiary's equipment. The subsidiary's profitability after taxes is 12%. Would manufacture and export to related firms in other countries offer a solution to the cash transfer problem?

SOLUTION:

Profit at full capacity = LC5,000,000(0.12) = LC600,000
Profit at 70% of capacity = 3,500,000(0.12) = 420,000
Profit on additional capacity = LC180,000
Retention of foreign exchange on export
    of added production = 1,500,000(0.20) = LC300,000

Presently no funds can be transferred out of the country. When operating at full capacity the subsidiary could transfer to the parent LC300,000. In addition, there would be available for local investment LC300,000. Other reasons for accepting this export developing proposal are:
1. The production costs for the subsidiary may be lower than the same for other parts of the multinational firm.
2. The percentage of profitability may increase with full production.

3. Adding to the volume of production in this country may permit the shutting down of obsolete or more costly production capacity in other countries.
4. Billing between this subsidiary and the parent or other subsidiaries may permit, through transfer pricing, some funds to be repatriated by shifting the location at which profits are realized.

PROBLEM 11-4

Davidson International's principal manufacturing plant in Europe is located in Paris. In-transfer and temporarily idle funds have been routed to and through this office. Since, however, forward market quotations on the French franc have been weakening lately, the manager of the international division is planning to reroute temporarily idle cash funds to the office of the company's German subsidiary. At present the company has been protecting itself by entering into forward 90-day contracts to purchase dollars with French francs at an annual discount of 5% to 6%. By comparison, 90-day forward contracts may be obtained to buy dollars with West German marks at a premium in relation to the present spot rate of 1½%. Short-term interest rates in France are 7½% and in West Germany approximately 7%.
A. Should West Germany become the transfer center of the firm's international funds flow? What would be the cost or benefit of any change that might be suggested?
B. What requirements for an international financial center are considered important to locate a cash concentration center in a particular city? Why?

SOLUTION:

A. Since the German currency is presently one of the strongest and the firm is in a positive net monetary position, protection in the form of forward contracts is not needed. Also premiums on forward contracts to buy dollars with German marks are not likely to be as high as the expected revaluation of the mark in relation to the U.S. dollar. Thus, cash funds for the time being may be kept in German marks. The benefit of the change from France to West Germany would be the elimination of forward contracts at a small sacrifice in interest income.
B. A cash center is meant to serve only as a location where idle funds can be accumulated and invested, on a temporary basis, in anticipation of their need and reassignment to other places in the world. Thus, these funds should be safely placed, with no undue burden of taxation, and be readily transferable to any part of the world. Specifically, the transfer center for cash funds should be located in a country with:
1. A strong currency.
2. A stable government.

3. A stable value, readily convertible currency.
4. No limitations on transfers of funds in or out.
5. No tax on foreign-earned income.
6. Laws that permit 100% foreign-owned corporations.
7. An active international financial market.
8. An active money market.
9. Sufficient capital markets to permit investment of funds for longer periods, if desired.
10. A foreign investment insurance or guarantee program.

III. The international flow of funds.
   A. Operating funds.
      1. Payments for goods and services received or sold.
      2. Interest payments on loans placed or obtained.
      3. Royalty payments made or received.
      4. License fees paid or earned.
   B. Investment funds.
      1. Direct investments made or received.
      2. Portfolio investments made or received.
      3. Interest payments made or received.
      4. Return of principal payments.
   C. The flow of funds between related firms.
      1. Subsidiary to parent.
         a. Dividends.
         b. Interest on loans.
         c. Principal reduction payments.
         d. Royalty payments.
         e. License fees.
         f. Technical service fees.
         g. Management fees.
         h. Export commissions.
         i. Payment for goods received which involves transfer pricing.
            (1) Capital equipment.
            (2) Parts and supplies.
            (3) Raw materials.
      2. Parent to subsidiary.
         a. Initial direct investment funds.
         b. Subsequent added investment funds.
         c. Loan of funds.
         d. Purchase of goods and services which involves transfer pricing.
      3. The flow of funds between subsidiaries.
         a. Loans from one to another.
         b. Payments and receipts of interest.
         c. Principal reduction payments from debtor to lender.

d. Purchase or sale of the following goods which permits transfer pricing.
   (1) Capital equipment.
   (2) Parts and supplies.
   (3) Raw materials.

PROBLEM 11-5

A number of methods exist for making remittances from foreign subsidiaries to the domestic parent.
A. Name six of these methods.
B. Are there any government constraints or national laws which make some methods preferable to others?

SOLUTION:

A. Remittances from foreign subsidiaries may be in the form of:
   1. Interest on loans.
   2. Return of loan principal.
   3. Royalty payments and licensing fees.
   4. Technical service and management fees.
   5. Payment for goods (transfer pricing).
   6. Dividends.
B. Some government policies affect the methods used.
   1. In many countries dividends may not be paid in foreign currency.
   2. Some countries limit the amount of dividends paid.
   3. Royalties, license fees, technical service and management fees, and transfer pricing are perhaps the least restricted.

IV. The management of the flow of funds. In view of the large variety in the components that make up the flow of funds between all parts of a multinational firm, it is possible to arrange the activities of the various parts of a firm in such a way that the net flow between all parts is kept to a minimum. This planning must by necessity be done on a worldwide basis at the head office or at the point of control of international operations.
   A. General policies.
      1. Dividend payout ratios should be similar in all parts of an organization.
      2. Overhead and management fee charges to subsidiaries should be consistent.
      3. Loan and local financial policies should be similar.
      4. The charges for licensing and patent fees must be uniform.
      5. Transfer pricing practiced on a sound basis is an effective means of transferring income from one subsidiary to another or to the parent.

6. Equity investments in foreign subsidiaries should be held at a minimum since quite often the payment of dividends is not as readily permitted as the payment of interest on loans. It may be possible to loan funds to a subsidiary in a strong currency country and then have this subsidiary sell to the subsidiary in a weak currency country the needed equipment and supplies on liberal credit terms.
7. All funds advanced to subsidiaries should be registered in the host country.
8. Local partners, if any, might object to loss of cash but might acquiesce if these orders come from the head office.
9. Idle funds should be concentrated in cash centers for accumulation and reassignment.
   a. The concentration of cash improves
      (1) The availability of the idle cash.
      (2) The income derived from idle funds prior to their reassignment.
   b. The concentration of cash will shorten the time interval between investment decisions and execution.
   c. Characteristics required in a country where a cash center is to be located.
      (1) A very stable government.
      (2) A government which permits a ready inflow and outflow of funds.
      (3) A strong currency which is readily convertible into other currencies in order to minimize foreign-exchange-rate risk.
      (4) Does not tax cash assets with a capital tax.
      (5) Taxes income only at the source.
      (6) A friendly attitude toward private enterprise, particularly 100% foreign-controlled subsidiaries.
      (7) An effective foreign exchange market, including a forward market where forward contracts in terms of most of the currencies of major trading nations can be entered into.
      (8) An active money market for temporary investment of idle funds.
      (9) Capital markets that offer opportunities for relatively risk-free investments on a medium-term basis.
      (10) A network of effective communications.
      (11) Available foreign investment insurance or guarantees to protect funds newly invested in other countries.
      (12) If possible, a government export promotion program that can be useful to the multinational firm.
B. Policies in strongly inflationary countries.
   1. When devaluation of the local currency occurs at frequent intervals, average quarterly, monthly, or weekly exchange rates should be adopted for purposes of translating local results into the home currency.

2. Under strongly inflationary conditions, foreign subsidiaries should never have any idle cash on hand. Such funds should be invested in inventories or other real assets if they cannot be moved out of the country.
3. Trade credit should be granted sparingly and only for short periods of time. Whenever possible, a rate of interest should be charged to cover any losses due to the fact that these are monetary assets.
4. Whenever purchases are made with the purchase price to be determined at the time of delivery, advance payments should not be made unless the supplier is willing to pay a rate of interest on such advances.
5. Borrow local currency funds from banks or other sources whenever these funds can be obtained at a rate of interest whose level above the United States or European rate is equal to or smaller than the anticipated rate of devaluation.
6. If supply conditions permit, attempt to obtain trade credit without the payment of a rate of interest.

C. Policies in countries trending toward revaluation.
1. Revaluations are not likely to occur as often as devaluations.
   a. Revaluation lowers the competitive position of the county's export industries.
   b. A country with a strong foreign exchange position is not as motivated to act as a country with a weak foreign exchange position that must devalue.
   c. Devaluation by one country in relation to others has the same effect as if all the others have revaluated in relation to it.
2. Therefore annual, semiannual, or quarterly exchange rates will most likely be suitable for the translation of financial statements into the home currency.
3. Operations on a positive net monetary position basis are likely to prove advantageous except during periods of temporary overvaluation.
4. Monetary liabilities, short-, medium-, or long-term, should not be large in relation to monetary assets.
5. If funds must be obtained for operations, they should be borrowed in other countries and loaned to the subsidiaries in countries that are candidates for revaluation.

PROBLEM 11-6

1. As a manager in a foreign subsidiary how would you actually proceed to protect your business from inflation and devaluation? Remember that your next promotion depends on headquarter's view of your profit, sales expansion, and earnings growth.
2. What might be different in the set of "books" you show the foreign country's IRS and the set you show headquarters?
3. Could transfer pricing help or hurt your record?

INTERNATIONAL WORKING CAPITAL MANAGEMENT

SOLUTION:

1. To protect the business against inflation and devaluation, acquire the services of local economic forecasters first and attempt to determine the probability, size, and timing of devaluations (and/or rate of inflation). When the *expected cost* of devaluation exceeds the *expected cost* of insuring against it, buy the insurance. Then, proceed to obtain local loans, use swaps, increase local accounts payable, accelerate foreign currency payables, buy hard currency inventory, enter into forward exchange contracts to purchase the local currency, encourage local equity participation, etc.
2. The local books would expense more than the books at the home office. The local books would show "full" payment of local interest charges; the home office books would show a gain on a negative net monetary position, after devaluation. Asset write-up would also be used where permitted for both subsidiary and home office books. Wherever permitted, the write-up of the value of the assets would create additional book value that would be depreciated in future periods, reducing earnings before taxes, taxes, and earnings after taxes, and increasing cash flow.
3. Transfer payments would be determined to minimize taxes for each set of books. If it were desired to repatriate funds to the parent, within limits, the sale prices to the parent could be lowered, reducing subsidiary profits. The effect of this must then be taken into account by the home-office staff when making an evaluation of the performance of the subsidiary.

PROBLEM 11-7

Discuss techniques that the manager of a foreign subsidiary can use to operate successfully (in a financial sense) in an environment characterized by:
1. Headquarters country inflation and subsidiary country stability.
2. Devaluation of the headquarter's currency and no change in the subsidiary's currency.
3. "Blocked" or tightly regulated exchange controls in the host country.
4. Switch trade financing.

SOLUTION:

1. Increase home office monetary receivables in the subsidiary's currency; increase home office payables in the home country currency; raising home country prices ahead of inflation, transfer pricing which will increase home office receivables in the subsidiary's currency (consider offsetting tax consequences), and postponing payments to the home office.

2. Same as any weak currency—reduce exposure, insure by forward exchange, swaps, HQ currency dominated debt, etc. (Perhaps sell HQ currency short, and/or "cover" any HQ currency holdings.)
3. If a currency in which a subsidiary operates is blocked, unless there are loopholes (free blackmarkets, transfer pricing, or netting of intersubsidiary debt), the best that can be done is to operate the subsidiary independently as an LC project. If surplus funds are available, use funds to buy other profitable ventures in that country. If the subsidiary needs parts not locally obtainable (or expensive), look into international barter or inventory trade.
4. Switch trade develops as the result of bilateral trade agreements that exist between developing countries and Eastern-bloc countries. These agreements provide for a specified volume of two-way trade between the countries. Usually the Eastern-bloc country falls behind in its obligation due to its inability to ship the promised goods. As the result of the Eastern-bloc country's desire to prevent the bilateral trade agreement from failing, it is willing to use convertible currency to purchase from third countries goods desired by its trading partner. Through a knowledgeable switch broker a firm can develop additional foreign sales paid for by the deficit country partner to the bilateral trade agreement.

V. The international movement of funds—implementation of policies.
   A. Factors that increase risks or costs.
      1. Longer transfer times—greater float.
      2. Exposure to exchange-rate risks while funds are in transit.
         a. Currency in which funds are transferred may be devalued in relation to:
            (1) The currency at the origin of the transfer.
            (2) The currency at the destination.
            (3) A third-country currency in which the transfer may have taken place.
         b. The currency at the destination may have been revalued during the transfer period.
      3. Rules and regulations in various countries may prohibit or restrict the transfer of currencies.
         a. Fund transfers should take place in the shortest possible time consistent with safety to minimize the risk of blocked or "frozen" funds.
         b. The loss of income during the transfer period must always be measured against the potential loss due to possible devaluation.
   B. The value of an international bank in the transfer of funds.
      1. It can aid in speeding the transfer of funds between all parts of an international organization. This
         a. Decreases the exposure of the funds to foreign exchange fluctuations.
         b. Makes funds otherwise in transfer available sooner for other business use, thereby increasing profitability.

INTERNATIONAL WORKING CAPITAL MANAGEMENT

2. It can advise on the appropriate currency to use in the transfer process to minimize foreign-exchange-rate risk.
3. It can provide consulting services in establishing cash flow systems. This can be of value to the international firm even though the advising bank is not itself directly involved in all phases of the cash transfer.
4. In addition, a multinational bank can advise the financial officer of a multinational firm on:
   a. The banking laws and required procedures in the various countries in which the firm is operating.
   b. Government restrictions and prohibitions of fund transfers or of contemplated changes in these rules.
5. It can advise and assist the firm in its efforts to move idle funds to locations of greater profitability and safety.
6. It can also arrange introductions in foreign countries that may be of great help in furthering the interests of its client.

PROBLEM 11-8

The international transfer of funds of the Ajax Company amounts to about $2 million monthly. Presently the average transfer time is 10 days. It has been proposed that the transfer of funds be turned over to one of the larger international banks which could reduce the transfer time to an average of 2 days. A charge of 0.5% of the volume of transfer has been proposed for this service. In view of the fact that the firm's opportunity cost of funds is 12%, should this offer be accepted?

SOLUTION:

$2,000,000 per month = $24,000,000 per year.
Time saved = 10 − 2 = 8 days funds are freed for other uses.
Investing $24,000,000 at 12% for 8 days:
Yield = 24,000,000(0.12)(8/360) = $64,000
% yield = 64,000/24,000,000 = 0.00267, or 0.267%

Since the firm saves less than 0.3% and the proposed charge is 0.5%, the service would not produce commensurate savings. However, the new transfer time would shorten the exposure of the funds to various risks by an average of 8 days. The firm must decide whether or not this reduction in risk is worth the difference between the proposed fee and the savings due to the shorter transfer time, 0.5% − 0.267% = 0.233%.

PROBLEM 11-9

The MNC Corporation has a number of subsidiaries located in various Asian countries. These subsidiaries collect the equivalent of U.S. $500,000 each month which are then transferred to the company's cash center in Hong Kong. The average transfer time has been 14 days. An international bank, eager to solicit business from MNC, offered to handle the transfer of these funds at a guaranteed average transfer time of not more than 2 days. The company's opportunity cost is 15%.

A. How much is this service worth to the company?
B. What are the advantages and disadvantages of this arrangement?

SOLUTION:

A. Value of the service is as follows:

Annual transfers = ($500,000)(12) = $6,000,000
Time savings = 14 − 2 = 12 days funds are available for other uses.
Investing $6,000,000 at 15% for 12 days:
Yield = ($6,000,000)(.15)(12/360) = $30,000

On a percentage basis of the funds transferred, this service is worth a yield of: $\frac{\$30,000}{\$6,000,000}$ = .005, or .5% to the company.

B. The advantages and disadvantages to the MNC Corporation of having this arrangement are as follows:

1. An advantage is the reduction of uncertainty as to when the funds will actually be available in the Hong Kong cash center. Although the average transfer time has been 15 days, transfer times for individual transactions sometimes may take longer than a month. From a cash planning point of view, the guarantee by the international bank of a specified transfer time is a big advantage.

2. Reducing transfer time reduces the firm's exposure to exchange-rate risk involved while the cash is in float for various periods of time. This is particularly a problem for the various Asian countries which have generally weak currencies.

3. A possible disadvantage is that MNC may miss the range of services and information that are provided by the local banks due to their knowledge of local conditions and relationships with government officials. These may not be provided by the international bank.

   Therefore, from a practical point of view, MNC may decide to have the transfer service performed by the international bank, but continue to hold balances of various amounts in the local banks in order to continue to receive information and nonfinancial services. Sometimes the international bank has a partial ownership arrangement with a local bank. In that case, there is no problem. It is then understood that the international bank will be responsible for the fund transfers and that other types of banking relationships will continue with the joint-ventured local bank.

REFERENCES:

Meister, Irene: *Managing the International Financial Function*, The Conference Board, New York, 1970.

Robbins, Sidney M., and Robert B. Stobaugh: *Money in the Multinational Enterprise: A Study in Financial Policy*, Basic Books, New York, 1973.

Rutenberg, David P.: "Maneuvering Liquid Assets in a Multinational Company: Formulation and Deterministic Solution Procedures," *Management Science*, **16**:B-671-683, June 1970.

_____: "Organizational Archetypes of a Multi-National Company," *Management Science*, **16**: B-337-349, February 1970.

Shapiro, Alan: "Optimal Inventory and Credit-Granting Strategies under Inflation and Devaluation," *Journal of Financial and Quantitative Analysis*, 8:37-46, January 1973.

Chapter 12

Financing Worldwide Commercial Sales

Theme: The foreign exchange earnings from worldwide commercial sales are important to the United States because they make possible the continuing and increasing imports of approximately 20 raw materials and other imports that are vital to the efficient functioning of the U.S. economy. The pricing of internationally traded goods is influenced by supply and demand conditions in particular markets, the currency in which the trade is denominated, the credit terms granted, the security offered by the buyer, and the availability of government credits, inducements, and insurance and guarantee programs. The proper selection of the variables affecting price will affect U.S. exports. This chapter discusses financing international transactions and other factors influencing export and import sales.

  I. A proper volume of world trade is important to the U.S. and world economies.
    A. The advantages of increased foreign trade to the United States.
      1. Greater efficiency in the world divisions of labor.
      2. Increased level of economic activity.
      3. A balance on goods and services consistent with a relatively stable U.S. dollar in its role as a reference currency.

B. The advantages of increased foreign trade to the individual firm.
1. A greater market for their products.
2. Increased volume may reduce costs of production.
3. Less dependency on the level of economic activity in the United States.
4. Products whose sales are leveling off in the United States may find increased sales in a foreign market.
5. Possibility of more favorable price-cost relationships than in domestic markets.
6. Lower tax rates on foreign sales if these sales are made via
    a. Western hemisphere trade corporations.
    b. Domestic international sales corporations.

II. Factors affecting the volume of U.S. exports.
A. Price of export goods. This is influenced by:
1. Choice of the billing currency.
    a. The currency of the seller.
    b. The currency of the buyer.
    c. The currency of a third country.
2. Terms granted by the seller to the buyer.
    a. Cash at the time of shipment.
    b. Credit with security.
    c. Open account basis.
3. Risk reduction by available credit instruments.
    a. Confirmed, irrevocable letter of credit.
    b. Irrevocable letter of credit.
    c. Banker's acceptance.
4. Risk reduction by action of governments.
    a. Credits which ease the problems of financing.
    b. Commercial and political risk insurance or guarantees which
        (1) Make it easier to obtain financing.
        (2) Lower the cost of financing.
5. The above factors all affect one another and the price of the export goods. Thus the exporter is presented with some choices of action and possible trade-offs when deciding on the best alternatives in connection with a particular export sale.

B. Market factors.
1. Demand and supply relationships in a particular market.
2. Characteristics of the market.
    a. Is it a market free of various restrictions?
    b. Are trade restrictions practiced by
        (1) Regional economic or trade groups attempting to achieve advantages for their members?
        (2) The individual country through the imposition of special taxes, licenses, and other forms of import and export controls?
        (3) Groups of producers of a raw material or commodity forming cartels, and controlling the price or movement of the goods?

FINANCING WORLDWIDE COMMERCIAL SALES

III. The basic documents in normal export-import transactions are the bill of exchange, the bill of lading, and the letter of credit.
   A. The *bill of exchange*, or draft, is an instrument that is used to effect payment for goods and services sold in export transactions.
      1. Two major types.
         a. Sight drafts—payment at sight.
         b. Time drafts—payment at the end of an agreed upon period. These exist either as
            (1) Plain, on an open account basis, or
            (2) Guaranteed, by the customer's bank by means of a banker's acceptance.
      2. Characteristics of a bill of exchange.
         a. It is an unconditional order in writing addressed by one person (drawer) to another (drawee).
         b. It requires that the drawee, upon demand or at a predetermined future time, pay a certain sum of money
            (1) To order, or
            (2) To bearer, the person in possession of the bill.
         c. It is a document to which shipping documents may or may not be attached.
            (1) Without attachment it is called a clean bill of exchange.
            (2) With attached document it is called a documentary bill of exchange.
      3. Definition of terms.
         a. The *drawer*, or *maker*, is the one that issues the bill.
         b. The *drawee* is the person against whom the bill is drawn, who eventually will accept it, and pay the specified amount at maturity.
         c. The *payee* is the person to whom the drawee will eventually pay the funds.
         d. The payee and drawer are one and the same person if the bill has not been discounted and signed over to somebody else.
   B. The *bill of lading* is a document that the transportation company gives to the shipper when he delivers the goods for shipment. It performs the following functions:
      1. It is a receipt that acknowledges that the specified goods have been received.
      2. It is a contract to transport the goods to a specified destination and deliver them to a designated person.
      3. It is also a document of title that gives its possessor the right to claim the goods at their destination.
      4. A bill of lading may be made out either
         a. To order, which makes it a negotiable instrument, or
         b. As a straight bill, which specifies the person to whom the goods are to be delivered. In some parts of South America this is the form required by shippers.

C. The *commercial letter of credit* is issued by a commercial bank on behalf of a foreign buyer.
1. These are the specifications of the letter.
   a. It states the maximum amount of credit that the bank will provide and the nature of the merchandise that can be purchased.
   b. It states the length of time that the letter is valid.
   c. It is addressed to the seller.
   d. It names the person for whom it was issued.
   e. It specifies the terms of the sale.
   f. It specifies the determination of the shipping charges, free on board (f.o.b.) or cost, insurance, and freight (c.i.f.).
   g. It specifies the papers that must be attached to the drafts issued in connection with the covered purchases.
   h. It is either revocable or irrevocable. From the point of view of the seller of the goods a revocable letter of credit does not have much value.
   i. It specifies the currencies in which the drafts drawn are to be issued.
      (1) The currency of the seller.
      (2) The currency of the buyer.
      (3) A third-country currency.
2. Definition of terms.
   a. The *opening bank* is the bank which issues the letter of credit on behalf of the buyer.
   b. The *notifying bank* is a bank in the country of the seller that notifies the seller of the existence of the letter of credit.
   c. The *negotiating bank* is one that buys or discounts the drafts that will be issued in connection with the letter of credit.
   d. The *paying bank* is the one on whom the drafts are drawn by the seller.
   e. The *confirming bank* in the country of the seller along with the opening bank assumes the obligation to honor the seller's drafts.

PROBLEM 12-1

You are the treasurer of ABC Corporation; your company to date has been selling its products exclusively in the United States and wishes to expand its sales to the international market. The board of directors has instructed you to investigate the following questions.
A. What are the principal risks involved in selling abroad?
B. To what degree can ABC Corporation eliminate, reduce, or minimize those risks?
C. To what extent can the domestic bank assist you?

FINANCING WORLDWIDE COMMERCIAL SALES

SOLUTION:

A. The risks.
  1. Commercial risks.
  2. Political risks.
  3. War, revolution, and insurrection.
  4. Convertibility.
  5. Expropriation.
  6. Foreign exchange risks.

B. How to minimize the risks.
  1. FCIA, Eximbank.
  2. FCIA, OPIC, Eximbank.
  3. OPIC, AID where applicable.
  4. OPIC, AID where applicable.
  5. OPIC, AID where applicable.
  6. Forward exchange contracts. Foreign currency swap. Achieving monetary balance. AID, only if not offered by host government in connection with Latin American housing projects.

C. How U.S. banks can help expansion.
  1. Identify areas where markets for the company's products exist.
  2. Finance credit sales.
  3. Make arrangements with FCIA, OPIC, AID, and/or Eximbank.
  4. Provide foreign exchange, etc.
  5. Coordinate transactions and provide other corresponding bank relations with foreign banks.
  6. Cooperate in letters of credit.
  7. Provide information on foreign areas.

PROBLEM 12-2

There are three basic documents used to facilitate export-import transactions. What are they? How do they originate?

SOLUTION:

A. Bill of exchange—an unconditional, written order calling on the person to whom it is addressed to pay on demand or at a future date, a sum of money to the order of a specified person or bearer, e.g., a commercial bank check and the draft used in import translations. Time drafts become bankers' acceptances when the bank agrees to substitute itself for the importer in honoring the liability.

B. Bill of lading—a receipt given by a carrier to a shipper for goods received stating that the goods have been accepted for shipment and detailing the terms and provisions under which they will be transported. The original copy of the bill of lading carries with it title to the goods shipped. When the original copy is attached to the bill of exchange used to effect payment for the shipment, it entitles the holder to receive the goods. Bills of lading may be negotiable if made out to order and not to a specified person.
C. Commercial letters of credit—a letter addressed by an importer's bank to the exporter, guaranteeing payment for goods received according to specified terms. The letter of credit greatly reduces the risk of the seller in connection with foreign export translations.
   1. Two types.
      a. Revocable—bank may revoke or cancel.
      b. Irrevocable—bank may not revoke or cancel.
   2. The strongest letter of credit is a confirmed, irrevocable letter of credit guaranteed by the issuing bank and confirming bank.

PROBLEM 12-3

What are Edge Act corporations and how do they function to expand and augment the domestic as well as foreign business of the parent corporation?

SOLUTION:

A. Essentially, Edge Act subsidiaries are simply international banking departments of commercial banks, capable of transacting any business of the parent except making domestic loans and accepting domestic deposits.
B. In areas of the United States where the parent has not penetrated, the establishment of an Edge Act subsidiary may enable it to generate new international and domestic business.
C. Edge Act subsidiaries are likely to know where the demand for U.S. products abroad is apt to be. By actively encouraging local producers to investigate these opportunities and by explaining how FCIA and Eximbank facilitate and encourage such trade, Edge Act subsidiaries may increase the volume of loan business.
D. In addition, Edge Act Subsidiaries can
   1. Make equity investments.
   2. Issue acceptances exceeding six months.

IV. Methods of financing export-import sales.
   A. Finance the sales in the home currency of the seller.
      1. Bankers' acceptances.
         a. A time draft accepted by the importer's bank.
         b. The credit of the accepting bank (the importer's bank) makes this form of time draft more readily negotiable.

FINANCING WORLDWIDE COMMERCIAL SALES

       c. The credit standing of a well-known bank is substituted for the less-known credit standing of individual business firms.
       d. The term is generally six months or less.
       e. The volume of dollar acceptances has grown greatly in recent years, from $7 billion in 1970 to $19 billion in 1976.
    2. Financial institutions.
       a. Edge Act financing subsidiaries of U.S. banks.
       b. Factors who finance foreign receivables.
          (1) May aid in credit evaluation of customers.
          (2) May be more costly than other sources of financing.
       c. U.S. export financing companies that limit their financing to exclusive foreign distributors of U.S. capital goods.
       d. Export-Import Bank of the United States.
          (1) Loans for the proprietors of large foreign projects.
          (2) Guarantees for financing additional amounts from
              (a) Commercial banks.
              (b) The Private Export Funding Corporation (PEFCO).
       e. The exporter may finance his exports through his commercial bank as a result of normal business borrowing arrangements. As a result his cost of financing is his normal borrowing rate.
B. Finance the sales in a foreign currency. Borrow in the country of the buyer and convert the loan into dollars at the prevailing rate of exchange and then pay off the loan plus interest at the end of the credit term when the seller's receivable is collected. This method avoids foreign-exchange-rate risk.
C. Use a foreign currency swap to obtain local currency funds, convert these funds into the home currency at the spot rate, and later on reverse the swap when paid by the buyer.
    1. This removes the exchange-rate risk.
    2. It may be more expensive because it temporarily requires more dollars since the swap rate is less than the spot rate. This may call for an increase in price of the goods sold, if competition permits.
D. P.L. 480 funds are not available to finance export sales as such. However, if the exporter has an operating subsidiary in the country of the buyer he can borrow P.L. 480 funds that may then be used in part to help finance his exports to that country.
E. Link financing, sometimes referred to as Arbi-loans, involves the borrowing of funds in a third country at a lower rate of interest than is offered in either the seller's or buyer's country. The lower cost of interest permits paying a commission to a broker and an exchange-rate risk protection by means of a forward market contract.

PROBLEM 12-4

A U.S. exporter sells $200,000 worth of merchandise on a 6-month open account basis. He requires a 10% down payment. His cost of financing the sale is 12% without insurance protection or credit guarantee. With an FCIA insurance coverage, this is reduced to 10%. The FCIA insurance covers only 90% of the amount to be financed and charges a premium of $0.55 per $100 of the insured amount. A confirmed, irrevocable letter of credit can also be arranged by the customer at a cost of $1,500. This credit guarantee would lower the FCIA premium to $0.35 per $100 and make possible the financing by the discounting of a banker's acceptance at 8%. Which of the methods of financing should the exporter use?

SOLUTION:

Alternative 1. Without an FCIA policy.

Total Sales	$200,000
Less down payment, 10%	20,000
To be financed	$180,000

Cost of financing = ($180,000)(12%)(6/12) = $10,800

Alternative 2. With an FCIA policy.
Since the FCIA policy only covers 90% of the financed portion ($180,000 × 90% = $162,000), this is the amount on which the lower interest of 10% applies. The remaining 10% ($18,000) carried at the exporter's own risk still costs 12%. In addition, there is the added cost of the FCIA insurance.

Total cost = cost of borrowing + cost of insurance

= ($162,000)(0.1)(6/12) + ($18,000)(0.12)(6/12) + ($162,000)(0.0055)

= 8,100 + 1,080 + 891

= $10,071

Alternative 3. Use of the confirmed, irrevocable letter of credit.

Total cost = cost of the letter of credit + cost of discounting the banker's acceptance

= $1,500 + ($180,000)(8%)(6/12)

= $1,500 + $7,200

= $8,700

Alternative 3 results in the least cost to the U.S. exporter, therefore he should finance by discounting the banker's acceptance backed by the confirmed, irrevocable letter of credit. The lowering of the FCIA premium results in a saving of 891 − 567 = 324. This is of no consequence in view of the lower cost of discounting the banker's acceptance.

PROBLEM 12-5

The SGV Company is contemplating the use of various financing policies with regard to its export sales. It estimates a sales volume of $1 million for the year mostly to base rate 1.17 and 1.37 countries. Normally these would be made on a 1-year open account basis with a down payment of 10%. However, the company estimates that customers would furnish confirmed, irrevocable letters of credit, if requested, on approximately half of its export sales. Its credit arrangements allow for that part of the exports to be financed by bankers' acceptances discounted at 7%. To the customer providing confirmed, irrevocable letters of credit, the company would grant a 1% discount.

Sales made on an open account basis require a financing cost of 10%. The FCIA insurance reduces this to 8.5% on the insured portion, but the insurance premium costs about $1.50 per $100 of the insured amount. FCIA requires the insured to carry at least 10% of the financed portion at his own risk on the sales to credit-worthy customers. On the other half of the sales, the company would be required to carry 30% of the risk. This averages out to carrying 20% of the risk on all of the sales. Also, it is estimated that 15% of the sales made to financially risky importers, who cannot obtain letters of credit, will not be collected.

Which policy should the company adopt?

SOLUTION:

The company faces 3 alternatives:

Alternative 1. Obtain no protection.

Total sales	$1,000,000	
Less down payment, 10%	100,000	
To be financed	$ 900,000	
Financing cost: (900,000)(10%)		$ 90,000
Plus potential loss due to noncollection:		
15% of half of $900,000		67,500
Total Cost		$157,500

Since the company is taking all the risk in selling on an open account basis, the cost of financing would be 10% on the financed portion for the 1-year period plus the potential loss due to noncollection, estimated at 15% of half of $900,000, representing risky sales to importers who cannot obtain letters of credit.

Alternative 2. Purchase FCIA insurance.

Financed portion	$900,000	
Less exporter's risk, 20%	180,000	
Insured portion	$720,000	

FCIA insurance premium = (720,000)(1.5%)		$ 10,800
+ Financing cost of insured portion = (720,000)(8.5%)		61,200
+ Financing cost of uncovered portion = (180,000)(10%)		18,000
+ Loss due to noncollection = 15% of half of 180,000		13,500
Total Cost		$103,500

The FCIA insurance covers 80% of the company's export sales to be financed. Half of the remaining 20% ($180,000) not covered, represents risky sales on which 15% is estimated to result in noncollection losses. This plus both the cost of the FCIA insurance premium and the 8.5% financing cost of the insured portion as well as the higher 10% financing cost on the uninsured portion add up to a total cost of $103,500.

Alternative 3. Obtain confirmed letters of credit on half the export sales and take a chance on the remaining half.

Portion to be financed:	$900,000
by letter of credit, 50%	450,000
by unprotected loan, 50%	450,000

Discount granted = $500,000(0.01)	=	$ 5,000
+ Cost of financing via letter of credit = 450,000(0.07)	=	31,500
+ Cost of financing by straight loan = 450,000(0.10)	=	45,000
+ Loss due to noncollection = 450,000(0.15)	=	67,500
Total cost	=	$149,000

It was assumed that half of the receivables would be discounted at 7% since these were backed by letters of credit for which the sale price was discounted 1%. A large part of the total cost was due to the assumption that 15% of the uncovered receivables would not be collectable.

Alternative 2 results in the lowest cost. Under alternative 1 the firm traded off highest sales yield and lowest insurance cost against highest risk. The financing cost was thus highest including the potential loss due to noncollection of $67,500. Under alternative 2 the firm retained the highest yield from sales but decided on a trade-off between the FCIA insurance expense and a lower financing cost, total cost $103,500. Under alternative 3 the firm made a trade-off between a lower sales price and greater safety and a lower financing charge. In this instance the higher cost of this alternate choice as under alternative 1 was largely due to the cost of noncollection of a percentage of the receivables. The total cost was $149,000 as shown above.

V. Foreign trade with countries suffering severe shortage of foreign exchange.
   A. Straight barter involves the exchange of one good for another.
      1. Normally these transactions take place directly between two countries.
      2. It is at times possible to effect three-country compensating agreements under which these countries join in an exchange of merchandise.
   B. Switch exchange transactions are made possible by existing imbalances in bilateral trade agreements between two countries. When one of the countries falls behind in its obligations to send goods to the other, it becomes a deficit country. It is, therefore, often quite willing to buy goods in third countries that are of interest to the surplus country. By shipping these goods to the bilateral trading partner, this imbalance is removed and the bilateral trade agreement is able to continue. These goods may be shipped either
      1. Directly from the third country to the surplus country, or
      2. From the third country via the deficit country to the surplus country.

VI. Variables in the sales transaction.
   A. Trade-offs between variables in the sales transaction.
      1. Figure 12-1 sets forth a schematic indicating how the terms and conditions of sale interact with the sales price.
      2. The denomination of billing, the extent of credit exposure, the use of letters of credit, and other insurance and risk reduction methods can be favorable to the buyer or seller. However, what the buyer receives or the

Figure 12-1 Trade-offs between Terms and Conditions with Negotiated Sale Prices

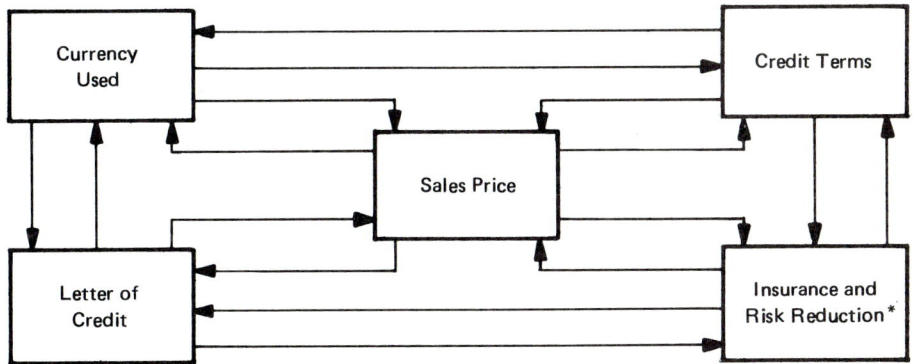

*This includes use of the forward market, borrowing or lending to adjust a firm's net monetary position, and a wide range of private and governmental insurance programs. Like other socially desirable insurance arrangements, for a relatively small premium the risk and uncertainty of a very large loss are avoided. Furthermore, as has been illustrated, the reduction in financing costs, by using insurance, may actually be greater than the insurance premium paid. Without this insurance protection, U.S. firms would not be able to quote prices to meet international competition.

seller provides with respect to any one of these variables may be offset (sometimes more than offset) by adjustment of the other terms and conditions of sale and/or in the sales price. The nature of these trade-offs is discussed for each of the variables.
- B. Currency or denomination of billing.
    1. Denomination in the domestic or the foreign currency.
        a. Does the foreign currency carry a risk of devaluation?
        b. Is the foreign currency likely to be revalued upward?
    2. A general principle often suggested is to always bill in the strong currency.
        a. No general answer can be given.
        b. If prevailing market prices have already reflected the anticipated inflation and the appropriate risk premium for uncertain inflation, it should make no difference in which currency the billing takes place.
        c. If the market has overvalued the strong currency, one may actually gain by taking denomination in the weak currency.
    3. Accepting the general principle that the foreign exchange and financial markets are efficient, it will make a difference only when there is a temporary aberration such as overvaluing the strong currency or undervaluing the weak currency or government intervention.
- C. Credit terms. An infinite number of variations of terms are possible. These vary at the one extreme from no risk on the part of the seller, due to terms calling for all cash prior to shipment, to all of the risk on the part of the seller when an open account line of credit is granted on a medium-term transaction.
    1. Cash terms may require one of the following payments.
        a. Cash with order.
        b. Cash prior to shipment.
        c. Cash prior to receipt of goods.
        d. A series of scheduled payments all prior to the receipt of the goods by the buyer.
    2. Credit terms are strongly influenced by competition at the time of sale.
        a. Shortest credit terms—a sight draft on a correspondent bank of the foreign buyer's bank.
        b. Slightly extended terms—a sight draft to the foreign buyer or his bank.
        c. Longer credits—time drafts from one month to 5 to 7 years.
    3. It is generally assumed that there is less risk, and therefore greater profit, if a firm does not extend credit terms.
        a. Any generalization can be misleading.
        b. One must consider all the factors involved.
        c. If the buyer has to use cash, he may use this as a bargaining point to demand.
            (1) A lower price.
            (2) A specified delivery schedule.
            (3) A form of transportation selected by the buyer.

FINANCING WORLDWIDE COMMERCIAL SALES

4. If credit is extended to the buyer, this may call for a slightly higher price. In addition, the seller may take the time draft, perhaps a banker's acceptance, and discount it with an intermediary. Again there may be a trade-off between the higher price and the cost of discounting the time draft.
5. It is also possible that by the use of an intermediary, risk may be reduced by diversification. A widely diversified intermediary may be able to achieve a lower loss ratio for the world as a whole and may require a lower risk premium for his financing.
6. If a transaction is denominated in a foreign currency and on a credit basis, there exists a possible trade-off between an increase in the price, the charge of a rate of interest during the credit period, and the possible devaluation of the currency used in the sale.

D. The risks of bill-of-exchange transactions.
   1. The risk is least if a confirmed, irrevocable letter of credit is used.
   2. The risk is slightly greater if an unconfirmed, irrevocable letter of credit is used.
   3. Considerably greater risk is present if a revocable letter of credit is used.
   4. The greatest amount of risk is present when credit is granted on an open account basis.
   5. Again, in this kind of a problem there are a number of trade-offs. The confirmed, irrevocable letter of credit is safest. However it may call for a reduction in price to offset the cost of the credit instrument to the buyer. The sale on open account is riskiest. However, it may be possible to balance this greater risk with a higher price. It is also possible that the discounting of the time draft may be less costly than the increase in price due to the greater diversification of risks on a worldwide basis on the part of the intermediary.

E. Risk reduction by action of government.
   1. Medium- to long-term credits are available to assist in the financing of qualified projects. These are available from
      a. Eximbank.
      b. PEFCO.
      c. OPIC. (See Chapter 13 for details.)
   2. Risk reduction may be achieved by the purchase of political and commercial risk insurance from
      a. Eximbank.
      b. FCIA. (See Chapter 9 for more details.)
   3. In this matter there are also a number of trade-offs available to the exporter.
      a. He can incur the cost of risk insurance protection and at the same time lower his financing costs.
      b. He may charge a higher price and use the increase to pay the insurance premium.

c. In this instance there is no trade-off between the seller's position and the buyer's position. It is simply good business to employ this protection since the uncertainty and the potential magnitude of these losses are too great in relation to the insurance premium required.
F. Recognition of adjustments required by the operation of efficient markets.
1. If all of the market relationships are in full equilibrium, it should not matter which of the risk protection measures is employed.
2. A reasonable number of trade-offs are always available in connection with export transactions as can be seen from Figure 12-1.

PROBLEM 12-6

A U.S. exporter sells farm equipment worth one million pesos to a Latin American country on a 1-year open account basis. The spot rate of the pesos is presently P20=$1. The dollar value of the peso is expected to continue to devalue at a rate of 10%. The exporter's opportunity cost of funds is 12%. He can borrow funds in the United States at 10%. He has the following choices:
1. Enter the forward market on a 1-year basis to sell P1 million at a discount of 20% of the present dollar value of the peso.
2. Borrow P1 million from a bank in the customer's country at an interest cost of 30% and convert the proceeds of the loan immediately into dollars at the existing spot rate. The loan will be liquidated at the end of the year with the pesos received from the customer. Due to competitive conditions the exporter will have to pay the interest on the loan.
3. Arrange a swap with a commercial bank in the customer's country at a swap discount of 20% on the peso value of the dollar and the borrowing rate on the pesos thus obtained is 15%. The pesos will be converted into dollars at the spot rate. The swap will be reversed using the funds obtained from the customer. The U.S. funds required for the swap will be borrowed by the exporter at 10% in the United States. His marginal income tax rate in the United States is 50%.

Evaluate the cost and risk of each alternative. Which should the exporter adopt?

SOLUTION:

Alternative 1. The 1-year forward contract purchased at a discount of 20% eliminates all further exchange-rate risk. In addition, since he will not have any receipts from this transaction until the end of the year, an opportunity cost of 12% must be charged under this alternative.

$$\text{Total cost} = \text{forward contract cost after U.S. taxes}$$
$$= F_o(E_o - E_f)(1 - t_{us})$$
$$E_o = 1/X_o$$

$$= (1{,}000{,}000)(.05-.04)(1-0.5)$$
$$= 50{,}000(.01)$$
$$= \$5{,}000$$

In this instance the cost of the forward contract is a tax deductible item in the home country of the exporter. It does not matter whether this is eventually listed as an expense of the forward contract or a loss on the sale; it still reduces income before taxes.

Alternative 2. Borrowing in the foreign country eliminates the exchange-rate risk on the principal. The borrowed funds will be converted at the spot rate into the home currency. It is reasonably certain that the expense of borrowing would be considered a tax deductible expense for income tax purposes.

$$\text{Total cost} = F_o R_f \bar{E}_1 (1-t_{us}) - F_o R_{us} E_o (1-t_{us})$$
$$= 1{,}000{,}000(0.30)(0.045)(1-0.50)$$
$$- 1{,}000{,}000(.10)(1-.5)(.05)$$
$$= \$6{,}750 - 2{,}500 = \$4{,}250$$

The opportunity return of the funds received immediately as a result of the conversion of the local currency funds into dollars will not be counted in this instance since the lack of these funds was charged as an expense under alternative 1.

Alternative 3. In this instance it is assumed that the exporter borrows the required dollars at home and would convert the pesos obtained into dollars at the spot rate. He also pays the foreign interest on the pesos at the end of the year when the exchange rate is P22=$1.

$$\text{Total cost} = F_o E_s R_{us}(1-t_{us}) + F_o R_s \bar{E}_1 (1-t_{us})$$
$$= (1{,}000{,}000)(0.0625)(0.10)(.5)+1{,}000{,}000(0.15)(0.045)(.5)$$
$$= 100{,}000(0.0625)(0.5) + 150{,}000(0.045)(0.5)$$
$$= \$3{,}125 + \$3{,}375$$
$$= \$6{,}500$$

In this instance, as in alternative 2, the exporter has the dollars obtained by conversion of the P1 million at the spot rate available for business purposes. The interest cost of the dollars borrowed for the swap and the foreign swap interest are tax deductible as an expense of doing business. Of the three alternatives, the second has the lowest cost and it is the least complicated.

It also makes the dollar equivalent of P1 million available to the exporter during the year. The foreign-exchange-rate risk is frozen at 20% in alternative 1 and is eliminated on the principal in alternatives 2 and 3. However, the elimination of this risk is not cost-free. There is no protection against the inability of the buyer to meet his obligations.

PROBLEM 12-7

The Williams Company has made a sale of machinery to a foreign customer, the AFC Corporation. The Williams Company has offered to provide one-year financing. The present spot rate is LC30 = $1 and the sale in dollars is $100,000. The expected devaluation of the local currency in terms of one dollar is 8%. The forward rate for one year is a discount of the LC value of the dollar of 10%. A swap is available at the discount of 20% on the LC value of a dollar and the swap interest rate is 6%. The opportunity cost of U.S. funds is 10%. The Williams Company can borrow foreign at 15% and at home at a rate of 8%. The income tax rate in the foreign country is 30% and in the United States it is 50%.

Due to his need, the foreign customer has agreed to pay all financing charges. He has asked that he be given the financing costs of various proposals in his currency. The various alternatives considered are as follows:

1. Make a U.S. dollar loan of $100,000 at 8%. Under this alternative AFC Corporation would repay $100,000 at the end of the year plus interest on $100,000 at 8%.
2. Extend the dollar credit at 8% for one year protecting the principal by a forward contract. This protects the customer on the principal against any devaluation in excess of the discount on the forward contract. However, he would still have to pay the interest at the end-of-the-year spot rate since the interest is not covered by the forward contract.
3. Finance the sale via a credit swap. As in alternative 2, the principal is protected against further devaluation but not the interest due at the end of the loan period.
4. The Williams Company borrows the funds on behalf of AFC in the foreign country since the customer is unable to do so directly. The customer will repay the loan and interest at the end of the year.

Which of the above methods would be the least expensive in local currency? What, if any, would be the risks to either the Williams Company or its customer?

SOLUTION:

Alternative 1. Under this alternative the loan and interest would be in dollars, removing all of the foreign-exchange-rate risk from the Williams Company and placing it fully on the shoulders of the AFC Corporation. As the devaluation progresses the local currency debt of customers increases. The greatest risk to the company is the potential inability of the customer to meet his obligation. For this eventuality, FCIA insurance would be available at a cost.

$$\begin{aligned}
\text{Cost} &= \text{cost of interest} + \text{cost of the decrease in foreign exchange value of LC} \\
&= A_o R_{us}(1-t_f)\bar{X}_1 + A_o(\bar{X}_1 - X_o) \\
&= \$100{,}000(0.08)(1-0.3)(32.4) + 100{,}000(32.4 - 30.0) \\
&= \text{LC}181{,}440 + 240{,}000 \\
&= \text{LC}421{,}440
\end{aligned}$$

Alternative 2. This alternative is similar to the one above except that here the risk of the deterioration of the foreign exchange value of the local currency above LC32.4 = \$1 is eliminated for the principal sum.

$$\begin{aligned}
\text{Cost} &= A_o R_{us}(1-t_f)\bar{X}_1 + A_o(X_f - X_o) \\
&= 100{,}000(0.08)(1-0.3)(32.4) + 100{,}000(33.0 - 30.0) \\
&= 181{,}440 + 300{,}000 \\
&= \text{LC } 481{,}440
\end{aligned}$$

The assumption here, as in the other alternatives, is that interest payments are tax deductible in the foreign country.

Alternative 3. Here the Williams Company is required to borrow \$125,000 to furnish to the swap bank free of interest. Therefore the buyer will reimburse the Williams Company for the interest on the U.S. loan. The swap protects the buyer from devaluation of his currency on the principal but does not protect his interest payment.

$$\begin{aligned}
\text{Cost} &= \text{cost of dollar funds} + \text{cost of interest on the local currency} \\
&= (F_o/S_o)(R_{us})(1-t_f)\bar{X}_1 + F_o R_s(1-t_f) \\
&= (3{,}000{,}000/24)(0.08)(1-0.3)(32.4) + 3{,}000{,}000(0.06)(.7) \\
&= 125{,}000(0.08)(0.7)(32.4) + 180{,}000(0.7) \\
&= 226{,}800 + 126{,}000 \\
&= \text{LC}352{,}800
\end{aligned}$$

The foreign currency received from the swap is converted into dollars at the spot rate. The firm considers this amount payment for the goods sold.

Alternative 4. Here the Williams Company borrows the LC3 million at 15% in the foreign country and converts the LC into dollars at the spot rate. This results in an immediate payment to the Williams Company of $100,000 and thus eliminates all foreign-exchange-rate risk for both firms. Since the customer's obligations are all in his currency, he also has no further exposure to exchange-rate risk.

$$\begin{aligned} \text{Cost} &= \text{cost of local currency borrowing} \\ &= F_o R_f (1-0.3) \\ &= 3{,}000{,}000 (0.15)(1-0.3) \\ &= 450{,}000 (0.7) \\ &= \text{LC}315{,}000 \end{aligned}$$

This is the least costly of the alternatives. It is also the most effective from a point of foreign exchange risk elimination. The company would be well advised to eliminate at least 70% to 90% of its commercial and political risks by a FCIA policy.

PROBLEM 12-8

The Anderson Company needs to finance an equipment purchase of $375,000 for a period of one year. The equipment will be used to initiate a new subsidiary in a foreign country. The parent wants the new organization to make payments out of income. Two methods of financing have been suggested.

1. The Anderson firm can provide funds to the new subsidiary at its cost of capital of 10%.
2. A credit swap can be arranged by the Anderson firm furnishing the required dollars. The local currency interest on the swap is to be paid by the subsidiary at a rate of 12%.

The present spot rate is LC8=$1. The spot rate at the end of the year is very uncertain. The swap rate demanded by the bank is LC6.25=$1. The profitability of the new enterprise is estimated to be 40% and the local tax rate 30%. Interest payments are deductible for tax purposes. Anderson Company wants to know the largest percentage of devaluation of the local currency value of a dollar that still permits the new firm to meet all its obligation without loss of capital. To solve this problem one can make use of the foreign investment profitability formulas discussed in Chapter 10.

SOLUTION:

1. The formula for the nonswap financing is

$$R_g^n = (X_o/X_1)[1 + g_f(1-t_f)] - [1 + k_p] = 0$$

The above relationship can be solved for X_1 the unknown quantity.

$$X_1 = \frac{X_o[1+g_f(1-t_f)]}{1+k_p} = \frac{8[1+.4(1-.3)]}{1+0.1}$$

$$= 8(1.28)/1.1 = 9.31$$

Now calculate the percentage change.

$$\text{Percentage change} = (X_1 - X_o)/X_o = (9.31-8.0)/8.0 = 16.4\%$$

2. The formula for the swap financing is

$$R_g^s = (S_o/X_1)(g_f - R_s)(1 - t_f) - k_p$$

Solve the above for X_1.

$$X_1 = \frac{S_o(g_f - R_s)(1-t_f)}{k_p} = 6.25(0.4-0.12)(1-0.3)/0.1$$

$$= 6.25(0.28)(0.7)/0.1 = 12.25$$

Now calculate percentage change.

$$\text{Percentage change} = (12.25 - 8.0)/8.0 = 53.1\%$$

The results show that under the use of the swap, the future spot rate can decline by 53.1% and still have the venture break even. Without the swap arrangement, a devaluation of the LC of only 16.4% would wipe out all profits. Hence, the swap financing assures the profitability of the new subsidiary under situations short of a catastrophic decline in the value of the local currency.

REFERENCES

Business International Corp.: *Financing Foreign Operations*, New York, 1976.

Greene, James: *Organizing for Exporting*, National Industrial Conference Board Business Policy Study Number 26, New York, 1968.

Hollis, Stanley E.: *Guide to Export Credit Insurance*, Foreign Credit Insurance Association, New York, 1971.

Lykes, Richard S.: *A Handbook on Financing U.S. Exports*, Machinery and Allied Products Institute, Washington, D.C., 1972.

Morgan Guaranty Trust Company: *The Financing of Exports and Imports*, New York, 1973.

Nehrt, Lee C.: *Financing Capital Equipment Exports*, International Textbook, Scranton, Pa., 1966.

Chapter 13

Financing International Operations

Theme: The general principles affecting financing decisions are the same for international financing as for domestic financing. However, the variables affecting financing decisions are expanded and the alternative financing methods and sources are increased. The forms and sources of financing are similar in the different countries of the world, but important differences provide new pitfalls and additional opportunities. A wide range of alternatives must be evaluated in both quantitative and qualitative terms in choosing between alternative sources, forms, and the localities of international financing. Financing in an international setting makes use of the increasingly important international financing markets—the Eurocurrency and Eurobond markets. In international financing, the facilities of private lending institutions are augmented substantially by international lending agencies, national development banks, and other government agencies performing important functions in financing international operations and projects.

I. Summary framework of alternative financing forms and sources.
   A. Alternative forms of financing.
      1. Regardless of the location of the firm or the sources of its financing, the forms of financing used will reflect some combination of the basic types of financing.

    a. Equity financing—internal and external.
    b. Long-term debt—secured and unsecured.
    c. Short-term financing—secured and unsecured.
    d. Debt forms with options on equity positions.
 2. Within these basic forms, variations exist with regard to the specific characteristics of each type of financing as shown in Table 13-1.

Table 13-1 Characteristics of Forms of Funds

Forms of Funds	Fixed Cost	Fixed Maturity Date	Tax Deductibility	Loss of Control	Flexibility for Future
Long-term Financing					
Common stock	Limited to dividends	No	No	Yes, if new shareholders	Widens financial base
Preferred stock	Limited to dividends	No	No	Some	Some restrictions
Debt (bonds)	Yes	Yes	Yes	Indenture provisions	Bond restrictions
Retained earnings	No	No	Avoids double taxation	No	No restrictions
Intermediate Financing					
Conditional sales contract	Interest	Yes	Yes	Some	Must meet payments
Leasing	Yes	Yes	Yes	Some	Must meet payments
Short-term Unsecured Financing					
Trade credit	No	Discount date and due date	Yes	Some	Frees cash
Commercial paper	Interest	Yes	Yes	Some restrictions	Restricts
Financial intermediaries	Interest	Yes	Yes	No	No effect
Short-term Secured Financing					
Accounts receivable financing	No	Yes	Yes	Some	Sales generate funds
Accounts receivable factoring	No	Yes	Yes	Some	Restrict buyers
Inventory financing	No	Yes	Yes	Some	Inventory controls

Source: From J. Fred Weston, "Sources and Costs of Obtaining Funds," in H. W. Stevenson and J. R. Nelson (eds.), *Profits in the Modern Economy*, University of Minnesota Press, Minneapolis, 1967, pp. 151–153.

FINANCING INTERNATIONAL OPERATIONS

3. The forms of financing differ with respect to five aspects.
   a. Is it a fixed obligation of the enterprise?
   b. Does it require fixed payments and have a fixed maturity date?
   c. What is the nature and extent of tax deductibility?
   d. What is its possible effect on voting control of the enterprise?
   e. Does it provide potential for additional financing in the future?

B. Alternative sources of financing.
   1. Alternative sources of financing differ with respect to these areas.
      a. Duration of the use of funds.
      b. Form of financing characteristically supplied.
      c. Degree of risk taken by the supplier of funds.
      d. Stability of the availability of funds.
      e. Facilities for administering mass financing.
      f. The nature of the contacts between the financing source and the borrower.
      g. The amount of management counsel provided.
   2. The main alternative sources of financing with their different characteristics are shown in Table 13-2.

C. Factors influencing the sources and forms of financing utilized by firms.
   1. Size and age of firm.
      a. New firms are restricted mainly to owner-supplied equity financing, credit from suppliers of goods, and secured short-term credits.
      b. As the firm establishes a high growth and profitability record, it may be able to obtain long-term debt financing and equity financing from the money and capital markets.
      c. As a firm matures, its growth rate and profitability levels are lower. The need for external financing is reduced and the firm utilizes internal financing to a greater degree.
   2. Industry characteristics.
      a. A new industry offers high growth and profitability opportunities and may stimulate the availability of external long-term debt and equity financing under favorable terms.
      b. Small business industries such as the wholesale and retail trades are characterized by easy entry of new firms and a tendency toward unfavorable sales-to-capacity relationships, with resulting high mortality rates. They depend heavily on financing by owners, by suppliers of goods, and by secured short-term financing.
      c. Industries that have reached maturity in their life cycle of growth are often characterized by the survival of a relatively small number of large firms which utilize internal financing to a high degree.
   3. Economic and financial environment.
      a. The high rate of inflation in recent years has increased the need for the use of external financing for most firms and industries.
      b. Improvements in transportation and communication have resulted in a greater degree of international operations by business firms.

Table 13-2 Summary of Characteristics of Alternative Sources of Financing

Source of Funds	Duration of Use of Funds	Form of Financing Supplied	Risk Taken by Source of Funds	Availability of Funds	Facilities for Mass Financing	Nature of Contact	Amount of Management Counsel
1. Commercial banks	Mainly short-term some medium	Debt	Low (high quality)	Cyclical variations	Limited	Close	Moderate to considerable
2. Interbusiness suppliers	Short, medium, and long	Debt and equity	Continuing low to high	Variable	Small	Close and direct	Small to considerable
3. Life insurance companies	Medium to long-term	Mostly debt	Low (high quality)	Secular growth	Limited	Limited but direct	Small to moderate
4. Finance companies	Continuing	Debt	Considerable	Cyclical	Considerable	Close	Small to considerable
5. Mutual savings banks	Long-term	Debt	Secured by real estate	Stable	None	Indirect	None
6. Fire and casualty insurance companies	Long-term	Debt and equity	Moderate	Variable	None	Indirect	Small
7. Investment companies	Long-term	Debt and equity	Low (high quality)	Variable	None	Indirect	None
8. Pension funds	Long-term	Debt and equity	Low (high quality)	Stable	None	Indirect	None
9. Savings and loan associations	Long-term	Debt	Medium to low	Stable	None	Direct	None
10. Educational and religious funds	Long-term	Debt and equity	Low (high quality)	Variable	None	Indirect	None
11. Investment development corporation	Long-term	Debt and equity	Moderate to high	Stable	None	Direct and close	Considerable
12. Open market sales of debt	Short, medium, and long	Debt	Low to medium	Variable	Small	Indirect	Moderate
13. Equity markets	Permanent	Equity Mostly equity	Full range	Erratic	None	Indirect	None
14. Employees	Long-term		Moderate to high	Erratic	None	Direct	None
15. Customers	Long-term	Debt and equity	Moderate to high	Erratic	None	Indirect	None

Source: From J. Fred Weston, "Sources and Costs of Obtaining Funds," in H. W. Stevenson and J. R. Nelson (eds.), *Profits in the Modern Economy*, University of Minnesota Press, Minneapolis, 1967, p. 151.

This has been associated with the greater use of international financing sources.

c. Restrictions on international capital flows, especially those employed by the United States from 1968 to 1974 contributed to the development of new international financing markets such as the Eurocurrency and Eurobond markets.

II. Financing in an international setting.
   A. Different currencies and issues of nationality of ownership and control introduce new variables affecting financing of the international firm.
      1. Figure 13-1 illustrates a range of possible relationships and their interactions.
      2. Although a number of possible relationships could develop within the framework of Figure 13-1, some predominant patterns have emerged.
         a. A preference for and predominance of 100% ownership of subsidiaries.
         b. Foreign investors can participate in the total by debt and equity ownership investments in the parent firm.
         c. Major decisions, with respect to financing of the operating foreign subsidiaries, are made by the parent firm.
   B. Financing forms distinctive to international business.
      1. The use of overdrafts in European business is similar to a line of credit in the United States.
      2. The growth of discounting trade bills as a form of financing is a relatively recent development in the United States, but has been more widespread in Europe.
         a. The growth of international trade has spurred the use of this form.
         b. Bankers' acceptances, arising from international transactions, account for more than half of the total outstanding volume of these investments in the United States.
      3. European commercial banks participate in more medium- and long-term foreign lending activities than do U.S. commercial banks. This stems from U.S. legal requirements which separate investment banking activities from commercial bank activities.
      4. Other financial practices distinct to international business are Arbi-loans and link financing.
         a. Arbi-loans represent international arbitrage financing.
            (1) Borrower obtains loans in a country where funds are more available and converts them to the local currency he needs for business.
            (2) The borrower simultaneously takes a forward exchange contract to protect the reconversion value of the local currency.
            (3) The cost of the Arbi-loan is the interest rate on the foreign loan and the differential on the forward exchange contract.

Figure 13-1 Schematic Representation of Financing Patterns in the MNC

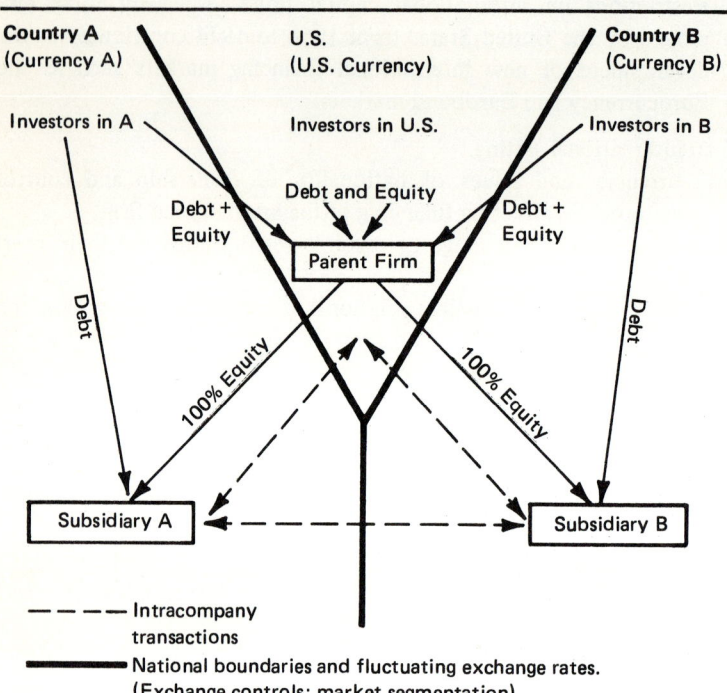

Source: Ruediger Naumann-Etienne, "A Framework for Financial Decisions in Multinational Corporations—Summary of Recent Research," *Journal of Financial and Quantitative Analysis,* 9:862, November 1974.

      (4) Commercial banks are involved in Arbi-loans both as lenders and as intermediaries in foreign exchange.
  b. Link financing.
      (1) A lender in a foreign country deposits funds with a bank in the borrower's country where interest rates are higher.
          (a) Funds may be earmarked for a specific borrower, or
          (b) May be channeled through a money broker.
      (2) Lender hedges his position in the forward exchange market, since repayment is in the currency of the country in which the bank deposit is made.
  c. Both of these help to equalize the supply and demand of loanable funds across interest-rate levels in different countries.

FINANCING INTERNATIONAL OPERATIONS

III. Financing subsidiaries are established to serve as a conduit in international financing. (See also Section III, B6 of Chapter 7, which deals with taxation.)
   A. Main reasons.
      1. Avoidance of withholding tax at the source in the country in which debt financing takes place.
      2. To supplement the thin equity base of the operating subsidiaries by placing the parent company's financial strength behind the issue through a guarantee by the parent.
   B. Domestic financing subsidiary.
      1. Under Section 861(a) of the Internal Revenue Code (IRC) when more than 80% of the gross income of a domestic corporation is from foreign sources, interest or dividends paid to nonresidents of the United States are not subject to the U.S. withholding tax.
         a. Most are incorporated in Delaware and known as 861 or 80-20 corporations.
         b. They are often highly leveraged.
            (1) The accepted debt-to-equity ratio is 5 to 1.
            (2) Equity subscribed in cash can be reloaned to parent.
            (3) Equity can be subscribed by a transfer of shares in other foreign operating subsidiaries of the parent.
         c. Ease of administration—parent company officers can fill executive positions.
         d. These subsidiaries had further advantages under Office of Foreign Direct Investment (OFDI) regulations until OFDI discontinued in 1974.
      2. Other tax aspects.
         a. Delaware subsidiaries are subject to regular U.S. income tax rates regardless of the source of their income, but their foreign taxes can be treated as a credit.
         b. Interest and dividend income of Delaware finance subsidiaries are subject to withholding taxes of foreign countries, but at reduced rates under U.S. tax treaties.
         c. Over 80% of income must be derived from foreign sources to be exempt from U.S. withholding tax.
            (1) If financing proceeds are invested overseas in operations, there is no problem.
            (2) If proceeds are used in the United States, the subsidiary's income will be considered American source income and its 80-20 status will be lost.
   C. Overseas financing subsidiary.
      1. Preferable when financing proceeds are used in the United States.
         a. Income could be from U.S. sources, but if its business is conducted outside the United States, it is not subject to U.S. withholding tax.

        b. Meetings of directors and shareholders and significant actions by officers should take place outside the United States.
    2. Use of Netherlands Antilles as a site.
        a. Low incorporation and annual operating costs.
        b. Tax treaties between Netherlands and United States include the Netherlands Antilles.

IV. Expanding role of U.S. commercial banks and investment bankers in international financing.
  A. Commercial banks.
    1. Have long performed an important role in export and import financing.
    2. Have participated in financing international operations with their Edge Act corporations through which commercial banks can make equity investments.
    3. Have increased the number of foreign branches and have expanded their operations and lending activities.
    4. Participation in consortia with foreign merchant banks and investment banking firms for the conduct of all forms of international financing services.
    5. Edge Act subsidiaries.
        a. Provided for by amendments in 1916 and 1919 to the Federal Reserve Act of 1913.
        b. U.S. commercial banks are permitted to engage in activities in international markets from which they are prohibited in their domestic activities.
            (1) Conduct all forms of international banking—issue or confirm letters of credit, finance foreign trade, engage in spot and forward foreign exchange transactions, etc.
            (2) May establish foreign banking subsidiaries and affiliates.
            (3) Can make direct investments in commercial and industrial firms in both debt and equity forms.
    6. European banking response.
        a. Many European banks form consortia or other groupings or agreements to meet the increasing competition from foreign branches of U.S. banks.
        b. Some immediate benefits of group cooperation, such as access to a broader branch network, have been gained and more are expected to come.
  B. Investment banking firms.
    1. Have actively participated in arranging Eurocurrency financing.
    2. Have developed joint participation activities with foreign merchant banks and with foreign investment banking houses.
    3. Have established offices in foreign countries and participated in the international underwriting groups which have led to the development of the Eurobond market.

C. International project financing[1]
1. Large investment projects usually involving joint ventures between government and private enterprise, financed from international and government sources as well as from private sources, often through a Eurodollar bank syndicate.
2. Characteristics.
   a. Large investment for development activities.
   b. Normally more than one equity owner of the project company.
   c. Equity owners collectively possess the requisite operating, technical, marketing, and financial strengths to achieve a successful project.
   d. Normal corporate guarantees of debt are not provided.
3. Financial characteristics.
   a. Relatively high debt leverage is employed.
   b. Since the projects provide output for international markets, debt is issued in several currencies.
   c. Sources of debt are commercial banks, export credit agencies, suppliers, product purchasers, international lending agencies, regional or national development banks, and local governments.
   d. International investment bankers serve as project financial advisors, fitting together the various types of financing needed to meet the requirements of the project.
   e. Each transaction will include various covenants related directly to the characteristics of the project.

PROBLEM 13-1

Discuss the role of foreign branches of U.S. banks in the financing of the multinational activities of U.S. business firms.

SOLUTION:

Essentially, foreign branches are capable of doing everything that Edge Act subsidiaries can do, except create bankers' acceptances of more than 6 months duration and make equity-type loans.
A. Original functions.
   1. Provide foreign exchange.
   2. Handle documentation of trade bills, letters of credit, etc.
   3. Provide funds to finance credit sales abroad.
B. Their growth has been spurred by the growth of U.S. MNCs.
   1. Provide long-term as well as short-term financing.

---

[1] For a more complete discussion see Robert L. Huston, Senior Vice President, White, Weld & Company, "Project Financing," Chapter 42 in J. F. Weston and M. G. Goudzwaard (eds.), *Treasurer's Handbook*, Dow Jones-R. D. Irwin, Homewood, Ill., 1976.

2. International cash management programs designed for MNCs.
3. An important source of foreign exchange.
C. Commercial banks are themselves becoming multinational corporations with interests in all aspects of financial asset management.

V. The Eurodollar system.
   A. The Eurodollar system provides an international money market.
      1. Developed in early 1950s as banks accepted interest-bearing deposits in currencies other than their own.
      2. Primarily took place in Europe where the predominant foreign currency used was the dollar (hence, Eurodollar market). Now the Eurodollar system is worldwide and includes many different currencies.
   B. Eurodollars are created when a depositor in a domestic U.S. bank transfers claims on domestic funds to a foreign bank or a foreign branch of a domestic bank.
      1. These transfers are often made in response to higher interest rates on deposits abroad.
      2. The foreign bank accepts these deposits because it can lend funds at higher rates.
   C. Factors behind growth of the Eurodollar market.
      1. Governmental controls on U.S. credit system sparked initial growth.
         a. Regulation Q restricts maximum interest payable on U.S. bank deposits, so funds flow out to foreign banks where allowable rates are higher.
         b. The Interest Equalization Tax (IET) raised the cost of foreign borrowing in the United States thereby making Eurodollar loans more attractive to foreign borrowers.
         c. Attempts by Office of Foreign Direct Investments to control the outflow of U.S. dollars made Eurodollars the primary source of financing foreign business activities of U.S. firms.
         d. Both (b) and (c) were lifted as of January 1974.
      2. Need of an international currency to facilitate international trade expansion.
         a. Dollar was strong and widely accepted as means of payment.
         b. Dollar provided short-term liquidity and long-term source of funds unavailable in other continental capital markets.
   D. Eurodollar deposits and loans.
      1. The Eurobanks, including foreign branches of many U.S. banks, accept Eurodollar deposits and loan these funds.
         a. Transactions are in large amounts.
         b. Small spreads between the interest rate on loans and the interest paid on deposits.
         c. Fast turnaround—most transactions are arranged over the phone or cable systems with the confirming documents following later in the mail.

2. Eurodollar deposits.
   a. Most have a maturity of less than a year.
   b. Time deposits.
      (1) For deposits with a maturity of less than 3 months or for amounts under $100,000.
      (2) In the form of overnight deposits, call money, or other accounts.
   c. Certificates of deposit (CDs).
      (1) For amounts over $100,000 in maturities longer than 3 months.
      (2) Negotiable certificates of deposit were introduced in 1966. Some are floating rate notes.
      (3) There is also a forward market for CDs in London. The bank commits itself to a certificate of deposit at a specific future date and rate.
3. Eurodollar loans.
   a. Amounts are typically multiples of $1 million. Maturities range from 30 days to 5 to 7 years.
   b. If the borrower is known to the bank, a loan of less than a year can be arranged over the phone or cable system. Parent guarantee, if required, can also be handled over the phone.
   c. Eurodollar loans are typically unsecured, but there may be other restrictions placed on the borrowing activities of the firm receiving the loan. The loans are also not typically amortized.
   d. Floating rate revolving loans (known as *revolvers* or *roll-over credits*).
      (1) The rate on the loan is quoted as a percentage above the London interbank offer rate (LIBO) reflecting rates on liquid funds that flow between the money markets of the developed nations. The intervals at which the LIBO rate will be changed are also specified.
      (2) The floating rate provision dampens borrowing based on speculation on future interest rates.
      (3) Prime borrowers typically pay from [LIBO + 3/4%] for 7- to 8-year maturities down to [LIBO + 3/8%] for 5-year maturities. Others pay [LIBO + 2% to 3%].
   e. Lines of credit.
      (1) For a given period not to exceed 12 months. The line of credit may be renegotiated at the end of the period.
      (2) There is usually a commitment fee of 1/4% to 1/2% on the unused portion of the credit.
      (3) Interest rates are set at the time a portion of the line of credit is used at a fixed percentage over an interbank rate.
E. Overview of the Eurodollar market process.
   1. A flow of the Eurodollar market is provided in Figure 13-2.

Figure 13-2 Flow Diagram of the Eurodollar Market

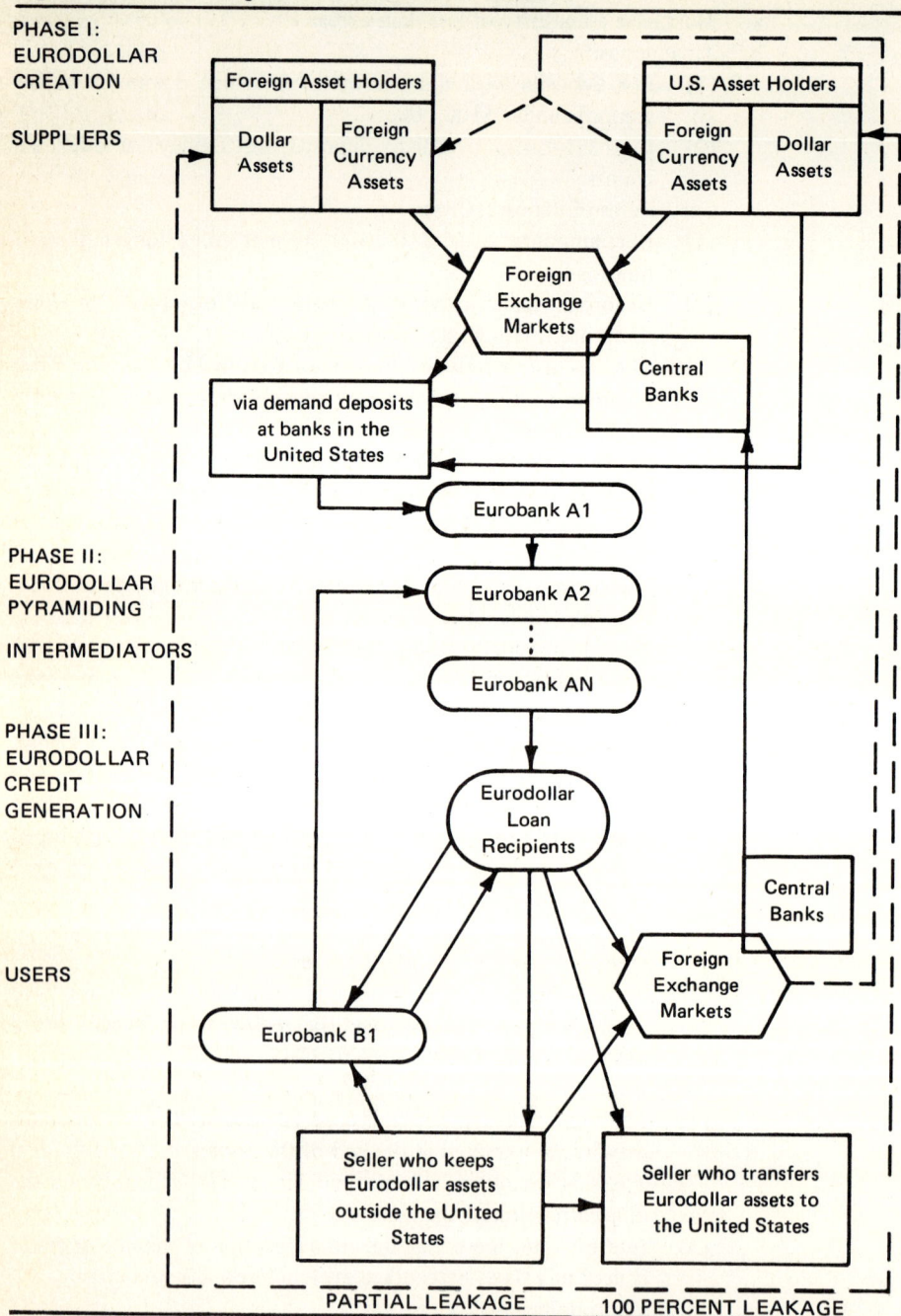

Source: Federal Reserve Bank of Cleveland, *Economic Review*, March 1970, p. 12.

2. The flow process of the Eurodollar market.
   a. A European holds a dollar deposit in a New York bank. He can hold the dollars in the form of a dollar deposit claim on his European bank by drawing a check on the New York banks and making a deposit in his European bank. The European bank can in turn make loans to other customers. Except for the fractional reserve held against its dollar deposit liabilities, the European bank has intermediated transfers of the dollar balances in the United States from its depositors to its borrowers. Yet its depositors still hold claims in dollars.
   b. Since Eurodollars do not circulate as a medium of exchange as do checks on demand deposits, the drainage or leakages out of the European banking system shown in the lower section of Figure 13-2 are likely to be larger than the deposit multiplier in a fractional reserve demand deposit system.
      (1) In this respect, the Eurobanks are like noncommercial bank financial intermediaries in the United States such as savings and loan associations that create noncirculating claims against themselves and serve as intermediaries in making loans.
      (2) The operations of financial intermediaries do not increase the money supply, narrowly defined, but they may increase its velocity.
         (a) If there were no excess reserves in the commercial banking systems of the United States or Europe before the movement of deposits, only the creation of time deposits not used as means of payment takes place.
         (b) If there were excess reserves in the commercial banking system before the movement of deposits, the Eurodollar system can thereby help to increase loans and result in expanding total loans and deposits.
3. Implications of the Eurodollar market.
   a. It contributes toward increasing and redistributing the world supply of international reserves or liquid resources.
   b. It has thereby facilitated the need to finance the growth in international transactions.
   c. It is an important addition to the development of a competitive and unified international money market.
   d. In redistributing the use of international liquid resources, it may cause exchange-rate movements, offsetting central bank actions, and create additional high-powered domestic commercial bank reserves.
   e. It thus increases the interdependence of the nation's money and capital markets with the economic and financial developments in other nations.

f. It expands the size of the upper layers in the inverted pyramid of money stocks on a given reserve base. Thus potential instability resulting from shocks to the international financial mechanisms might thereby be increased.
g. Its future development will be influenced by the pattern of locations where Arab oil dollars are invested or spent.

PROBLEM 13-2

A. Make the appropriate T-account entries to illustrate the operations of the Eurodollar market for the transactions which follow. (Key your entries by the letters of the transaction, (a), (b), etc.)
B. Make up a table recording
   1. The outstanding deposit liabilities of banks in New York.
   2. The total outstanding Eurodollar deposit liabilities of banks located abroad as of the end of each of the transactions (a) through (i).

Transactions to be recorded in T-accounts.

(a) A British bank transfers its demand deposits of $20,000 at New York bank A to make a time deposit in a German bank which has a demand deposit in New York bank B.
(b) The German bank uses its demand deposit of $20,000 at New York bank B to make a time deposit in a Swiss bank which has a demand deposit account in New York bank C.
(c) The Swiss bank uses its demand deposit of $20,000 at New York bank C to make a time deposit in a French bank which has an account in the New York bank D.
(d) The French bank uses its demand deposit of $20,000 at New York bank D to make a loan to a French importer who pays by check the New York commodity seller who deposits it in his account at New York bank E.
(e) The French trader sells the goods and repays the $20,000 loan to the French bank.
(f) The French bank pays off its $20,000 liability to the Swiss bank at maturity.
(g) The Swiss bank pays off its liability to the German bank at maturity.
(h) The German bank pays off its liability to the British bank at maturity.
(i) The British bank redeposits its $20,000 deposit at New York bank A.

FINANCING INTERNATIONAL OPERATIONS

SOLUTION:

A. T-accounts (amounts in thousands).

New York Bank A

(a)	Reserves to New York bank B	−20	(a)	Demand deposit of British bank B	−20
(i)	Cash	+20	(i)	Demand deposit of British bank B	+20

British Bank

			(a)	Demand deposit at New York bank A	−20
			(a)	Demand deposit at German bank	+20
			(h)	Time deposit at German bank	−20
			(h)	Cash	+20
			(i)	Cash	−20
			(i)	Demand deposit at New York bank A	+20

New York Bank B

(a)	Reserves from New York bank A	+20	(a)	Demand deposit of German bank	+20
(b)	Reserves to New York bank C	−20	(b)	Demand deposit of German bank	−20

German Bank

			(a)	Demand deposit at New York bank B	+20
			(a)	Time deposit due British bank	+20
			(b)	Demand deposit at New York bank B	−20
			(b)	Demand deposit at Swiss bank	+20
			(g)	Time deposit at Swiss bank	−20
			(g)	Cash	+20
			(h)	Cash	−20
			(h)	Time deposit due British bank	−20

New York Bank C

(b)	Reserves from New York bank B	+20	(b)	Demand deposit of Swiss bank	+20

Swiss Bank

			(b)	Demand deposit of New York bank C	+20
			(b)	Time deposit due German bank	+20

T-accounts (continued)

New York Bank C

(c)	Reserves to New York bank D	−20	(c)	Demand deposit of Swiss bank	−20

New York Bank D

(c)	Reserves from New York bank C	+20	(c)	Demand deposit of French bank	+20
(d)	Reserves to New York bank E	−20	(d)	Demand deposit of French bank	−20

New York Bank E

(d)	Reserves from New York bank D	+20	(d)	Demand deposit of New York commodity dealer	+20

Swiss Bank

			(c)	Demand deposit of New York bank C	−20
			(c)	Time deposit at French bank	+20
			(f)	Time deposit at French bank	−20
			(f)	Cash	+20
			(g)	Cash	−20
			(g)	Time deposit due German bank	−20

French Bank

			(c)	Demand deposit at New York bank D	+20
			(d)	Demand deposit at New York bank D	−20
			(d)	Loan outstanding to French importer	+20
			(e)	Loan outstanding to French importer	−20
			(e)	Cash	+20
			(f)	Cash	−20
			(c)	Time deposit due Swiss bank	+20
			(f)	Time deposit due Swiss bank	−20

French Trader

			(d)	Inventory of goods	+20
			(e)	Inventory of goods	−20
			(e)	Cash	+20
			(e)	Cash	−20
			(d)	Loan from French bank	+20
			(e)	Loan from French bank	−10

New York Commodity Dealer

			(d)	Inventory of goods	−20
			(d)	Demand deposit at New York bank E	+20

B. Deposit Liabilities

		1. Outstanding Deposit Liabilities of Banks in New York.	2. Outstanding Eurodollar Deposit Liabilities of Banks Located Abroad.
(a)	British bank places demand deposits of $20,000 at New York bank in Eurodollar market with German bank.	$20,000	$20,000
(b)	German bank places Eurodollar deposit with Swiss bank.	20,000	40,000
(c)	Swiss bank places Eurodollar deposit with French bank.	20,000	60,000
(d)	French bank makes Eurodollar loan to French importer.	20,000	60,000
(e)	French importer sells the goods and repays loan to French bank.	20,000	60,000
(f)	French bank pays off Eurodollar liability to Swiss bank at maturity.	20,000	40,000
(g)	Swiss bank meets its Eurodollar liability to German bank at maturity.	20,000	20,000
(h)	German bank repays Eurodollar liability to British bank at maturity.	20,000	0
(i)	British bank redeposits $20,000 at New York bank.	40,000	0

PROBLEM 13-3

Discuss the alternative views of the reasons for the development of the Eurodollar market and the extent to which its growth has resulted from new funds versus multiple expansion of initial dollar balances.

SOLUTION:

A. F. H. Klopstock (1970) has put forth the view that the ability of European banks to attract new dollar deposits is the primary reason for the development of the Eurodollar market. This view proceeds from the assumption that new deposits are necessary since leakages of Eurodollar-loan proceeds are so large that the market would not be viable without them. As a consequence, this position relies on chronic U.S. balance-of-payments deficits to generate the Eurodollar market structure. It is unlikely that this analysis can fully explain the size and adaptability of the existing market. Furthermore, it does not contain a specific mechanism by which dollars are attracted to Europe.

B. J. S. Little in her book, *The Eurodollar Market: Its Nature and Impact,* modifies the Klopstock view. She argues that the major reason for the existence of the Eurodollar market is that it helped restore convertibility of the European currencies. Specifically, U.S. investors were willing to exchange direct dollar claims for European time deposit claims because of the higher interest rate obtainable. In addition, confidence in the convertibility of the time deposits was established since, with chronic U.S. balance-of-payments deficits, European currencies were appreciating relative to the dollar. Little's modification improves the Klopstock position, but, since its effect is only indirect, it is doubtful that this is the complete story.

C. Other specific influences include:
1. Regulation Q, by placing a ceiling on the interest payment allowed on domestically held time deposits, makes it attractive to hold such deposits abroad. At one point, competition forced a 1/4% interest rate spread between American-held time deposits and those held in Europe. This allowed a brisk market for such accounts in London.
2. The Interest Equalization Tax made it difficult for foreign-based firms to obtain loans on favorable terms in the United States. Europeans found it difficult to raise dollar funds for investment purposes. Banks in Europe thus began to handle large dollar volumes to fill the gap.
3. Finally, regulations of the Office of Foreign Direct Investment made it difficult for American firms to raise funds in the United States for use in their European subsidiaries. Because of this, American banks began losing business to their European counterparts. The American banks then aggressively expanded their foreign branches to engage in such lending, thus, creating another segment of the Eurodollar market.

    But these specific influences cannot be regarded as the complete explanation because when (2) and (3) were repealed in January 1974, no great decline in the magnitude of Euromarket activity was observed. Also the Regulation Q influence would not be binding at a time when interest rates in the United States were high in relation to Western Europe. Another variable to consider is that the costs of holding reserves may be lower for the European banks (they have lower reserve requirements and the reserves need not be deposited with their central banks) and competition produces the interest rate differential in favor of European banks. If so, this is a more basic and continuing influence than the Regulation Q influence.
4. Friedman (1969) emphasizes what Machlup (1971) has called "multiplying rabbits out of the Eurodollar hat." That is, the market for Eurodollars is symptomatic of a multiplier-type process resulting from the redeposit of dollar loan proceeds with European banks,

i.e., a dollar loan from the United States is multiplied several times through the European fractional reserve system. This has allowed American-based and European-based firms to obtain dollar loans in Europe, thus avoiding a transaction in New York. This view is probably partially correct also, but since part of its effect rests on shifting investments from New York to Europe, it is a weak candidate for a full explanation. It is more likely that the complete answer lies somewhere between the Friedman/Klopstock views. Makin (1972) has tried to measure the effect of these positions. He attributes 40% of the growth of the Eurodollar market to multiple expansion and 60% to new funds.

5. Helmut Mayer concludes as follows:

> ... the growth of the Euromarket may, of course, have at times expansionary or inflationary effects by reducing balance-of-payments constraints for example, by swelling the flow of funds from countries with easy, to countries with tight, monetary conditions; by contributing to payment outflows from the United States as the reserve currency country; or by serving as a way around reserve requirements or national credit ceilings. In other words, the problem is not that when the national monetary authorities all succeed in containing the growth of their domestic money supplies, there will nevertheless be inflation because of money creation in the Euromarket, but rather that the Euromarket might make it more difficult for them to control their domestic money supply. Thus the liquidity offered by the Euromarket might make it necessary for the monetary authorities to adhere to slightly more restrictive domestic money supply targets.
>
> On the other hand, and quite apart from its allocative role, the financial possibilities offered by the Euromarket have often been welcome to the authorities in many countries; and at certain times, such as in 1974 when it helped to finance the international payments disequilibrium caused by the oil price increase and thus to contain the downward movement of world economic activity and to prevent the spreading of restrictive trade practices, its macro-economic consequences have been beneficial to the world economy as a whole. Nor is the market's influence always expansionary. In 1968-69, for instance, when the market drew in money to the United States from the rest of the world, its overall impact was contractionary.[2]

VI. The Eurobond market.
A. Historical background.

---

[2] Helmut W. Mayer, "The BIS Concept of the Eurocurrency Market," *Euromoney*, May 1976, p. 66.

1. In July 1963, President Kennedy proposed the Interest Equalization Tax (IET). The act was signed by President Johnson on September 2, 1964, and was made retroactive to July 18, 1963.
    a. This tax placed a levy, initially up to 15%, on all subsequent purchases by Americans of foreign debt and equity securities of developed countries.
    b. This caused a reduction in foreign-issue bonds in the United States.
2. The IET helped revive London as a capital market where international securities could be floated to attract funds from all over the world.
    a. Because of the weakness of the British pound it was necessary to issue securities in other than sterling to minimize the outflows of domestic funds for the purchase of nonresident issues.
    b. Issuing bonds denominated in dollars achieved this objective and the first major private issue was for an Italian company, Autostrade, in July 1963.
3. Foreign bonds, which were a precursor to Eurobonds
    a. Are issued by a borrower in a foreign country, but denominated in the currency of the lending country.
    b. Are sold by a national underwriting group of the lending country.
B. Eurobonds.
    1. Conventional type.
        a. Offered for sale in more than one country through *international* syndicates of underwriting and selling banks.
        b. Denomination of the Eurobond is in
            (1) A strong currency such as the German mark.
            (2) The U.S. dollar because:
                (a) It is the principal transaction currency.
                (b) Availability of large pool of Eurodollars.
    2. Eurobonds involving more than one currency.
        a. Multiple-currency bonds—creditor can request payment of the interest and principal in any predetermined currency at a previously established parity.
        b. European Monetary Unit (EMU) bonds—a multiple currency bond based upon the currency values of the six original Common Market countries.
        c. European Unit of Account bond.
            (1) Bond denominated in the unit of account of the European Payments Union.
            (2) Value of European Unit of Account (EUA) after 1972 linked to the reference values of the enlarged (to 9) Common Market currencies.
    3. Convertible Eurobonds.
        a. Stimulated by entry of U.S. firms into the Eurobond market.
        b. Advantages to issuing firms.

FINANCING INTERNATIONAL OPERATIONS 301

    (1) Lower interest rates are paid.
    (2) Larger amounts can be sold.
    (3) A method to internationalize the ownership of the common stock of U.S. MNCs with large direct investments and operations in foreign countries.
  c. Advantages to investors.
    (1) Fixed rate of interest higher than dividend yields plus potential capital gains.
    (2) The downside protection of selling on a yield basis similar to a straight bond.
4. Implications of the Eurobond market.
  a. While stimulated by the U.S. Interest Equalization Tax, has led to the development of underwriting activity and purchase of such bonds by investors in individual European countries.
  b. Has tended to internationalize the formerly local character of capital markets in individual European countries.
  c. Stimulates outflow of funds from countries such as Germany with balance-of-payments surpluses; substitutes for flow of funds from the United States when the United States has balance-of-payments deficits.

PROBLEM 13-4

What are the advantages and disadvantages of Eurodollar/Eurobond financing?

SOLUTION:

A. Advantages.
  1. Because of tight credit (or OFDI regulations prior to 1974), U.S. firms unable to transfer funds from the United States would be able to obtain these funds from an Edge Act bank or from other sources in Europe to meet their overseas commitments.
  2. Where LC funds market may not be broad enough or have sufficient equity financing available, or restrictions are placed on LC borrowing by foreign subsidiaries, Eurobond/Eurodollar financing often provides the only external source of the much needed funds.
  3. Eurodollar financing increases (or conserves) the amount of financing available in the U.S.
  4. It may be cheaper to raise funds in Europe, e.g., large American corporations were able to float 4.5% convertible bonds in the Eurodollar market early in 1972, when the U.S. prime rate was 5% and higher.
  5. Real costs may be cheaper as European banks lend at a rate to make some spread over their costs, whereas domestic lenders usually require compensating balances of 10 to 20%.

6. If the account is large and the customer well known at a bank, a short-term loan may be obtained at relatively easier terms and with minimal documentation in the Eurodollar market.

B. Disadvantages.
1. The parent corporation may be required to guarantee the subsidiary's loan.
2. There are controls on repayment of debt in foreign currencies in some countries.
3. The rates may be higher than comparable U.S. rates.
4. Investors are vulnerable to Interest Equalization Tax and other similar charges that may be instituted in the countries involved, hence wiping out the relative advantages of such types of financing.
5. Eurodollar deposits are not negotiable instruments, and cannot be readily liquidated.
6. Nonfractional reserve system and deposit/loan maturity dates differences may cause European banks to foreclose "shaky" creditors instead of working with them.

PROBLEM 13-5

Why would a Japanese firm issue securities in the United States which involves the SEC registration requirements when most of the issue is sold to European investors?

SOLUTION:

This involves the actual sale of $50 million convertible debentures by Mitsui in October 1975. The transaction is discussed in the *Institutional Investor*, (International edition), March 1976, p. 6. Most of the underwriting fees went to the U.S. underwriters invited to participate by the comanagers—Smith, Barney; Goldman Sachs; Nomura Securities. Yet most of the initial sales were to European institutions buying through European members of the underwriting syndicate.

This raised a number of questions. Why didn't Mitsui avoid the requirements of SEC registration and float the issue in Europe? Tatsuo Nagashima, Vice President for Finance of Mitsui's U.S. subsidiary, explained that while the European capital market may become unavailable during a period of tight money, the depth of the U.S. capital market insures that funds are always available. Why didn't Mitsui use a private placement? The answer here was that Mitsui preferred to have its financing be as visible and broadly based as possible to keep its future alternatives as broad as possible.

PROBLEM 13-6

"If a country is engaged in large foreign borrowing, we can expect that while the borrowing is taking place its currency will exhibit weakness in the foreign exchange markets." Comment on this "obviously correct practical statement."

SOLUTION:

Direct material on this statement is provided by an article in the *Wall Street Journal*, April 26, 1976, p. 10. The article comments on the continued increasing strength of the Canadian dollar, stating,

> The Canadian dollar's strength has come largely from a very heavy schedule of external borrowings by Canadian corporations and provinces to take advantage of lower interest costs available in other lands . . . Canada's large overseas debt placements (outside the U.S.) have created strong demand for Canada's currency because lenders must round up Canadian dollars to acquire the Canadian-dollar denominated issues. Canadian debt issues placed in the U.S. are denominated in U.S. currency, but [since the money is spent in Canada for projects in Canada] this must be converted into Canadian dollars by the borrowers, putting further upward pressure on Canada's currency.

The article notes concern that the strength of the Canadian dollar makes Canadian exports less competitive in world markets. This factor plus the need to make interest payments and loan repayments in the future could be offsetting influences. But if the money is used to achieve returns greater than interest rates paid, it leads to strengthening of the Canadian economy. In this connection, the article comments that "Forex Research Ltd., a London currency forecasting concern, says the Canadian dollar could slip below parity later this year. But even it predicts the Canadian currency 'should be trading back at around par with the U.S. dollar . . . by mid-1977'."

PROBLEM 13-7[3]

In planning the forthcoming year's operations of its Rudelia-based subsidiary SOR, U.S. based Omnicorp is determined that SOR will require additional debt financing for one year in the amount of LC2 million. Omnicorp is considering five alternative methods of raising the funds.
1. A loan from Omnicorp to SOR.
2. A Eurodollar loan.
3. A local currency loan from a bank in Rudelia.
4. Selling a draft on a discounted basis to a bank in Rudelia.
5. A foreign currency swap through the central bank of Rudelia.

---

[3] Based on the article by Alan C. Shapiro, "Evaluating Financing Costs for Multinational Subsidiaries," *Journal of International Business Studies*, 6:25–32, Fall 1975.

The comparative costs for each alternative financing source can be calculated by use of the expressions listed below.[4]

This analysis is from the standpoint of the parent. The effect of changes in the dollar value of the local currency could be handled in one of two ways. For example, if the dollar value of the local currency falls, and gains are recorded on soft currency loans, no loss is recorded on hard currency loans. The logic is that the gain recorded on soft currency loans represents the smaller number of dollars required to repay the loan. On the hard currency loan, the larger number of local currency units required to repay it is translated into the same original number of dollars, so no loss is recorded; however, since a larger number of local currency units are involved, a local tax deduction can be claimed and represents a reduction in the cost of the loan. Conversely, if losses were recorded on hard currency loans, no gains would be recorded on the soft currency loans. Under either approach, the *relative* costs of each alternative will result in the same ranking. In the previous chapters we illustrated the method of showing losses on the hard currency loans, so no gain or loss was shown on soft currency loans. To illustrate both methods, we adopt the other alternative in the present chapter to show a gain on soft currency loans and therefore no loss (just a tax shelter benefit) on the hard currency loans.

C_1 = Cost of a loan from parent

$$C_1 = E_o F_o R_{us}(1-t_{us}) + E_o F_o R(1-t_f) - E_o F_o R(1-t_p) - (E_o - E_1) F_o t_f$$

C_2 = Cost of a Eurodollar loan

$$C_2 = E_o F_o R_e(1-t_f) - (E_o - E_1) F_o t_f$$

C_3 = Cost of a local currency loan

$$C_3 = E_1 F_o R_f(1-t_f) - (E_o - E_1) F_o$$

C_4 = Cost of selling a draft on a discounted basis

$$C_4 = E_1 \frac{F_o d}{(1-d)} (1-t_f) - \frac{(E_o - E_1) F_o}{(1-d)}$$

C_5 = Cost of a foreign currency swap

$$C_5 = E_s F_o R_p(1-t_{us}) + E_1 F_o R_s(1-t_f) - (E_o - E_1)$$

The symbols used and the values assumed for each are:

E_o = present \$/LC exchange rate = \$0.50

E_1 = unknown future exchange rate —

---

[4] Extended explanations of the logic of these formulations is provided in Shapiro, 1975.

FINANCING INTERNATIONAL OPERATIONS

E_f	= forward exchange rate	=	$0.40
E_s	= swap rate	=	$0.60
R_{us}	= parent cost of debt	=	0.1
R	= interest charged by parent	=	0.1
R_e	= interest on Euroloan	=	0.12
R_f	= interest on LC loan	=	0.25
R_s	= interest rate on swap	=	0.15
F_o	= LC funds to borrow	=	2,000,000
d	= discount rate	=	0.30
t_f	= subsidiary's tax rate on regular income	=	0.40
t_{us}	= U.S. tax rate	=	0.50
t_p	= parent effective tax rate on foreign income	=	0.45

A. Calculate the cost of each alternative source in terms of the unknown future exchange rate E_1. Assume that the hard currency loans are not hedged in the forward exchange market.

B. Calculate the cost of each alternative method of financing for the following values of E_1 – $.55, .48, .45, .43, .40,$ and $.35$.

C. Which method of financing is lowest for each of the above values of E_1?

D. 1. What are the breakeven values of the future exchange rate, E_1, for the least cost alternatives.

   2. For each of the least cost alternatives, give the range over which it is the least cost.

   3. What rate of devaluation D_{df} is represented by the breakeven values? (D_{df} = rate of devaluation measured on the dollar value of LC currency.)

SOLUTION:

A. 1. With a loan from the parent the cost is (in $000):

$$C_1 = E_o F_o R_{us}(1-t_{us}) + E_o F_o R(1-t_f) - E_o F_o R(1-t_p) - (E_o - E_1) F_o t_f$$

$$= E_o F_o R_{us}(1-t_{us}) + E_o F_o R(t_p - t_f) - (E_o - E_1) F_o t_f$$

$$= .50 \times 2000 \times .1 \times .5 + 2000 \times .50 \times .1(.45-.40) - (.50 - E_1) 2000 \times .4$$

$$= 50 + 5 - 400 + 800 E_1$$

$$= -345 + 800 E_1$$

2. With a Eurodollar loan the cost is (in $000):

$$C_2 = E_o F_o R_e (1-t_f) - (E_o - E_1) F_o t_f$$
$$= .50 \times 2000 \times .12(1-.4) - (.50 - E_1) 2000 \times .4$$
$$= 72 - 400 + 800 E_1$$
$$= -328 + 800 E_1$$

3. A local currency loan from a bank in Rudelia will cost (in $000):

$$C_3 = E_1 F_o R_f (1-t_f) - (E_o - E_1) F_o$$
$$= 2000 \times .25 \times (.6) E_1 - (.50 - E_1) 2000$$
$$= 300 E_1 - 1000 + 2000 E_1$$
$$= -1000 + 2300 E_1$$

4. Selling a draft on a discounted basis to a bank in Rudelia costs (in $000):

$$C_4 = E_1 \frac{F_o d}{(1-d)} (1-t_f) - (E_o - E_1) F_o$$
$$= E_1 \frac{2000 \times .3 \times .6}{.7} - .50 \times 2000 + 2000 E_1$$
$$= 514 E_1 - 1000 + 2000 E_1$$
$$= -1000 + 2514 E_1$$

5. With a foreign currency swap the cost will be (in $000):

$$C_5 = E_s F_o R_{us} (1-t_{us}) + E_1 F_o R_s (1-t_f) - (E_o - E_1) F_o$$
$$= .6 \times 2000 \times .1 \times .5 + E_1 \times 2000 \times .15 \times .6 - (.50 - E_1) 2000$$
$$= 60 + 180 E_1 - 1000 + 2000 E_1$$
$$= -940 + 2180 E_1$$

B. The results under Part A can be summarized into a series of equations which are listed below along with the evaluation of the results of the equations for a range of values of the future spot exchange rate.

Financing Method	Cost Equations ($000)	Costs of Each Financing Alternative for Alternative Values of E_1						
		.55	.50	.48	.45	.43	.40	.35
Parent loan	$C_1 = -345 + 800E_1$	95	55	39	15	(1)	(25)	(65)
Eurodollar loan	$C_2 = -328 + 800E_1$	112	72	56	32	16	(8)	(48)
Local currency loan	$C_3 = -1000 + 2300E_1$	265	150	104	35	(11)	(80)	(195)
Discounted draft	$C_4 = -1000 + 2514E_1$	383	257	207	131	81	6	(120)
Swap	$C_5 = -940 + 2180E_1$	259	150	106	41	(3)	(68)	(177)

Each cost is a straight-line equation whose intercept is a negative amount and whose slope is determined by the coefficient of the term which involves the future spot exchange rate, E_1. These straight-line equations are plotted in Figure 13-3. This figure illustrates that at an improvement in the foreign exchange rate from its present value of .50 the cost of a loan from the parent will be the lowest of the financing methods. For the largest degree of devaluation in the table, an exchange rate of .35 (a devaluation of 30% in terms of the dollar value per LC) a local currency loan represents the lowest cost method of financing.

C. Specifically, for values $E_1 = .55, E_1 = .50, E_1 = .48$, and $E_1 = .45, C_1$ is the lowest cost alternative. For $E_1 = .43, E_1 = .40$, and $E_1 = .35, C_3$ is the lowest cost alternative.

D. 1. The best method for determining the least cost alternative is to graph the alternatives and find which of the alternatives make up the least cost frontier. Then find the breakeven points between the neighboring least cost alternatives. In the Omnicorp case, the alternatives are plotted in Figure 13-3. The least cost frontier is the solid line through C_1-C_3. Thus, find the breakeven point between C_1 and C_3.

Find E_1^*, where $C_1 = C_3$.

$$-345 + 8000E_1^* = -1000 + 2300E_1^*$$

$$1500E_1^* = 655$$

$$E_1^* = .4367$$

2. Thus, for

$$E_1 > E_1^* = .4367, C_1 \text{ is the lowest cost.}$$

3. The rate of devaluation D_{df} represented by E_1^* is

$$D_{df} = \frac{E_o - E_1^*}{E_o} = \frac{.50 - .4367}{.50} = .1266 = 12.66\%$$

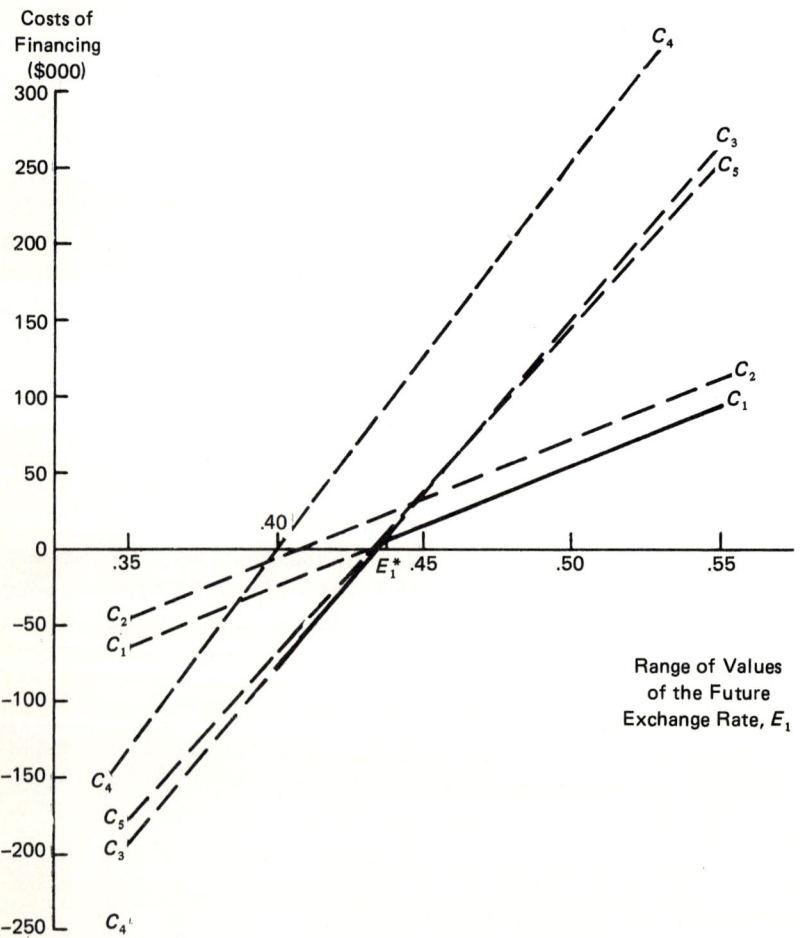

Figure 13-3 Costs of Alternative Sources of Financing Debt Funds for a Foreign Subsidiary

VII. International financing agencies.

In addition to financing from private lending institutions, international lending agencies perform important functions in financing international operations and projects.

A. The International Bank for Reconstruction and Development, also known as the World Bank, was started in 1944 as a companion to the IMF.
   1. The World Bank normally finances the foreign exchange portion of projects.
      a. Loans are made only when other private sources are unavailable.
      b. Loans are made to member governments, or firms with guarantees from member governments.
      c. The project must aid the productivity of the borrowing country.
   2. World Bank loans have been directed to less developed countries.
      a. Emphasis has been on development lending, designed to build the economic infrastructure of these nations.
      b. Major categories of loans are: electric power, transportation, water supply, agriculture, and education.
   3. World Bank financed projects must be soundly conceived and must provide a basis for repayments.
      a. Loans are amortized over maturity periods from 10 to 30 years.
      b. A waiting period may be included before repayment commences, in order to allow time for sufficient generation of earnings.
   4. Repayment of principal to the Bank has aggregated over $3 billion and no defaults have been realized on any of its loans. This excellent lending record has served to generate trust among private lenders and has encouraged their participation in more than $2 billion of World Bank loans.

B. The International Finance Corporation (IFC) was formed in 1956 to supplement activities of the World Bank by making higher risk loans.
   1. The IFC makes nonguaranteed loans to private enterprises in developing countries. It expects private financial participation to account for more than 50% of the total cost of the project.
   2. The IFC invests in both the debt securities and equities of business firms. Its activities have provided a basis for investment activity about ten times the size of its own portfolio.
   3. The IFC also invests in development banks that in turn lend to other institutions.
   4. Other institutions with which the IFC may engage in joint participation projects include:
      a. U.S. commercial banks.
      b. Foreign commercial banks.
      c. Foreign development banks.
      d. Foreign and domestic suppliers of the firm undertaking the project.
      e. The firm or firms holding equity positions in the project.

C. The International Development Association (IDA) was formed in 1960 to provide "soft loans" to nations with limited capacity to service conventional loans.
  1. The IDA is open to all World Bank members.
  2. IDA loans emphasize social overhead projects such as power, transportation, education, and housing.
  3. These projects require many years to generate income for servicing the loan. Thus, IDA loans carry generous terms.
     a. Loans are generally interest-free and have a minimum annual service charge.
     b. Maturity period is generally 50 years.
     c. The repayment schedule starts after a 10-year waiting period.
D. The Inter-American Development Bank (IDB) is a western hemispheric version of the World Bank.
  1. The IDB, founded in 1959, was composed of the United States and Latin American countries. Its goals are to promote economic development and regional economic integration.
  2. The IDB had two funds for financing business: the ordinary capital resources fund and the fund for special operations (which now includes the former Social Progress Trust Fund).
     a. Ordinary capital resources fund.
        (1) Loans are repayable in the currency that was borrowed.
        (2) Loans are made to private and public entities of member nations.
        (3) Maturities are of 10 to 20 years.
     b. The fund for special operations provides for loans with terms and conditions determined by the special circumstances surrounding projects.
        (1) Maturities range from 10 to 30 years.
        (2) Interest rates are below market levels.
        (3) Purchases can be made anywhere in the free world.
E. The Asian Development Bank (ADB), founded in 1966, was modeled after the IDB.
  1. The United States is a participating member.
  2. The ADB makes development loans under criteria similar to that used by the World Bank.
  3. The ADB operates through several funds and also gives liberal terms in special circumstances.
F. The European Investment Bank (EIB) was formed in 1958 to aid in the goals of the European Common Market.
  1. Goals.
     a. Designed to facilitate economic integration over the whole Common Market area.

b. Assists in financing projects involving two or more national governments.
   c. Responsible in helping make necessary adjustments to achieve marketwide economies of scale. This requires the specialization and expansion of firms in countries with a particular comparative trade advantage.
  2. Functions—the EIB is an international mechanism for mobilizing the resources of a group of nations.
   a. The EIB provides only a portion of the needed funds.
   b. The borrower may have to obtain the other funds from third parties.
   c. EIB projects may be carried out jointly with the World Bank.
   d. By pooling resources and sponsoring joint projects, the EIB can carry much larger risks than can the development banks of individual nations.
   e. Loan amortization periods are related to the durability of the project, and interest rates are determined by market conditions alone.
    (1) The predominant monetary arrangement for EIB loans is that the borrower receives and repays in whatever member currency the EIB chooses.
    (2) An alternative is that the borrower chooses the currency he receives and the EIB selects the currency for repayment.
  3. Related to the EIB are the European Development Fund (EDF) and the European Social Fund (ESF).
   a. The EDF provides financial aid for overseas territories to supplement their productive development projects.
   b. The ESF aids the improvement of employment possibilities and increases the geographic and occupational mobility of labor.
 G. The African Development Bank (AFDB) has excluded nonregional partners. This may be viewed as an effort to avoid excessive outside influence.

VIII. National development banks conduct activities to support economic growth of their nation as well as support international business operations.
 A. The Eximbank provides financial assistance to encourage exports from the United States.
  1. Since 1934 the Eximbank has supported $32 billion of credits, guarantees, and insurance for U.S. exports.
  2. Long-term direct loans to foreign borrowers for the purchase of U.S. goods comprise the major program of the Eximbank.
   a. The objective of direct loans is to supplement private capital which is unable to assume the risks involved.
   b. This also aids the competitive ability of U.S. suppliers by extending generous credit terms.

c. The interest rate charged is the average of the rates paid by the U.S. Treasury on its debt obligations.
d. These direct loans have great significance to financial managers in facilitating the sales programs of their companies.
3. Financial guarantee programs of the Eximbank provide guaranteed repayments to commercial banks which finance medium-term transactions for exporters. Eximbank also works with the FCIA to provide credit protection for exporters.
4. Participation financing is the combination of Eximbank's direct lending with loans from private sources.
    a. This will reduce the overall rate of interest paid on total project financing.
    b. This financing is available up to 15% of the total value of U.S. exports in the transaction.
5. Relending credits are lines of credit extended by the Eximbank directly to foreign financial institutions.
    a. Purpose is to stimulate subloans or relending for private purchases of U.S. goods.
    b. The subloan rate of interest was at 8½% per annum in the mid-seventies.
6. Cooperative financing is another program in which the Eximbank participates with foreign institutions to finance U.S. exports. Eximbank will provide up to 50% of the loan.
7. The Export Expansion Facility of the Eximbank was created in 1968 to allow participation in higher risk transactions.
8. Eximbank programs have many significant implications for financial managers of firms.
    a. They provide sources of financing for foreign firms at rates generally lower than those in the foreign country.
    b. This reduces the need of U.S. firms to provide financing of exports.
    c. Thus the risks of export financing are not borne by the firm.

B. The Agency for International Development lends money to foreign governments and to other qualified foreign borrowers.
1. Loans take three forms:
    a. Development loans.
    b. Alliance for Progress loans.
    c. Supporting assistance loans.
2. Loans are repayable in dollars and are used to pay for U.S. services in an economic development project.
    a. Maximum 40-year maturity, with 10-year grace period.
    b. Interest rates are below general international money market rates.
3. AID also handles P.L. 480 loans, which are in local currencies.
    a. These funds represent U.S. owned foreign currency received in payment for surplus agricultural commodities.

FINANCING INTERNATIONAL OPERATIONS

      b. These funds are used to finance direct investment, not export sales.
      c. Another aim is to expand foreign markets for U.S. agricultural products.
  4. AID has an investment guarantee program to cover extended risks of currency exchange, expropriation, war, etc.
      a. This program has been largely taken over by OPIC.
      b. AID's portion of the extended risk guarantee program applies mainly to Latin American housing projects.
C. The Private Export Funding Corporation provides intermediate-term financing of U.S. exports.
  1. PEFCO was established in 1971 by joint ownership of 55 banks, 7 industrial corporations, and one investment banking concern.
  2. Its purpose is to mobilize private capital to assist in the intermediate-term financing of U.S. exports. This fills the vacuum between the short-term financing generally provided by commercial banks and other private sources and the long-term financing provided by the Eximbank.
  3. PEFCO purchases medium- and long-term debt obligations arising from the sale of U.S. products and services to foreign importers.
      a. PEFCO finances its purchases of guaranteed foreign importer notes through the sale of its own securities, principally secured notes, to investors in the United States and abroad. The maturities of the debt instruments are closely matched with the due dates of the purchased notes.
      b. In addition, PEFCO has a revolving line of short-term credit from Eximbank.
      c. PEFCO charges a commitment fee of 0.5% on the undisbursed balance of each of the commitments at the time a financing agreement is worked out with a borrower.
  4. PEFCO's financing operations are entirely without risk since all of its activities are guaranteed as well as controlled by the Eximbank.
      a. The debt obligations purchased by PEFCO are fully guaranteed as to both principal and interest by the Eximbank.
      b. PEFCO has an arrangement with the Eximbank whereby the Eximbank agrees to increase its financial participation in the financing of a particular venture at a lower interest rate to allow PEFCO a higher interest on its share and still keep the overall lending rate constant should the market borrowing rate rise above the quoted lending rate. This virtually guarantees PEFCO a sure income on its financing ventures.
      c. In view of the above arrangements, Eximbank has the power to exercise rather close control over PEFCO's financial operations.
  5. PEFCO seeks maximum flexibility in its lending operations.
      a. There are no set forms and there are few procedures that cannot be adjusted to meet the needs of borrowers and the desires of PEFCO's sponsoring shareholders.

b. PEFCO normally undertakes intermediate-term financing from three to eight years. This can, however, be lengthened as required. It will not participate in short-term lending though, as this falls under the sphere of its shareholder banks.
c. Loans are made by PEFCO on either a fixed or floating rate basis and borrowers generally have the option to convert from a floating rate to a fixed rate in the future.

D. Foreign national development banks provide programs for the support of their country's exports similar to those provided by the Eximbank and AID for U.S. exports.
1. In the United Kingdom, the Industrial Reorganization Corporation (IRC) makes loans up to 10 years.
2. The Crédit Nationale (CN) in France provides long-term financing, and discounts medium-term loans from commercial banks.
3. The Kreditanstalt für Wiederaufbau (KFW) is Germany's primary industrial development bank.
4. Italy's largest financing agency, the Instituto Mobiliare Italiano, primarily extends loans of 10- to 15-year maturity, and also makes equity investments.

E. Private industrial development banks (international venture capital firms), are characterized by three major activities.
1. They make high-risk investments in new industries or in new economies.
2. These firms make equity investments, provide managerial and technical assistance, but they avoid taking management control.
3. They place emphasis on international activities in developing countries. This represents a private sector contribution to economic development.

PROBLEM 13-8

Briefly describe the international lending agencies and the types of loans which they usually make.

SOLUTION:

A. World Bank group.
1. IBRD—normally finances the foreign exchange portion of development projects of members.
2. IFC—supplements IBRD (World Bank) by making higher risk loans to businesses.
3. IDA—provides interest-free "soft loans" to nations for social overhead projects.

B. Regional lending agencies.
1. IDB—"Western Hemisphere World Bank," provides ordinary capital, special operations, and social progress funds.

FINANCING INTERNATIONAL OPERATIONS

2. ADB—(Asian Development Bank, though the United States is included as a member) provides development loans similar to those provided by IBRD and IDB.
3. EIB—helps with objectives of EEC and assists in financing multi-European projects.
4. AFDB—excludes nonregional partners, otherwise similar to IDB.

C. National development banks.
1. Eximbank—provides financial aid to encourage exports from United States.
2. AID/OPIC—administers nonmilitary U.S. foreign assistance programs.

PROBLEM 13-9

Some governmental bodies provide various types of international financing. Discuss why the U.S. government may want to get involved in international financing and mention some of the means by which it provides this financing.

SOLUTION:

A. Reasons.
1. To aid U.S. firms and U.S. employment.
2. To help U.S. balance of payments.
3. To develop favorable relations with other nations.
4. To maintain U.S. competitive position in world market.

B. Means.

Governmental Financing Agencies.	Main Functions
Eximbank	Finance medium- and long-term exports.
	Develop projects in LDCs.
AID	Provide grants and loans to other governments.
FCIA, Eximbank, OPIC	Provide export insurance.
P.L. 480	Local currency loans from sales of agricultural surplus.

PROBLEM 13-10

The B.C. Company is seeking to expand its operations abroad. It plans to set up a manufacturing plant in a developing Asian country that is encouraging

this type of foreign direct investment in joint venture with local capital. As part of its planning process, the company has to determine the availability of financing sources for the local operation.
- A. What is the range of possibilities for the venture?
- B. How would the financing alternatives differ if it were a wholly owned subsidiary versus a joint venture with a local group?

SOLUTION:

A. The range of possibilities include:
1. World Bank, under special conditions, with government guarantees.
2. IFC, especially on a joint basis with a local development bank.
3. The regional development bank, since the project will contribute to the economic development efforts of the host country.
4. Eximbank, which provides direct loans for purchases of U.S. goods, participation financing, and local financing up to 15% of cost of U.S. goods sold.
5. AID, which administers P.L. 480 loans for the benefit of U.S. multinational firms and the local economy.
6. The local government development bank, particularly since the government is encouraging such investments.
7. Private industrial development banks.
8. The customary private domestic financing sources.
9. Financing from Edge Act subsidiaries of U.S. commercial banks.
10. Open-market financing—equity or debt—in U.S. or European capital markets.

B. If the company forms a joint venture with a local firm, it has access to the following sources of funds:
1. Equity capital.
    a. The parent company.
    b. The participating local firm.
    c. The International Finance Corporation.
2. Debt capital.
    a. The International Finance Corporation.
    b. Local government development bank.
    c. Eximbank.
    d. AID P.L. 480 loans.
    e. Foreign country suppliers of goods and equipment credits.
    f. Edge Act subsidiaries of U.S. private commercial banks.
    g. Foreign country private banks.

If the B.C. Company wanted to form a wholly owned subsidiary instead of a joint venture, it would not be able to secure equity capital from the local firm or the International Finance Corporation. It would also not be able to obtain debt capital from the local government bank and possibly, the foreign country private banks. Thus, if the U.S. firm wants to operate a wholly owned subsidiary, it should be in a position to undertake most of the financing itself or to secure it from U.S. or European capital markets.

PROBLEM 13-11

How would the financing strategy of a U.S. company differ if it were operating with subsidiaries in a strong-currency country such as Germany rather than in a weak-currency country such as the Philippines? Compare in terms of:
A. Financing sources and forms.
B. Financial structure and terms of sale.

SOLUTION:

A. Financing sources and forms.

A U.S. company financing a subsidiary in Germany is likely to use funds from an equity source with the parent owning most of the equity interest. Debt financing would most likely be obtained in Western Europe either by floating a straight loan or a convertible debt issue in the Eurobond market with the debt guaranteed by the parent. The subsidiary will also be able to borrow from Western European private banks or insurance companies an amount up to the amount of its equity investment.

Because of greater pressure from the government as well as the need to deal with special local problems, the U.S. parent would most likely form a joint venture with substantial local interests in operating in the Philippines. Debt capital could be obtained through various U.S. government agencies or local government and private sources.

B. Financial structure.

In Western Europe, where the dollar has been declining in value in relation to the Western European currencies, the subsidiary should be in a net monetary asset position, i.e., its monetary assets should exceed its monetary liabilities. Its monetary assets will rise in dollar values as the foreign currencies continue to rise in value compared with the U.S. dollar. The firm should finance in the United States rather than in the foreign country where the repayment obligations will rise over time in terms of U.S. dollars. It can provide extended sales terms because the future value of foreign currencies will be higher in relation to the U.S. dollar.

The converse would be true for the Philippine subsidiary operating under conditions in which the value of the local currency might be falling in relation to the dollar. There the subsidiary should be in a net monetary debtor position. It should obtain as much local financing as possible. It should sell on as short-credit terms as possible or charge a very high rate of interest to compensate for the declining value of the local currency.

REFERENCES

Altman, Oscar L.: "Euro-Dollars," *Finance and Development*, vol. 4, March 1967.

Borsuk, Mark: "The Future Development of Offshore Capital Markets in Asia," *Columbia Journal of World Business*, **9**:48-60, Spring 1974.

Dufey, Gunter: *The Euro-Bond Market: Function and Future*, University of Washington Graduate School of Business, Seattle, Wash., 1961.

──────────: "The Euro-Bond Market: Its Significance for International Financial Management," *Journal of International Business Studies*, **1**: 65-81, Summer 1970.

Einzig, Paul: *The Euro-Bond Market*, St. Martin's Press, New York, 1969.

Friedman, Milton: "The Euro-Dollar Market: Some First Principles," *The Morgan Guaranty Survey*, October 1969, pp. 1-11.

Hendershott, Patrick H.: "The Structure of International Interest Rates: The U.S. Treasury Bill Rate and the Eurodollar Deposit Rate," *Journal of Finance*, **22**:455-465, September 1967.

Hinshaw, Randall: "The Euro-Dollar Market: A Comment," *Journal of Money, Credit and Banking*, **4**:688-690, August 1972.

Hoffmann, Diether H.: "German Banks as Financial Department Stores," *Review*, **53**:8-13, Federal Reserve Bank of St. Louis, November 1971.

Klopstock, Fred H.: "Money Creation in the Euro-Dollar Market—A Note on Professor Friedman's Views," *Monthly Review*, Federal Reserve Bank of New York, **52**:12-15, January 1970.

Little, Jane Sneddon: "The Euro-Dollar Market: Its Nature and Impact," *New England Economic Review*, Federal Reserve Bank of Boston, May-June 1969, pp. 2-31.

──────────: *Euro-Dollars: The Money Marker Gypsies*, Harper & Row, New York, 1975.

──────────: "The Impact of the Euro-Dollar Market on the Effectiveness of Monetary Policy in the United States and Abroad," *New England Economic Review*, Federal Reserve Bank of Boston, March-April 1975, pp. 3-19.

Machlup, Dr. Fritz: "The Magicians and Their Rabbits," *Morgan Guaranty Survey*, May 1971, pp. 3-13.

Makin, John H.: "Demand and Supply Functions for Stocks and Euro-dollar Deposits: An Empirical Study," *Review of Economics and Statistics*, **54**:381-391, November 1972.

Mayer, Helmut W.: "The BIS Concept of the Eurocurrency Market," *Euromoney*, May 1976, pp. 60-67.

―――: "Some Theoretical Problems Relating to the Euro-Dollar Market," *Essays in International Finance*, No. 79, Princeton University, Princeton, N.J., 1970.

Mikesell, Raymond F.: "The Euro-Dollar Market and the Foreign Demand for Liquid Dollar Assets," *Journal of Money, Credit and Banking*, **4**:643-683, August 1972.

Park, Yoon S.: *The Euro-Bond Market: Function and Structure*, Praeger, New York: 1974.

Potter, David R. W.: "The London Dollar CD—Liquid Tool for International Cash Management," *Columbia Journal of World Business,* Summer 1973, pp. 5-10.

Rich, Georg: "A Theoretical and Empirical Analysis of the Euro-Dollar Market," *Journal of Money, Credit and Banking*, **4**:617-635, August 1972.

Shapiro, A. C.: "Evaluating Financing Costs for Multinational Subsidiaries," *Journal of International Business Studies,* **6**:25-32, Fall 1975.

Stem, Carl H.: "The Euro-Dollar Market and the Foreign Demand for Liquid Dollar Assets: A Comment," *Journal of Money, Credit and Banking*, **4**: 691-703, August 1972.

Wai, U Tan, and H. T. Patrick: "Stock and Bond Issues and Capital Markets in Less Developed Countries," *IMF Staff Papers,* July 1973, pp. 253-317.

Chapter 14

The Cost of Capital and Financial Structure of the International Firm

Theme: The cost of capital of an international firm or project is determined by the same basic relationships as for a domestic firm or project. Because interest on debt is deductible for tax purposes there are tax advantages through the use of debt. Financial leverage from the use of debt magnifies gains and losses for the firm. A number of influences result in a greater use of leverage for foreign subsidiaries than for the parent firm. Also, the tax laws of most of the major trading nations provide some inducements to foreign investments resulting in a lower effective tax rate on the retained earnings of foreign subsidiaries than for the retained earnings of the parent company. Foreign investments may have greater total risk than domestic investments, but as a part of the firm's portfolio of investments the overall risk of the international firm may be reduced. The cost of capital of an international firm may, therefore, be no greater and perhaps even lower than the cost of capital for a domestic firm. But the final comparison would be greatly influenced by the product and industry areas in which the firms are operating

I. Cost of different forms of capital.
    A. Cost of debt capital.
        1. The present value of a bond is calculated as shown in equation (14-1).

2. $$P_b = \frac{a}{(1+k_b)} + \frac{a}{(1+k_b)^2} + \cdots + \frac{a}{(1+k_b)^n}$$ (14-1)

$$+ \frac{M_n}{(1+k_b)^n} = aP_{n,kp} + \frac{M_n}{(1+k_b)}$$

where:

P_b = price of a bond

a = annual interest coupon payment

M_n = value of the bond at maturity

k_b = cost of debt capital before taxes for a firm in a given risk class

$P_{n,kb}$ = present value of annuity factor for n years at kb percent.

3. Equation (14-1) is illustrated for a 3-year bond with a face value of $1,000 ($M$), and a coupon rate of 7%, so that the annual interest payment is $70; the current cost of debt for the firm is 8%.

$$P_b = \frac{70}{(1+.08)} + \frac{70}{(1+.08)^2} + \frac{1{,}070}{(1+.08)^3} \quad (14\text{-}1a)$$

$$= 70(.926) + 70(.857) + 1{,}070(.794)$$

$$= 65 + 60 + 849$$

$$= \$974$$

4. The cost of debt is calculated from information on the coupon payment and the current price. From this information, we solve for the value of k_b in equation (14-1).
   a. The yield to maturity, or the value of k_b, is the cost of debt before taxes.
   b. Since debt interest is deductible for tax purposes, the cost of debt is $k_b(1-t_j)$. The subscript j refers to the tax rate applicable in the location of the international operations.

B. Cost of preferred stock capital.
   1. Valuation formula.

$$P_p = \frac{D}{k_p}$$ (14-2)

THE COST OF CAPITAL AND FINANCIAL STRUCTURE

where:

P_p = price of a share of preferred stock

D = annual dividend on preferred stock

k_p = cost of capital for preferred stock for a firm of a given risk class

2. Preferred stock dividends are not deductible for tax purposes so k_p is the cost of preferred stock.

II. The cost of equity capital.
   A. New factors.
      1. Earnings and dividends on common stocks are subject to greater variations than coupon rates of interest on bonds or dividends on preferred stock.
      2. Expectations of growth in earnings and dividends.
   B. The valuation formulas for common stock reflect these two factors.
      1. The expected return on common stock is equal to the dividend yield plus the market appreciation yield as shown in equation (14-3).

      Return on common stock = dividend yield

      + market appreciation yield   (14-3)

      2. In equations (14-4a) and (14-4b) the relationships in equation (14-3) are set forth in symbols.

$$k_e = \frac{D_1}{P_o} + \frac{P_1 - P_o}{P_o} \qquad (14\text{-}4a)$$

$$k_e = \frac{D_1}{P_o} + g \qquad (14\text{-}4b)$$

where:

k_e = the rate of return on equity [$\equiv E(R_j)$]

D_1 = the expected end-of-year dividend

P_o = the current price

P_1 = the expected end-of-year price

g = the expected rate of capital gain and growth in dividends

3. Solving equation (14-4b) for P_o, we obtain:

$$P_o = \frac{D_1}{k_e - g} = \frac{D_o(1 + g)}{k_e - g} \qquad (14\text{-}5)$$

4. Equation (14-5) has a high degree of versatility which can be illustrated by numerical examples.
   Assume that $D_o = 3.81$; dividend payout ratio = 50%; $k_e = 10\%$; and $g = 5\%$; then $P_o = [\$3.81(1.05)]/(.10 - .05) = \$4/.05 = \$80$

PROBLEM 14-1

Assume that $k_e = .2$, g without foreign investment is .05, and the end of period dividend is 15.
1. What will the price of the stock be?
2. Assume that because of foreign investment, growth goes to .10 and the end-of-period dividend goes up to $18. What will the value of the company be?

SOLUTION:

1. $P_o = \dfrac{D_1}{k_e - g} = \dfrac{15}{.2 - .05} = \dfrac{15}{.15} = \$100$

2. $P_o = \dfrac{D_1}{k_e - g} = \dfrac{18}{.2 - .10} = \dfrac{18}{.1} = \$180$

This illustrates how the increased growth in earnings and dividends from foreign operations may contribute to a higher rate of growth in earnings and dividends and thus increase the value for the common stock of a company.

III. Applications of Capital Market Theory.
   A. Provides a general market equilibrium framework.
   B. In equilibrium, the capital market pricing mechanism can be described by a linear equation showing the relationship between expected return and risk for efficient portfolios.
   C. The equation for individual securities is shown in equation (14-6).

$$E(R_j) = R_F + \lambda \, Cov(R_j, R_M) \qquad (14\text{-}6)$$

THE COST OF CAPITAL AND FINANCIAL STRUCTURE

where:

$E(R_j)$ = expected return on an individual security

R_F = risk-free return

λ = price of risk for securities = $[E(R_M) - R_F]/\sigma_M^2$

$Cov(R_j, R_M)$ = covariance of the returns from individual securities with market returns

D. Illustration:

If $E(R_M) = .10$, $R_F = .05$, $\sigma_M^2 = .04$, and $Cov(R_j, R_M) = .08$

Then: $\lambda = \dfrac{.10 - .05}{.04} = 1.25$ and

$$E(R_j) = R_F + \lambda\, Cov(R_j, R_M) \qquad (14\text{-}7)$$
$$= .05 + 1.25(.08) = .15 = 15\%$$

E. The risk index can also be expressed in terms of the *beta coefficient* which is defined by equation (14-8).

$$\beta_j = \dfrac{Cov(R_j, R_M)}{\sigma_M^2} \qquad (14\text{-}8)$$

β_j is measured by the ratio of the covariance of the returns of the individual security with market returns, divided by the variance of market returns. The security market line for individual securities, using betas is:

$$E(R_j) = R_F + [E(R_M) - R_F]\,\beta_j \qquad (14\text{-}9)$$

F. Illustration continued for β.

$$\beta = .08/.04 = 2$$
$$E(R_j) = .05 + .05(2) = .15 = 15\%$$

G. The risk adjustment factor.
   1. The Capital Market Theory provides a measure of the risk adjustment factor.
   2. The risk adjustment factor for an individual security is a market risk factor multiplied (weighted) by the risk index computed for the individual security or investment project.
   3. The risk adjustment factor also influences the required rate of return for different classes of securities or investment projects.

IV. Leverage and the cost of capital.
   A. The design of the firm's capital structure.
      1. To determine the optimal capital structure of the firm requires an application of the theory of financial leverage. If the return on assets exceeds the cost of debt, leverage may increase the returns to equity, the shareholders' investment.
      2. However, leverage also increases the degree of fluctuations in the returns to equity for any given degree of fluctuations in sales and the return on assets.
      3. These generalizations are now illustrated. Table 14-1 provides data for calculating the return on equity under 3 alternative leverage and profitability conditions.

Table 14-1 Return on Common Stock under Alternative Leverage and Profitability Conditions (Dollar amounts are in millions)

	Profitability Conditions		
	Poor	Average	Good
Rate of return on total assets*	4%	20%	30%
Earnings before interest and taxes (EBIT)	$4	$20	$30
Firm A: Leverage factor is zero			
EBIT	$4	$20	$30
Less: Interest expense	0	0	0
Taxable income	4	20	30
Taxes	2	10	15
Profit after taxes	$2	$10	$15
Return on equity	2%	10%	15%
Firm B: Leverage factor is 50%. Total debt is $50 million.			
Earnings before interest and taxes (EBIT)	$4	$20	$30
Less: Interest expense @ 10%	5	5	5
Taxable income	(1)	15	25
Taxes	(.5)	7.5	12.5
Profit after taxes	$(.5)	$7.5	$12.5
Return on equity	(1%)	15%	25%
Firm C: Leverage factor is 80%. Total debt is $80 million.			
Earnings before interest and taxes (EBIT)	$4	$20	$30
Less: Interest expense @ 10%	8	8	8
Taxable income	(4)	12	22
Taxes	(2)	6	11
Profit after taxes	$(2)	$6	$11
Return on equity	(10%)	30%	55%

*Total assets are $100,000,000.

a. Firm A has no debt in its capital structure — it is unlevered.
b. Firm B's debt is 50 percent of total assets. At a 10 percent interest rate on debt of $50 million, its interest expense would be $5 million. The percent return on equity for firm B ranges from -1 percent to +25 percent. Its range is 26 percentage points as compared with the range of 13 percentage points for firm A.
c. For firm C the leverage factor is 80%—the ratio of debt to equity is four times. Its interest expense would be 10% times $80 million, or $8 million. The percentage return on common stock ranges from -10% to +55%, a total range of 65%.

4. This example shows how leverage increases the variability of the return on common stock. The results are graphed in Figure 14-1. At rates of return on total assets below 10%, the before-tax interest cost of debt, the unlevered firm has the highest return on net worth. At rates of return on total assets above 10%, the unlevered firm has the lowest return on net worth. At 10% the three firms have the same return on net worth.

Figure 14-1 Return on Net Worth as a Function of the Return on Assets under Alternative Leverage Rates

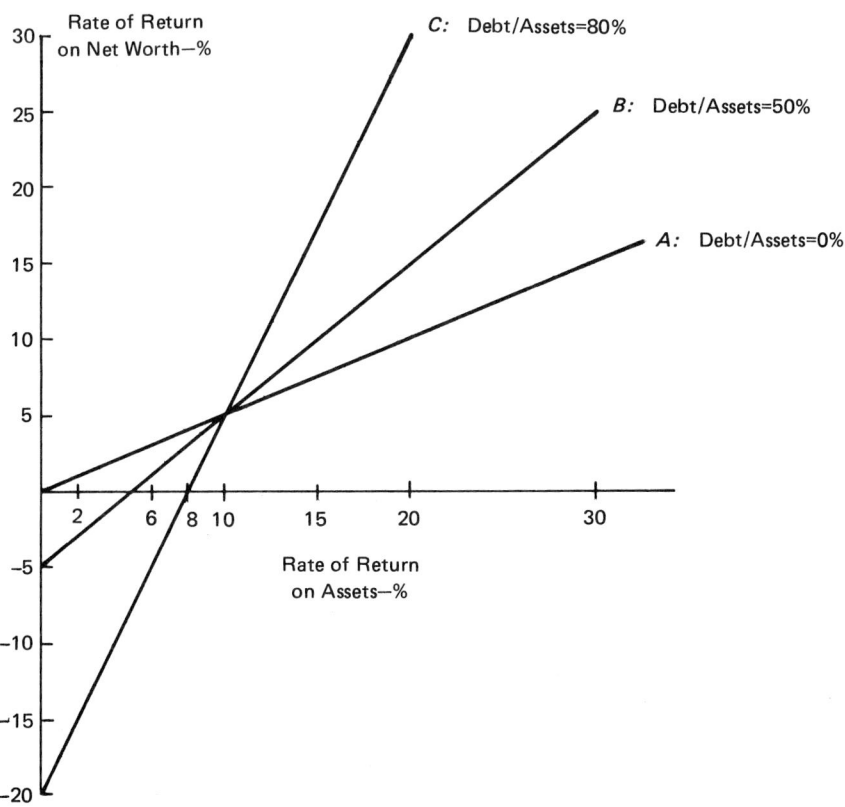

B. The cost of capital with corporate income taxes.
1. The weighted average cost of capital is

$$k = k_b(1-t)\frac{B}{V} + k_e\frac{S}{V} \qquad (14\text{-}10)$$

where:

k = the weighted average cost of capital
k_b = cost of debt
t = tax rate
B = market value of debt
S = market value of equity
V = value of the firm

2. The cost of equity capital is increased by leverage, but leverage decreases the weighted cost of capital. Illustrative income statement data are set forth in Table 14-2. The value of the unlevered firm V_a is $320,000; the debt of the levered firm is $200,000 at 10%; the tax rate is 40%.

Table 14-2 Illustration of MM's Propositions—with Taxes

Facts	No Leverage	50% Leverage
Income statement		
Sales	$800,000	$800,000
Total costs	720,000	720,000
EBIT = X	$ 80,000	$ 80,000
Interest	0	20,000
PBT	$ 80,000	$ 60,000
Taxes	32,000	24,000
Profit after tax	$ 48,000	$ 36,000

Calculations: Modigliani and Miller (1966) have shown that, for an unlevered firm, the cost of capital is

$$k_u = \frac{\overline{X}(1-t)}{V_u} = \frac{\$80,000(.6)}{\$320,000} = 15\% \qquad (14\text{-}11)$$

Since an unlevered firm has no debt, this is also its cost of equity capital, $k_u = k_{eu}$. The cost of equity capital for a levered firm is

$$k_e = k_{eu} + (k_{eu}-k_b)\frac{B(1-t)}{S} = .15+(.15-.10)\left(\frac{200,000}{200,000}\right)(.6) \qquad (14\text{-}12)$$

$$k_e = .18$$

The value of a levered firm, as demonstrated by Modigliani and Miller, is

$$V = V_u + tB \qquad (14\text{-}13)$$

Since B was given as \$200,000,

$$V = \$320{,}000 + .4(200{,}000)$$
$$= \$400{,}000$$

The value of a levered firm also is

$$V = B + S \qquad (14\text{-}14)$$

Since $V = \$400{,}000$ and $B = \$200{,}000$,

$$S = V - B = \$400{,}000 - \$200{,}000 = \$200{,}000$$

The weighted average cost of capital can now be calculated by equation (14-11).

$$k = k_b (1\text{-}t) \frac{B}{V} + k_e \frac{S}{V}$$
$$= .10(.6)(.5) + .18(.5)$$
$$= .03 + .09 = .12 = 12\%$$

Recall that $k_u = k_{eu}$ was 15%. The cost of equity of the levered firm rises to 18%, but its weighted cost of capital falls to 12%.

3. The weighted average cost of capital for the levered firm is lower than for the unlevered firm because of the tax shelter benefits achieved by the levered firm, but not achieved by the unlevered firm.
4. The cost of equity capital rises with increased debt because of the greater variability in the return on equity produced by increased leverage.
5. However, the overall cost of capital for a leveraged firm is smaller because of the tax shelter benefits of debt.
6. Business firms would seek to use very high debt ratios because of the tax advantages of debt, but the risk of losses to the bondholders limits the percentage of total assets that may be financed by debt.

PROBLEM 14-2

An American company that is 50% leveraged judges it worthwhile to be a net monetary creditor with respect to its investments in West Germany. The financial structure of its German subsidiary there consequently has only a 25% debt-to-total-assets ratio, half that of the U.S. parent. Discuss the effects that the foreign subsidiary has on the parent's leverage position and its cost of capital.

SOLUTION:

The consolidated leverage position of the MNC is lower because the lower leveraged West German subsidiary is combined with the U.S. parent. This makes the combined firm less subject to the fluctuations in its combined net income. The combined sales may be subject to opposite influences so the combined sales may be more stable, contributing to further stability of the combined net income. As a consequence, the parent company in the United States might be justified in using a higher leverage ratio than debt-to-total-assets ratio of 50%. It may thereby decrease its weighted cost of capital.

V. Illustrative calculations of the cost of capital.
   A. No growth.
      1. Earnings yield approach.

$$k_e = \frac{\overline{EPS}}{P}$$

where:

k_e = cost of equity capital

$\overline{EPS}$ = expected earnings per share

P = market price per share

For example on July 14, 1976, Chrysler Corporation was selling for $20 per share. Its average earnings per share from 1966 to 1973 were $3.39. No growth trend is exhibited in the earnings so the historical average is used as an estimate of the expected earnings per share. Hence,

$$k_e = \frac{3.40}{20} = 17\%$$

2. Use of the capital asset pricing model.
   a. First, the market parameters are calculated. This is illustrated in Table 14-4. From Table 14-4, we estimate the market return to be 9%. Its variance is 1%.
   b. Second, the risk-free return is calculated. This is shown in Table 14-5 to be 5%.
   c. Third, the expected return from Chrysler is calculated as shown in Table 14-6. It is 17%. A check can be made on this result. The expected return on a company, $E(R_j)$ is

$$E(R_j) = R_F + [E(R_M) - R_F] \frac{Cov(R_j, R_M)}{Var(R_M)}$$

$$= R_F + \beta_j [E(R_M) - R_F]$$

THE COST OF CAPITAL AND FINANCIAL STRUCTURE

Table 14-3 Estimation of Market Parameters Based on Historical Data

Year	(1) S&P Index Market Index (500 stocks)	(2) Capital Gain or (Loss)	(3) Dividend Yield	(4) Return on the Market (2+3) R_{Mt}	(5) $[R_{Mt} - E(R_{Mt})]$	(6) $[R_{Mt} - E(R_{Mt})]^2$
1960	55.85					
1961	66.27	.1860	.0298	.216	.128	.0164
1962	62.38	(.0587)	.0337	(.025)	(.113)	.0128
1963	69.87	.1201	.0317	.152	.064	.0041
1964	81.37	.1646	.0301	.195	.107	.0114
1965	88.17	.0836	.0300	.114	.026	.0007
1966	85.26	(.0330)	.0340	.001	(.087)	.0076
1967	91.93	.0782	.0320	.110	.022	.0005
1968	98.70	.0736	.0307	.104	.016	.0003
1969	97.84	(.0087)	.0324	.024	(.064)	.0041
1970	83.22	(.1494)	.0383	(.111)	(.199)	.0396
1971	98.29	.1811	.0314	.213	.125	.0156
1972	109.20	.1110	.0284	.139	.051	.0026
1973	107.43	(.0162)	.0306	.014	(.074)	.0055

$$\sum_{t=1}^{13} R_{Mt} = 1.146 \qquad \sum_{t=1}^{13} [R_{Mt} - E(R_{Mt})]^2 \cong .1212$$

$$E(R_M) = \sum_{t=1}^{13} R_{Mt}/13 = 1.146/13 = .088 \cong .09$$

$$Var(R_M) = \sum_{t=1}^{13} [R_{Mt} - E(R_M)]^2/12 = .1212/12 = .0101 \cong .01$$

In Table 14-6 we see that the covariance of Chrysler with the market is .025. The variance of the market is .01, so Chrysler's β is 2.5. The market risk premium is $[E(R_M) - R_F]$. Inserting the values from Tables 14-4 and 14-5, the risk premium for Chrysler is:

$$\beta_j [E(R_M) - R_F] = 2.5[.09 - .05]$$
$$= 2.5(.04) = .10$$

The $E(R_j)$ for Chrysler, using the security market line relationship is, using equation (14-9),

$$.05 + .10 = .15 = 15\%$$

Thus, using the historical security market line, Chrysler's cost of equity capital is 15%. Recent inflationary influences would require an upward adjustment as discussed below.

Table 14-4 Estimate of R_F Based on Historical Data*

Year	R_{Ft}
1960	.029
1961	.024
1962	.028
1963	.032
1964	.035
1965	.040
1966	.049
1967	.043
1968	.053
1969	.067
1970	.065
1971	.043
1972	.041
1973	.070

$$\sum_{t=1}^{13} R_{Ft} = .619$$

$$\text{est. } R_{Ft} = \sum_{t=1}^{13} R_{Ft}/13 = .619/13 = .0476 \cong .05$$

*R_F is the economy-wide risk-free return measured by the average annual yields on 3-month Treasury bills.

B. Growth companies.
1. Constant growth approach.
   a. This approach is based on the following equation.

$$P_o = \frac{D_1}{k_e - g}$$

where:

P_o = current price
D_1 = expected dividend
k_e = cost of equity capital
g = expected growth in dividends per share

THE COST OF CAPITAL AND FINANCIAL STRUCTURE

This can be solved for k_e, the cost of equity capital.

$$k_e = \frac{D_1}{P_o} + g$$

b. For example, the growth in earnings per share for the Kellogg Company between 1966 and 1975 was about 10.5%. Kellogg's dividend yield has been approximately 4%. Hence, Kellogg's cost of equity capital would be about 14.5%.

Table 14-5 Chrysler Corporation—Use of the CAPM* to Calculate the Required Return, Covariance, and Beta

Year (t)	P_t	$\frac{P_t}{P_{t-1}} - 1$	$\frac{D_{t+1}}{P_t}$	R_{jt}	$[R_{jt}-E(R_j)]$	$[R_{jt}-E(R_j)]^2$	$[R_M-E(R_M)]$ $[R_{jt}-E(R_{jt})]$
1960	13						
1961	12	(.08)	.02	(.06)	(.23)	.0529	(.0294)
1962	14	.17	.02	.19	.02	.0004	(.0023)
1963	33	1.36	.01	1.37	1.20	1.4400	.0768
1964	51	.55	.02	.57	.40	.1600	.0428
1965	54	.06	.02	.08	(.09)	.0081	(.0023)
1966	45	(.17)	.04	(.13)	(.30)	.0900	.0261
1967	44	(.02)	.05	.03	(.14)	.0196	(.0031)
1968	60	.36	.03	.39	.22	.0484	.0035
1969	44	(.27)	.05	(.22)	(.39)	.1521	.0250
1970	25	(.43)	.02	(.41)	(.58)	.3364	.1154
1971	30	.20	.02	.22	.05	.0025	.0063
1972	35	.17	.03	.20	.03	.0009	.0015
1973	33	(.06)	.04	(.02)	(.19)	.0361	.0141
				2.210		2.3474	.2744

1. est $R_{jt} = \sum_{t=1}^{13} R_{jt}/13 = .17$

2. $Cov(R_j, R_M) = \sum_{t=1}^{13} [R_M-E(R_M)][R_{jt}-E(R_j)]/11 = .2744/11 = .0249$

3. $\beta_k = \frac{Cov(R_j, R_M)}{Var(R_M)} = \frac{.0249}{.010} = 2.490$

*CAPM—Capital Asset Pricing Model

2. Temporary supernormal growth.
   Illustrative example. A firm has present earnings of $5 per share and pays dividends of $2 per share. Dividends are expected to grow at a 20% rate for 5 years, then decline to a normal growth of 6% per year when a 10 times multiplier will be applicable. Its current price is $70.32. What is its cost of equity capital?

Its cost of equity capital is the value of k_e that solves the following equation.

$$P_o = D_o \sum_{t=1}^{n} \frac{(1+g)^t}{(1+k_e)^t} + ME_o \frac{(1+g)^n}{(1+k_e)^n}$$

$$= 2(5.5416) + 10(5)(1.1847)$$

$$= 11.08 + 59.24$$

$$= \$70.32$$

where the new symbols are:

M = standard earnings multiplier

g = temporary supernormal growth

The value of k_e, which is consistent with the price of $70.32, is 16%, which is the firm's cost of equity capital.

C. The weighted average cost of capital.
1. Assume that project beta $(\beta_j) = 1.3$, market price of risk = $[E(R_M) - R_F]$ = .06, and risk-free return = .06.
2. Required return.

$$E(R_j) = R_F + [E(R_M) - R_F]\beta_j$$

$$= .06 + .06(1.3)$$

$$= .14 = 14\%$$

3. For a firm of this risk category, the cost of debt is 10% and the applicable tax rate is 40%. The leverage ratio assumed to be appropriate for this firm is a debt-to-total-capital ratio of 40%.
4. The weighted cost of capital for the firm.

$$(1-t)k_b \frac{B}{V} + k_e \frac{S}{V} \qquad (14\text{-}15)$$

The firm has 1 million shares outstanding at a price of $60 per share, with a total value of equity of $60 million. The total debt outstanding is $40 million and V is $100 million. We now have the information to use equation (14-15).

$$.6(.1)(.4) + .14(.6) = .024 + .084 = .108$$

Thus, based on the facts given, the firm's weighted cost of capital is 10.8%.

THE COST OF CAPITAL AND FINANCIAL STRUCTURE

5. Influence of inflation.
   a. The Fisher effect states that the nominal interest rate, cost of equity, and cost of debt will be increased by the anticipated inflation rate.
   b. Assume that a 2% per annum rate of price increase is reflected in the above relations and that the rate of price increase anticipated is 6% per year. The cost of debt would rise to 14%, the risk-free rate would become 10%, and the cost of equity 18%.
   c. If the debt to total capital rises to 50%, the weighted cost of capital becomes:

$$(.14)(.6)(.5) + (.18)(.5) = 4.2 + 9.0 = 13.2\%$$

VI. International financial markets and the use of debt.
   A. Comparative costs of borrowing in domestic versus foreign markets.
      1. For many years debt costs were lower in the U.S. markets because of the breadth of the capital markets and the high rate of savings possible in an affluent society.
      2. However, in recent years interest rates in the United States have fluctuated above as well as below interest rates in other countries. (See Table 14-6.)
      3. Even when interest rates are higher abroad, it may be advantageous to raise debt abroad.
         a. To protect against devaluation by being in a net monetary debtor position.
         b. When covered interest arbitrage opportunities make it desirable to bring funds into the United States by borrowing them abroad.
         c. When there are controls on the use of domestic funds to make foreign direct investments.
   B. Special factors that may be operating.
      1. U.S. companies may issue debt convertible into the common stock of the parent.
         a. European investor interest in the equity of the parent may result in favorable terms.
         b. Interest rates, maturity, and sinking fund requirements may be more favorable on the foreign issue.
      2. Investors in the foreign country in which the U.S. company has a plant may enable the merchant banks in the foreign country to sell debt issues to the public.

VII. The sale of equity issues in foreign countries.
   A. Breadth of U.S. equity market.
      1. For a given amount of foreign funds to be invested in equity, the large size of the U.S. equity market enables equity investments to be made

Table 14-6 Comparative Interest Rate Levels, 1968–1975

Central Bank Discount Rates
(End of period quotations in percent per annum)

	1968	1969	1970	1971	1972	1973	1974 I	1974 II	1974 III	1974 IV	1975 I	May	June	July	Aug
Industrial Countries															
United States	5.50	6.00	5.50	4.50	4.50	7.50	7.50	8.00	8.00	7.75	6.25	6.00	6.00	6.00	6.00
Canada	6.50	8.00	6.00	4.75	4.75	7.25	7.25	8.75	9.25	8.75	8.25	8.25	8.25	8.25	8.25
Japan	5.84	6.25	6.00	4.75	4.25	9.00	9.00	9.00	9.00	9.00	9.00	8.50	8.00	8.00	7.50
Austria	3.75	4.75	5.00	5.00	5.50	5.50	5.50	6.50	6.50	6.50	6.50	6.00	6.00	6.00	6.00
Belgium	4.50	7.50	6.50	5.50	5.00	7.75	8.75	8.75	8.75	8.75	7.50	6.50	6.50	6.50	6.00
Denmark	6.00	9.00	9.00	7.50	7.00	9.00	10.00	10.00	10.00	10.00	9.00	8.00	8.00	8.00	8.00
France	6.00	8.00	7.00	6.50	7.50	11.00	11.00	13.00	13.00	13.00	11.00	10.00	9.50	9.50	9.50
Germany	3.00	6.00	6.00	4.00	4.50	7.00	7.00	7.00	7.00	6.00	5.00	4.50	4.50	5.00	4.00
Italy	3.50	4.00	5.50	4.50	4.00	6.50	9.00	9.00	9.00	8.00	8.00	7.00	7.00	7.00	7.00
Netherlands	5.00	6.00	6.00	5.00	4.00	8.00	8.00	8.00	8.00	7.00	6.00	6.00	6.00	6.00	5.50
Norway	3.50	4.50	4.50	4.50	4.50	4.50	5.50	5.50	5.50	5.50	5.50	5.50	5.50	5.50	5.50
Sweden	5.00	7.00	7.00	5.00	5.00	5.00	5.00	6.00	7.00	7.00	7.00	7.00	7.00	7.00	6.00
Switzerland	3.00	3.75	3.75	3.75	3.75	4.50	5.50	5.50	5.50	5.50	5.00	4.50	4.50	4.50	4.00
United Kingdom	7.00	8.00	7.00	5.00	9.00	13.00	12.50	11.75	11.50	11.50	10.00	10.00	10.00	11.00	11.00

Source: *International Financial Statistics*, International Monetary Fund, **28**:27, October 1975.

THE COST OF CAPITAL AND FINANCIAL STRUCTURE

without driving down the yields to very low levels in the foreign countries, e.g., Western European countries.
   2. Especially true from the standpoint of Swiss banks receiving funds from all over the world. The amount of funds held by the Swiss banks is so large that, if placed in European equities, it would drive down their yields and therefore returns to unattractive levels.
B. Advantages to U.S. firms of selling their common stock in foreign countries.
   1. The sale of common stock and listing on foreign stock exchanges increases familiarity with the U.S. company.
      a. This may be supported by advertising of its products and trademarks.
      b. Foreign shareholders will be more disposed to buy the products of "their company."
      c. Widespread foreign ownership of common stock may also contribute to management and employee loyalty to the company. Management stock option and employee stock-purchase plans will assist in this.
   2. Familiarity with the company may facilitate the acquisition of foreign companies by exchanging the common stock of the U.S. company for their assets in the foreign country.
   3. The concept of transnational ownership.
      a. The U.S. company may desire wholly owned foreign subsidiaries for management efficiency reasons.
         (1) Manufacturing and marketing may require a unified decision-making source.
         (2) Production rationalization, transfer pricing, and dividend policy should be decided on a worldwide basis which may conflict with a local point of view.
      b. Local investors are able to participate in the broader diversified activities of the parent firm as well as in its profits from the local subsidiary.
   4. Local participation in ownership may reduce the risks of nationalization by foreign governments.

PROBLEM 14-3

What are the advantages to an American company of selling convertible debentures abroad that are convertible into the equity of the parent?

SOLUTION:

1. The interest cost on the convertible debenture is likely to be as low or lower than a convertible debenture would require if sold in the United States.
2. This is particularly true if the convertible debenture is sold in the countries in which the American company conducts its foreign operations, for

example, West Germany and France. When the price of the parent stock rises, the parent could conceivably force conversion. It would thereby create common stockholders in the equity of the U.S. parent. Thus the investors in foreign countries may develop favorable attitudes toward the parent company because they are owners of its common stock. This may help the U.S. parent company in terms of social and political attitudes toward its operations in the foreign countries.

VIII. The influence of international operations on the selection of a firm's capital structure.
   A. The main influences on capital structure.
      1. Taxes.
      2. The expected rate of inflation.
      3. The expected relative exchange-rate values.
      4. Risks of bankruptcy.
      5. Agency and monitoring costs.
   B. Impact of the above for a multinational corporation.
      1. These influences would tend to be similar for a given country but vary between countries.
      2. Therefore, one would expect that, for industrial corporations, financial structures would be quite similar for companies operating mainly in one particular country.
      3. The elements under (A) have unique influences and impacts on the multinational corporation.
      4. In comparing the capital structures of companies in different countries, one would expect to find differences because of the different effects of the influences under (A).
   C. The financial structures of multinational corporations.
      1. These corporations should structure their worldwide operations on a consolidated basis.
      2. Structure may be influenced by the major areas in which operations take place.
   D. The risk of multinational operations as compared with domestic operations alone.
      1. Political risks can be projected from analysis of underlying conditions in a country.
         a. Risks can be controlled to some degree by selection of countries and exposures.
         b. Insurance can be purchased to reduce political risks. (See Chapter 9.)
      2. Inflation and exchange-rate risks are reflected in the cost of capital.
      3. The special factors and special risks of international operations may increase the risks of multinational corporations.
      4. However, multinational corporations also benefit from the portfolio effects of their investments in diversified international operations. (See the Appendix to this chapter for a demonstration of this point.)

E. The advantages of a centralized global viewpoint avoid *overhedging*.
   1. Illustration of potential overhedging. Consider a large company using an accounting system where both inventories and long-term debt are exposed. The currency of a country threatens to revalue, but overall the company is covered because the long inventory position of subsidiary A (on which there will be an exchange gain) happens to offset the long-term debt position of subsidiary B (on which there will be an exchange loss). Subsidiary A is happy, but subsidiary B is not, and may try to protect its exposed position.
   2. With decentralized management, particularly where the accounting system leads to too much coverage, there may be the additional problem of subsidiaries covering themselves at cross-purposes. Sometimes these anomalies are avoided by adjusting a subsidiary's profits to leave out foreign exchange losses made "for the greater good."
   3. Decentralized foreign exchange management presents the danger that lower-level officials, sometimes deficient in production or sales success, will try to recoup fallen fortunes with a speculative flyer in foreign exchange markets. Potential losses can be substantial.

IX. The determination of an international firm's cost of capital.
   A. Global viewpoint versus local financial structure.
      1. Both influences should be taken into account.
      2. The initial approach should be to relate the financial structure of the foreign subsidiary to the economic and financial environment of the country in which it operates.
      3. The corporate headquarters of the multinational corporation should then take a global point of view and modify the financial structures of the individual financial subsidiaries so that the resulting pattern for the multinational firm as a whole is sound in relation to its total complex financial and economic environment.
   B. Illustrative example.[1]
      1. The cost of capital for the parent company is 10% for debt (k_b) and 18% for equity (k_e) with a debt-to-total-capital ratio of 40%. Total capital of the parent is $500 million. The nominal cost of debt in the local currency for the subsidiary is 20% with an annual expected devaluation rate in the local currency of 4% per year over the life of the loan.

      The subsidiary proposes to undertake a new project which will involve a total capital outlay of $50 million. The foreign tax rate is 40% (t_f); the U.S. tax rate is 50% (t_{us}). The subsidiary can contribute $10 million of retained earnings toward financing the project. Local debt of $30 million can be raised at a nominal interest rate of 20%.

[1] This general approach and the related theory are developed by Professor Alan C. Shapiro in a manuscript, "Financial Structure and Cost of Capital in the Multinational Corporation," dated March 1976.

The parent company will provide the remaining $10 million on a debt basis.

What is the applicable cost of capital for the proposed project?

2. The solution is as follows.
   a. Parent cost of capital.

$$.40 \times .05 = .020$$
$$.60 \times .18 = .108$$
$$\text{Weighted average} = .128 = 12.8\%$$

Since the parent's capital structure is 40% debt and 60% equity, its weighted cost of capital is determined by applying these proportions to the after-tax cost of debt and to the cost of equity capital. The resulting weighted average cost of capital is 12.8%.

   b. Cost of subsidiary's retained earnings

$$\frac{(1-t_{us})}{(1-t_f)} (k_e) = \frac{.50}{.60}(.18) = .15$$

The effective cost of the subsidiary's debt is

$$R_f^* = R_f(1-t_f)(1-D_{fd}) - D_{fd}$$
$$= .20(.6)(.96) - .04$$
$$= .1152 - .040 = .0752$$

The cost of the subsidiary's retained earnings reflects the benefit of the lower corporate income tax in the foreign country. By multiplying the ratio of 1 minus the U.S. tax rate over 1 minus the foreign tax rate times the parent and subsidiary's cost of equity, the cost of retained earnings of 15.6% is obtained. The effective cost of subsidiary's debt reflects the discussion in previous chapters. While the nominal cost of subsidiary debt is 20%, its cost after taxes and after the devaluation factor is 7.52%.

   c. Required adjustment in financial structure of the parent.

	(1) Before Project	(2) Impact of Project	(3) Required Capital Structure for 40% D/TC Ratio	(4) Adjustment Required
Debt	200	230	220	−10
Equity	300	310	330	+20
From parent	—	10	—	—
Total	500	550	550	+10

THE COST OF CAPITAL AND FINANCIAL STRUCTURE

The required adjustment in the financial structure of the parent is necessary to bring the overall capital structure of the consolidated firm back to the 40-60% debt and equity percentages. Before the project, debt was $200 million and equity was $300 million. The project added $30 million of debt and $10 million of equity as well as requiring $10 million of funds from the parent. Hence, the new total capital is $550 million. To have a required capital structure of 40% debt requires debt of $220 million and equity of $330 million. Thus, the total consolidated debt must be $220 million and the total consolidated equity must become $330 million. Therefore, as shown in column 4 of (c), equity must be increased by $20 million and debt reduced by $10 million. The net change is an increase of $10 million.

d. Cost of capital of the project.

Subsidiary's retained earnings	$10 @ .150	1.50
Subsidiary's debt	30 @ .0752	2.256
Increased parent equity	20 @ .180	3.60
Reduced parent debt	-10 @ .05	-.50
	50	6.856

$$\frac{6.856}{50} = 13.71\% = \text{cost of capital for the project}$$

The cost of capital of the project was calculated. The subsidiary's retained earnings and subsidiary's debt are costed at their applicable rates. The increased required parent equity of 20 is also included in the analysis. The cost of the reduction of debt of 10 is also shown. The result is a cost of capital for the project of 13.71%. We see that the cost of capital of the project therefore is 1.03% higher than the parent cost of capital. The difference reflects the differential cost of retained earnings and the effective cost of debt in the subsidiary operation. The cost of capital of the parent applied in the analysis is the cost of capital applicable to a project of this risk. The overall cost of capital of the parent reflecting the weighted average of the risks of all projects reflected in the parent's operations could be lower or higher than the 12.8% on the project under analysis. The cost of equity of the parent overall might be 15% or 20%. The cost of debt for the parent overall could also be lower or higher than the 10% cost of debt applicable to this project. This analysis, therefore, takes the view that it is the cost of capital related to the risk of the individual project that is relevant. As pointed out earlier in this chapter, a useful guideline to the risk of the project is the measurement of the covariance of the returns from the project with the total market returns or the project's beta. Hence, although the risk of the individual project is measured, the measure used relates the characteristics of the project to total market behavior.

PROBLEM 14-4

Analyze the differences in the financial data and financial ratios for two Japanese steel companies and two American steel companies of similar size, as shown in Tables 14-7 and 14-8.

Table 14-7 Financial Data and Financial Ratios for Two Japanese Steel Companies

Key Financial Data	Nippon Steel Amount ($ mil. 4/74)	%	Kawasaki Steel Corporation Amount ($ mil. 4/74)	%
Current assets	$3,269		$1,256	
Short-term interest-bearing debt	680	8.20	451	12.86
Other current liabilities	2,419	29.17	1,089	31.04
Current liabilities	3,099	37.37	1,540	43.90
Long-term interest-bearing debt	3,165	38.17	1,167	33.27
Other long-term debt	840	10.13	392	11.17
Total long-term debt	4,005	48.30	1,559	44.44
Total debt	7,104	85.67	3,099	88.34
Stockholders' equity	1,188	14.33	409	11.66
Total liabilities and equity	$8,292	100	$3,508	100
Sales	$6,777		$2,006	
Interest	363		128	
Net income	185		64	
Financial Ratios				
1. Total interest-bearing debt to stockholders' equity	3.24		3.96	
2. Total debt to stockholders' equity	5.98		7.58	
3. Current ratio	1.05		.8156	
Current liabilities to stockholders' equity	2.61		3.77	
Sales to total assets	.817		.5718	
4. Net income to sales	.0273		.0319	
5. Net income + interest to total assets	.0661		.0547	
6. Net income to stockholders' equity	.1557		.1565	
Short-term interest-bearing debt to stockholders' equity	.5724		1.10	

THE COST OF CAPITAL AND FINANCIAL STRUCTURE

Table 14-8 Financial Data and Financial Ratios for Two American Steel Companies

Key Financial Data	United States Steel Corporation Amount ($ mil. 74)	%	Bethleham Steel Amount ($ mil. 74)	%
Current assets	$2,889		$1,682	
Short-term interest-bearing debt	28	.36	8	.18
Other current liabilities	1,710	22.16	1,023	22.67
Current liabilities	1,738	22.52	1,031	22.85
Long-term interest-bearing debt	1,323	17.14	648	14.36
Other long-term debt	203	2.63	343	7.60
Total long-term debt	1,526	19.77	991	21.96
Total debt	3,264	42.29	2,022	44.81
Stockholders' equity	4,454	57.71	2,490	55.19
Total liabilities and equity	$7,718	100	$4,512	100
Sales	$9,186		$5,381	
Interest	93		44	
Net income	635		342	

Financial Ratios

	United States Steel Corporation	Bethleham Steel
1. Total interest bearing debt to stockholders' equity	.303	.263
2. Total debt to stockholders' equity	.73	.81
3. Current ratio	1.66	1.63
Current liabilities to stockholders' equity	.390	.414
Sales to total assets	1.19	1.19
4. Net income to sales	.0691	.0636
5. Net income + interest to total assets	.0943	.0855
6. Net income to stockholders' equity	.1426	.1373
Short-term interest-bearing debt to stockholders' equity	.0063	.0032

SOLUTION:

Some sharp contrasts stand out when the financial ratios of the two large Japanese steel companies are compared with those of the two large American steel companies. Total interest-bearing debt is 300 to 400 percent of stockholders' equity for the Japanese companies. For the American steel companies total interest-bearing debt is only 30 percent of stockholders' equity. The ratio of total debt to stockholders' equity of the Japanese companies ranges from 600 to 700 percent. For the American companies the ratio is

70 to 80 percent. The current ratio for the Japanese companies is around 1. For the American steel companies it is 1.6 times.

These differences in financial ratios have an impact on profitability. The Japanese companies are able to operate with a net income to sales ratio of about 3 percent as compared to 6 to 7 percent for the American companies. The ratio of net income plus interest to total assets is 6 to 7 percent for the Japanese steel companies and 9 percent for the American companies. However, the Japanese companies with half the ratio of net income to sales produced a return on net worth of 16 percent, 2 percentage points higher than the return of 14 percent on net worth for the two American companies. It should be noted that 1974 was a year of very strong steel demand resulting in a high water mark in rate of return on net worth for steel companies.

How is it possible for the Japanese steel companies to utilize such high leverage ratios in an industry such as steel which experiences the greatest cyclical fluctuations in sales and profits of the major industries? One possibility is the close relationship between the Japanese government, the financial groups which invest in the Japanese steel industry, and the important role of the Japanese steel industry in developing export earnings for the Japanese economy. Another influence may be that, if the financial groups invest (by the same percentage) in both the debt and equity of the Japanese steel companies, it is equivalent to being an equity investor by the same percentage. Nevertheless, this would still raise questions as to why foreign banks have provided long-term debt to the Japanese steel companies given the high leverage ratios of the Japanese steel companies. However, long-term loans supplied from external sources including the World Bank, Eximbank, and banks in the United States, Canada, the United Kingdom, Switzerland, and West Germany, totaled only 5 percent of the total long-term loans of Nippon Steel, for example. It would appear that there are some direct or indirect guarantees by the Japanese government that enable the Japanese steel companies to operate with ratios of total debt of 600 to 700 percent of stockholders' equity.

REFERENCES

Adler, M.: "The Cost of Capital and Valuation of a Two-Country Firm," *Journal of Finance,* **29**:119-132, March 1974.

de Faro, C., and J. V. Jucker: "The Impact of Inflation and Devaluation on the Selection of an International Borrowing Source," *Journal of International Business Studies,* **4**:97-104, Fall 1973.

Lessard, Donald: "World, National, and Industry Factors in Equity Returns," *Journal of Finance,* **29**:379-391, May 1974.

Miller, Merton H., and Franco Modigliani, "Some Estimates of the Cost of Capital to the Electric Utility Industry, 1954-57," *American Economic Review*, 56:333-391, June 1966.

Ness, W. L., Jr.: "U.S. Corporate Income Taxation and the Dividend Remittance Policy of Multinational Corporations," *Journal of International Business Studies*, 5:67-75, Spring 1975.

Robbins, S. M., and R. S. Stobaugh: "Financing Foreign Affiliates," *Financial Management*, 1:56-65, Winter 1972.

Shapiro, A.C.: "Exchange Rate Changes, Inflation and the Value of the Multinational Corporation," *Journal of Finance*, 30:485-502, May 1975.

Solnik, Bruno H.: "An Equilibrium Model of the International Capital Market," *Journal of Economic Theory*, 8:500-524, August 1974.

———: *European Capital Markets*, Lexington Books, Lexington, Mass., 1973.

———: "An International Market Model of Security Price Behavior," *Journal of Financial and Quantitative Analysis*, 9:537-554, September 1974.

Stonehill, A., and T. Stitzel: "Financial Structure and Multinational Corporations," *California Management Review*, 12:91-96, Fall 1969.

Weston, J. F., and E. F. Brigham: *Managerial Finance*, 5th ed., Dryden Press, Hinsdale, Ill., 1975.

Appendix to Chapter 14

ILLUSTRATION OF THE BENEFITS OF FOREIGN INVESTMENT WITH THE MARKET MODEL

Given:

s	p	$\tilde{R}_w$	$\tilde{X}_a$	$\tilde{X}_d$
1	.1	−.15	1040	−795
2	.3	.05	−795	240
3	.4	.15	−45	140
4	.2	.20	1790	540

where:

s = state of the world

p = probability

$\tilde{R}_w$ = market return

$\tilde{X}_a$ = dollar return to foreign investment

$\tilde{X}_d$ = dollar return to domestic investment

APPENDIX TO CHAPTER 14

t = tax rate
R_F = risk-free rate
S = equity
B = debt
R_a = return on equity of foreign firm = $\dfrac{\overline{X}_a}{S_a}$
R_d = return on equity of domestic firm = $\dfrac{\overline{X}_d}{S_d}$
$\sim$ indicates random variable, $-$ indicates expected value.

Also:

$R_F = .08;\ S_a = S_d = 500;\ t = .4;$
$V_d = V_a = 1000;\ B_a = B_d = 500$

σ = standard deviation of returns
c.v. = coefficient of variation of returns

A. Determine the expected return, variance, and standard deviation for the market, the foreign investment, and the domestic investment.
B. Obtain the covariance between the foreign investment and the market. Do likewise for the domestic investment. Using the security market line relationship, calculate the required return for each of the foreign and domestic investments.
C. Assume a portfolio made up of both the foreign investment and the domestic investment in equal proportion. Calculate the portfolio expected return, variance, standard deviation, covariance with the market, and its required return based on the security market line.
D. Graph the security market line and plot the expected returns from the foreign investment, the domestic investment, and the portfolio. How do they compare?

SOLUTION:

A. Calculations of expected return, variance, and standard deviation.
   1. Market parameters.

s	p	$\tilde{R}_w$	$p\tilde{R}_w$	$(\tilde{R}_w - \overline{R}_w)$	$(\tilde{R}_w - \overline{R}_w)^2$	$p(\tilde{R}_w - \overline{R}_w)^2$
1	.1	−.15	−.015	−.25	.0625	.00625
2	.3	.05	.015	−.05	.0025	.00075
3	.4	.15	.060	.05	.0025	.00100
4	.2	.20	.040	.10	.0100	.00200

$E(\tilde{R}_w) = .10$

$Var(\tilde{R}_w) = .01$

$\sigma_w = .1$

APPENDIX TO CHAPTER 14

2. Foreign investment.

s	p	$\tilde{X}_a$	R_{FB_a}	$(\tilde{X}_a - R_{FB_a})$	$\hat{X}_a = (\tilde{X}_a - R_{FB_a})(1-t)$	$\tilde{R}_a = \dfrac{\hat{X}_a}{S_a}$
1	.1	1040	40	1000	600	1.20
2	.3	−795	40	−835	−501	−1.00
3	.4	−45	40	−85	−51	−.10
4	.2	1790	40	1750	1050	2.10

s	p	$\tilde{R}_a$	$p\tilde{R}_a$	$(\tilde{R}_a - \bar{R}_a)$	$(\tilde{R}_a - \bar{R}_a)^2$	$p(\tilde{R}_a - \bar{R}_a)^2$
1	.1	1.20	.12	1.00	1.00	.100
2	.3	−1.00	−.30	−1.20	1.44	.432
3	.4	−.10	−.04	−.30	.09	.036
4	.2	2.10	.42	1.90	3.61	.722

$E(\tilde{R}_a) = .20$

$Var(\tilde{R}_a) = 1.29$

$\sigma_a = 1.14$

$CV = 5.7$

3. Domestic firm.

s	p	$\tilde{X}_d$	R_{FB_d}	$(\tilde{X}_d - R_{FB_d})$	$\hat{X}_d = (\tilde{X}_d - R_{FB_d})(1-t)$	$\tilde{R}_d = \dfrac{\hat{X}_d}{S_d}$
1	.1	−795	40	−835	−501	−1.00
2	.3	240	40	200	120	.24
3	.4	140	40	100	60	.12
4	.2	540	40	500	300	.60

s	p	$\tilde{R}_d$	$p\tilde{R}_d$	$(\tilde{R}_d - \bar{R}_d)$	$(\tilde{R}_d - \bar{R}_d)^2$	$p(\tilde{R}_d - \bar{R}_d)^2$
1	.1	−1.00	−.100	−1.14	1.2996	.1300
2	.3	.24	.072	.10	.0100	.0030
3	.4	.12	.048	−.02	.0004	.0002
4	.2	.60	.120	.46	.2116	.0423

$E(\tilde{R}_d) = .14$

$Var(\tilde{R}_d) = .1755$

$\sigma_d = .42$

$CV = 3.0$

B. Calculations of covariance with the world market.

s	p	$(\tilde{R}_a-\bar{R}_a)(\tilde{R}_w-\bar{R}_w)$		s	p	$(\tilde{R}_d-\bar{R}_d)(\tilde{R}_w-\bar{R}_w)$
1	.1 × 1.00 × −.25 =	−.025		1	.1 × −1.14 × −.25 =	.0285
2	.3 × −1.20 × −.05 =	.018		2	.3 × .10 × −.05 =	−.0015
3	.4 × −.30 × .05 =	−.006		3	.4 × −.02 × .05 =	−.0004
4	.2 × 1.90 × .10 =	.038		4	.2 × .46 × .10 =	.0092
	$Cov(\tilde{R}_a,\tilde{R}_w)$ =	.025			$Cov(\tilde{R}_d,\tilde{R}_w)$ =	.0358

$$\lambda = (\bar{R}_w - R_F)/\sigma_w^2 = (.10-.08)/.01 = 2$$

1. Required return.

Domestic	Foreign
$\bar{R}_d = R_F + \lambda Cov(\tilde{R}_d,\tilde{R}_w)$	$\bar{R}_a = R_F + \lambda Cov(\tilde{R}_a,\tilde{R}_w)$
$= .08 + 2(.0358)$	$= .08 + 2(.025)$
$= .152 = 15.2\%$	$= .13 = 13\%$

C. Calculations for the portfolio. (*Note*: $\tilde{R}_p = .5\tilde{R}_a + .5\tilde{R}_d$.)

s	p	$\tilde{R}_p$	$p\tilde{R}_p$	$(\tilde{R}_p-\bar{R}_p)$	$(\tilde{R}_p-\bar{R}_p)^2$	$p(\tilde{R}_p-\bar{R}_p)^2$
1	.1	.10	.010	−.07	.0049	.00049
2	.3	−.38	−.114	−.55	.3025	.09075
3	.4	.01	.004	−.16	.0256	.01024
4	.2	1.35	.270	1.18	1.3924	.27848
			$\bar{R}_p = .17$		$Var(\tilde{R}_p)$ =	.38
					σ_p =	.62
					CV =	3.65

s	p	$(\tilde{R}_p-\bar{R}_p)$	$(\tilde{R}_w-\bar{R}_w)$	
1	.1 ×	−.07 ×	−.25 =	.00175
2	.3 ×	−.55 ×	−.05 =	.00825
3	.4 ×	−.16 ×	.05 =	−.00320
4	.2 ×	1.18 ×	.10 =	.02360
			$Cov(\tilde{R}_p,\tilde{R}_w)$ =	.0304

APPENDIX TO CHAPTER 14   351

$$\bar{R}_p = R_F + \lambda Cov(\tilde{R}_p, \tilde{R}_w)$$
$$= .08 + 2(.0304)$$
$$= .141 = 14.1\%$$

D. Graph of the security market line.

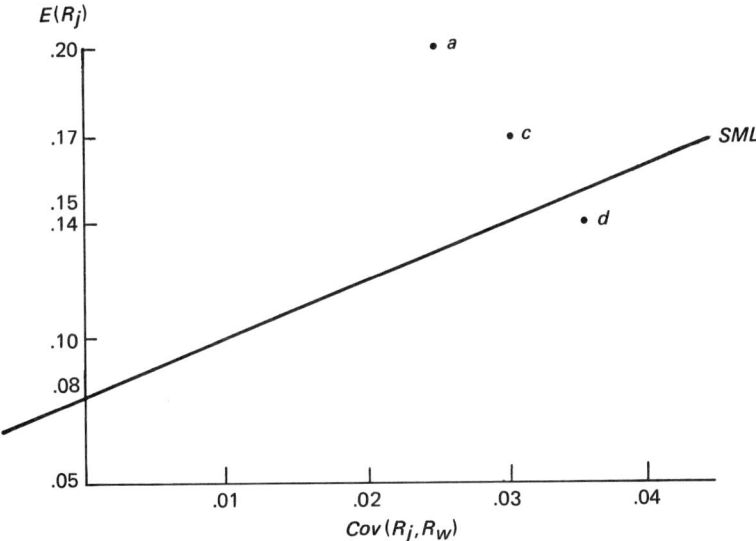

Figure A14-1 The Expected Returns on Domestic and Foreign Operations in Relation to the Security Market Line

Comments on the role of a foreign subsidiary: While the data in the example are hypothetical, they illustrate some patterns which are supported by considerable empirical data. Note that the foreign investment is more profitable than the domestic investment. The expected return on the foreign investment is 20% while that on the domestic investment is 14%. In part, this may result from the general practice of not assigning fixed costs from domestic operations to foreign operations.

While the foreign investment has a greater expected return, it also has a greater dispersion in its returns as measured by the variance and standard deviation of the returns. A normalized measure of dispersion is the coefficient of variation (CV). This is measured by dividing the standard deviation by the means. By this measure also the foreign investment has greater risk. The coefficient of variation for the foreign investment is 5.7 while it is only 3.0 in the domestic investment.

However, the total risk as measured by the variance of returns or the coefficient of variation is composed of two elements: unsystematic risk and systematic risk. Unsystematic risk is the risk that can be diversified away.

Systematic risk is the risk that remains even after diversification. It is measured by the covariance of the returns of the individual investment with the world-market returns. As shown in (B), the foreign investment has a covariance of 2.5% while the domestic investment has a covariance of 3.58%. Hence, the systematic risk, the risk that cannot be diversified away, is greater for the domestic operations than for the foreign subsidiary.

Furthermore, using the security market line relationship, the required return on the domestic investment is 15.2% while its expected return is only 14%. The required return for the foreign investment is 13% while its expected return is 20%. Thus, the foreign investment is very favorable since the return expected from the foreign investment is substantially in excess of the requirement indicated by the security market line relationships. On the other hand, the expected return from the domestic investment of 14% is below the requirement indicated by the security market line relationship.

Another aspect of the foreign subsidiary is dealt with in (C). By combining the domestic operations and the operations of the foreign subsidiary, the firm achieves some portfolio effects. The expected return for the firm as a portfolio of domestic and international operations is 17%. In addition, the covariance of the combined operation is only slightly over 3%. Thus, the systematic risk of domestic operations has been reduced by adding the foreign operations which have greater variability in returns. However, by combining the two operations, some of the variability in the returns of both the domestic and foreign operations is removed by portfolio effects and the systematic risk of the combined operations as compared with the systematic risk of the domestic operations is reduced. Utilizing the security market line, we observe also that the required return on the combined operations of the portfolio is 14.1%. Since the expected return is 17%, this is a favorable relationship. Thus, without the international operations, the domestic operations would plot below the security market line. The expected return would be less than that required by security market relationships. However, by combining with international operations the portfolio expected return is above that required by security market line relationships. Thus, in the framework of the capital asset pricing model, the financial rationale for foreign operation is illustrated.

Chapter 15

The Foreign Investment Decision

Theme: Foreign investments may be of a short-term, temporary nature, or they may be long-term portfolio or direct investments. In this chapter we focus on direct investments in controlled entities operating abroad. The general principles of capital budgeting apply to foreign direct investments—the aim is to generate the most profitable projects. However, the range of variables affecting the investment decision is increased. In addition, new elements of cost such as insuring against the risks of foreign-exchange fluctuations and political events must be taken into account. While foreign investments may have greater risks, when combined into a portfolio of investments by the firm, the benefits of diversification may reduce unsystematic risks and result in lower risks for the total operation of the firm.

I. The general principles of international investments concern comparative advantages in the supply of capital, labor, raw materials, and technology among trading nations.
    A. The country with a relative abundance of capital and a shortage of labor would have declining returns from investments and rapidly rising wage rates.
        1. This country would need to export capital or import labor.
        2. Direct investments abroad are a means of exporting capital.

B. In a country with capital shortages and abundant labor the situation would be reversed. This country would likely be the recipient of the foreign direct investment, thus importing capital.
C. These differences may only represent comparative advantages in particular industries among nations. The advantages may result from physical technology, managerial know-how, or raw materials and labor supply conditions.
D. The foregoing logic is illustrated in the recent trading history of Japan.
 1. High levels of exports over imports gave Japan a large surplus capital position compared to its Asian trading partners.
 2. Japan's labor shortage resulted in domestic wage increases of 15 to 20 percent per year.
 3. Thus, Japan had to export capital by investing in other countries in order to balance its Asian trade position and to make use of the comparative labor advantage of other countries.
 4. This type of foreign investment program is closely correlated to the desire of foreign trading partners to reduce imports and to increase domestic industrialization.
 5. These host countries may provide economic incentives to stimulate the direct investment of foreign industrial firms.

II. The U.S. position in foreign investment.
 A. The United States is a net creditor to the rest of the world in its international direct investment position. However, this has unfavorable effects on the balance of payments from a liquidity standpoint.
 1. Most of U.S. assets abroad are of a nonliquid nature.
 2. Almost half of U.S. liabilities to foreigners are in the form of liquid claims on the United States.
 3. The U.S. investment position is strong, but its liquidity position is weak.
 B. Rates of return on U.S. direct investments are higher in less developed countries, although risks are also higher.
 1. Alternative measures of direct investment earnings are used. Each provides information on only limited aspects of investment returns.
 2. Returns vary by industry and by country and do not fully reflect investments that do not survive to be included in a continuing time series of data.

III. The stimuli to direct foreign investment are so numerous and diverse that a single theory cannot provide a complete explanation.
 A. The basic principles of capital budgeting and cost of capital in international investments are the same as for domestic investments. However, significant new variables influence the implementation of the principles.
 B. Investments flow to areas in which rates of return are favorable in relation to risks. But diverse factors bring about attractive investment opportunities and vary by industries as well as for individual firms.

THE FOREIGN INVESTMENT DECISION

C. The special character of economic stimuli in international finance is illustrated by the major U.S. investments in Western Europe.
 1. These investments were the responses to opportunities and threats created by the European Common Market.
 2. The Common Market afforded opportunities for American firms to use their mass-production and mass-merchandising skills.
 3. The Common Market also posed the threat of limiting competition from other countries by creating tariff barriers against nonmember nations.
 4. Direct investments by U.S. firms in the Common Market countries provided opportunities to use their capabilities and avoided barriers to other forms of participation.

D. There are other factors that may favor the establishment of foreign manufacturing facilities compared with exporting finished products to these areas.
 1. Geographic diversification is one of the incentives for investing abroad.
 2. Governments wishing to conserve their nation's foreign exchange reserves may also provide incentives to investing firms.
 3. The requirements for different types of products in the foreign market might make it more efficient to utilize foreign production facilities.
 4. The high cost of transportation may dictate that only certain raw materials and parts can be profitably exported, while manufacturing and assembling must be performed abroad.

E. Other theories to explain foreign direct investment were discussed in Problem 10-5 of Chapter 10. These include:
 1. Utilization of knowledge and experience in high technology areas in foreign operations.
 2. The product-cycle thesis suggests that, since the growth in sales of individual products in the United States slows as their markets mature, new growth stimuli may be provided by foreign markets in which experience and successful products may be sold.
 3. The skill, knowledge, or organizational efficiency of a firm can be utilized abroad without the necessity of incurring the same investments in learning and experience expended in developing domestic business.
 4. This relates to the general idea of superior management skills that may be utilized abroad.
 5. Some have viewed foreign investments as a part of a long-range strategy in response to emerging domestic problems of firms.
 6. Cash flows in foreign subsidiaries may stimulate follow-on investments.
 7. A higher level of exchange risk in some foreign countries leads to higher required capitalization rates on earnings.
 8. Foreign investment is viewed by some as an opportunity to develop consumer attachments to differentiated advertised products such as soap, cosmetics, and foods over wider geographic markets.

PROBLEM 15-1

A. What are the factors that stimulate direct foreign investment?
B. In the case of the United States, have direct foreign investments contributed measurably to balance-of-payments problems?

SOLUTION:

A. Factors that stimulate direct foreign investment.
1. Management skills and capabilities in some U.S. firms which are not found in foreign countries, and which will yield good returns when utilized abroad.
2. Tariffs and other barriers to export sales (i.e., if you want to share in the foreign market, you must do so by producing the goods locally).
3. The need for different types of products in the foreign market.
4. New growth opportunities for products whose markets have matured in the United States.
5. Savings in transportation expenses.
6. The opportunity for geographic diversification, which may stimulate growth of the firm.
7. Greater utilization of corporate staff personnel.
8. Employment of local talent.
9. The favorable policies of host governments.

B. While direct investments are being made, they are a negative factor in the U.S. balance of payments. Some direct investments have resulted in manufacturing activity abroad that produced products that otherwise would have been exports from the United States. On some direct investments, the United States would have lost these export sales if production had not moved abroad. It is estimated that a substantial volume of parts and materials are sold to these foreign subsidiaries and used in production that is mostly sold abroad. Also, investment income cumulates as the total volume of direct investments abroad grows. A point is reached at which the new foreign investment made in a given year is exceeded by the investment income from those investments. For example, in 1974 the net direct investment income for the United States was $10 billion while the U.S. direct investment abroad in the same year totaled $7.5 billion. Therefore, the net effect for 1974 was a positive contribution to the U.S. balance of payments of $2.5 billion.

PROBLEM 15-2

How does the multinational company assess proposed entry into a foreign country or market in which it is not allowed majority ownership or control?

THE FOREIGN INVESTMENT DECISION

SOLUTION:

A. It may still be able to serve the market by utilizing one of the following:
   1. Exporting to the market.
   2. Entering a licensing agreement with a local manufacturer.
   3. Entering into a joint venture with local partners.
   4. Signing a management contract.
B. Disadvantages of having a minority position.
   1. Firm may disagree on policies.
   2. Firm may be "frozen out."
   3. Firm may give up some know-how.
   5. No independent decisions can be made on divided policy, profit reinvestment, or transfer payment policy.
C. Advantages of being in the market with a local partner.
   1. This may be the only method available to enter the market.
   2. Firm may learn from local partners (patents, licenses, local marketing techniques).
   3. Firm may sell domestically produced materials and parts to the foreign joint venture.
   4. It may also be permitted to sell some domestic finished products.
   5. Firm may thereby avoid trade barriers (tariffs, quotas).

PROBLEM 15-3

A historical trend for multinational companies has been to finance their foreign affiliates and/or subsidiaries with a minimum of equity capital. What are the reasons for this and what conditions are necessary for debt capital to be the preferred source of financing?

SOLUTION:

This assumes that an equity ownership has been established. Reasons for the use of debt financing are:
1. Tax advantages; interest paid is deductible expense in foreign country.
2. It is easier to repatriate funds via *debt repayments* rather than through dividends, which are often perceived as withdrawal of ownership capital.
3. Under former OFDI (Office of Foreign Direct Investment) regulations before 1974, debt funds could be raised from foreign banks, foreign branches of U.S. banks, and in the Eurobond markets.
4. It allows the parent to guarantee debt if necessary and also make it convertible into equity of parent.
5. It provides favorable monetary balance in a nation where devaluation is a risk.

6. The debt is considered guaranteed; it is therefore a form of equity from the standpoint of foreign investors and countries.
7. If the debt is sold to investors in the foreign country, nationalization is less likely. This would also be true of equity sold to local investors.

IV. Project evaluation in foreign investment decisions.
   A. The same general pattern of analysis applies to foreign and domestic investment decisions.
      1. Compare cash inflows and outflows on the project.
      2. Apply the appropriate cost of capital to discount cash flows to obtain the net present value of prospective investment projects.
      3. Accept projects with positive net present values to the extent permitted by availability of financial resources.
   B. At least three aspects of foreign investments differ from domestic investments.
      1. A larger number of factors influencing cash flows and discount factors need to be considered.
      2. Estimates of cash flows may have wider margins of error because of additional factors more difficult to predict and to control.
      3. Analysis of risks and returns is likely to be more complex.
   C. In reviewing foreign project proposals, the following financial statements are required covering the life of the project.
      1. A capital budgeting analysis from the standpoint of the project.
      2. A pro forma income statement from the standpoint of the project to determine applicable taxes in the capital budgeting analysis.
      3. A pro forma balance sheet from the standpoint of the project, required for determination of charges to income and applicable taxes.
      4. A cash flow analysis (cash budget) of the project to take into account liquidity considerations.
      5. The computations of the tax obligations of the U.S. parent over the project horizon for use in the capital budgeting analysis from the point of view of the parent.
      6. The parent company cash flows and cumulative net present values from the project calculated at the appropriate discount rate.
   D. New elements of costs that must be included in the above statements are:
      1. Costs of hedging against foreign exchange losses.
      2. Costs of insuring against higher commercial credit risks.
      3. Costs of guarantees against political risks.
      4. Additional foreign taxes.
      5. Management fees charged by the parent company to the foreign project.
      6. An indirect cost resulting from the potential loss of export sales to customers of the new foreign project.

THE FOREIGN INVESTMENT DECISION   359

    E. Transfer of used equipment from the parent to the new foreign subsidiary may be advantageous.
        1. It may allow the parent to realize higher salvage values on the old equipment.
        2. The appropriate cost to charge the project for this equipment is not depreciated book value but the opportunity cost of acquiring similar equipment in the foreign country.
    F. On international projects, it is useful to make an analysis of the terminal value at the end of the planning horizon.
        1. Some funds may be blocked for periods of time.
        2. Judgments of what will be received from the project during its lifetime and on liquidation must be made.
    G. The appropriate cost of capital to assign the project is the project's cost of capital, not the company's overall cost of capital.

PROBLEM 15-4

This problem is used to illustrate an analysis of a foreign investment decision.

The Magnacorp operating in the United States exports 10,000 units per month to the nation of Zorba, a less developed country. The price per unit sold is $6. The direct cost of manufacturing and transporting the product to the major distribution center of Zorba is $4 per unit. The government of Zorba has contacted Magnacorp with an invitation to establish a manufacturing operation in Zorba. After analysis it was determined that an equity investment of $1 million would be made, half of which would represent working capital and the other half fixed assets. At the end of five years, Magnacorp would sell the firm to Zorba nationals for $1 and the central bank would repay Magnacorp for the working capital (5,000,000 flattos).

In return for protection against imports by other firms, Magnacorp would be required to sell its product in Zorba for $5. Also it would buy raw materials and parts from local suppliers and utilize local managers. The total of labor and materials purchased locally would be $1.50 per unit. In addition, materials would be purchased from the parent at $1 per unit on which the parent would have variable costs of $.50 per unit. The current exchange rate is 10 flattos to the dollar.

The depreciation on fixed assets would be over a 5-year period on a straight-line basis. The effective tax rates in Zorba would be 50% which is also the current rate of tax paid by Magnacorp in the United States and Zorba is a LDC for tax purposes. Initially, assume no restrictions on cash flow repatriation, and assume further that exchange rates will remain constant. The applicable cost of capital for the project is 15%.

A. Should Magnacorp accept the proposal?
B. Magnacorp has been informed that, if it decides to reject the project, Competo, one of Magnacorp's competitors, has expressed an interest in the project. How does this affect the decision by Magnacorp?
C. Assume (B) still applies. Suppose that the equipment cost included in the $500,000 represents a book value of equipment transferred to the Zorba manufacturing site by Magnacorp at its cost on the books of $100,000, but the equipment could have been sold in the United States for $150,000 and in Zorba for $200,000. Reevaluate the proposal taking this information into account.
D. Return to question (B) and assume that the development minister of Zorba states that Zorba will cut the tax rate to 20%. Reevaluate the proposal.
E. Return to question (B) and assume further that Magnacorp will not be permitted to remit the earnings from Zorba until the end of the fifth year. The funds are blocked with no earnings on them in the interim. What is your recommendation?
F. Instead of the assumption under (E), assume that the blocked funds can be invested at a reinvestment rate of 10%. Calculate the net terminal values instead of the net present values as a basis for your recommendation.
G. Return to question (B) again and assume a decline in the foreign exchange value of the flatto by 50% in the fifth year. All prices and costs except depreciation are indexed. The devaluation is the result of a 50% inflation in Zorba at the beginning of the fifth year. Assume that the price of the raw material purchased from the parent has been fixed at 10 flattos. Again, recalculate the returns from the project.
H. Comment on the implications of the above variables affecting the foreign investment decision.

SOLUTION:

Basic cash flow analysis.
1. Cash flow from Zorba.
   a. Monthly revenue   10,000 × fl50 =   fl500,000
   b. Variable cost, local   10,000 × fl15 = 150,000
      purchase
   c. Variable cost, U.S.   10,000 × fl10 = 100,000   250,000
      purchase
         Monthly operating   fl250,000
         cash flow

THE FOREIGN INVESTMENT DECISION

Annual operating cash flow	fl3,000,000
Depreciation (5,000,000/5)	1,000,000
Earnings before taxes	2,000,000
Local taxes (50%)	1,000,000
Net income in Zorba	1,000,000
Depreciation	1,000,000
Annual cash flow form Zorba	fl2,000,000 = $200,000
	(fl10 = $1)

Cash flow to parent for materials purchased in United States.

Price per unit (P_u) = $1

Variable costs per unit (VC_u) = $.50

Contribution margin = $P_u - VC_u$ = $.50

Annual cash flow = $(P_u - VC_u)Q(1 - t_{us})$ = 120,000 × $.50 × .5
= $30,000

Cash flow foregone from loss of export sales (annual).

(120,000)($2)(.5) = $120,000

Note that since the local tax rate = U.S. tax rate = 50%, the parent will not have to pay U.S. taxes on the earnings in Zorba. (The normal basis applies.)

A.

	Item	Amt. ($000)	Yr.	Present Value Factor (PVF)	Amt. ($000)
1.	Cost of project	(1,000)	0	1	(1,000)
2.	Annual cash flow (200+30−120)*	110	1−5	3.3522	369
3.	Remit. of working capital	500	5	.49718	249
					(382)

*$200 is annual cash flow
30 is cash flow in materials sold by parent
−120 is export sales lost to local production

Reject the project.

B. Here the cash flow foregone is irrelevant because the sales would be lost anyhow.

Item	Amt. ($000)	Yr.	Present Value Factor (PVF)	Present Value (PV) ($000)
1. Cost of project	(1,000)	0	1	(1,000)
2. Annual cash flow (200+30)	230	1–5	3.3522	771
3. Remit. of working capital	500	5	.49718	249
			Net present value (NPV) =	20

Accept the project.

C. The relevant cost for the equipment is the opportunity cost. Hence the cost of the project should be $1,100,000.

Item	Amt. ($000)	Yr.	Present Value Factor (PVF)	Present Value (PV) ($000)
1. Cost of project	(1,100)	0	1	(1,100)
2. Annual cash flow	230	1–5	3.3522	771
3. Remit. of working capital	500	5	.49718	249
			NPV =	(80)

Reject the project.

D. The parent will have to pay U.S. taxes on the amount remitted from Zorba.

1. Foreign earnings before taxes   fl2,000,000
2. Local taxes (20%)   400,000
3. Dividend to parent   fl1,600,000 ($160,000)
4. U.S. income tax $80,000
5. Credit (20% of 3)   32,000
6. Net U.S. tax $48,000

Item	Amt. ($000)	Yr.	PVF	PV ($000)
1. Cost of project	(1,000)	0	1	(1,000)
2. Annual cash flow (160+100−48+30)*	242	1–5	3.3522	811
3. Remit. of working capital	500	5	.49718	249
			NPV =	60

*160 is dividend to parent
100 is depreciation cash flow
30 is cash flow on materials sold
48 is U.S. taxes

Accept the project.

THE FOREIGN INVESTMENT DECISION

E. The cash flow to the parent for U.S. material purchases will be annual, the rest will be at the end of the fifth year (5 × 200,000 + 500,000 = $1,500,000).

Item	Amt. ($000)	Yr.	PVF	PV ($000)
1. Cost of project	(1,000)	0	1	(1,000)
2. Annual purchases from United States	30	1-5	3.3522	101
3. Remit. of earnings and working capital	1,500	5	.49718	746
				(153)

Reject the project.

F.

Item	Amt. ($000)	Yr.	Future Value Factor (FVF)	Future Value (FV) ($000)
1. Cost of project	(1,000)	0	(@15%) 2.0114	(2,011)
2. Annual purchases from United States	30	1-5	(@15%) 6.7424	202
3. Working capital	500	5	1	500
4. Annual earnings in Zorba	200	1-5	(@10%) 6.1051	1,221
			Net Future Value (NFV) =	(88)

Reject the project.

G. Calculate the cash flow for the fifth year in flattos.

Monthly revenue	10,000 × 75	=	fl750,000
Variable cost, local purchase	10,000 × 22.5	= 225,000	
Variable cost, U.S. purchase	10,000 × 10	= 100,000	325,000
Monthly operating cash flow			fl425,000

Annual operating cash flow	fl5,100,000
Deprec. (5,000,000/5)	1,000,000
Earnings before taxes	4,100,000
Local taxes (50%)	2,050,000
Net income in Zorba	2,050,000
Depreciation	1,000,000
Cash flow from Zorba in 5th year	fl3,050,000
Cash flow in $ (15fl = $1)	$203,333

The working capital received is fl5,000,000/15 = $333,333. The profit to the parent on materials purchased from United States will be reduced:
$P_u = fl10/X_1 = \$10/15$ $VC_u = \$.50$ $P_u - V_c = (\$2/3) - \$.50$
$120,000[(\$2/3) - \$.50]$ $(1 - t_{us}) = \$10,000$.

	Item	Amt. ($000)	Yr.	PVF	PV ($000)
1.	Cost of project	(1,000)	0	1	(1,000)
2.	Annual cost flow (Yrs. 1–4)	230	1–4	2.8550	657
3.	Cash flow year 5 + working capital (203 + 10 + 333)*	546	5	.49718	271
				NPV =	(72)

Reject the project.

H. This case highlights the complexities involved and high level of managerial judgments required in making foreign investment decisions. Among the variables to be considered are:
1. Tax arrangements in the foreign country.
2. Extent to which the foreign government may change tax laws, government regulations, and other "rules of the game."
3. Effect on export sales if a competitor establishes operations in the foreign country.
4. Patterns of revenues, costs, and investment requirements under inflationary conditions.
5. Rate of possible inflation and exchange-rate movements.
6. Extent to which repatriation of earnings will be permitted.
7. Investment opportunities if funds are required to remain in the foreign country.
8. Possible changes in U.S. tax laws on income from foreign investments.

PROBLEM 15-5

This problem provides an illustrative example of a foreign investment project evaluation.

The J. J. Peterson Company is contemplating the establishment of a manufacturing plant in Latin America. For evaluation purposes, it developed the following information: Sales are estimated to be LC20,000 the first year, LC40,000 each for the second and third year, and LC60,000 per year for the fourth and the fifth year. An investment of LC25,000 in new fixed assets and of LC5,000 in used equipment will be made at the beginning of the first year. Raw materials costs will be 30 percent of sales. Labor costs will be 10 percent of sales. Selling and administrative costs will also be 10 percent of sales. Assume for simplicity that there are no accounts receivable, all sales being for cash. All goods are sold in the year produced and all expenses are paid as incurred. The parent company will charge the project a supervisory fee of LC1,000 per annum for the first three years and LC2,000 for each of the remaining two years to cover its actual dollar costs. Local taxes will be 40 percent of the before-tax profits.

In determining the profit and loss of the project, assume straight-line depreciation over a 10-year period with 0 salvage value for both the new fixed assets and the used equipment. Assume further that both the new fixed assets

THE FOREIGN INVESTMENT DECISION

and the used equipment can be sold at their depreciated value as of the end of the fifth year. The parent made an additional cash contribution of LC4,000 on an equity basis at the start of the first year. This investment in working capital will be returned at the end of the investment period.

The project will return dividends to the U.S. parent as shown in Table B. These dividends will be subject to a 10-percent withholding tax in the country of operation. A tax treaty between the two governments allows the 10 percent withholding tax to be offset against U.S. income taxes. The U.S. income tax will be calculated under the normal basis at a U.S. corporate income tax rate of 50 percent.

The foreign country does not tax the sale of used equipment at book value. Neither does it tax the supervisory fee charged by the parent company. The equipment will be sold and all the unremitted retained earnings and cash from the equipment sale will be returned home. The exchange rate is LC10 to $1; no devaluation is expected. A 12 percent cost of capital is considered appropriate for evaluating the project.

A. Make a cash budget from the point of view of the project for each of the five years in the life of the project in terms of the local currency.
B. Calculate the profit or loss after taxes for each year in the local currency (LC).
C. Prepare a pro forma balance sheet for the project in LC. (Note that since no time lags are involved in the production process, there are no inventories shown on the balance sheet.)
D. Determine the U.S. income tax obligations of the parent on the dividends received from the Latin American project.
E. Determine the cash flows from the point of view of the project on a capital budgeting basis.
F. Make a capital budgeting analysis of the project from the standpoint of the parent company.

Where applicable, separate the analysis of the fifth year flows into before and after liquidation of the fixed assets cases.

SOLUTION:

Table A   Pro Forma Cash-Flow Statement of the Project (Cash Budget Analysis)
(in thousands of LC)

	\multicolumn{7}{c}{Years}						
	0	1	2	3	4	5	5_t
Inflows							
Cash from parent	34	—	—	—	—	—	—
Cash sales	—	20	40	40	60	60	—
Equipment sold	—	—	—	—	—	—	15
Total inflows	34	20	40	40	60	60	15

Table A Pro Forma Cash-Flow Statement of the Project (Continued)

	Years						
	0	1	2	3	4	5	5_t
Disbursements							
Raw Materials (30% of sales)	—	6	12	12	18	18	—
Equipment	30	—	—	—	—	—	—
Labor (10% of sales)	—	2	4	4	6	6	—
Selling and admin. expense (10% of sales)	—	2	4	4	6	6	—
Parent fee	—	1	1	1	2	2	—
Dividends (see Table B)	—	3	8	8	7.5	0	26.3
Income taxes of subsidiary (see Table B)	—	2.4	6.4	6.4	10	10	—
Total disbursements	30	16.4	35.4	35.4	49.5	42	26.3
Net inflow	4	3.6	4.6	4.6	10.5	18	(11.3)
Cash on hand	0	4	7.6	12.2	16.8	27.3	45.3
Cash at end of period	4	7.6	12.2	16.8	27.3	45.3	34

Inflows result from the cash sales of each period and the initial capital contribution of the parent (investment in equipment of LC30,000 + initial cash contribution of LC4,000). The equipment sold at the end of the fifth year at its depreciated value contributes another LC15,000. Disbursements calculated are based on the relationships given in the problem. Both dividends and local taxes are derived from Table B.

The difference between the inflows and the disbursements of each period gives the net inflow for the period. This is added to the cash on hand to obtain a cumulative cash-at-the-end-of-period schedule. This is the source of the cash item that appears on the balance sheet statement in Table C.

Table B Pro Forma Income Statement
(in thousands of LC)

	Years					
	0	1	2	3	4	5
Sales		20	40	40	60	60
Less:						
Raw materials		6	12	12	18	18
Labor		2	4	4	6	6
Selling and admin. expense		2	4	4	6	6
Supervisory fee		1	1	1	2	2
Equipment depreciation (10% of gross fixed assets)		3	3	3	3	3
Total cost		14	24	24	35	35
Income before taxes		6	16	16	25	25
Income taxes (40%)		2.4	6.4	6.4	10	10
Income after taxes		3.0	9.6	9.6	15	15
Dividends		3.0	8.0	8.0	7.50	26.3
Withholding tax (10%)		0.3	0.8	0.8	0.75	2.63
Net dividend to parent		2.7	7.2	7.2	6.75	23.67

THE FOREIGN INVESTMENT DECISION

All expenses including depreciation are offset against income from sales to obtain income before taxes. Local taxes take 40% from this. Dividend payments made to the parent are subject to a 10% local dividend withholding tax. Dividends for the fifth year include the usual payment of LC7,500 plus a liquidating payment to the parent. This liquidating payment at the end of the investment period consists of the sum of all undistributed earnings.

Table C Pro Forma Balance Sheet Statement
(in thousands of LC)

	Years						
	0	1	2	3	4	5	5_t
Cash (see Table A)	4	7.6	12.2	16.8	21.3	45.3	34
Gross fixed assets	30	30	30	30	30	30	—
Less: reserve for depreciation	—	3	6	9	12	15	—
Net fixed assets	30	27	24	21	18	15	—
Total assets	34	37	45	53	60.5	60.3	34
Common stock	34	34	34	34	34	34	34
Retained earnings	—	3	11	19	26.5	26.3	—
Total liabilities and net worth	34	37	45	53	60.5	60.3	34

Cash here is derived from Table A. Fixed assets worth LC30,000 are depreciated on a straight-line basis over 10 years. These are, however, sold at the end of the fifth year at their depreciated value as shown in 5_t. Common stock consists of the initial parent capital contribution and retained earnings are simply the cumulative sum of the undistributed earnings.

Table D Calculations of U.S. Income Tax
(in dollars)

	Years					
	0	1	2	3	4	5
Net dividend received (Table B)		270	720	720	675	236.7
+ Dividend withholding tax (Table B)		30	80	80	75	26.3
Taxable income		300	800	800	750	263.0
U.S. income tax (50%)		150	400	400	375	131.5
− Foreign tax credit*		150	400	400	375	131.5
Net U.S. tax		0	0	0	0	0

*Withholding tax plus 40% of gross dividends.

The U.S. income tax is calculated on a normal basis. The 10% dividend withholding tax is added back to the net dividend received by the parent (from Table B) to obtain the taxable income on which the 50% U.S. corporate tax rate is applied. The resulting U.S. income tax is then reduced by the amount of the deductible foreign tax credit to obtain the net U.S. tax. Note that all values have been converted into dollars at LC10 to the $. Also, all foreign tax not absorbed by the parent in prior years is charged to the parent in year 5 upon liquidation of the investment project.

Table E Five-Year Capital Budgeting Analysis of the Project
(in thousands of LC)

	\multicolumn{7}{c}{Years}
	0	1	2	3	4	5	5_t
Cash inflows							
Cash sales	0	20	40	40	60	60	—
Total cash collections	0	20	40	40	60	60	—
Cash outflows							
Cash investment	4	—	—	—	—	—	(4.0)
New fixed assets	25	—	—	—	—	—	(12.5)
Used equipment	5	—	—	—	—	—	(2.5)
Raw materials	—	6	12	12	18	18	—
Labor	—	2	4	4	6	6	—
Selling and admin. expense	—	2	4	4	6	6	—
Parent fee	—	1	1	1	2	2	—
Local taxes (Table B)	—	2.4	6.4	6.4	10	10	—
Total outflows	34	13.4	27.4	27.4	42	42	(19)
Net cash inflows	(34)	6.6	12.6	12.6	18	18	19
Cumulative cash inflows	(34)	(27.4)	(14.8)	(2.2)	15.8	33.8	52.8

The capital budgeting analysis of the project starts with the identification of the cash flows involved. Cash inflows consist primarily of cash sales. Other items include the return of the original cash investment by the parent and the liquidation of the fixed assets at depreciated value. These are, however, treated as negative outflows here. The difference between the inflows and the outflows results in the net cash inflows.

Table F J. J. Peterson Company—Capital Budgeting Analysis of Project
(in U.S. dollars)

	\multicolumn{7}{c}{Year}
	0	1	2	3	4	5	5_t
Cash inflows and outflows							
Net cash flow from project*	(3,400)	270	720	720	675	2,367	3,400
Supervisory fee, net	—	50	50	50	100	100	—
Total inflow	(3,400)	320	770	770	775	2,467	3,400
Present value factor (12%)	1	.893	.797	.712	.636	.567	.567
Present value	(3,400)	285.76	613.69	548.24	492.90	1,398.79	1,927.8
					Cumulative net present value =		$1,867.18

*For parts 1–5, last line of Table B. Years 0 and 5_t represent the investment and its recovery.

The capital budgeting analysis from the standpoint of the parent is presented in Table F.

The cash flows from the point of view of the parent include (1) the initial investment of $3,400, (2) the recovery of this investment on liquidation, (3) the net dividends received, and (4) the after U.S. tax supervisory fee. The net cash flows are discounted at the 12 percent cost of capital considered appropriate for this project. The firm experiences positive net cash inflows after the initial investment outlay. The cumulative net present value of the project is $1,867.18. The project, therefore, earns a return greater than the 12 percent applicable cost of capital and would be considered profitable at this point of the analysis.

Comments:

1. Note that different flow patterns are reflected in the cash budget, the pro forma income statement, and the capital budgeting analysis of the project. Depreciation expenses are recorded in the income statement, but not in the other two. Dividends do not enter the project capital budgeting analysis, but are reflected in the other two and in the first line of the capital budgeting analysis from the standpoint of the parent. The investment of LC4,000 cash is a part of "cash on hand" in the cash budget, but is shown as a return cash flow in the project capital budgeting analysis. Thus the flows and accounts in Tables A through F are all interrelated.
2. The analysis of the project as presented with liquidation at the end of the fifth year can be considered as one alternative. Another alternative is that the project is so successful that the Peterson Company will want to continue the venture and possibly even expand it. As such, this analysis presents the addition to the value of the firm under one unfavorable alternative.

V. Risk considerations are especially important in foreign investment decisions.
   A. The range of possible outcomes may be much greater for the foreign investment than for a domestic one.
      1. A large number of uncertainties over which the firm has little control may be faced.
         a. Changes in government taxation treatment and other governmental regulations.
         b. Foreign-exchange-rate fluctuations.
      2. Changes in the total world economic environment may more directly affect the firm in international operations.
      3. A firm in international operations becomes exposed to the numerous and diverse forces of competition in international markets.
         a. As foreign exchange rates fluctuate, the competitive position of the international firm can be greatly affected regardless of its own operating efficiency. For example, the decline in the value of the dollar in relation to the German mark made the Volkswagen much more expensive in the United States and adversely affected Volkswagen's competitive position in the United States.

b. U.S. companies must deal with the problem of more favorable treatment of international companies domiciled in other countries as compared with the environment of their own operations created by the U.S. government.
B. Risk analysis requires the evaluation of cumulative net present values that occur under alternative future outcomes. Compare the expected returns and their standard deviations.
C. Some portions of risk may be diversified away in a portfolio of domestic and international investments as shown in the following illustrative problems.

PROBLEM 15-6

The Arbee Company is contemplating the desirability of diversifying through foreign investments. There are currently a number of attractive investment opportunities in Southeast Asia with a total funds requirement of $20 million. For evaluation purposes, estimates of probabilities of returns for both the foreign investment and the domestic operation for the coming year were made. These are given below:

Probability Factor (p)	Estimated Rates of Return	
	Foreign (R_b)	Domestic (R_d)
.3	−.10	.20
.5	.30	.10
.2	.15	−.05

Make a risk-return analysis of the foreign investment project and its effect on the company. Assume that total foreign investment amounts to 25 percent of the company's total assets.

SOLUTION:

The objective here is to determine if diversifying by making the foreign investment will improve the overall risk-return relationship of the total portfolio of the firm; the portfolio here consists of both the domestic operation and the foreign investment. Thus, we need to compare the performance of the firm before and after it adds the foreign investment to its portfolio. The steps leading to the final determination of the expected return on the portfolio [$E(R_p)$] and its dispersion factor as measured by the standard deviation of the portfolio (σ_p) are illustrated as follows:

From the probabilities of the various estimated returns given in the problem, we first make independent evaluations of the expected return and standard deviation of the domestic operation $[E(R_d), \sigma_d]$ and the foreign investment project $[E(R_b), \sigma_b]$. Calculations are set forth below.

For the domestic operation:

p	R_d	pR_d	$[R_d - E(R_d)]$	$[R_d - E(R_d)]^2$	$p[R_d - E(R_d)]^2$
.3	.20	.06	.10	.0100	.0030
.5	.10	.05	0	0	0
.2	−.05	−.01	−.15	.0225	.0045
	$E(R_d)$ =	.10		Var (R_d) =	.0075
				σ_d =	.0866

For the foreign investment project:

p	R_b	pR_f	$[R_b - E(R_b)]$	$[R_b - E(R_b)]^2$	$p[R_b - E(R_b)]^2$
.3	−.10	−.03	−.25	.0625	.01875
.5	.30	.15	.15	.0225	.01125
.2	.15	.03	0	0	0
	$E(R_b)$ =	.15		Var (R_b) =	.03
				σ_b =	.1732

The expected return is obtained by getting the sum of the estimated returns weighted by their respective probabilities. The deviations of the individual estimated returns from the expected mean are then squared, weighted by their respective probabilities, and summed to obtain the variance (*Var*). The standard deviation (σ) is the square root of the variance. These last two are measures of dispersion from the expected mean.

The results of the calculation show that the foreign investment has both a higher expected return (15%) and a higher risk (17.3%) as compared to a lower expected return (10%) and standard deviation (8.66%) for the domestic investment.

In order to determine the extent of the influence between the returns on the foreign investment and those of the domestic investment, we first calculate the covariance factor between them ($Cov_{f,d}$). This is obtained by multiplying their corresponding deviations, weighting these by their respective probabilities, and finally summing them up. The calculations below give a covariance factor of −.0075.

$$[R_b - E(R_b)] \; [R_a - E(R_a)] \qquad p[R_b - E(R_b)] \; [R_a - E(R_a)]$$

−.25	×	.10 =	−.025	−.0075
.15	×	0 =	0	0
0	×	−.15 =	0	0
			$Cov_{b,d}$ =	−.0075

The covariance is also equal to the product of the correlation between the returns for the two investments ($Cor_{b,d}$) and their individual standard deviations. From this relationship, we can obtain the correlation between their returns by:

$$Cor_{b,d} = Cov_{b,d}/(\sigma_b \sigma_d)$$

to obtain a correlation factor of -0.5. This shows that there is a negative correlation between the pattern of returns from the two investments. This negative correlation has important implications for portfolio diversification, as we shall see later.

At this point we have obtained:

$$E(R_b) = .15 \quad \sigma_b = 17.32\%$$
$$E(R_d) = .10 \quad \sigma_d = 8.66\% \quad Cor_{b,d} = -.5$$

and, given the proportion of the foreign investment (x_b) = .25, we can now obtain the expected return and the risk of the portfolio using the relations:

$$E(R_p) = x_b E(R_f) + x_d E(R_d)$$

$$\sigma_p = \sqrt{x_b^2 \sigma_b^2 + x_d^2 \sigma_d^2 + 2 x_b x_d \, Cor_{b,d} \sigma_b \sigma_d}$$

The calculations are made as follows:

$$E(R_p) = (.25)(.15) + (.75)(.10)$$
$$= .0375 + .075$$
$$= 11.25\%$$

$$\sigma_p = [(.25)^2(.1732)^2 + (.75)^2(.0866)^2 + 2(.25)(.75)(-.5)(.1732)(.0866)]^{1/2}$$
$$= [(.0625)(.03) + (.5625)(.0075) + (2)(.25)(.75)(-.0075)]^{1/2}$$
$$= [.001875 + .004219 - .002813]^{1/2}$$
$$= [.003281]^{1/2}$$
$$= 5.73\%$$

Notice in the last part of the equation solving for σ_p, we could have simply substituted $Cov_{b,d}$ for its equivalent terms: $[Cor_{b,d} \sigma_b \sigma_d]$. Also, since we know that foreign investment makes up a fourth of the firm's total assets (x_b = .25), domestic investment would obviously make up the remaining three fourths $[x_d = (1 - .25)]$.

THE FOREIGN INVESTMENT DECISION

In conclusion, we see that even though the foreign investment is highly risky when considered on its own, its addition to the firm's portfolio reduces the firm's overall risk to 5.73%, significantly below the risk derived from either the domestic or the foreign investment alone. This reduction occurs because of the negative correlation between the returns from the two investments, which has a smoothing effect on the firm's overall portfolio performance.

This illustrates the underlying principle involved in portfolio diversification: Combine activities that are less than perfectly positively correlated ($Cor < +1$). In fact, combining in the right proportion activities that are perfectly negatively correlated ($Cor = -1$) would totally eliminate the risk. Finally, the higher expected return from the foreign investment also favorably affects the firm's returns by increasing them 1.25%.

PROBLEM 15-7

1. What discount rate should be used for evaluating projected overseas investments? Does the possibility of added risk change the rate to be used?
2. Is it possible for the overseas investment to lower the corporate business risk?
3. Does this have any effect on the corporation's financial structure? How might this happen?

SOLUTION:

1. The appropriate discount rate to use for evaluating foreign investments should be the same discount rate that would be applied to a similar project (in a similar risk class) undertaken in the headquarter's country (which may be different than the firm's risk class prior to this present project), plus a risk differential for the "special risks of the internationality" of the project.
2. It is possible for an overseas project to lower a firm's risk from diversification effects, as discussed in the previous problem.
3. This reduced risk might make possible the use of more leverage by the firm and possibly a reduction in the firm's cost of capital.

PROBLEM 15-8

The International Division of Olson Worldwide, Inc., is planning to establish an electronic manufacturing subsidiary. The firm has sales and/or manufacturing subsidiaries in a number of developed and developing countries. Some of these are 100% owned, but the latest ones are mostly on a joint-venture basis involving investors from the host and other countries.

Under the proposed plan the investment would require LC800,000 or $200,000. Additional funds needed can be borrowed in the host country. The Olson firm would initiate the undertaking on a 100% basis and then sell the operation at the end of the fifth year to a joint-venture group of which the Olson firm might or might not be a partner. The sale price agreed upon is LC1,500,000.

Environmental Factors

The government of the host country has assured the company that there would be no interference with the flow of funds out of the country for purposes of the payment of interest, dividends, or the repatriation of capital. There will be no foreign tax on a capital gain at the end of the 5-year period.

The government of the country has been stable since the country became an independent nation.

Inflation is no worse than the average in the world.

Exports do not balance imports, but this deficit is made up from the foreign exchange earned from a very active tourist industry. In general, the country's balance of payments is neutral.

Foreign exchange and import and export controls presently do not exist and are not contemplated.

Taxes are lower than in the United States.

An adequate system of social security has been in existence for many years.

There are provisions for vacation allowances, bonuses and severance payments, and reasonable work standards.

The company has been assured that the planned venture fills a need of the country's economy and that a large domestic demand exists within the country as well as in neighboring countries.

A system of major paved roads exists. There is adequate air transportation, but only one rail line out to the coast.

The population is mainly black, with arab, oriental, and white minorities. Much of the business of trading is done by the orientals. Whites and blacks are involved in the government of the country.

Education is available to all children with the exception of those of some of the nomadic tribes in the desert areas.

Nationals of the country are very much interested in participating in the joint venture at the end of five years.

The country's banking system is reasonably developed so that loans may be obtained under normal circumstances.

There is no international financial market in the country.

Financial Information

Sales volume for the first five years is estimated as LC200,000, 400,000, 1,300,000, 1,450,000, and 1,600,000 in that order. Sales for the first year of the joint-venture management are estimated to be LC1,800,000.

THE FOREIGN INVESTMENT DECISION

Beginning cash will be LC150,000.

Accounts receivable are estimated to be 1/6 of annual sales.

Inventories are estimated to be LC50,000 plus 10% of the annual sales of the following year. Accounts payable equal 1/12 of cost of goods sold.

Other payables are estimated to be 1/12 of the overhead expenses which are estimated to be LC50,000 plus 10% of sales for the first two years and 90,000 plus 15% of sales later.

Short-term funds can be obtained at 10% from commercial banks.

Taxes are paid on a quarterly basis in the month following each calendar quarter.

Minimum cash need will be LC100,000; borrowing and repayment will be done in units of LC1,000.

Depreciation is straight-line on a 10-year basis. The amount of the depreciation is included in the estimates of the cost of goods sold.

No dividends will be paid for the first two years. Thereafter, 50% of earnings will be paid to the shareholders with a dividend withholding tax of 10% applying.

The government of the host country has concluded a tax treaty with the U.S. government.

The company's contribution to equity capital will be LC300,000 to common stock and 500,000 to be paid in capital.

The exchange rate of the local currency in terms of the U.S. dollar is LC4 per $1 at the beginning of the investment. Depreciation of the currency is expected to be 10% per year in terms of LC/$.

The firm's U.S. tax rate is 50% and the foreign rate is 30%.

The firm would use the gross-up method in reporting its foreign income on this investment.

The firm's cost of capital is 12%.

The firm will charge the subsidiary a management fee of $5,000 for the first two years and $10,000 per year thereafter. This fee is included in the estimated overhead expenses.

Prior to the sale to the joint-venture group all earnings not previously remitted will be transferred to the home office in the form of a dividend.

Cost of goods sold are estimated to be LC10,000 + 50% of annual sales.

Added equipment of LC200,000 will be purchased in years 3 and 4 at the beginning of each year from internal cash flows of the subsidiary.

A. Set forth the expected exchange rates at the end of each year.
B. Analyze the relevant cash flows from the standpoint of the parent, including:
1. The initial investment.
2. Management fees.
3. Selling price in the fifth year, including the U.S. tax on the capital gain or loss.
4. Dividends before U.S. taxes received by parent.

5. A schedule of yearly taxes ending with the after-tax cash flows to the parent.
6. Summary of net cash flows by year after tax, discounted at the 12% cost of capital, with a final net present value calculation.

C. Prepare balance sheets at the end of each of the five years.

SOLUTION:

A. The information on expected devaluation rates is used to compute the expected exchange rates at the end of years 0-5. Let X_t be the exchange rate at the end of year t.

Then, $D_{fd} = \dfrac{X_t - X_{t-1}}{X_{t-1}} = \dfrac{X_t}{X_{t-1}} - 1.$

Thus, $X_t = X_{t-1}(1+D_{fd}) = X_{t-1}(1.10)$

t	0	1	2	3	4	5
X_t	4	4.40	4.84	5.32	5.86	6.44

B. In analyzing this project as an investment decision, two factors must be considered: (1) the cash flows for the project and (2) the cost of capital for projects of this risk class, given as 12%. The relevant cash flows are the dollar cash flows from the standpoint of the parent. Any local purchases, borrowings, or exchange-rate gains or losses are considered only through their influence on the final dollar cash flows to the parent. The relevant cash flows for the parent are: the initial investment, the management fee, the sale price at the end of the fifth year, and the dividends received by the parent.

1. The initial investment is $200,000 in year 0.
2. The management fee is as follows:

Years	$ Amount	$ Amount after Taxes
1-2	$ 5,000	$2,500
3-5	$10,000	$5,000

3. The sales price of the investment in year 5 = LC1,500,000/6.44 = $232,919

Capital gain on sale = selling price − cost basis
= $232,919 − $200,000 = $32,919

With a capital gains tax at $.5 t_{us}$ the applicable tax rate will be .25.

Capital gains tax on investment sale = .25(32,919) = $8,230

THE FOREIGN INVESTMENT DECISION

4. The dividends received are computed as follows. First compute the net dividend remitted to the parent in LC.

Item	Year 1	Year 2	Year 3	Year 4	Year 5
Estimated sales	LC200,000	LC400,000	LC1,300,000	LC1,450,000	LC1,600,000
Earnings before taxes (EBT)*	20,000	100,000	355,000	407,500	460,000
Local taxes (30%)	6,000	30,000	106,500	122,250	138,000
Earnings after taxes	LC 14,000	LC 70,000	248,500	285,250	322,000
Dividends declared in LC			124,250	142,625	672,875
Dividend withholding tax			12,425	14,263	67,288
Net LC dividend			LC 111,825	LC 128,363	LC 605,588
Exchange rate (LC/$)			5.32	5.86	6.44
$ dividend received			$21,020	$21,905	$94,035

*For years 1, 2: EBT = Sales − (.50+.10) Sales − (LC50,000+LC10,000)
                     = .40(Sales) − LC60,000

For years 3, 4, 5: EBT = Sales − (.50+.15) Sales − (LC10,000−LC90,000)
                     = .35(Sales) − LC100,000

5. Next compute taxes and the net dollar cash flow after taxes.

Item	Year 3	Year 4	Year 5
Dividends received	$21,020	$21,905	$94,035
Applicable foreign taxes	10,009	10,431	44,779
Dividend withholding taxes	2,336	2,434	10,448
Grossed-up income	33,365	34,770	149,262
U.S. tax (50% of previous line)	16,683	17,385	74,631
Foreign tax credit	12,345	12,865	55,227
Net U.S. tax	4,338	4,520	19,404
Net cash flow from operations	$16,682	$17,385	$74,631

6. Summary of net cash flows by year (after tax)

Item	Year 0	Year 1	Year 2	Year 3	Year 4	Year 5
Initial investment	($200,000)	—	—	—	—	—
Management fees	—	2,500	$2,500	$ 5,000	$ 5,000	$ 5,000
Dividends received	—	—	—	16,682	17,385	74,631
Sale of firm	—	—	—	—	—	232,919
Capital gains tax on sale	—	—	—	—	—	(8,230)
Total cash flow by year	($200,000)	$2,500	$2,500	$21,682	$22,385	$304,320
PVF	1	.89286	.79719	.71178	.63552	.56743
PV	($200,000)	$2,232	$1,993	$15,433	$14,226	$172,680

NPV = $ 6,564

The positive *NPV* (net present value) would provide one basis for accepting the project. In addition, the general environmental factors in the host country are favorable.

C. Balance sheets.
1. In the initial year (before operations begin), the balance sheet would consist of the following items only:

Cash	LC150,000	Common stock	LC300,000
Inventory	50,000	Paid in capital	500,000
Plant and equipment	600,000	Total equity	LC800,000
Total Assets	LC800,000		

2. In preparing the subsequent pro forma balance sheets all items except cash are entered. Then all liability and capital items are added to get a total. This total is transferred to the total asset location, and the total of all noncash asset items is then subtracted from the total. In this way cash is the residual item on the pro forma balance sheet. For this problem the cash balance did not fall below the required minimum. Should this happen, the required amount to bring the cash amount above the required minimum is then borrowed short-term by increasing notes to banks. Following this, the liabilities and capital items are added again and the total transferred to the position for total assets. Then when the asset items are subtracted from the total noncash asset amount, the residual item cash will be above the required minimum.

Pro Forma Balance Sheets in LCs

	Years				
	1	2	3	4	5
Current assets					
Cash	167,167	189,833	101,958	116,646	344,708
Accounts receivable	33,333	66,667	216,667	241,667	266,667
Inventory	90,000	180,000	195,000	210,000	230,000
Total current assets	290,500	436,500	513,625	568,313	841,375
Plant and equipment	600,000	600,000	800,000	1,000,000	1,000,000
Reserve for depreciation	60,000	120,000	200,000	300,000	400,000
Net plant and equipment	540,000	480,000	600,000	700,000	600,000
Total Assets	830,000	916,500	1,113,625	1,268,313	1,441,375
Current liabilities					
Accounts payable	9,167	17,500	55,000	61,250	67,500
Notes payable	—	—	—	—	—
Other payables	5,833	7,500	23,750	25,625	27,500
Taxes payable	1,500	7,500	26,625	30,563	34,500
Total current liabilities	16,500	32,500	105,375	117,438	129,500

Pro Forma Balance Sheets in LCs (Continued)

	Years				
	1	2	3	4	5
Long-term debt	—	—	—	—	—
Common stock	300,000	300,000	300,000	300,000	300,000
Paid in capital	500,000	500,000	500,000	500,000	500,000
Retained earnings	14,000	84,000	208,250	350,875	511,875
Total liabilities and capital	830,500	916,500	1,113,625	1,268,313	1,441,375
Exchange rate LC/$	4.40	4.84	5.324	5.856	6.442

3. At the end of the fifth year, the total retained earnings to be remitted to the parent is LC511,875. Cash in excess of the required minimum of LC100,000 is LC244,708. Thus, if LC511,875 is to be remitted, additional financing of LC267,167 will be required. This illustrates that retained earnings are not the same as cash since retained earnings are likely to be invested in part in noncash items. Hence, outside financing will be required in the amount of LC267,167.

REFERENCES

Adler, Michael, and Guy V. G. Stevens: "The Trade Effects of Direct Investment," *The Journal of Finance*, **29**:655-676, May 1974.

Aharoni, Yair: *The Foreign Investment Decision Process*, Graduate School of Business Administration, Harvard University, Boston, Mass., 1966.

Chenery, H. B.: "Comparative Advantage and Development Policy," *American Economic Review*, **51**:18-51, March 1961.

Dunn, Robert M.: "Flexible Exchange Rates and Oligopoly Pricing: A Study of Canadian Markets," *Journal of Political Economy*, **78**:140-151, January-February 1970.

"Foreign Investment," *Business International*, **23**:41-42, February 6, 1976.

Horst, Thomas: "The Theory of the Multinational Firm: Optimal Behavior Under Different Tariff and Tax Rates," *Journal of Political Economy*, **79**:1059-1072, September-October 1971.

Miller, Norman C., and Marina V. N. Whitman: "Alternative Theories and Tests of U.S. Short-Term Foreign Investment," *Journal of Finance*, **28**:1131-1147, December 1973.

————, and ————, "A Mean-Variance Analysis of United States Long-Term Portfolio Foreign Investment," *Quarterly Journal of Economics*, **85**:175-196, May 1970.

Scaperlanda, Anthony E., and Laurence J. Mauer: "The Determinants of U.S. Direct Investment in the E.E.C.," *American Economic Review*, **59**: 558-568, September 1969.

Vernon, Raymond: "International Investment and International Trade in the Product Life Cycle," *Quarterly Journal of Economics*, **80**:190-207, May 1966.

Wells, Louis: "Test of a Product Cycle Model of International Trade: U.S. Exports of Consumer Durables," *Quarterly Journal of Economics*, **83**: 152-162, February 1969.

————(ed.): *The Product Life Cycle and International Trade*, Division of Research, Harvard Business School, Boston, Mass., 1972.

Chapter 16

The Finance Function in International Operations

Theme: This chapter seeks to provide a perspective on the finance function in international operations. The turbulence of the international economic environment produces continuous changes, which have impacts upon business firms. To function effectively, business firms must adapt to these changes. The central characteristic of the international financial market is that it is efficient—new information is rapidly reflected in market price relationships. In choosing between alternative methods of managing risks and in comparing the costs of alternative methods of limiting the potential losses from risk exposure, trade-offs are possible. The characteristics of these trade-offs are reviewed in this chapter.

I. The scope of international financial functions.
    A. The organization of the international finance functions.
    B. Financial policies and practices carried out consistently on a worldwide basis.
        1. Evaluation and control of international operations.
        2. Management of foreign assets.
    C. International tax planning.
    D. Management of international cash flows.

E. Financing international sales.
F. Financing foreign operations.
G. Planning and evaluating foreign ventures.
H. Some central themes in analyzing the trade-offs between expanding profit possibilities, exposure to the risks of the international financial markets, and the costs of limiting risks.

II. The general patterns of organizational relationships in the international company. (See Figure 16-1.)
   A. The evolution of the organization of an international firm.
   B. The international financial function must be at the location where top-level management makes foreign operations decisions. Depending on the firm's organizational structure this may be
      1. The overall corporate head office if
         a. The scope of foreign operations is small.
         b. The nature of the firm's business is such that foreign and domestic operations must be closely coordinated.
         c. The success of the overall firm depends greatly on the performance of the foreign part of the business.
      2. The head office of a foreign operations subsidiary if
         a. All foreign business is managed by that subsidiary.
         b. The country of location of the firm's overall head office presents disadvantages that interfere with effective worldwide management. This may be due to:
            (1) National currency that cannot be readily converted into other currencies.
            (2) Laws, rules, or regulations that prevent the free flow of funds into and out of the country.
            (3) Tax laws that would unnecessarily subject foreign-earned funds to national taxation.
   C. The volume of a firm's international operations strongly influences the choice among the above alternatives.
      1. If operations are small, the international finance function may be represented by
         a. One financial expert, or
         b. One expert and a small staff.
      2. If worldwide operations are large in scope, the financial function may include:
         a. A top-level international financial executive.
         b. A number of financial specialists in each area of international finance with their own staffs to manage particular phases of international financial management.

THE FINANCE FUNCTION IN INTERNATIONAL OPERATIONS

Figure 16-1 Types of Organization in International Companies

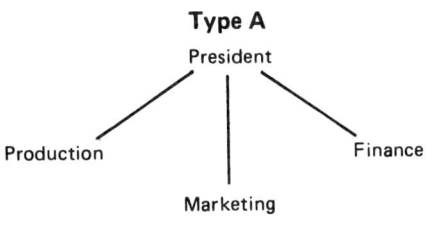

Type A Organized by management functions

1. Small firm.
2. New to international business.
3. One operation for both domestic and international production and sales
4. Use of export agents and brokers.

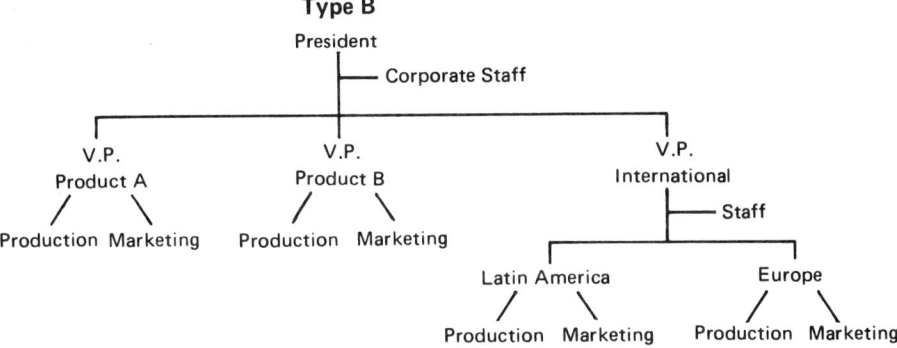

Type B Organized by product with an international division

1. Treats international as another activity with special characteristics.
2. Needs to coordinate product and geographical activities.

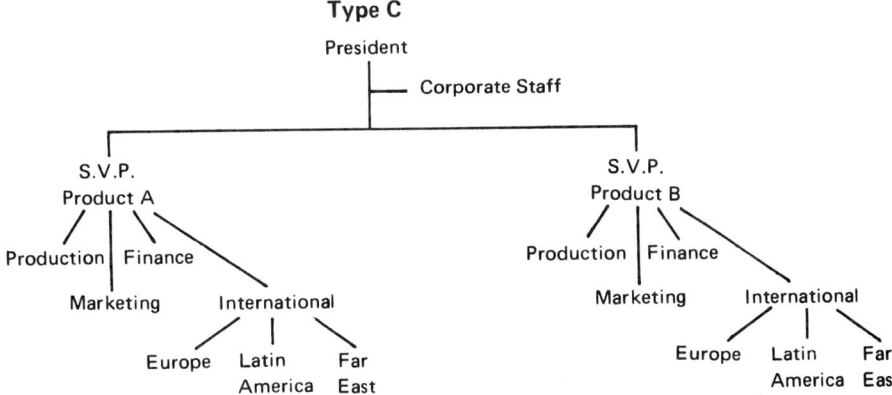

Type C Organized by product with functional and geographic departmentation

1. International fully integrated by product.
2. Most appropriate for a basic staple such as cornstarch.
3. Lends itself to standardization of production policies with some flexibility in marketing in different areas.

Figure 16-1 Types of Organization in International Companies (Continued)

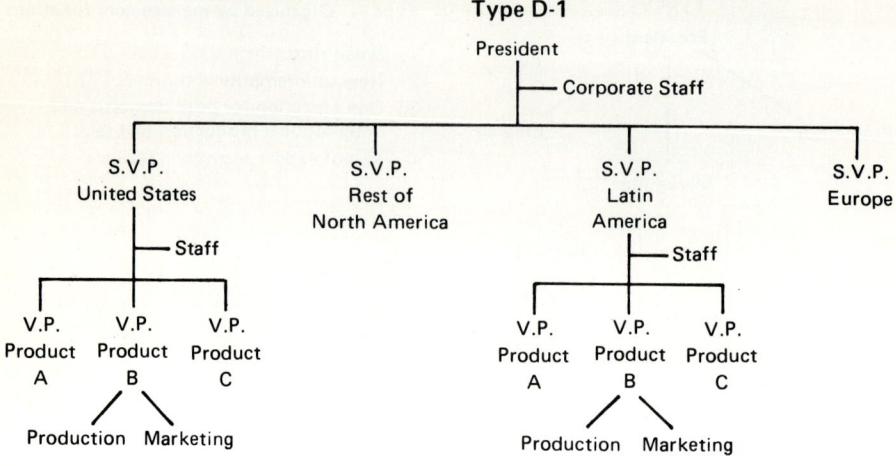

Type D-1 Basic organization geographic with product departmentation

1. Facilitates adapting operations to the characteristics required by geographical areas.
2. Most appropriate for products such as drugs and autos which must differ for different areas.

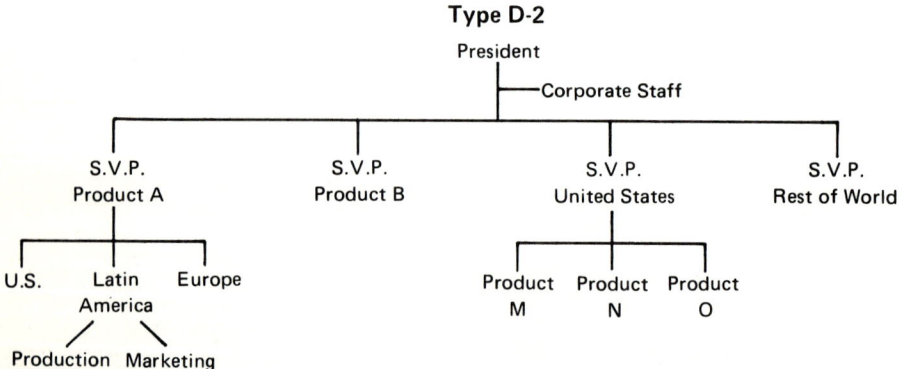

Type D-2 Combination of product and geographic organization

1. Product organization for staple products.
2. Geographic organization for products that require adaptation to different areas.

THE FINANCE FUNCTION IN INTERNATIONAL OPERATIONS 385

      3. Whenever individual foreign operations are large, their accounting and finance functions must be of sufficient size to satisfy local requirements. All of the personnel involved have
         a. Line responsibility to the local management.
         b. Responsibility, as a staff, to their counterparts at the location that controls international operations.
   D. The evolution of a firm into an international company involves the combination and interaction of the characteristics of the firm and the characteristics of the environment in the host country. Figure 16-2 shows how a firm progressed from export and import sales activities to become an international company financed by sales of equity in countries throughout the world.
      1. A small firm with limited international experience selling to a country in which uncertainty affects the conduct of foreign operations will be limited to export and import activity.
      2. A large firm with well-established products in the United States, long experience in international operations, and a broad range of managerial capabilities will ultimately develop into a firm with wholly owned foreign subsidiaries. In addition, the parent's equity will be widely owned by foreign nationals, particularly in countries in which it conducts business operations.

III. Financial policies and practices must be carried out consistently on a worldwide basis.
   A. Recommended financial operating practices.
      1. Practice a neutral net monetary position if possible. A net monetary liability position in countries of weak currencies and a net monetary asset position in countries of strong currencies represent defensive postures, but also require forecasting ability.
      2. In inflationary countries, charge interest on accounts receivable granted, whenever competition permits. Also avoid the payment of interest on accounts payable, whenever possible.
      3. Invest idle funds that cannot be removed from inflationary countries in real assets such as raw materials or parts inventory.
      4. Equity investments should be held to a minimum in countries with a weak foreign exchange position because interest payments are more likely to be permitted to foreign owners than dividend payments.
      5. Transfer pricing may be used whenever possible to move funds out of countries with foreign exchange controls.
      6. Exchange ratios may have to be determined weekly, semimonthly, monthly, quarterly, semiannually, or annually, depending upon the rate of devaluation in order to obtain meaningful results from financial data representing the foreign operations during an accounting period.

Figure 16-2 Scope of International Operations as a Result of both the Firm's Strengths and the Environmental Opportunities and Risks

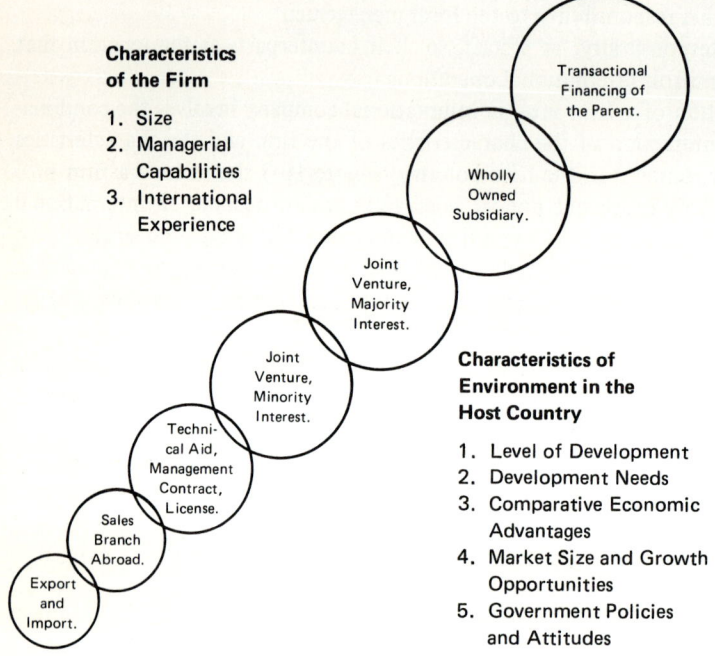

7. Forward market contracts, as well as the use of foreign currency swaps whenever available at reasonable costs in relation to the potential foreign-exchange-rate risks, should be employed to limit the cost of exposed positions.
8. Whenever possible, the local currency for foreign working capital requirements should be obtained on a loan basis in the country of operations to serve as a hedge against possible future devaluations.

B. Evaluation of international operations.
1. Most important is the development of a planning and control system, encompassing international operations and providing for an effective information flow and communication system among all parts of the international firm.
2. For financial accounting purposes, the temporal approach to foreign currency translation, which is similar to the monetary-nonmonetary approach, must now be used by U.S. firms in line with a recent opinion of the Financial Accounting Standards Board (FASB No. 8, October 1975).
3. Inflation or holding gains should be isolated in the evaluation process.
4. Financial interrelationships for each foreign operation should be studied continuously to detect changes in trends that may strongly influence earnings in future periods.

5. Observations of the financial results should be performed on an exception principle basis to permit the checking of large amounts of data. Deviations from previous standards of performance should be reported to responsible management so that corrective actions may be taken.
6. The effects of unusual environmental factors in a particular country that may influence financial outcomes must be taken into account when making comparisons between operations in different countries.

C. Recommended general international financial policies.
1. Dividend payout ratios should be similar for all parts of an organization.
2. License and patent fees must be uniform on a worldwide basis.
3. Overhead and management charges to subsidiaries and branches must be consistent.

D. The management of foreign assets. All assets owned in foreign countries must be recorded in detail so that this information is available at all times.
1. Plant and equipment assets and other long-term assets. These should be
   a. Carefully evaluated at the time of acquisition and at regular intervals during their economic life.
   b. Recorded both in the foreign and home countries. The government of the host country will always insist that records be kept on a local currency basis in the country of operations. Detailed records must also be kept in the home country on a home country basis to be able to defend depreciation schedules.
   c. Replaced on a timely basis when technologically obsolete.
2. Acquisition and disposal values.
   a. The costs of real assets must be converted into the home currency at the time of acquisition.
   b. Proceeds from the sale of real assets must be converted into the home currency using the exchange rate existing at the time of sale in order to determine whether or not a profit or a loss has resulted.
3. Inventory assets. These must also be recorded on a local currency as well as home currency basis. In many strongly inflationary countries, when inventory items are sold or used in local production, the local currency price is obtained by taking the home currency value determined at acquisition and converting it back into the local currency at the current spot rate. This updates the current values of inventories.

IV. International tax planning.
A. Taxes on a worldwide basis have major effects on the profitability of international business ventures. This requires a continuing study of the tax laws, rules, and practices in countries of present operations as well as in countries of intended future operations.
B. Study the local tax laws in regard to:
1. Income taxes on domestic and foreign earned income.
2. Property taxes. Can these be deducted from income before income taxes?

3. Capital taxes that would seriously erode investment values during the investment period.
4. Value added taxes. How will these affect the profitability of operations?
5. Magnitude of social security taxes.
6. Requirements for annual bonuses and severance payments at the end of employment.

V. Management of international cash flows and temporary investments.
   A. Available funds should always migrate towards points of highest profitability and safety.
      1. The opportunity cost of funds must be considered in making decisions involving the transfer of funds.
      2. Temporarily idle funds should be moved into strong currencies and away from currencies subject to possible devaluations.
      3. The international transfer of funds must take place in accordance with overall company needs.
      4. Temporarily idle cash should be moved to one or a few cash concentration centers that satisfy the following requirements. The country must have
         a. A stable government.
         b. No laws preventing the free inflow or outflow of funds.
         c. Strong, readily convertible currency.
         d. No taxes on capital.
         e. Taxation on income only at the source.
         f. Effective foreign exchange market with forward contracts available.
         g. An active money market for temporary investment of idle funds.
   B. Fund transfers should take place in the shortest possible time to decrease transfer risk.
      1. Whenever possible, the transfer of funds should take place in the strongest possible currency.
      2. Whenever possible, the movement of funds should be speeded up by using the services of international banks and their foreign affiliates to reduce the transfer time and thereby the amount of funds tied up in float.

VI. Financing international sales.
   A. Sales on an international basis can be financed from a number of alternative sources.
      1. Funds loaned to the seller by:
         a. A commercial bank.
            (1) On a general credit basis.
            (2) With risks covered by Eximbank or FCIA insurance policies or guarantees.

b. Accounts receivable financing.
      (1) With recourse.
      (2) Without recourse (factoring).
   2. Funds advanced to the customer in the case of large projects by:
      a. Eximbank.
      b. Overseas Private Investment Corporation, in the case of qualified projects (see Chapter 9).
   3. Making effective use of time drafts that become bankers' acceptances upon acceptance by the customer's bank.
   4. Borrowing on a local currency basis in the country of the customer with the receivable pledged to the local bank.
   5. Borrowing on a link financing basis from a lender in a foreign country where funds are more plentiful. This requires the cooperation of a broker and a commercial bank.
   6. Direct barter or the use of a switch broker.
B. The cost of financing, in many instances, can be reduced by encouraging or requiring the customer to furnish letters of credit on the following bases:
   1. Confirmed and irrevocable.
   2. Irrevocable.
   3. Revocable.
C. Variables in the international sales transaction include the following:
   1. The terms and conditions of sale interact with the sales price.
   2. The denomination of billing, the extent of credit exposure involved in the sale, the use of letters of credit, and other risk protection methods can be favorable to the buyer or seller. Any advantage gained or granted may be offset by adjustment of the other terms and conditions of sale and/or in the sales price.
   3. Trade-offs between these variables should be taken into account in the negotiations.

VII. Financing foreign operations.
   A. Private financing institutions.
      1. Financial institutions are similar in the developed countries.
      2. The United States now has money and capital markets of the greatest breadth.
      3. Financial institutions abroad combine commercial banking functions and investment functions to a greater degree than in the United States.
      4. U.S. commercial banks and investment banking firms have developed active and effective organizations for financing international firms.
      5. International financing subsidiaries are utilized to avoid the U.S. withholding taxes on interest paid by U.S. firms to foreign creditors.
      6. The Eurodollar system has developed into a substantial international market in which both short-term and long-term financing is obtained.

7. A framework has been developed for analyzing the advantages and disadvantages of a number of alternatives for financing a foreign subsidiary. The alternatives include:
   a. Funds from parent.
   b. Financing in the Euromarket.
   c. A local currency loan.
   d. Selling a draft on a discounted basis.
   e. A foreign currency swap.
B. International and governmental financing agencies.
   1. International development programs include provisions for financing assistance on a wide range of projects involving sales of goods, equipment, and services by international firms.
   2. When new foreign investments are made, particularly on a joint-venture basis with foreign nationals, the World Bank, the International Finance Corporation, the various regional development banks, and the Export-Import Bank of the United States should be considered as possible sources of investment funds.
   3. When capital goods are obtained from third countries, financing should be sought from the foreign equivalent of the Eximbank.
   4. When equity participation is desired, the International Finance Corporation is a potential source for development projects.
   5. The development banks of individual countries are also sources of financing sales to local projects.
C. Insurance sources.
   1. A number of alternative sources for protecting sales against commercial and political risks are available to exporters, including the FCIA and the Eximbank.
   2. Sales to foreign subsidiaries of capital goods and other goods should be protected against commercial and political risk since the cost of this protection is relatively low.
   3. Whenever possible, investments in connection with foreign operations should be protected by OPIC insurance against the risks of
      a. Convertibility.
      b. Expropriation.
      c. War.
   4. Funds advanced to a subsidiary on a loan basis should be protected by an OPIC guarantee.

VIII. Planning and evaluation of foreign ventures.
A. A foreign-business study group for the continuing evaluation of foreign environmental factors affecting the firm's present and future business ventures is essential. Among the many environmental factors to be studied are
   1. Demographic factors.
      a. Demands that only nationals of the host country be employed.
      b. The influence of the social stratification of the population.

THE FINANCE FUNCTION IN INTERNATIONAL OPERATIONS

  c. The potential vertical and horizontal mobility of the work force.
  d. The effect that the country's educational system has on the labor force.
  e. The influence of social customs, habits, and attitudes on the effectiveness of national labor.
2. The legal system of countries and their effect on business operations and decisions.
3. Governmental factors.
  a. The attitude towards private enterprise.
  b. The stability of governments.
  c. Laws and regulations that affect foreign investors in regard to
    (1) Safety of investments.
    (2) Ability to transfer funds into and out of a country for
      (a) Investment funds.
      (b) Interest payments.
      (c) Dividend payments.
    (3) Import and export restrictions.
4. Tax structures and the administration of tax laws.
5. Social legislation as it affects the cost of doing business.
  a. Social security taxes.
  b. Annual bonus rules.
  c. Annual vacation requirements.
  d. Severance pay laws.
6. Business customs.
  a. Informal agreements in industries.
  b. Methods of conducting business.
  c. Involvement of government corporations in particular industries.
7. Monetary and fiscal policies of governments.
  a. Foreign exchange value of the national currency and its trend.
  b. Ease of conversion of national currency into others.
  c. The restrictions on the inflow and outflow of funds.
  d. The growth rate of the local economy.
8. The financial markets of countries.
  a. Are funds readily obtainable on a short- as well as long-term basis?
  b. What are the interest rates on funds?
  c. Is trade credit used and available?
9. Government aid to business.
  a. Is protection available for import-replacing industries?
  b. Does the national government aid the expansion of exports by providing
    (1) Export financing?
    (2) Commercial and political risk insurance?
    (3) Investment insurance and/or guarantees?
    (4) Tax incentives to exporters?

- **B.** The planning of new foreign ventures.
    1. Foreign business expansion is undertaken for
        a. Expansion of the production of existing products.
        b. New products.
    2. This requires study of the countries of the world in regard to their
        a. Stage of economic development.
        b. Availability of required raw materials.
        c. Available labor.
        d. Internal demand for the planned product.
        e. Government's attitude toward the planned investment.
    3. Financial studies are needed to determine the
        a. Availability of the required investment funds.
        b. Permitted potential use of these funds.
        c. Effect of the new venture on the existing structure of the firm's present business.
    4. Profitability and risk.
        a. The basic principles of capital budgeting for international investments are the same as for domestic investments.
        b. Operating expenses and other costs are likely to be higher in a developing country than in a developed part of the world.
        c. Due to essentially greater risks associated with foreign investments, a more careful analysis of all of these risks is required.
        d. Even though the total risk of an international project may be greater than that of a domestic one, the addition of the international activities and operations may, through diversification effects, reduce the systematic risk of the firm. Since the systematic risk of the firm as a whole is the sum of the systematic risks of its parts, the effect of the foreign operation on the systematic risk of the firm as a whole is the best measure of the risk of the foreign operation.
        e. The cost of capital applicable to foreign investments is determined by the risk of the individual investment rather than by the overall risk of the firm, and by the cost of financing the foreign project.

IX. Central themes of this book.
- **A.** Communication and transportation have reduced the size of the world so that it is becoming one market in which nations and firms interact. Thus most firms are increasingly affected by the opportunities and costs in international financial markets.
- **B.** The international financial markets are characterized by continuous turbulence and change, requiring adjustments by individual firms.
- **C.** Foreign exchange rates fluctuate as price levels vary and interest-rate changes are experienced in different countries. The forward exchange rates also vary in response to the above influences. A firm's sales, purchases, investment, and financing positions will be affected by these changes. The nature and

magnitude of a firm's exposure will change in response to the changing patterns of price movements, exchange rates and interest structure relationships.

D. If a firm is in an exposed position—for example a net monetary position, positive or negative—costs must be incurred by the firm to limit the degree of its exposure.

E. In limiting its risk exposures, a firm may be tempted to seek gains from prospective changes in exchange-rate relationships and financing alternatives. Considerable evidence supports the generalization that the international financial markets are efficient. Hence attempts to "play the international financial markets" will require the development of considerable sophisticated knowledge and involve substantial risks. The yield may not be more than a normal rate of return in relation to the expertise applied.

F. Since the international financial markets are efficient, a firm must learn how to avoid losses from the rapid and substantial adjustments continuously taking place.

G. Alternative methods are available for limiting the risks of movements in the international financial markets. The interaction between the structure of relationships in the international financial markets and the circumstances of the individual firm may point to one alternative rather than another for a particular situation. However, given the consistent relationships between price-level movements, interest-rate levels, and exchange-rate movements which are developing in the markets, it is probable that the least-cost alternative will generally mean a greater risk. Thus a trade-off between cost and risk is usually involved in the choice between alternatives.

H. Similar trade-offs are also involved in alternative costs of financing. The differences in anticipated costs of alternative sources of financing reflect assumptions of future levels of exchange rates and interest rates.

I. In international sales, trade-offs will be made between the extent of credit-risk exposure, the degree of protection afforded by the type of letters of credit used, the currency in which the transaction is denominated, and the price at which the transaction is made. Favorable terms and conditions of sale can be offset by price differences and vice versa.

J. The services offered by agencies insuring the risks of international sales and investments are generally advantageous and should be used. The cost of insurance—substituting a small outlay to avoid the risk of a large loss—is lowered by the competition between governments in their efforts to encourage international sales and investment by their national firms. In effect, the insurance is government-subsidized.

K. Advantageous financing arrangements can also be obtained from governments that wish to encourage the growth of their international firms and to strengthen foreign-exchange-reserve positions. International financing agencies are also an important source of funds for sales and for participation in projects that meet their economic development objectives in individual countries.

L. While risks are inherent in international operations, they can be controlled to some degree. Commercial and political risks can largely be eliminated by insurance. Furthermore, the increased understanding of the variables that cause political instability makes it possible to predict conditions likely to produce unfavorable political developments. But since prediction is not perfect, a firm can either avoid the risky countries, utilize various forms of insurance, or seek protection in the form of a higher required rate of return.

M. Since there is some correlation between unstable governments, inflation, and resulting devaluations, another protective policy is to use local financing in unstable countries whenever possible. Financing by debt locally protects against losses from the declines in the foreign exchange value of the local currency. Financing locally, by either debt or equity, may also develop a substantial local ownership stake in the company—thus reducing the risks of nationalization or other adverse actions by the host government.

N. In planning its international operations strategy, a firm should recognize an even broader extension of the general principle of seeking an identity of interests with foreign countries. It should emphasize those product-market areas and activities (whether in the form of imports, exports, purchase of raw materials, or production and investment activities) that contribute to the economic health of the countries affected by its operations. A firm is less likely to be the object of adverse political treatment and unfavorable government rules and regulations if its continued operations are viewed as vital to the country's economic well-being and future development.

Appendix

Compound Interest Tables

TABLE A–1

Compound sum of \$1; $S_n = P(1 + r)^n$

Year	1%	2%	3%	4%	5%	6%	7%	8%
1	1.010	1.020	1.030	1.040	1.050	1.060	1.070	1.080
2	1.020	1.040	1.081	1.082	1.102	1.124	1.145	1.166
3	1.030	1.061	1.093	1.125	1.158	1.191	1.225	1.260
4	1.041	1.082	1.126	1.170	1.216	1.262	1.311	1.360
5	1.051	1.104	1.159	1.217	1.276	1.338	1.403	1.469
6	1.062	1.126	1.194	1.265	1.340	1.419	1.501	1.587
7	1.072	1.149	1.230	1.316	1.407	1.504	1.606	1.714
8	1.083	1.172	1.267	1.369	1.477	1.594	1.718	1.851
9	1.094	1.195	1.305	1.423	1.551	1.689	1.838	1.999
10	1.105	1.219	1.344	1.480	1.629	1.791	1.967	2.159
11	1.116	1.243	1.384	1.539	1.710	1.898	2.105	2.332
12	1.127	1.268	1.426	1.601	1.796	2.012	2.252	2.518
13	1.138	1.294	1.469	1.665	1.886	2.133	2.410	2.720
14	1.149	1.319	1.513	1.732	1.980	2.261	2.579	2.937
15	1.161	1.346	1.558	1.801	2.079	2.397	2.759	3.172
16	1.173	1.373	1.605	1.873	2.183	2.540	2.952	3.426
17	1.184	1.400	1.653	1.948	2.292	2.693	3.159	3.700
18	1.196	1.428	1.702	2.026	2.407	2.854	3.380	3.996
19	1.208	1.457	1.754	2.107	2.527	3.026	3.617	4.316
20	1.220	1.486	1.806	2.191	2.653	3.207	3.870	4.661

Year	9%	10%	11%	12%	13%	14%	15%	16%
1	1.090	1.100	1.110	1.120	1.130	1.140	1.150	1.160
2	1.188	1.210	1.232	1.254	1.277	1.300	1.322	1.346
3	1.295	1.331	1.368	1.405	1.443	1.482	1.521	1.561
4	1.412	1.464	1.518	1.574	1.631	1.689	1.749	1.811
5	1.539	1.611	1.685	1.762	1.842	1.925	2.011	2.100
6	1.677	1.772	1.870	1.974	2.082	2.195	2.313	2.436
7	1.828	1.949	2.076	2.211	2.353	2.502	2.660	2.826
8	1.993	2.144	2.305	2.476	2.658	2.853	3.059	3.278
9	2.172	2.358	2.558	2.773	3.004	3.252	3.518	3.803
10	2.367	2.594	2.839	3.106	3.395	3.707	4.046	4.411
11	2.580	2.853	3.152	3.479	3.836	4.226	4.652	5.117
12	2.813	3.138	3.499	3.896	4.335	4.818	5.350	5.936
13	3.066	3.452	3.883	4.363	4.898	5.492	6.153	6.886
14	3.342	3.797	4.310	4.887	5.535	6.261	7.076	7.988
15	3.642	4.177	4.785	5.474	6.254	7.138	8.137	9.266
16	3.970	4.595	5.311	6.130	7.067	8.137	9.358	10.748
17	4.328	5.054	5.895	6.866	7.986	9.276	10.761	12.468
18	4.717	5.560	6.544	7.690	9.024	10.575	12.375	14.463
19	5.142	6.116	7.263	8.613	10.197	12.056	14.232	16.777
20	5.604	6.728	8.062	9.646	11.523	13.743	16.367	19.461

TABLE A-2
Present value of $1; $P = S_n(1 + r)^{-n}$

Periods until Payment	1%	2%	2½%	3%	4%	5%	6%	8%	10%	12%	14%	15%	16%	18%	20%	22%	24%	25%	26%	30%	40%	50%
1	0.990	0.980	0.976	0.971	0.962	0.952	0.943	0.926	0.909	0.893	0.877	0.870	0.862	0.847	0.833	0.820	0.806	0.800	0.794	0.769	0.714	0.667
2	0.980	0.961	0.952	0.943	0.925	0.907	0.890	0.857	0.826	0.797	0.769	0.756	0.743	0.718	0.694	0.672	0.650	0.640	0.630	0.592	0.510	0.444
3	0.971	0.942	0.929	0.915	0.889	0.864	0.840	0.794	0.751	0.712	0.675	0.658	0.641	0.609	0.579	0.551	0.524	0.512	0.500	0.455	0.364	0.296
4	0.961	0.924	0.906	0.888	0.855	0.823	0.792	0.735	0.683	0.636	0.592	0.572	0.552	0.516	0.482	0.451	0.423	0.410	0.397	0.350	0.260	0.198
5	0.951	0.906	0.884	0.863	0.822	0.784	0.747	0.681	0.621	0.567	0.519	0.497	0.476	0.437	0.402	0.370	0.341	0.328	0.315	0.269	0.186	0.132
6	0.942	0.888	0.862	0.837	0.790	0.746	0.705	0.630	0.564	0.507	0.456	0.432	0.410	0.370	0.335	0.303	0.275	0.262	0.250	0.207	0.133	0.088
7	0.933	0.871	0.841	0.813	0.760	0.711	0.665	0.583	0.513	0.452	0.400	0.376	0.354	0.314	0.279	0.249	0.222	0.210	0.198	0.159	0.095	0.059
8	0.923	0.853	0.821	0.789	0.731	0.677	0.627	0.540	0.467	0.404	0.351	0.327	0.305	0.266	0.233	0.204	0.179	0.168	0.157	0.123	0.068	0.039
9	0.914	0.837	0.801	0.766	0.703	0.645	0.592	0.500	0.424	0.361	0.308	0.284	0.263	0.225	0.194	0.167	0.144	0.134	0.125	0.094	0.048	0.026
10	0.905	0.820	0.781	0.744	0.676	0.614	0.558	0.463	0.386	0.322	0.270	0.247	0.227	0.191	0.162	0.137	0.116	0.107	0.099	0.073	0.035	0.017
11	0.896	0.804	0.762	0.722	0.650	0.585	0.527	0.429	0.350	0.287	0.237	0.215	0.195	0.162	0.135	0.112	0.094	0.086	0.079	0.056	0.025	0.012
12	0.887	0.788	0.744	0.701	0.625	0.557	0.497	0.397	0.319	0.257	0.208	0.187	0.168	0.137	0.112	0.092	0.076	0.069	0.062	0.043	0.018	0.008
13	0.879	0.773	0.725	0.681	0.601	0.530	0.469	0.368	0.290	0.229	0.182	0.163	0.145	0.116	0.093	0.075	0.061	0.055	0.050	0.033	0.013	0.005
14	0.870	0.758	0.708	0.661	0.577	0.505	0.442	0.340	0.263	0.205	0.160	0.141	0.125	0.099	0.078	0.062	0.049	0.044	0.039	0.025	0.009	0.003
15	0.861	0.743	0.690	0.642	0.555	0.481	0.417	0.315	0.239	0.183	0.140	0.123	0.108	0.084	0.065	0.051	0.040	0.035	0.031	0.020	0.006	0.002
16	0.853	0.728	0.674	0.623	0.534	0.458	0.394	0.292	0.218	0.163	0.123	0.107	0.093	0.071	0.054	0.042	0.032	0.028	0.025	0.015	0.005	0.002
17	0.844	0.714	0.657	0.605	0.513	0.436	0.371	0.270	0.198	0.146	0.108	0.093	0.080	0.060	0.045	0.034	0.026	0.023	0.020	0.012	0.003	0.001
18	0.836	0.700	0.641	0.587	0.494	0.416	0.350	0.250	0.180	0.130	0.095	0.081	0.069	0.051	0.038	0.028	0.021	0.018	0.016	0.009	0.002	0.001
19	0.828	0.686	0.626	0.570	0.475	0.396	0.331	0.232	0.164	0.116	0.083	0.070	0.060	0.043	0.031	0.023	0.017	0.014	0.012	0.007	0.002	
20	0.820	0.673	0.610	0.554	0.456	0.377	0.312	0.215	0.149	0.104	0.073	0.061	0.051	0.037	0.026	0.019	0.014	0.012	0.010	0.005	0.001	
21	0.811	0.660	0.595	0.538	0.439	0.359	0.294	0.199	0.135	0.093	0.064	0.053	0.044	0.031	0.022	0.015	0.011	0.009	0.008	0.004	0.001	
22	0.803	0.647	0.581	0.522	0.422	0.342	0.278	0.184	0.123	0.083	0.056	0.046	0.038	0.026	0.018	0.013	0.009	0.007	0.006	0.003	0.001	
23	0.795	0.634	0.567	0.507	0.406	0.326	0.262	0.170	0.112	0.074	0.049	0.040	0.033	0.022	0.015	0.010	0.007	0.006	0.005	0.002		
24	0.788	0.622	0.553	0.492	0.390	0.310	0.247	0.158	0.102	0.066	0.043	0.035	0.028	0.019	0.013	0.008	0.006	0.005	0.004	0.002		
25	0.780	0.610	0.539	0.478	0.375	0.295	0.233	0.146	0.092	0.059	0.038ª	0.030	0.024	0.016	0.010	0.007	0.005	0.004	0.003	0.001		
26	0.772	0.598	0.526	0.464	0.361	0.281	0.220	0.135	0.084	0.053	0.033	0.026	0.021	0.014	0.009	0.006	0.004	0.003	0.002			
27	0.764	0.586	0.513	0.450	0.347	0.268	0.207	0.125	0.076	0.047	0.029	0.023	0.018	0.011	0.007	0.005	0.003	0.002	0.002			
28	0.757	0.574	0.501	0.437	0.333	0.255	0.196	0.116	0.069	0.042	0.026	0.020	0.016	0.010	0.006	0.004	0.002	0.002	0.001			
29	0.749	0.563	0.489	0.424	0.321	0.243	0.185	0.107	0.063	0.037	0.022	0.017	0.014	0.008	0.005	0.003	0.002	0.002	0.001			
30	0.742	0.552	0.477	0.412	0.308	0.231	0.174	0.099	0.057	0.033	0.020	0.015	0.012	0.007	0.004	0.003	0.002	0.001	0.001			
40	0.672	0.453	0.372	0.307	0.208	0.142	0.097	0.046	0.022	0.011	0.005	0.004	0.003	0.001	0.001							
50	0.608	0.372	0.291	0.228	0.141	0.087	0.054	0.021	0.009	0.003	0.001	0.001	0.001									

TABLE A-3

Present value of $1 received annually; $A_{\overline{n}|r} = \$1 \left[\dfrac{1-(1+r)^{-n}}{r} \right] = \$1 P_{n,r}$

Periods to Be Paid	1%	2%	2½%	3%	4%	5%	6%	8%	10%	12%	14%	15%	16%	18%	20%	22%	24%	25%	26%	30%	40%	50%
1	0.990	0.980	0.976	0.971	0.962	0.952	0.943	0.926	0.909	0.893	0.877	0.870	0.862	0.847	0.833	0.820	0.806	0.800	0.794	0.769	0.714	0.667
2	1.970	1.942	1.927	1.914	1.886	1.859	1.833	1.783	1.736	1.690	1.647	1.626	1.605	1.566	1.528	1.492	1.457	1.440	1.424	1.361	1.224	1.111
3	2.941	2.884	2.856	2.829	2.775	2.723	2.673	2.577	2.487	2.402	2.322	2.283	2.246	2.174	2.106	2.042	1.981	1.952	1.923	1.816	1.589	1.407
4	3.902	3.808	3.762	3.717	3.630	3.546	3.465	3.312	3.170	3.037	2.914	2.855	2.798	2.690	2.589	2.494	2.404	2.362	2.320	2.166	1.849	1.605
5	4.853	4.713	4.646	4.580	4.452	4.330	4.212	3.993	3.791	3.605	3.433	3.352	3.274	3.127	2.991	2.864	2.745	2.689	2.635	2.436	2.035	1.737
6	5.795	5.601	5.508	5.417	5.242	5.076	4.917	4.623	4.355	4.111	3.889	3.784	3.685	3.498	3.326	3.167	3.020	2.951	2.885	2.643	2.168	1.824
7	6.728	6.472	6.349	6.230	6.002	5.786	5.582	5.206	4.868	4.564	4.288	4.160	4.039	3.812	3.605	3.416	3.242	3.161	3.083	2.802	2.263	1.883
8	7.652	7.325	7.170	7.020	6.733	6.463	6.210	5.747	5.335	4.968	4.639	4.487	4.344	4.078	3.837	3.619	3.421	3.329	3.241	2.925	2.331	1.922
9	8.566	8.162	7.971	7.786	7.435	7.108	6.802	6.247	5.759	5.328	4.946	4.772	4.607	4.303	4.031	3.786	3.566	3.463	3.366	3.019	2.379	1.948
10	9.471	8.983	8.752	8.530	8.111	7.722	7.360	6.710	6.145	5.650	5.216	5.019	4.833	4.494	4.192	3.923	3.682	3.571	3.465	3.092	2.414	1.965
11	10.368	9.787	9.514	9.253	8.760	8.306	7.887	7.139	6.495	5.938	5.453	5.234	5.029	4.656	4.327	4.035	3.776	3.656	3.544	3.147	2.438	1.977
12	11.255	10.575	10.258	9.954	9.385	8.863	8.384	7.536	6.814	6.194	5.660	5.421	5.197	4.793	4.439	4.127	3.851	3.725	3.606	3.190	2.456	1.985
13	12.134	11.348	10.983	10.635	9.986	9.394	8.853	7.904	7.103	6.424	5.842	5.583	5.342	4.910	4.533	4.203	3.912	3.780	3.656	3.223	2.468	1.990
14	13.004	12.106	11.691	11.296	10.563	9.899	9.295	8.244	7.367	6.628	6.002	5.724	5.468	5.008	4.611	4.265	3.962	3.824	3.695	3.249	2.478	1.993
15	13.865	12.849	12.381	11.938	11.118	10.380	9.712	8.559	7.606	6.811	6.142	5.847	5.576	5.092	4.676	4.315	4.001	3.859	3.726	3.268	2.484	1.995
16	14.718	13.578	13.055	12.561	11.652	10.838	10.106	8.851	7.824	6.974	6.265	5.954	5.668	5.162	4.730	4.357	4.033	3.887	3.751	3.283	2.488	1.997
17	15.562	14.292	13.712	13.166	12.166	11.274	10.477	9.122	8.022	7.120	6.373	6.047	5.749	5.222	4.775	4.391	4.059	3.910	3.771	3.295	2.492	1.998
18	16.398	14.992	14.353	13.754	12.659	11.690	10.828	9.372	8.201	7.250	6.467	6.128	5.818	5.273	4.812	4.419	4.080	3.928	3.786	3.304	2.494	1.999
19	17.226	15.678	14.979	14.324	13.134	12.085	11.158	9.604	8.365	7.366	6.550	6.198	5.878	5.316	4.844	4.442	4.097	3.942	3.799	3.311	2.496	1.999
20	18.046	16.351	15.589	14.877	13.590	12.462	11.470	9.818	8.514	7.469	6.623	6.259	5.929	5.353	4.870	4.460	4.110	3.954	3.808	3.316	2.497	1.999
21	18.857	17.011	16.185	15.415	14.029	12.821	11.764	10.017	8.649	7.562	6.687	6.312	5.973	5.384	4.891	4.476	4.121	3.963	3.816	3.320	2.498	2.000
22	19.660	17.658	16.765	15.937	14.451	13.163	12.042	10.201	8.772	7.645	6.743	6.359	6.011	5.410	4.909	4.488	4.130	3.970	3.822	3.323	2.498	2.000
23	20.456	18.292	17.332	16.444	14.857	13.489	12.303	10.371	8.883	7.718	6.792	6.399	6.044	5.432	4.924	4.499	4.137	3.976	3.827	3.325	2.499	2.000
24	21.243	18.914	17.885	16.936	15.247	13.799	12.550	10.529	8.985	7.784	6.835	6.434	6.073	5.451	4.937	4.507	4.143	3.981	3.831	3.327	2.499	2.000
25	22.023	19.523	18.424	17.413	15.622	14.094	12.783	10.675	9.077	7.843	6.873	6.464	6.097	5.467	4.948	4.514	4.147	3.985	3.834	3.329	2.499	2.000
26	22.795	20.121	18.951	17.877	15.983	14.375	13.003	10.810	9.161	7.896	6.906	6.491	6.118	5.480	4.956	4.520	4.151	3.988	3.837	3.330	2.500	2.000
27	23.560	20.707	19.464	18.327	16.330	14.643	13.211	10.935	9.237	7.943	6.935	6.514	6.136	5.492	4.964	4.524	4.154	3.990	3.839	3.331	2.500	2.000
28	24.316	21.281	19.965	18.764	16.663	14.898	13.406	11.051	9.307	7.984	6.961	6.534	6.152	5.502	4.970	4.528	4.157	3.992	3.840	3.331	2.500	2.000
29	25.066	21.844	20.454	19.188	16.984	15.141	13.591	11.158	9.370	8.022	6.983	6.551	6.166	5.510	4.975	4.531	4.159	3.994	3.841	3.332	2.500	2.000
30	25.808	22.396	20.930	19.600	17.292	15.372	13.765	11.258	9.427	8.055	7.003	6.566	6.177	5.517	4.979	4.534	4.160	3.995	3.842	3.332	2.500	2.000
40	32.835	27.355	25.103	23.115	19.793	17.159	15.046	11.925	9.779	8.244	7.105	6.642	6.234	5.548	4.997	4.544	4.166	3.999	3.846	3.333	2.500	2.000
50	39.196	31.424	28.362	25.730	21.482	18.256	15.762	12.233	9.915	8.304	7.133	6.660	6.246	5.554	4.999	4.545	4.167	4.000	3.846	3.333	2.500	2.000

Source for Tables A-2 and A-3: Jerome Bracken and Charles J. Christenson, *Tables for Use in Analyzing Business Decisions* (Homewood, Ill.: Richard D. Irwin, Inc., 1965), except for the data on 2½%, the source for which is *Mathematical Tables from Handbook of Chemistry and Physics*, 6th ed. (Cleveland: Chemical Rubber Publishing Co., 1938).

TABLE A-4
Sum of an annuity of $1 for n years

$$S_{\overline{n}|r} = \$1 \left[\frac{(1+r)^n - 1}{r} \right] = \$1 C_{n,r}$$

Year	1%	2%	3%	4%	5%	6%	7%	8%
1	1.000	1.000	1.000	1.000	1.000	1.000	1.000	1.000
2	2.010	2.020	2.030	2.040	2.050	2.080	2.070	2.080
3	3.030	3.060	3.091	3.122	3.152	3.184	3.215	3.246
4	4.060	4.122	4.184	4.246	4.310	4.375	4.440	4.506
5	5.101	5.204	5.309	5.416	5.526	5.637	5.751	5.867
6	6.152	6.308	6.468	6.633	6.802	6.975	7.153	7.336
7	7.214	7.434	7.662	7.898	8.142	8.394	8.654	8.923
8	8.286	8.583	8.892	9.214	9.549	9.897	10.260	10.637
9	9.369	9.755	10.159	10.583	11.027	11.491	11.978	12.488
10	10.462	10.950	11.464	12.006	12.578	13.181	13.816	14.487
11	11.567	12.169	12.808	13.846	14.207	14.972	15.784	16.645
12	12.683	13.412	14.192	15.026	15.917	16.870	17.888	18.977
13	13.809	14.680	15.818	16.627	17.713	18.882	20.141	21.495
14	14.947	15.974	17.086	18.292	19.599	21.051	22.550	24.215
15	16.097	17.293	18.599	20.024	21.579	23.276	25.129	27.152

Year	9%	10%	11%	12%	13%	14%	15%	16%
1	1.000	1.000	1.000	1.000	1.000	1.000	1.000	1.000
2	2.090	2.100	2.110	2.120	2.130	2.140	2.150	2.160
3	3.278	3.310	3.342	3.374	3.407	3.440	3.473	3.506
4	4.573	4.641	4.710	4.779	4.850	4.921	4.993	5.066
5	5.985	6.105	6.228	6.353	6.480	6.610	6.742	6.877
6	7.523	7.716	7.913	8.115	8.323	8.536	8.754	8.977
7	9.200	9.487	9.783	10.089	10.405	10.730	11.067	11.414
8	11.028	11.436	11.859	12.300	12.757	13.233	13.727	14.240
9	13.021	13.579	14.164	14.776	15.416	16.085	16.786	17.518
10	15.193	15.937	16.772	17.549	18.420	19.337	20.304	21.321
11	17.560	18.531	19.561	20.655	21.814	23.044	24.349	25.733
12	20.141	21.384	22.713	24.133	25.650	27.271	29.002	30.850
13	22.953	24.523	26.212	28.029	29.985	32.089	34.352	36.786
14	26.019	27.975	30.095	32.393	34.883	37.581	40.505	43.672
15	29.361	31.772	34.405	37.286	40.417	43.842	47.580	51.659

Glossary of Symbols Used

a Annual interest coupon payment

A_t Dollar amount at the end of time period t

A_t^s Dollar amount using a swap at the end of time period t

B Market value of debt of a levered firm

$\beta_j = \dfrac{Cov(R_j, R_M)}{\sigma_M^2}$ The β for security j

$\bar{C}_e$ Expected loss due to exchange-rate changes

C_k Cost of alternative k

C_p Cost of a net monetary position due to exchange-rate changes

C_s Cost of a swap

$Cor(R_j, R_k) = Cor_{j,k}$ Correlation coefficient of returns j with k

$Cov(R_j, R_k) = Cov_{j,k}$ Covariance of returns R_j with R_k

CV_j Coefficient of variation = $\sigma(R_j)/E(R_j)$

d Discount on a local currency discounted draft

D_{df} Percentage change of the dollar value of one local currency unit

D_{fd} Percentage change of the local currency value per dollar

D_s Swap discount rate given in terms of local currency value per dollar

D_t Dividend per share paid at the end of time period t

E_f Forward contract exchange rate given in terms of the dollar value of one local currency unit

E_s Swap exchange rate given in terms of the dollar value of one local currency unit

E_t Dollar value of one local currency unit at the end of time period t

$EBIT$ Earnings before interest and taxes

EPS Earnings per share

$E(R_j)$ Expected return on portfolio j

$E(R_M)$ Expected return on the market

$E(R_p)$ Expected return on a portfolio p

$E(R_W)$ Expected return on the world market

F_0, F_1 Amount in local currency units at the beginning of a time period, and at the end of a time period

GLOSSARY

FV — Future value

FVF — Future value factor

g — Expected rate of growth or of capital gain

g_f — Expected gain on funds invested in a foreign country

k — Weighted cost of capital

k_b — Cost of debt

k_e — Cost of equity capital (levered firm)

k_{eu} — Cost of equity capital for the unlevered firm

k_p — Parent's after-tax opportunity cost of funds, or equivalently parent's after-tax weighted cost of capital

k_{ps} — Cost of preferred stock

k_u — Cost of capital for the unlevered firm, $k_u = k_{eu}$

$\lambda = \dfrac{[E(R_M)-R_F]}{\sigma_M^2}$ The market price of risk

M — Standard earnings multiplier

M_n — Value of a bond at maturity

MA — Monetary assets

ML — Monetary liabilities

n — Number of years

NFV — Net future value

NMP — Net monetary position

NPV	Net present value
O	Percent ownership in a firm
p	Probability value
P	Price of a share of common stock
P_b	Price of a bond
P_{dt}	Domestic price-level index at time period t
P_{ft}	Foreign country price-level index at time period t
$P_{n,r}$	Present value factor of an annuity for n periods at r per period
P_o, P_1	Price of a common share at the beginning and end of a period
P_p	Price of a share of preferred stock
P_t, P_{t-1}	Price level at beginning of time periods t and t-1
P_u	Price per unit quantity sold
PV	Present value
PVF	Present value factor
Q	Quantity sold
r	Real rate of interest
R	Interest rate charged to a subsidiary or a foreign customer by a U.S. firm
R_a, R_b, R_g	Returns on foreign investment projects a, b, or g
R_d	Returns on domestic investment project d
R_{dt}	Domestic interest rate during time period t

GLOSSARY

R_e Rate of interest on a Eurodollar loan

R_f Nominal interest rate paid on local currency loans borrowed in a foreign country

R_{ft} Foreign interest rate during time period t

R_g^n Profit rate on an investment without using a swap

R_g^s Profit rate on an investment using a swap

R_{jt} Return on security j in time period t

$\overline{R_k} = E(R_k)$ Expected return on security k

R_n Nominal rate of interest

R_p Returns on a portfolio

R_s Interest rate paid on a local currency loan obtained via a swap

R_{us} Interest rate paid by the parent on funds borrowed in the United States

R_F Risk-free rate of interest

R_{Ft} Risk-free rate in time period t

R_{Mt} Return on the market for time period t

σ_j Standard deviation of returns of security j

$\sigma_j^2 = Var(R_j)$ Variance of returns of security j

σ_M Standard deviation of returns on the market

$\sigma_M^2 = Var(R_M)$ Variance of returns on the market

σ_p Standard deviation of portfolio returns

s States of the world

S	Market value of equity
S_a, S_d	Market value of investment projects a or d
S_o	Swap exchange rate given in terms of the local currency value per dollar
t	Marginal tax rate or time index as indicated by context
t_f	Marginal income tax in a foreign country
t_p	Parent's effective marginal tax rate on foreign source income received
t_{us}	Marginal income tax rate in the United States
V	Value of a levered firm
V_a, V_d	Value of firms a and d
V_u	Value of an unlevered firm
$Var(R_j)$	Variance of the returns of security j
$Var(R_m)$	Variance of the returns on the market
VC_u	Variable cost per unit
X_a, X_d	Dollar return to investment projects a and d
x_b, x_d	Proportions of investment in a portfolio
X_f	Forward contract exchange rate given in terms of the local currency value per dollar
X_t	Local currency value per dollar at the end of time period t

Index

Accounting for international operations, 116–123
  accounting systems, 115–116
  principles, 116–120
Accounting treatment of foreign operations, 115–144
African Development Bank (AFDB), 311
Agency for International Development (AID), 177, 192, 206–209, 265, 312–313
Aid to international business, government, 391
Alliance for Progress loans, 312
Alternative financing sources:
  costs of, 304–308
  methods of raising funds, 303–308
Arbi-loans, 267, 285–286
Arbitrage:
  definition of, 91
  illustration, 93–95
Asian Development Bank (ADB), 310, 315

Balance of payments, 75–77, 81–90
  adjustment process, 53–55
  construction of, 85–86, 100–104
  major categories, 82–83
  major developments in U.S., 110
  monetary view of, 110–112
  new format, 90
  statements, 82
  summary measures, 86–90
  transactions affecting, 83
Balance sheet, pro forma, 367, 378–379
Bankers' acceptances, 285
Banks, foreign development, 309
Barter, 271
Beta coefficient, 325
Bill of exchange, 263, 265
Bill of lading, 263, 266
Bonds:
  European Monetary Unit, 300
  European Unit of Account, 300
  value of, 321–22
Borrowing in a foreign country, 275

Breakeven point, 308
Bretton Woods system:
  characteristics of, 70–71
  problems with, 71–73

Canadian dollar, strength of, 303
Capital asset pricing model, use of, 330
Capital budgeting:
  analysis of, 358, 368–369
  problems with, 40
Capital Market Theory, 324–326
Capital structure:
  design of, 326
  influence of international operations on, 338–339
Cash concentration, 388
Cash flows, 375–377
  analysis, 358, 360–366
  pro forma statement, 365–367
Cash management, international, 244–246, 290
Central themes, 392–394
Certificates of deposit (CDs), 291
Chicago Mercantile Exchange, 186
Commercial banks:
  European, 285
  foreign, 309
  U.S., 309
Commercial letter of credit, 264, 266
Commercial risks, 176–177, 182–184, 192
Commercial sales financing, examples of, 267–271
Common Market, 355
Common stock:
  convertible, 335
  international ownership of, 301
  return on, 323, 326
  variability of return on, 327
Comparative advantage, 65
Consistent cross rates, 92
Controlled Foreign Corporation, 155–160
Convertibility of the dollar, reasons for suspension of, 60–61, 65
Convertible debentures, 337

Cost of capital, 321–335
   with corporate income taxes, 328–334
   illustrative example, 339–344
   influence of inflation on, 335
   for an international firm, 339–344
   weighted average, 334
Cost of debt capital, 321–322
Cost of equity capital, 323–324
Cost of preferred stock capital, 322–323
Covariance, 325, 350, 372
Covered interest arbitrage, 91–92, 104–107, 213–214
Crédit Nationale (CN), 314
Credit swaps, 219, 247
Credit terms, 272
Currency swap, 218–227
   cost of, 219–220
   evaluation of, 223–227
   foreign, 304, 306
   use of, 267

Debt financing, 316, 357
Debtor position, 233
Demographic factors, 390
Devaluation, 57
   as adjustment device, 57
   effects of, 77–80
   measuring, 215–216
Development banks, 309, 312
   national, 315
   private industrial, 314
Direct foreign investment:
   exporting capital, 353–354
   stimuli, 354–358
Discount rate, 373
Domestic International Sales Corporation (DISC), 149–152
Draft, discounted basis, 306

Edge Act subsidiaries, 266, 288–289, 301
Environmental factors:
   analysis of, 6–11
   demographic, social, and legal, 4–5
   government, 5
   influence of, 178–182
   influence on risk exposure, 178
   local business customs, 6
Equilibrium market relationships, 95–99
   Fisher effect, 96
   Interest Rate Parity Theorem, 97–98
   Purchasing Power Parity Theorem, 98–99
Equity capital, cost of, 323
Equity issues, 316, 335–338

Eurobond market, 299–302
Eurobonds, 300
Eurodollar market, 290–299
   convertible bonds, 301
   flow process of, 293
   implications of, 293–294
   loans, 304, 306
   reasons for development of, 297–299
European Development Fund (EDF), 311
European Economic Community (EEC), 59–60, 66–67
European Investment Bank (EIB), 310–311
Exchange-rate risk, 176, 187
   and position of firm, 233–234
   protection, 211–241
      examples, 234–238
      global view, 239
Exchange rates, 90–91
   adjustment processes, 92–93
   advantages and disadvantages of floating system, 66
   consistent cross rates, 92
   and risk analysis, 187–90
Eximbank, 177, 191, 198–201, 265, 267, 273, 311–312, 388–389, 390
   commercial bank plans, 200
   exporter guarantee program, 199
   premiums, basis for, 200
Expected return, 348–350
Export-import transactions:
   basic documents, 263–264
   examples, 264–266
Export trade corporation, 152
Exports:
   efforts to increase, 146–147
   use of brokers, 14

FASB Statement No. 8, 127–144, 243, 246
   foreign currency transactions, 129
   foreign operations, 135–144
   forward contracts, 130
FCIA, 265, 388, 390
   combination policy, 194
   master policy, 194
   medium-term policy, 193
   policy analysis, 194–198
   policy premiums, 193
   short-term policy, 192
   small exporter policy, 194
FIFO, 245–246
Finance function, international, 381–394
Financial Accounting Standards Board (*see* FASB Statement No. 8)

Financial policies, worldwide, 381-382
Financial structure, 317, 335-344, 373
Financial swaps, 219
Financing:
  Eurodollar, 301-302
  export-import sales, 266-271
  industry characteristics, 283
  international business, 285-286
  international and governmental agencies, 390
  international sales, 388-389
  sources and forms, 317
  strategy, 317
  worldwide commercial sales, 261-280
Financing subsidiaries, 287
  domestic, 287
  overseas, 287-288
Fisher effect, 96, 212
Float, 245
Floating exchange rate, effects of, 66
Floating exchange rates, 56
Forecasting foreign exchange rates, 81-113
Foreign borrowing, 302-303
Foreign branch sales office, 14
Foreign Credit Insurance Association (see FCIA)
Foreign currency:
  "long position," 90
  "short position," 91
Foreign direct investment:
  assessment of foreign country, 356-357
  leading theories, 22-27
Foreign-exchange-rate risks, 43-44, 249-251
Foreign exchange rates, 54, 56
Foreign exchange reserve position, 145-146, 179
Foreign exchange systems, 55-58
Foreign financing alternatives, 390
Foreign investment:
  diversification, 347-52
  U.S. position, 354
Foreign investment decision, 353-386
  analysis of, 359-364
  diversification, 370-373
  project evaluation, 358-369
  risk considerations, 369-373
Foreign source income of U.S. corporations, 158
Foreign subsidiary:
  compared with domestic operation, 46-47
  role of, 351
  tax aspects of, 154
Forms of financing, 281-283

Forward contract, 131, 215, 247, 274
  for a specific identifiable commitment, 132
  used with exposed net asset or net liability position, 132-134
  used in speculation, 134-135
Forward exchange market, 91, 185-186, 215-218, 247
Fund transfers, 388

Geographical organization, regional center, 39
Gliding peg exchange rate, effects of, 56, 66
Gold exchange standard, 56
Gold standard, 55-56
Governmental factors, 391
  fiscal policy, 178
  monetary policy, 178
  policies affecting international business, 145-174
Gross-up basis, 159-160

Inflation, 68
  anticipated, 187
  effects on U.S. export prices, 60
Instituto Mobilare Italiano, 314
Insurance and Guarantee Programs, 191-209
Inter-American Development Bank (IDB), 310
Interest Equalization Tax (IET), 290, 293, 300
Interest Rate Parity Theorem (IRPT), 97, 213
International Bank for Reconstruction and Development (IBRD), 309
International business finance:
  environment, 1-12
  new variables, 3
International Development Association (IDA), 310
International Finance Corporation (IFC), 309
International finance function, 3
  areas of decision making, 4
  environmental factors, 4-11
  organization of, 391
  representation of, 382-85
  scope of, 381-382
International financial markets, 335
International financial policies, 387
International financial system, 61-65
  differences of opinion on, 64-65
  proposals for reform of, 63-65
International financing:
  agencies, 309-318
  commercial banks, 288-289
  investment bankers, 288-389
  possibilities of, 316
  reasons for, 315

International firm, development of, 13–29, 383–384
International lending agencies, 314–315
International Monetary Fund (IMF), 58
International monetary system, 63–64, 71–73
International operations:
  evaluation of, 386–387
  scope of, 386
International sales transactions:
  trade-offs, 393
  variables in, 389
International working capital management, 243–259
Investment banking firms, 288–289
Investment decisions:
  foreign and domestic, 371
  and foreign environmental factors, 374
  problems of, 44
Investment guarantees, 206–207, 313
Investment insurance, 201–203

Jamaica agreements, 73
Japanese companies, financial structure, 342–343
Joint ventures, 14, 316

Kreditanstalt für Wiederaufbau (KFW), 314

Letters of credit, 270, 389
Leverage, 326–328
Licensing, 14
LIFO, 245–246
Link financing, 267, 285, 389
Long position, 90, 176–177

Monetary position, 247
  balance, 227–233
  creditor, 329
  exposure, 229–241
  liabilities, 227
Multinational corporation, 15, 338
  and the development of a financial system, 36–37
  effect on U.S. economy, 16
  financial structure of, 338
  organization of, 31–36
  requirements for, 13–14
  subsidiary of, 37–38

Office of Foreign Direct Investment (OFDI), 293, 301, 357
Organization and control, 31–51
  organization relationships, 382–384
  organization types, 32–36

Organization of Petroleum Exporting Countries (OPEC), 62
Overseas Private Investment Corporation (OPIC), 177, 192, 201–206, 265, 273, 389
  analysis of insurance, 203–204
  direct investment fund loans, 204–208
  eligible investments, 203
  eligible investors, 202
  ineligible investments, 203
  insurance requirements, 202
  investment guarantees, 204–208
  policies, 202
  programs, 201
  requirements for participation, 205–206
  risk management, 201
  sponsor requirements, 205

P.L. 480:
  funds, 267
  loans, 312
Performance:
  evaluation, 42–43
  measurement, 41-43
Planning and control systems, 39–41, 47–48
Planning international operations, 17–18
Political risks, 176–179, 192, 338
  coverage, 200
  exposure, 182
Price-level accounting, 120–122
Private Export Funding Corporation (PEFCO), 199, 267, 273, 313
  commitment fee, 313
  financing, 313
  line of credit, 313
  sponsoring shareholders, 313
Project evaluation, 373–380
Project financing, international, 289
Purchasing Power Parity Theorem (PPPT), 98, 212–213

Regulation Q, 290, 293
Revenue Act of 1962, 155–161, 169–170
Risk:
  analysis of, 182–184, 187–190, 370
  exposure, 178
  foreign operations, 175–176
  foreign subsidiary, 184–185
  insurance, 197–198
  systematic, 352
Risk premium, 331
Risk reduction by government, 273–274
Risk-return analysis, 370–373
Ruble, 112–113

INDEX

Sales transaction, variables, 271–274
Security market line, 351–352
Short position, 91, 176–177
Sight drafts, 263
Smithsonian Agreement, 62–63
Social Progress Trust Fund, 310
"Soft loans," 314
Sources of financing, 283–285
Special Drawing Rights (SDRs), 61–62, 70
Stages of economic development, 16–22
Swap discount, 218
Swap partner, 247
Swiss banks, 337
Switch broker, 389
Switch exchange transactions, 271

Taxation of international operations, 45, 148–174
 on personal foreign earned income, 148–149
 policies, 162–169
 subpart F income, 156–157
 tax calculations, 367
  gross-up basis, 159–160

Taxation of international operations, tax calculations *(Cont.)*:
  normal basis, 159–160
 tax planning, 387–388
 tax theories, 147–148
 tax treaties, 147–148
Time drafts, 263
Transfer of funds, 257–259, 266–267
Transfer pricing, 44–46, 49–50
Translation of accounting statements, 123–124
 current-noncurrent approach, 124–125
 historical background, 123–124
 monetary-nonmonetary approach, 125
 practices, 126–128
 reporting gains or losses, 246–251
 temporal principle, 125–126
Transnational ownership, 337

Value added tax (VAT), 170–174

Western Hemisphere Trade Corporation, 149
Working capital management policies, 243–244, 254–256
World Bank (*see* International Bank for Reconstruction and Development)